dreadful
    desires

Thought in the Act
A series edited by Erin Manning and Brian Massumi

CHARLIE YI ZHANG

dreadful desires

The Uses of Love in Neoliberal China

Duke University Press   Durham and London   2022

© 2022 DUKE UNIVERSITY PRESS

All rights reserved

Printed in the United States of America on acid-free paper ∞

Designed by A. Mattson Gallagher

Typeset in Utopia, B612, and Source Han Serif by Westchester
Publishing Services

Library of Congress Cataloging-in-Publication Data

Names: Zhang, Charlie Yi, [date] author.

Title: Dreadful desires : the uses of love in neoliberal China /
Charlie Yi Zhang.

Other titles: Thought in the act.

Description: Durham : Duke University Press, 2022. | Series:
Thought in the act | Includes bibliographical references and index.

Identifiers: LCCN 2021022858 (print)

LCCN 2021022859 (ebook)

ISBN 9781478015376 (hardcover)

ISBN 9781478017998 (paperback)

ISBN 9781478022619 (ebook)

Subjects: LCSH: Work and family—China. | Work and family—
Government policy—China. | Work-life balance—China. |
Women—China—Social conditions—21st century. | Women—
Employment—China. | Neoliberalism—China. | Rural-urban
migration—China. | Migration, Internal—China—History. |
Globalization—China. | Nationalism—China. | BISAC: SOCIAL
SCIENCE / Gender Studies | SOCIAL SCIENCE / LGBTQ Studies /
General Classification: LCC HD4904.25 .Z445 2022 (print) |
LCC HD4904.25 (ebook) | DDC 306.3/60951—dc23

LC record available at https://lccn.loc.gov/2021022858

LC ebook record available at https://lccn.loc.gov/2021022859

Cover art: Zheng Lu, *Honour's Grave*, 2015. Stainless steel,
63 × 63 × 78½ in. (160 × 160 × 200 cm). Image courtesy of
Sundaram Tagore Gallery.

For my dear mother, Suhua Yan

Contents

Acknowledgments

This book is the result of a personal journey of learning and unlearning driven by numerous fellow sojourners' unquenchable aspiration for a good life. I was born into a working-class family in a small town in southwestern China in the late 1970s, right after Deng Xiaoping announced the economic reform and plan for opening China up for the global market. In the year I was born, the policy of allowing only one child per family was also introduced by the state to reshape the population and facilitate economic restructuring. Marketizing practices started in coastal regions and mainly focused on southern and eastern urban areas throughout the 1980s, and the polarizing effects of neoliberal economy did not fully unfold in my hometown at the time. Like my working-class peers, I enjoyed an array of benefits unavailable to rural Chinese citizens, including good public education; affordable rationed food and medical care because of my urban residential status in the state-controlled registration system of *hukou*; and free housing, which came with my parents' state-sponsored jobs. Moreover, the soft, literary masculinity associated with the Confucian tradition that I embodied placed me in an advantaged position at school. These taken-for-granted privileges took me years to realize and unpack, a process that was the starting point of this book project.

China's marketizing transition started to accelerate in the early 1990s, unsettling my habituated way of living and revealing the brutal facades of the social systems of class, gender, and sexuality that took new forms in neoliberal China. In the wake of the whole country's opening up, westernized dimorphic gender discourse and discriminatory terminology for homosexuality became prevalent, turning my ambiguous masculinity into a source of shamefulness and rendering my burgeoning same-sex desire a target of surveillance and disciplining that haunted me throughout puberty. In the late 1990s, with the hope of restoring my so-called normality and changing my life, I left my hometown to attend college in Nanjing, a big city in eastern China. My first attempt at self-rejuvenation, however, turned out to be more disturbing than freeing. As someone from a working-class background and an underdeveloped area, I experienced firsthand the devastating effects of neoliberalism in this metropolitan area. For marginalized students like me, the meritocratic dream that a good education will finally bring you a good life was embraced as the only viable solution to our problems, beckoning us into the self-help neoliberal fantasy by having us invest more time and energy to remake ourselves according to its rule. In 2004, I was admitted to a graduate program in Shanghai, winning a ticket that I expected to help me achieve my goal. However, in the face of soaring housing prices resulting from a rapidly growing market economy, I soon realized that I might not even be able to afford to find a place in this megacity that I could call home. Like other subaltern migrants who persist against all odds, I did not lose hope. In 2008, three days before the opening ceremony of the Beijing Olympics, I boarded a flight to the United States—which I saw as a land of opportunity—looking to revitalize my dream in uncharted places on the other side of the Pacific Ocean.

My learning experience in the United States provided me with a much-needed hiatus and, more importantly, critical tools that allow me to revisit the questions that have defined the dream-pursuing journeys of countless Chinese migrants. Why do we keep returning to our aspirational dreams even after they repeatedly fail us? How do the systems of gender, class, sexuality, and ethno-race shape our dreams and sustain our hope, which often works in opposition to our rational thinking and well-being? How do our self-defeating efforts contribute to the so-called self-serving market subjectivity and neoliberal restructuring that happens as or in the background? What does it take for us to unlearn our intangible yet poignant dreams for a good life and break down the detrimental cycle that these dreams refuel? These questions are at the heart of this book. There are innumerable people who have challenged me to push my inquiry in new ways; provided unswerving support during the process of learning and writing; shared their thoughts, which opened my mind; read my manuscript and offered constructive feedback; and inspired me to continue my journey simply by being who they are. I hope my acknowledgments do justice to their invaluable contributions.

H. L. T. Quan, Mary Margaret Fonow, Jacqueline Martinez, and Charles Lee were instrumental in how this project emerged. Quan's insights into critical theories were pivotal and inspired my own thinking in multiple ways, and Fonow's knowledge about labor and feminist methodology shaped my approach to the topic. My project also benefited from Martinez's expertise in phenomenology and queer theory and Lee's work on globalization and citizenship. Moreover, I am deeply indebted to Karen Leong and Ann Koblitz for pushing me to expand my study to a transnational scope. Sally Kitch and Lisa Anderson mentored me in intersectionality and cultural analysis. Georganne Scheiner Gillis taught me the essence of feminist pedagogy, and Alesha Durfee showed me how to combine different methodologies into my unique voice. I am very thankful for my fellow graduate students at Arizona State University: Debjani Chakravarty, Elena Frank, Alicia Woodbury, Tiffany Lamoreaux, Corie Nixon, Mary Jatau, Sarah Suhail, Aundrea Janae, Katie Harper, Julie Nagoshi, Dongling Zhang, Jack Cheung, Kishonna Gray, Jie Gong, Jieyoung Kong, Lijing Jiang, Shuzhen Huang, Terrie Wong, and Roberta Chevrette. Their friendship and conversations made my graduate studies meaningful and enjoyable.

My former colleagues, friends, and the Chinese community at South Dakota State University provided tremendous support that enabled me to survive the chilly weather and climate and emerge stronger. They include Xiaoyang Zhang, James Burns, Richard Meyers, Laura Renée Chandler, Jaime Nolan, Jihong Cole-Dai, Phyllis Cole-Dai, and Yan Lin. The North American Asian Feminist Caucus of the National Women's Studies Association has been another source of strength and inspiration for me, and special thanks go to Xin Huang, Dong Isbister, Yi-Chun Tricia Lin, Jo-Anne Lee, Vivien Ng, Wen Liu, Lin Li, Shana Ye, Mignonette Chiu, Xiumei Pu, Jennifer Yee, Cecilia Herles, Rui Shen, and Shuxuan Zhou.

I finished writing this book while serving on the faculty of the University of Kentucky, which has provided vital resources for sustaining my scholarly and political engagement. My colleagues in the Department of Gender and Women's Studies—Karen Tice, Srimati Basu, Carol Mason, Michelle Del Toro, Melissa Stein, Ellen Riggle, Cristina Alcalde, Anastasia Todd, Jennifer Hunt, Elizabeth Williams, Susan Bordo, Frances Henderson, Aria Halliday, and Lance Poston—have all provided important support for my intellectual ventures. It is a great pleasure to work with them. Additionally, I am privileged to work alongside a group of amazing colleagues in the College of Arts and Sciences, including Liang Luo (and the Asian Studies group that she organizes and leads), Sharon Yam, Jack Gieseking, Douglas Slaymaker, Akiko Takenaka, Francie Chassen-López, Monica Udvardy, Melinda Price, Rusty Barrett, Anastasia Curwood, Anna Secor, Ted Schatzki, Kathi Kern, Richard Schein, Rachel Farr, Mark Kornbluh, Arnold Farr, DaMaris B. Hill, Michael Samers, Karen Petrone, Patricia Ehrkamp, Jacqueline Couti, Tad Mutersbaugh, Mónica Díaz, Vanessa Holden, Sue Roberts, Robyn Brown, Ana Liberato, Dierdra Reber, Keiko Tanaka, Rachel Elliott, Jianjun He, Ann Kingsolver, Kristin Monroe, Mark Whitaker, Janice Fernheimer, Michelle Sizemore, Emily Mokros, and Lisa Cliggett. The experience of coteaching Affect, a social theory seminar, fundamentally reshaped this book project, and I am profoundly thankful to Sharon Yam, Anna Secor, Arnold Farr, and Dierdra Reber—as well as our guest speakers Brian Massumi, Deborah Gould, and Shannon Sullivan—for stimulating my thinking. Conversations with the graduate students in the seminars Feminist Theory and Politics of the Body were also helpful for me in developing my project. These students included Mel Lesch, Leif Johnson, James Lincoln, Christine Woodward, Miles Feroli, Ruwen Chang, and Rachel Davies, among others.

I am fortunate to have met a group of scholars and friends and to have had many thought-provoking conversations with them that shaped my writing in this book: Adam K. Dedman, Kate Black, Judy Tzu-Chun Wu, Cricket Keating, Sasha Su-Ling Welland, Hongwei Bao, Howard Chiang, Amy Lind, Sandra Soto, Patti Duncan, Ashwini Tambe, Larin McLaughlin, Alicia Christensen, Michelle Rowley, Calvin Hui, Brena Tai, Louisa Schein, Jigna Desai, Karma Chávez, Jennifer Suchland, Petrus Liu, Alvin Wong, Jaime J. Zhao, Maud Lavin, Ling Yang, James Welker, Chris Jingchao Ma, Thomas Baudinette, Emily Wilcox, Marlon Bailey, Martin F. Manalansan, Yi-Li Wu, Heather Switzer, Aren Aizura, Kimberly Scott, Sujey Vega, Wendy Cheng, Aimee Bahng, Seung-kyung Kim, Tammy Ho, Rachel Afi Quinn, John Cho, Yige Dong, Yan Long, Juno Salazar Parreñas, Tiantian Zheng, Xiqing Zheng, Annie Isabel Fukushima, Dredge Kang, Iris Ai Wang, Eileen Boris, Fan Yang, Jill Bystydzienski, Emily Burrill, Michelle Stuckey, Ling Zhang, Patricia Hill Collins, Michelle Ho, Daisy Yan Du, Elizabeth Canfield, Toby Beauchamp, Mishuana Goeman, and Guldana Salimjan. I am especially grateful to Zheng Wang, who introduced me to the field of gender and sexuality studies and has provided unwavering support for my professional career ever since.

Outside the academy, a group of migrant workers, farmers, and female *danmei* fans shared with me their stories, which have been central to my writing of this book. They invested much time and energy in the book, hoping that it could bring positive change to their lives. I cannot express my gratitude enough, and I hope that my book meets their expectations in at least some way. My friends Cunfu Li and Dan Li provided tremendous help that allowed me to complete my fieldwork in Hai'an and Wuxi. Without their contributions, this book could have never been completed.

Srimati Basu, Karen Tice, Adam K. Dedman, Noah J. Springer, Lin Li, and Sharon Yam have read different parts or versions of this book and provided indispensable feedback that made it stronger. Basu's suggestion to include love as part of the central framework and title, and the detailed reading and editing of multiple drafts by Tice and Dedman were crucial in helping me finalize the manuscript. In addition to her careful reading of the manuscript, Li provided valuable suggestions about the book cover. I am also indebted to Dedman for pushing me to expand my scope to Southeast Asia, which has paved the ground for my next book project, and to Springer for the editorial expertise that helped me revamp and reorganize the whole manuscript in a more coherent way.

This book would not have been possible without institutional support. I received a summer fellowship in 2013 at Arizona State University that allowed me to complete my dissertation. I also received mini-grant awards provided by the College of Arts and Sciences and two Research and Creative Activities Support Program Grants at the University of Kentucky for professional editorial support that enabled me to complete the book manuscript.

The consistent support from the editorial team at Duke University Press has been essential to this book project. I am grateful to Brian Massumi and Erin Manning for generously including the book in the Thought in the Act series. I am also very thankful to Elizabeth Ault for her belief in this project and careful nurturing of its development, and to Ken Wissoker for supporting the publication of my manuscript. The generous reports from three anonymous readers provided very insightful and clear guidance that allowed me to revise and improve my manuscript, and their enthusiasm for the direction it has taken encouraged and motivated me to complete the project. At Duke University Press, I also thank Kate Herman, Benjamin Kossak, and the rest of the team for taking great care with this project.

Finally, I wish to express my infinite gratitude to my family for the love and care they have demonstrated. My father, Hongshu Zhang, has been a role model for me as a tireless learner from the very early stages of my life. My uncle Hongxuan Zhang has always believed in me at each turn of my life. My partner, Kunzheng Deng, has been my most adamant supporter, and he allows me to explore my potential in every possible way. His mother, Yanli Liu, also provided substantial support throughout the process of writing the manuscript. This book is written in the memory of and dedicated to my mother, Suhua Yan, whose steadfast and unforgettable love has always been the main driving force in my life.

An earlier version of chapter 1 was published in *Frontiers: A Journal of Women's Studies* 37, no. 2 (2016): 1–27. An earlier version of chapter 5 was published in *Feminist Formations* 29, no. 2 (2017): 121–46.

Introduction

One early summer afternoon, after a long day of fieldwork in a silk factory in suburban Hai'an, a small town located on the northern bank of the Yangtze River in Jiangsu province, I stopped by a grocery store at the front gate of the factory to purchase a gift for the woman who had helped organize the trip. My conversation with her about gender inequality in China's labor market soon attracted the attention of the male store owner, who, perturbed by the topic, tried to persuade us that women had taken over control of the family and society at large, to the detriment of all Chinese men. Apparently, the prickly man's misogyny was inspired by, and chiefly levied against, his wife, Liu, who was about to replace him to start her shift for the day. Intrigued by our exchanges and after several hesitant attempts and retreats, Liu finally divulged her story after her husband had left the store.[1]

As a teenager in the mid-1980s, Liu had left her home in the nearby village and taken a job in the silk factory. After working there for over thirteen years, she had left to start this grocery store, which she had run with her husband ever since. Before her resignation from the factory, the manager had planned to promote her to a more challenging leadership position. There, she could have explored her business talents in performing more important tasks. However, this potentially life-changing opportunity met with vehement opposition from Liu's husband, who insisted that "any virtuous women should let their husband take care of them and never get involved in the business world." Liu used the term *virtuous women* almost like a verbal stab, infusing it with poignancy and self-derision steeped in piercing cynicism about such restrictive gender norms. After a marathon of impassioned arguments, silent protests, and even physical altercations, Liu gave up her career plan and resigned from her position. "People like me would sacrifice for the sake of our family and happiness of our children. When my sons date girls, their girlfriends' parents will say our family is not very harmonious," she commented with a shaky voice and tense countenance, which conveyed meanings far graver than her words did. Her narrative then took a drastic turn, and she began to stab the air with her fingers, while her speech became a punchy staccato punctuated by searing rage: "Actually, I did everything for my sons. I am a woman. My husband is so sexist, and he can say anything. Sometimes I am worried about my face, so I just suppress myself." To salvage her sons' romantic prospects and preserve her femininity, Liu had subordinated her personal aspirations to the gendered and sexual scripts of a family-focused love, which ironically impeded her original aim.

As the following chapters show, Liu's self-defeating love is by no means singular. Instead, it reveals a life-sustaining fantasy looming large in China's boundless landscape of love that entraps innumerable rural migrants like Liu in dreadful ways. As China shifts from socialism to neoliberalism, countless women have wrestled with dilemmas similar to hers. Their full participation in the newly minted market economy—one that, to no small extent, is developed through and built upon men's consumption of women's sexuality—profoundly undercuts their chances for a good family life. Women's qualifications for love have been redefined in contradictory terms that require both self-made success in the market and self-sacrifice for the family.[2] Learning that our conversation would be included in my research project, which might be published at some point, Liu—her voice quavering and her eyes welling up with tears—insisted that I should write down the following words, which she stated emphatically: "We, Chinese women, are different from American women. We have big love (*daai*) for our family, but they only prioritize small love (*xiaoai*) for themselves." Of course, this sweeping generalization begs for contextualization and further scrutiny for nuanced understanding. Still, it provides a glimpse into the daunting lovescape that this book aims to unfold: in China, love has contributed to a collective hallucination that cajoles numerous disenfranchised subjects to expect that the possession of the correct format of love, or even proximity to it, will help their lives become different in the right way, no matter what that format of love looks and feels like on an everyday basis.

Its delusively promissory feature aside, love is hard to capture. According to Lauren Berlant, love can be seen as an affective structure of enduring attachments that "might feel like anything, including nothing" at any moment.[3]

In addition, it flies repeatedly in the face of our linguistic and cognitive capacities, taking shape as shifting and often contradictory personal feelings and interpersonal attachments. From day to day, the apparatus of love finds its way into our capacity "to affect and to be affected that pushes a present into a composition, an expressivity."[4] Furthermore, it encircles us as an incipient but freighted affectsphere that can suddenly immerse us in "something that feels like something" and motivate our collective sensibilities to "pulse in plain sight."[5] With her emotionally imbued words, Liu tried to impress me with the self-value and -esteem that she derived from the family-centered love so as to distinguish her from the selfish Others—that is, the "American women." Yet based on her gestures, I could sense that she did not feel much happiness, excitement, passion, or any of the other warm feelings usually associated with love. Instead, the love that she articulated chilled me with the glaring regret and anguish that it registered both sonically and visually. Drawn partially by the affective valence of Liu's dreadful experience and partially by her propositional content, women workers who had finished their day started to gather around us to share their own pitiable stories, amplifying the atmosphere that she had activated and attracting more passersby to join in the denunciation of love's false promises. Transmitted between and across different bodies, love's affectivities generated far greater effects than the sum of its parts and created a sense of "living together" and "relations made flesh" that accompanied the bursts and circulations of the messages and objects that it brought into shape.[6] Before disappearing into the air again, this contagious love created an intangible but thick ambience that produced a group of woeful women. This "might not be [directly] visible, but at any given point it might be sensed" through these women's conflicted feelings as "the sociocultural expression of [its] felt intensity."[7] Circulating among these women, the embodied weight of love furthered their world building by disturbing and creating "what is continuous, anchoring [them] enough in the scene to pull in other things as [it] goes," such as a rekindled hope of a promising tomorrow.[8]

As this book sets out to show, despite its ever-morphing and fleeting nature, the structure of love has taken on an unsettling pattern in the milieu of neoliberalization in China and beyond. On the day of an interview with a group of male construction workers in Hai'an, after briefly introducing the nature of my project, I explained that there would be an audio recording of our conversations and my research would be made available to the public. This disclosure is common in Western academia, and I was surprised when it triggered overwhelmingly positive responses. I was inundated by a deluge of stories about my interviewees' unremitting fight with the government for better working conditions and treatment, which, they hoped, could rouse some transnational repercussions that would tame the unruly state and make their life easier. Like these workers, many other informants tried to secure a spot for their long-subdued experiences in my notebook, bringing into focus the sacrificial love that had sustained them as children who had given up educational opportunities to help with family finances, mothers or daughters who had terminated careers to move back home to care for underage and aging loved ones, outcasts living alone in cities and struggling to support their rural families, and hopeful migrants following fellow villagers' footsteps in search of job opportunities in China's proliferating overseas construction sites to provide a better life for the people they care about. Out of a shared sense of family-centered love, they had re-created themselves as pursuers of dreams who were motivated to work for all but their own well-being, and as indentured laborers shoring up the interests of the Chinese state and transnational capital alike. Divergent though the starting points of their migratory route might be, the ends remain distressingly identical to what Jasbir Puar calls "slow death," as they all move toward the premeditated destination of a decaying segment of the population meted out by the state for wearing out.[9] Instead of the self-interested individuals intent on personal optimization who are touted by neoliberal ideologues as the epitome of rational market subjectivity, these migrants were motivated by their love for their family, and they toiled for the benefits of the state and capital to their own detriment. Thus, they constitute the obscured source of China's presumably inexhaustible labor force, which is pivotal to its neoliberalizing transformation. Like the workers, I came from a lower-class background, and I had left my home at the age of eighteen, moving out of China and across the Pacific to pursue my family dream in my late twenties.[10] As a former migrant and now a diasporic subject, I share their feelings about the love-ignited aspiration and fully identify with them. Having frequently returned to promissory love only to find it unfailingly chimerical rather than salvific, I feel obligated to find ways to end its illusory spell and release the potentials that it subdues.[11]

Dreadful Desires: The Uses of Love in Neoliberal China invites readers to reencounter love—not to accept love as it is, but to shift the way we look at love from a transparent form of feeling ingrained in all human beings to a complex set of potentials for embedded actualization in polarized terms. Taking cues from the affective turn in critical theories, the book reframes love as a social apparatus that transpires sustainably into variegated emotions and feelings with grounded effects.[12] This study draws upon both a discursive analysis of media and cultural products and ethnographic data to trace how disparate emotive responses are generated on personal and interpersonal levels to reproduce different subjects and social groups for energizing China's neoliberal transition. The book not only adds new materials from a different context to enrich the discussions of affect that have heretofore mostly focused on Western societies, but it also employs affect as a heuristic device to reexamine the critical issues that human beings are facing together at this moment—that is, the rampant neoliberalizing process and its dire consequences. To deepen our knowledge of the kaleidoscopic landscape of love, I take a feminist intersectional approach to interrogate and untangle the mechanism that the Chinese state relies upon to define and redefine the affective parameters of desire and intimacy in binaristic terms of gender, class, sexuality, and ethno-race.[13] Such an analysis enables me to delineate how these manipulative practices are integrated with other exploitative biopolitical policies through the bifurcated engineering of differences. Following insights from queer of color critiques, I am also attentive to hidden aspects of the institutionalized disparities, and I keep track of emerging forms of differences that are re-created by the party-state for profit-seeking purposes to build a robust platform of solidarity for social change.[14]

Taken together, these issues and concerns bring forth the central questions that my study intends to answer: What constitutes the driving forces that render China at once a part of the global neoliberal system and yet apart from it? Using the case of China as an optic, what larger picture can we capture to identify the mechanism that informs and enables neoliberalism's global control and, more recently, the mounting nationalist backlash against that control? Given the disturbing arrangements built upon this mechanism, what are the conditions in which new forms of livability and sociality can emerge, survive, and thrive? And if we believe that all social life is material, grounded, and embodied on a daily basis, how can critical scholars committed to positive social change uncover and access these potentialities for a more humane future?

This book argues that love sets up the daily flow of our affective energies as a fantasmatic apparatus of desire and intimacy that inhabits a nonlinear temporal logic operating recursively between the past, present, and future and works along and across multiscalar sociospaces to mediate and fuse our processes of becoming self and world making into symbiotic ones. My analysis probes the ways in which love is fabulated both by the Chinese state and by capital as an expansive spatiotemporal matrix that I call the borderless Loveland for serving their collective interests. Since China initiated economic reforms and reopened its door to the world in the late 1970s, the state has developed a series of rationalized policies to regenerate precarious migrant workers to boost China's marketization and reintegration with the global economy.[15] This has attracted plenty of critical attention.[16] However, that coverage generally misses how affective forces—in particular, those related to love—are used to complement stringent biopolitical management.[17] As Lisa Rofel shows, the constitution of desires—aspirations, needs, and longings—is central to the remaking of human subjects vital for China's neoliberal transition.[18] Neoliberalism, Berlant posits, is not simply "a world-homogenizing sovereign with coherent intentions that produces subjects who serve its interests, such that their singular actions only seem personal, effective, and freely intentional," but also "the messy dynamics of attachment, self-continuity, and the reproduction of life that are the material scenes of living on in the present."[19] More broadly, as Brian Massumi demonstrates, "affectivity and rationality" that function by the divergent "feedforward" and "feedback" logic "circle creatively through each other" to subtend and buttress all economistic relationships.[20] Building on her genealogical analysis of modern liberalism and settler colonialism, Lisa Lowe lays bare how the capitalistic system was established and expanded through the mixture of the affective traction created by enticing offers of rights, emancipation, wage labor, and free trade with geographic, national, racialized, gendered, sexualized, and religious asymmetries to re-create docile laboring subjects.[21] Likewise, showing how legions of nonwhite migrants were drawn to Canada and the United States by their aspirational dreams of settler family life in the second half of the twentieth century, but were simultaneously confronted with the gendered and sexualized norms that denied them enough political voice and social status and thus perpetuated their enslaved labor, Nayan Shah identifies the collusional connection between the biopolitical regulation of populations and the manipulation of affective potentials that fostered the capitalistic system from its early stages.[22]

To answer the questions and explore alternatives to the present dire setup, this book develops an approach that includes an engaged scrutiny of the borderless Loveland and an embedded inquiry into people's mundane lives as the Loveland's grounded effects to identify the mechanism that subtends and upholds the transnational neoliberal system. I call this mechanism the difference-making machinery. My study integrates the discursive with the ethnographic and combines grave scrutiny of political economies and empirical data with upbeat examinations of popular cultures to unpack the entanglements of affect, rationality, capital, labor, market, and state in contemporary China with the goal of finding transformative possibilities.

Following this approach, I provide a broad view of China's dramatic love-scape and its variegated articulations, and I dissect how the state relies upon the difference-making machinery to shuffle and reshuffle disparities of gender, class, sexuality, and ethno-race to preregister the affective tendencies of myriad rural migrants before they are actualized in unfavorable terms and align the migrants' life trajectories with neoliberal restructuring in the Chinese and transnational contexts. Drawing upon a critical analysis of state-sponsored cultural spectacles, such as the televised ceremony of China's sixtieth anniversary in 2009 and the popular TV dating game show *If You Are the One*, my investigation brings into focus the phantasmagoric terrains of the Loveland to cast light on the ways in which love is orchestrated to serve different needs of the party-state and capital. Through ethnographic engagement with the migrant worker communities in Hai'an and Wuxi (a metropolitan area eighty miles west of Hai'an), I explore how the apparatus of love facilitates and sustains the biopolitical exploitation of disenfranchised and so-called irrational groups to stabilize China's turbulent neoliberalization and demonstrate how the dreadful Loveland can be dismantled. Drawing attention to the resistant praxes of well-educated single urban women demonized as being unlovable and unable to love in China's daunting marriage market, my query also maps fissures across the landscape of love that create room for concrete change. Diverse and divergent as the materials for analysis are, they are all clustered around China's fantasmatic apparatus of desire and intimacy—serving as its normative articulation embedded in the neoliberal condition or as willful or resistant subjects impelled by its possibilities and impossibilities.

Dreadful Desires can thus be viewed as an intervention in contrast to the claim of universal rationality and its incarnation, homo economicus (the figurative human being driven solely to maximize personal interests), as the epistemic foundation of neoliberalism and ideological leverage of its global domination. Instead, the book identifies the ways in which affect and rationality are imbricated to enable and sustain the transnational unfolding of neoliberal relationships, while also spawning insolvable contradictions for subversions. It disentangles the transactional relationships between affective forces and biopolitical calculus, as well as dismantling the difference-making machinery that accommodates their disparate functioning to undergird China's neoliberal transition. Tracing how this mechanism also sets China apart as an emerging threat to the capitalist world, my analysis unpacks the recent nationalist backlash against globalization to envision possibilities of substantive change from within the transnational neoliberal regime.

Reencountering the Borderless
Apparatus of Love

Certainly, the manipulative orchestration of love is central to China's neoliberal and neocolonial agenda, which has been met with escalating pushback. In May 2017, *China Daily*, the state-run flagship English-language newspaper, released a five-episode web series intended to promote and defend the Belt and Road Initiative (BRI), the largest infrastructure construction project in history.[23] Packaging the aggressive plan into affectionate dialogues between a genteel white American father and his studious daughter, "Belt and Road Bedtime Stories" attempts to mitigate the growing concern about China's debt-funded plan to bend other nation-states to its will and create new markets for its excess production capacity of steel, cement, and aluminum. Episode 4, for example, centers on a bedtime storytelling scene that turns into a blatant propaganda tool. As the man relaxes in bed, lying against the headboard and playing the ukulele, his five-year-old daughter cuddles next to him, tapping on her pink toy bunny in time with the tune. "Time for bed, kiddo," says the man as he stops playing and turns toward the girl. "Story time!" the girl demands. The father grabs a globe and starts to mark on it the various countries connected by the BRI. "Wow! So it really is globalization! Like all around the world," the girl exclaims with a knowing smile. The father continues, "But some countries are moving away from globalization." The BRI, in his account, is "an opportunity to move globalization forward. Especially since a lot about it is about building infrastructure." Ostensibly, the heart-melting videos employ affable storytelling to ease the brewing tension between the world and the aspiring imperial giant intent on increasing its global presence. Even China's harshest critics might find solace in the daughter's seemingly spontaneous reactions to such fatherly storytelling. But these videos are only part of China's paternalist affective agenda.

In the wake of the 2008 global financial meltdown imputed to the failure of the Washington Consensus—the US-backed global restructuring plan through market fundamentalism developed by a group of Washington-based organizations and institutions—many of its critics embraced the Beijing Consensus, which relies on larger policy tool kits, more regulated resources, long-term state planning, and the stringent control of enterprises as an alternative way of advancing global economic integration.[24] Xi Jinping, China's president, has largely accrued his authoritarian power to expand the Beijing Consensus through his meticulously crafted persona as a loving father, symbolized not least by the well-popularized moniker "*xi dada*" (or "Big Daddy

Xi"). Since he assumed the presidency in 2013, Chinese media have used a wide range of discursive tropes—including animated ditties, video clips, musical odes, and comic images—to cultivate his chivalrous, gallant, and paternalistic personality, extolling him as a strong leader born with a kind heart. At home, he is lauded as an affectionate husband who puts his wife's needs ahead of his own.[25] He is also praised as a softhearted man who is unashamed of shedding tears in public and who "feels deeply about family, friends, average citizens and model officials."[26] In addition, he is presented as an unpretentious and genuine commander in chief who is willing to pay his own way and carry his own tray to share street food around cheap folding tables with average Chinese citizens.[27] Abroad, he is portrayed as a reliable champion who makes every effort during crises to ensure the safety of Chinese nationals, citizens or not.[28] And he is shown as an unfaltering guardian of China's revival and return to the world stage after hundreds of years of war, colonized humiliation, poverty-stricken disarray, and other calamities.[29] Xi's embodied heteropatriarchal love for his own nuclear family and, by proxy, the family of the nation has been measured and used repeatedly as nothing less than a vessel to rally nationalist momentum to propel China into its role as a new global leader.

In stark contrast to China's love-paved road into a more cosmopolitan world, far-right groups have recently come to power through fearmongering campaigns across Europe, Asia, and the Americas, giving rise to a nationalist groundswell that is ready to reshape and curtail our putatively unified future.[30] For instance, Xi's geopolitical nemesis, Donald J. Trump, rode a virulent racist, xenophobic, misogynist, and ableist campaign into the White House to the surprise of both ends of the political spectrum. By demonizing marginalized groups such as Mexicans and Muslim immigrants as a direct threat to the American people, he spoke directly about the failed American dream, inspiring an inward-looking nationalist vision for remaking the United States. Meanwhile, by touting himself as the only person who could deliver on the unfulfilled promise of America, Trump created and retained thick affective forces that drew many disillusioned voters to him as his most loyal electoral base.[31]

However, China's love-gilded cosmopolitan dream proves no less pernicious than the hate-filled paranoia stoked by incendiary nationalists. In November 2017, the Beijing municipal government's forces stormed migrant worker communities, cut off their water and electricity with no notice, and bulldozed their homes.[32] Under mounting pressure from the public and media, the state defended its act as part of a broad plan to purge "low-end populations" and "modernize, beautify, and gentrify the Chinese capital as a showcase for the Communist Party."[33] Predictably, this reckless justification increased tensions, inadvertently revealing the heart of the state's developmental agenda: the consistent intrusive management of the Chinese population and individual lives. Stuck in these baffling developments, we might ask how love, as a human emotion that is often celebrated as a self-evident good, is inspired, retained, and spread in such a way that has led to dire consequences like presumably negative feelings—say, hate and fear. And when heterogeneous feelings are persistently provoked by tyrannical politicians to sponsor their comparably dangerous agendas and the consequential boundaries between positive and negative emotions appear to be incrementally blurred, how can we retrieve the good ones such as love to build a truly blissful world?

This book develops a novel approach to tracing the genealogies and topologies of love that are embedded in and extend beyond China's social upheavals and provide a panoramic view of the fantasmatic lovescape to release love from its grim entrapment by neoliberal logic and reopen its boundless potential. As Sara Ahmed reminds us, no feelings "simply reside within subjects and then move outward toward objects," and human beings' innate desires and presumably transcendent emotions are in actuality all directed by outside-in forces toward certain ends.[34] Using happiness as an example, Ahmed adeptly unpacks how emotions treated as self-evidently good are frequently "used to redescribe social norms as social goods," with unhappy consequences.[35] As Mishuana Goeman has observed, in North America liberal discourses of love and marriage re-create the intimate couple as a transference point within liberalism and partake in the ideology as part of a complex of "freedom producing subjects and institutions" that operates around the autonomous subject to support settler colonialism.[36] In the global context, Elizabeth Povinelli expounds on how love "secures the self-evident good of social institutions, social distributions of life and death, and social responsibilities for these institutions and distributions" as an ongoing event, anchoring the construction of liberalism as a Western sociopolitical project to further transnational colonial and imperial expansion.[37] Love, in these accounts, begs for more critical attention to unravel how different social forces are woven into the texture of the affective apparatus, which in turn shapes and reshapes our desire and intimacy in varied directions with tangible consequences.

As will be clear from my analysis, the borderless Loveland functions as a public structure of sensing and perceiving that modulates our potentialities to love and be loved, incorporating its effectual tapestry into our subjectivities as expanding lovabilities and love-abilities. Meanwhile, it creates an embedded matrix of sentiments that tunes our love-associated feelings, cognitions, and actions to habituate our sovereign individuality and collective existence, enfolding its sprawling affectsphere in the worlding process that we all inhabit as conjoined experiences. Along the Loveland's morphing spatiotemporal terrains, love is frequently registered as "the anticipatory reality in the present," a promissory future that materializes our being by "the felt reality of the nonexistent, loomingly present as the affective fact of the matter."[38] Retrieving the past and present and thrusting their recurrence into our emerging existence, it also takes shape as a form of "future anteriority," the anticipated future embedded in the past and present.[39] Love, in our lifeworld, cannot be fully captured but only briefly sensed as a cluster of spatialities—both physical and imaginary—best understood topologically "as attenuated, squeezed, pliant, and labile-like textiles," which are "dense with circulating expressive forms that effect transnational belonging" that in turn is textured by local forces and attributes.[40] Every now and then, it surges into being as "a speculative topography of the everyday sensibilities," reaching us as "a state of alert saturated with the potentiality of things in the making in a personal, political, and aesthetic ambit that has not yet found its form but is always promising and threatening to take shape."[41] In the midst of China's neoliberal transition, the prismatic lovescape permutes its affective ambience along the shifting metrics of gender, class, and sexuality, reframing the idealized projection of love from the state-supervised version that Haiyan Lee calls "revolutionary romanticism" to the one based on private property ownership, upward mobility, and endurable heteronormative intimacy.[42] By predetermining the scope of our desire and intimacy, the unbounded Loveland plays an integral role in reorienting Chinese people from self-effacing subjects, whose interests are subordinated to the state's socialist cause, to agential selves motivated to seek familial opulence and prosperity in market competition—a collective subjective transition affectively modulated to accommodate societal changes at a structural level.

Building on the holistic view of China's extensive Loveland, this book also opens up a new horizon to reexamine the alarming nationalist waves that have set the stage for a new Cold War, while reconstructing solidarities through feminist and queer lenses for more humanitarian and just futurities beyond the neoliberal singularity of the present. Offering a critical optic to revisit the Cold War legacy and probe how it proliferates the communist specter and protracts its haunting into antiglobalist resurgences, it enables readers to delve into the difference-making machinery that begets the germination of gendered, classed, sexualized, and racialized polarities—which in turn remake barriers in calculative and affective terms, both allowing China's integration into the global market as a central player and, at the same time, re-creating it as the new primary adversary of the capitalist world. I propose a different perspective for understanding the ways that the competing relationships of structurally induced biopolitics and the speculative manipulation of affective tendencies, profiteering capital and laborers seeking a better life, border-crossing markets and border-reclaiming nation-states, and politico-economic materialities and cultural formations of identities are fused into contingent balance to ground the operation of the neoliberal matrix and forward its global reign. It is my hope that this book will provide a vantage point from which we can initiate generative discussion and concerted efforts to find a path through the chaotic moment and build a more peaceful world.

Identifying the Difference-Making
Neoliberal Mechanism

Francis Fukuyama declared that history "ended" with the demise of the Soviet-led socialist bloc and human beings became united as a global community founded on cosmopolitan solidarity and Western-style democracy.[43] However, the Cold War mentality persists into the present, spawning growing agitation that has erupted into an antiglobalist tsunami. As Jinhua Dai suggests, although China freed itself from the frenzied competition between the socialist and capitalist camps in the old Cold War as an independent, self-sufficient nation and major advocate of third world solidarity, its active participation in neoliberal globalization has implicated it in the current Cold War as the new emblem of the socialist or communist threat.[44] By re-creating communist China as their major geopolitical adversary, right-wing groups in the West recharge nationalist frenzy to consolidate their political power across the world.[45] Instead of building up the anticipated bountiful cosmopolitan community, we are rapidly backtracking into the dark days of divisive, parochial, and war-torn disarray, with conservatives fully rallied against their new opponent.

To be sure, since its reform and opening up in 1978, China has grown from a newly founded regime sandwiched between two ideological camps, carrying the potential to tip their power balance at the height of the arms race in the 1980s, into a giant set on using its immeasurable economic clout to reshape the world. Capitalizing on the turbulence of financial deregulation and trade liberalization afforded by globalization, the so-called socialist monster with Chinese characteristics has siphoned off tremendous amounts of capital and numerous jobs from its capitalist adversaries to subsidize its own development. For decades, the world envied China for the double-digit growth in its gross domestic product (GDP). In 2009, after pulling itself swiftly out of the Great Recession—the devastating aftershock from one of the worst financial meltdowns since the Great Depression in the 1930s—and acting as a generous lender to the troubled Western economies, it emerged as the savior of the capitalist world and the leader of the global recovery.[46] By 2010, China had leapfrogged Japan and was in the second position in the global economic hierarchy, trailing only the United States.[47] In January 2017, three days before Trump's seismic inauguration, Xi defended globalization in his plenary speech at the World Economic Forum meeting at Davos, Switzerland, announcing his commitment to shepherding the globalizing process.[48] Four months later, he opened China's own globalization forum with a pledge to provide $78 billion to advance the BRI project that supported the country's view of itself as the founder and advocate of the "community of common destiny with mankind."[49]

Despite their contrasting affective appeals and worldviews, right-wing nationalists in the West and Chinese globalists converge via the difference-making strategies they develop to realize their rival visions. By turning pluralist identity politics on its head and into vengeful masculinist and white supremacist rhetoric and braiding it into his inflammatory prolabor populist narrative, Trump reinforced the resentful nationalist ethos that propelled him to his 2016 electoral victory and gave him the opportunity to carry out his neoliberal agenda.[50] Comparably, Xi's plan to "comprehensively deepen China's reform" and revitalize its imperial multiplication for markets and resources is delivered in and shored up by gendered and classed biopolitics that reaggregate the Chinese population and individual lives in line with his grandiose restructuring plan—and in turn, its implementation is justified by love-defined cosmopolitanism.[51] Paradoxically, their affectively registered counterviews vying to lead "the people"—however defined—and find the path forward converge via an identity-induced differentiation working toward a common telos. Through incessant affection and propagation by these politicians to manipulate the general public, such contradictory narratives and fragmented realities are pieced together into a bewildering scenario that challenges any conventional wisdom and surely confounds the view of even the savviest pundits.

Dreadful Desires develops a road map to shed light on the inner workings of this neoliberal apparatus while seeking a path through the present turbulence. What refuels and upholds the transnational neoliberal regime and its neo-nationalist backfire, I argue, is the difference-making machinery that regenerates oppositional relationships and binaristic categorizations of gender, race, sexuality, and class, as well as concealing the connections in between to balance the competing factors, agents, components, and institutions implicated in transnational trading relationships. Working against the polarizing logic of this machinery and tracking how it weaves China into the global network of capital as the menacing Other, this book furthers critical understanding of the difference-fostering and -managing core of the neoliberal apparatus to coordinate our rationalized beings and affective potential in the service of the planetary banquet of interests for capital and rescaled nation-states.

In contrast to oppositional Cold War thinking, copious connections exist between China's reform and the neoliberal restructuring across the capitalist world. In response to the financial crisis that broke out in Britain in 1973 and quickly spread to the United States, neoliberal theories were road tested in Latin America first and then adopted in the West.[52] Under Augusto Pinochet's aegis and with US support, Chile became "the first country in the world to make that [neoliberal] momentous break with the past—away from socialism and extreme state capitalism toward more market-oriented structures and policies."[53] When the Conservative Party took power in 1978 in Britain, Prime Minister Margaret Thatcher launched drastic initiatives to privatize the public sector, deregulate financial and labor markets, and withdraw the state from the provision of welfare, laying the cornerstones of neoliberalization for other powerful politicians, such as Ronald Reagan and Deng Xiaoping.[54]

Amid the grueling socioeconomic crisis in the late 1970s, China also adopted neoliberalism as an "exception" for state-controlled experimentation.[55] And "if it wasn't merely reciting the neoliberal canons that originated in the West, then it was at least adding an effective footnote."[56] In 1978, the state replaced the system of the People's Commune with a family-based farming system to test the waters of the market, allowing farmers to sell the produce they had left after giving their quotas to the state. In 1980, the Communist leadership established four special economic zones in southern coastal regions to expand this marketizing thrust to nonagricultural sectors, and in 1984, it opened fourteen more coastal cities to overseas investment.[57] As reform edged its way into the late 1980s, Beijing introduced a two-track system, which included state-set prices applied to means of production and market prices for consumer items to create competing market subjects within the planned economy.[58] As effective as this price reform proved to be, it created the perfect conditions for rent seeking by government officials, who monopolized the access to material goods and triggered severe inflation in 1988, exacerbating the public's discontent with corruption and spiraling inequality.[59] The resulting social mobilization raged across the country and soon sprawled into the Tian'anmen Square (or June 4th) movement. One of the world's earliest mass protests against neoliberalism, it was soon forcibly suppressed by the state.[60]

While resistance movements waxed and waned in China, a transformative momentum swept across Europe, clearing the way for global neoliberal restructuring. Culminating in the fall of the Berlin Wall in 1989, these fundamental policy changes redirected societies toward a capital-leaning avenue. In the same year, the Washington-based International Monetary Fund and World Bank—in collaboration with the US Treasury Department (the so-called Washington Consensus)—prescribed a reform package for Latin American countries to liberalize and open up their markets to address the problems of their crisis-ridden economies. Purged of Keynesian influences in the 1980s, supranational institutions established under the Keynesian-Westphalian frame to stabilize and facilitate the postwar reconstruction were turned into mouthpieces of neoliberal ideology and imposed a series of disastrous structural adjustment programs on developing countries to consolidate free-market economies around the globe.[61]

China undoubtedly occupies a vital and pivotal point in the global network of capital, and the undeterred US efforts to integrate it into this network for broadening the scope of capital reproduction—even in the apogee of anti-China sentiment after the Tian'anmen Square movement among the European allies of the United States—finally bore fruit with Deng's so-called Southern Tour, which resumed reforms in 1992. The decision to open up Shanghai's Pudong area marked China's full embrace of the market mechanism, and soon afterward previously sporadic experiments were moving ahead at full steam.[62] Under the tutelage of two subsequent leaders (Jiang Zemin [1989–2003] and Hu Jintao [2003–2013]), China was transformed from a semi-autarkic economy into a major player in the global market, appealing to transnational capital with new facilities and reliable infrastructures; favorable policies and legal support; and, most importantly, a seemingly inexhaustible supply of cheap labor and raw materials.

China's reopening to the world also created "an important condition for the formation of neoliberal globalization."[63] In 2001, under pressure from the

United States, China compromised and sacrificed substantial national interests to secure its seat in the World Trade Organization. The global market quickly took advantage of its abundant labor force and resources, earning China the title of the (new) world's factory. By outsourcing low-value-added manufacturing jobs and offshoring sunset labor-intensive industries in decline to China, Western investors and multinationals exponentially reduced their costs and increased their profit margins.[64] This subjected Chinese workers to exploitation by transnational capital, multinational corporations, and supranational organizations, which siphoned off values to maximize their interests via the conduit of the party-state.

By altering its interconnected parameters of gender, class, and sexuality, the difference-making machinery also plays a key role in integrating China into global neoliberal infrastructures. In the early 1990s, following the discursive shift that heralded the gentrified lifestyle in tandem with global restructuring, media representations of daily life in China switched their focus from working-class people or peasants to the newly minted middle class, justifying the massive structural changes and soaring inequalities.[65] In contradiction to the Maoist goal of building a classless society, class struggles and social injustice became a suppressed topic that warranted the implicit value extraction of poor workers by both the state and capital. Meanwhile, the homogenizing gender egalitarianism of socialism gave way to a mélange of binaristic gender concepts, and the polarized gender essentialism that had been held at bay earlier was unleashed to shore up middle-class normativity.[66] For example, Chinese began to celebrate entrepreneurship as the new hallmark of manhood, with business masculinity assuming hegemonic status in a globalized world.[67] Like their Western counterparts, Chinese women are confronted with prescribed roles that instruct them, along with their male counterparts, to pursue education and hone their professional skills as independent, competitive, and successful people in a market-driven society.[68] However, women also have contradictory roles, as they are told to take on the role of caretaker and homemaker to facilitate the privatization of public services previously provided by the state.[69] Alongside the dichotomized installations of class and gender, the dualistic concept of homo- and heterosexuality emerged as a new taxonomic vector in the 1990s.[70] The discursive construction of sexual identities as a new label replaced Mao's heavy-handed punitive policies in regard to homosexual behavior. To compete for more jobs at the lower end of the global division of labor with its Southeast Asian neighbors and tackle the challenges from developed countries to build its advantages in high-tech sectors, the state is poised to redraw the lines of gender, class, and sexuality to further extract Chinese people's biopolitical values. Consequently, it has substantially increased the social splintering that keeps unfolding with massive rebellions, epidemic suicidal protests, and organized serial strikes.[71]

Tracking how the difference-making machinery works to incorporate China into the global neoliberal matrix and foster cross-border reproduction of capital, my study dismantles the Cold War legacy for new understandings of the present crisis. By imposing neoliberal principles as the blueprint of global restructuring, the Washington Consensus paved the way for the disastrous Great Recession and unrelenting resistance to globalization across the world.[72] Showing that the China model is not quintessentially different from its Western counterpart, my investigation provides a tool kit to dissect the various modes of neoliberal governance—in particular, the antigovernment discourse trafficked transnationally by right-wing nationalists to reinforce and perpetuate the neoliberal mantra.[73]

Following the paths through which this machinery reconfigures categories of differences to segregate human beings into competing groups and sets the stage for the global exploitation of laborers by the Chinese party-state, foreign countries, and multinationals, my study also builds an epistemic ground for fundamental change. As Aihwa Ong and Nancy Fraser both note, current studies of globalization treat it as a set of either rationalized structural changes or cultural dynamics that have shaped human identities and subjectivities.[74] Either way, these frameworks prevent us from fully accounting for, much less dismantling, the relationship between neoliberalism and the formations and re-formations of identities on both individual and societal levels. Far from bringing forth a borderless cosmopolitan world, the systematic and oppressive reordering of social control over populations in the form of reentrenched gendered, sexualized, classed, and ethno-racialized differences has accompanied the promotion of open markets and free traffic of capital, creating new tensions of reterritorialization of nation-state boundaries.[75] Focusing on the daily operation of the difference-making machinery, my analysis untangles the braided vectors of gender, sexuality, class, and ethno-race to expose the oppositions that are re-created in transnational settings to pit disenfranchised groups against one another, thus allowing for their compound exploitation by nation-states and multinational corporations. This grounded scrutiny clarifies how social hierarchies are remade at the local levels to thwart collective resistance of people on the periphery.

More critically, my investigation traces the ways in which China's marketization has been pushed forward through the integration of rational market subjectivity and love-induced fantasies and desires by the difference-making machinery. It also addresses the theoretical lacunae that leave affect, emotions, and feelings fatally underdiscussed in scholarly examinations of neoliberal subject and world making. This analytical inadequacy contributes to our inability to fathom the innermost layers of the transnational neoliberal matrix, an inability that prevents us from enacting far-reaching changes. In practice, neoliberalism depends on its ideological basis, which touts personal optimization through quantifiable market value maximization, as much as it does on motivation to increase the qualitative surplus value of life—which is infinitely deferred to elsewhere and elsewhen. During the course of China's neoliberalization, erratic feelings, emotive responses, and affective tethering have been unceasingly provoked and spread to engineer the marketized relationships and meet the changing needs of industrial and financial capital. In the following sections, drawing upon critical scholarship that has addressed these topics from various perspectives, I propose a new approach and elaborate how it can be used both to develop a different understanding of global neoliberalism and to transform the current system.

Tracing the Multidirectional and Multidimensional Governing Machinery

To move beyond antagonistic Cold War thinking, we might readdress neoliberalism as the set of contingent and flexible practices that Michel Foucault calls "governmentality" to produce self-serving subjects and, in turn, create and consolidate market mechanisms for managing all social relationships.[76] As the most important means as well as the end of neoliberal governance, the state embeds the market in a symbiotic relationship aimed to facilitate and sustain the efficacious running of the market—which, in turn, provides the ultimate legitimacy for the state's raison d'être. As chapter 4 shows, the adoption of neoliberal governance by the party-state has transformed all levels of the Chinese government from de jure bastions of social justice into de facto entrepreneurial entities wielding sovereign power to maximize their own interests. In short, China has turned into "a capitalistic society in terms of administration, fiscal system, and social structure . . . and socialist in terms of political bureaucracy," as a rural migrant with decades of experience in the housing development industry put it succinctly.[77] To stabilize this transition, nationalism comes to the fore as the primary resource for the state to use in garnering public support for advancing its marketizing agenda, as I show in chapter 1.

At its core, the neoliberal governing machinery relies upon the production of agential subjects to exert and extend market rule, and the administration of individual bodies and populations becomes two poles that are coordinated by the difference-making mechanism. At one end, generative biopower circulates and refuels itself in horizontal ways to produce new singular subjects who are willing to practice market rule.[78] At the other end, calculative biopolitics to catalogue, differentiate, and stratify populations are waged in totalizing vertical ways to set the stage for the practicing of market rule by these individualized subjects.[79] To coordinate the crosscurrents of biopower and biopolitics, the governing machine regenerates bifurcated differences to accommodate the diagonal working of biopower and biopolitics. Citing sexuality in eighteenth- and nineteenth-century Europe, Foucault explained how this polarizing mechanism constituted homosexuality as the categorical antithesis to heterosexuality in the burgeoning capitalist system via discursive formations; scientific archiving; medical practices; judicial protocols; legal practices; and the social institutions of state, family, and education. Meanwhile, the difference-making mechanism produced other so-called abnormal sexual categories (such as child sex and extramarital relationships) in the same manner as homosexuality, limiting the human sexual spectrum and valorizing the heterosexual conjugal relationship as normative. By inserting sexuality as a wedge between the macromanagement of the population and the microregimentation of self making, this normalized selfhood helped channel people's heterogeneous desiring fantasies into the monolithic purpose of reproduction of quality bodies, consolidating the bourgeois nuclear family as a bastion in which to foster subjects best suited for capital's needs.[80]

Feminist scholarship, especially scholarship about women of color and transnational feminism, substantially expand the single-axis and flattened Foucauldian framework by shedding light on the multidirectional and multidimensional operation of the difference-making machinery.[81] For example, Patricia Hill Collins aptly disentangles how race, gender, and class interact with one another to create the multilayered and multifaceted architecture of the matrix of domination, which modifies its structures and textures to serve the contingent socioeconomic and political interests of the United States.[82] At the apex of globalization, the machinery extends its layered parameters well beyond nation-state boundaries, taking a far more complicated shape to set up, distribute, and administer variously organized disciplinary regimes that invigorate neoliberalism's global reign.[83] The difference-making machinery drastically redraws the lines between central and peripheral, privileged and disadvantaged, and first and third worlds to match globally distributed capital, subjecting the marginalized majority to the joint exploitation by a global minority of elites.[84]

Taking these observations further, I argue that the difference-making machinery has created a multidirectional and multidimensional network in which disciplinary biopower and totalizing biopolitics collude to prop up the day-to-day running of the neoliberal regime. Out of its overlapping parameters of gender, sexuality, class, and race/ethnicity, oppositional differences are regenerated to pit the working majorities against one another and squeeze the most out of their labor values. The neoliberal machinery fixes these disenfranchised subjects in differentiated positions for comparative biopolitical devaluation, to maximize the benefits of state and capital by drawing upon the established patterns of dichotomized inequalities.

Given its elastic nature, the multidirectional and multidimensional machinery calls for a supple approach to avoid reducing its eclectic governing parameters to static categories simply for the purpose of naming identities, and to keep track of its grounded articulation to build "a gathering place for open-ended investigations of the overlapping and conflicting dynamics of race, gender, class, sexuality, nation, and other inequalities" that undergirds its daily operation.[85] For this purpose, I do not aim to provide an exhaustive account of all the parameters at play. Instead, my inquiry focuses on singular events, localized practices, and historiographic flash points as the nodal points to develop a broad view of its embedded functioning.[86] For instance, although I use the terms *race/ethnicity* and *ethno-race* interchangeably for making overarching arguments, my analysis shifts between race and ethnicity throughout the book for contextually relevant and culturally specific meanings, shedding light on details about the systematic pattern of the governing machine. My goal is to retain analytical sharpness related to structural inequalities that are key to biopolitical management, while remaining attentive to fictive and becoming aspects of the machinery that are instrumental to the speculative manipulation of affective tendencies and potentials.[87]

Feeling Love's Tempo with the Pulsating Body

Unarguably, building upon the polarized differences that it regenerates, the neoliberal machinery does not simply use feedback to capture and remake existing patterns of asymmetries to effectuate biopolitical control: it also uses feedforward to preregister people's affective tendencies to forestall their inauspicious concretization and better serve the state and capital.[88] On top of the retrospective ordering to create "a world-homogenizing sovereign with coherent intentions that produces subjects who serve its interests, such that their singular actions only *seem* personal, effective, and freely intentional," the difference-making machinery incorporates visceral forces and autopoietic shifts for preemptive registering of "the messy dynamics of attachment, self-continuity, and the reproduction of life that are the material scenes of living on in the present."[89] With life-changing hope for many people and life-affirming prospects for others, the machinery invigorates "a fantasy of the good life" that ensures the continuity of human subjects' sense of "what it means to keep on living on and to look forward to being" in our lifeworld that creates inseverable attachments by moving people out of themselves and toward its enticing offers.[90] These fantasmatic relationships help establish and retain the neoliberal system as "a thing that is sensed and under constant revision" by plunging people into a ceaseless search for a better life to facilitate the post–World War II restructuring across Europe and the United States.[91] Regardless of what happens in actuality, the pleasures of proximity to the aspirational dreams become the life-sustaining habitus that is essentially cruel rather than remedial, since neoliberal governance has turned the world into "a landfill for overwhelming and impending crises of life-building and expectation whose sheer volume so threatens what it has meant to 'have a life'"; it is the sticky attachment wrought by the promise of the good life that yokes people in ways that have reinforced and perpetuated the status quo.[92] As Berlant sees it, the hollow-sounding promise of the neoliberal dream is concretized in the binaristic terms of gender, class, and sexuality as "upward mobility, job security, political and social equality . . . durable intimacy . . . meritocracy" in the West.[93]

Through the antithetical and detached differences, life-improving neoliberal aspirations remap infinitely onto other times or places to recharge their affective traction. As Massumi argues, the futuristic and other-place-oriented neoliberal dreams operate in the "logic of the would-have/could-have," implying that "if I had . . . , I would/could have."[94] The difference-making machinery prevents people from seeing the broad picture by enacting a nonstop renewal of the future-oriented and other-object-projected affective attachments, displacing their unfulfilled neoliberal aspirations onto an ensemble of the Otherized items, people, relationships, and worlds. Thus, "the nonexistence of what has not happened" is rendered "more real than what is now observably over and done with."[95] The affective forces that such aspirational dreams generate are contemporary and very real, driving people toward the never-to-be-fulfilled promise offered by the delusive dreams against their calculative rationality.

In China, the unbounded difference-making machinery has contributed to an embedded structure of affective tethering that is comparable to what Berlant observes in Western societies, integrating people's becoming self with their world making into a symbiotic genesis that subtends and grounds the neoliberalizing process. Taking form as the kaleidoscopic Loveland, the structure of the sensorium does not simply dig up and reinforce enamoring feelings out of its burial ground, but fabulates love as a set of potentials that Massumi calls "the virtual" to be actualized in the wake of promissory things, items, or relationships.[96] Passing through our body, love lands on us, "ending up in a facial tic or passing fast, a one-time only smirk," and its intensified impacts on the body become our "new jumping-off point" and "seeds for a worlding."[97] The suspension of love's unobstructed flow in particular forms of bodily posture, felt tingling, or spontaneous kinesthetic reaction—as seen in the love-informed group of woeful women discussed above—is when and where the edgeless Loveland manifests its amorphous sensual registers both linguistically and prelinguistically. Anchored in the volatile vectors of the difference-making machinery, the Loveland nimbly extends its affectsphere along and across diverse spatiotemporal scales, transducing disciplinary biopower and totalizing biopolitical forces structured by the dimorphic categories of gender, class, sexuality, and race/ethnicity into sovereign selves to carry forward the worlding process in neoliberal terms.

As the contact sheet of the phantasmagoric lovescape, the pulsating body is the grounded venue we use to sense and chart the quotidian rhythm of love that perpetually takes and loses shape, appears and disappears. As Gilles Deleuze and Félix Guattari suggest, instead of a collective organism of flesh, sinews, blood, cartilages, and bones, the body is an ongoing event, an open-ended process of becoming and an assemblage of zones defined by intensity, thresholds, gradients, and flux.[98] At its core, "a body affects other bodies, or is affected by other bodies," and "it is this capacity for affecting and being affected that also defines a body in its individuality."[99] A body, in this sense, is defined not by insulation from but by interaction with other bodies. Via the vessel of the body, the intensification of transactional biopower and biopolitics produces individual subjects latched onto the body as residual effects that reshape the world these subjects coinhabit. With the focus being "less about its [the body's] nature as bounded substance or eternal essence and more . . . as an interface that becomes more and more describable when it learns to be affected by many more elements," a Deleuzian approach is instrumental to tracing people's emerging lovabilities and love-abilities and throwing into relief the indeterminate boundaries of the Loveland.[100]

In this book, I use the body as a telescope to develop an overview of the Loveland and as a microscope to zoom in on its metamorphic working and effects on the ground. Focusing on the "national bodies" of the performers spotlighted in the ceremony for the sixtieth anniversary of the People's Republic of China, chapter 1 explores how the state deploys an array of epidermal-cultural and fleshy-organic techniques on the metabolic body as a chronobiopolitical tool to re-create a coherent timeline and reunite its polarized socialist past and neoliberal present.[101] Reading against the historiography pieced together through these performing bodies, my analysis unearths the gendered, classed, and sexualized basics of the difference-making machinery that works to align the Loveland's shifting temporalities with the state's evolving biopolitical agenda for stabilizing China's neoliberal transition. Switching to the mass-mediated body as the prosaic extension of the corporeal body, chapter 2 diagnoses the articulation (both spatialized and despatialized) of the Loveland and shows how it recasts "normative constructions of body and corporeality" and confounds "assumptions about propinquity and distance, physicality and virtuality" to affect people's love capacities for fusing China's national interests with the transnational interests of capital.[102] The expansive Loveland, as chapters 3, 4, and 5 continue to delineate, complements and contradicts calculative biopolitics to regenerate subjects who work volitionally for the benefits of the state and capital, while it also spawns incessant contradictions from within the neoliberal apparatus as a contingent space for change.

Building a Robust Future from Within

Indeed, the difference-making machinery stretches its vibrant parameters and braids them into multifarious aspects of market activities, linking varying capitalistic relationships into a stabilized entity. For example, Roderick Ferguson notes that throughout US history, oppositional differences are continuously re-created out of the intersection of race, gender, and sexuality to disaggregate the working majorities into surplus populations that are antagonistic to one another and satisfy capital's incremental needs to reduce labor costs and increase profits.[103] While different racialized, gendered, and sexualized Others are re-created for capital reproduction, heterosexual white men, as Grace Hong posits, are reified as the emblem of US citizenship to demarcate and enforce the ambiguous borders of an imagined national community.[104] Via the centripetal apparatus of gender, race, and sexuality, the contradictory needs of freewheeling capital and the border-making nation-state are unified into a daunting US empire.

Building on its preemptive capacities to capture people's becoming tendencies, the difference-making machinery is also instrumental in the speculative proliferation of capital—the defining feature of the neoliberal economies that David Harvey calls "financialization."[105] Industrial capital depends on cheap labor, identified through retrospective differentiation based on race, gender, class, and sexuality. Yet for financial capital, profits are generated not directly by productive labor but by fantasy-engineered circulation to translate unknowable futurities into manageable probabilities.[106] With the oppositional differences that it foments and sustains, this polarizing machinery efficaciously preconditions and directs the future- and other-place-oriented projection of fantasies with the goal of fueling and furthering financial capital's predatory circulation.

China's swelling housing bubble—probably the largest in history—is the best example for expounding how the difference-making machinery coordinates the divergent needs of capital and labor, market and state, and rationalized biopolitics and affective apparatus of love to set the stage for hyper neoliberalization. Created and sponsored as a developmental powerhouse by the Zhu Rongji (1998–2003) and Wen Jiabao (2003–2013) administrations to accelerate the transitioning process, China's housing market is essentially driven by binaristic differentiation. As chapter 3 shows, precluding rural migrants who are building the urban housing sprawl out of its future existence and preventing these workers' preset-to-be-wasted bodies from compromising that sprawl's life-improving potential, the reordered disparities not only secure the unperturbed supply of low-cost labor for construction but also recharge its ever-better futurities to maintain skyrocketing prices and realize high market values. In particular, building on the manipulative formulation of love, the state-imposed rural identity and binaristic gender norms are interlocked into an enclosed route that captures numerous migrants working tirelessly toward their slow deaths to build China's glamorizing skyline. Almost all of the male construction workers I interviewed were over thirty years old and married but living alone in cities. Their wives, impelled by sacrificial love for their family members, had quit their own jobs in the cities (where educational resources for their school-age children are restricted) and moved back home (where state-sponsored care is minimal to none) to take care of their aging parents and in-laws. Also out of the familial love, the male migrants, now positioned as their family's sole breadwinner, chose to stay and struggled in abysmal conditions to work toward the family's aspirational dream. However, their love-incentivized striving has invariably left marks on them that cast them as perpetual outsiders to the spellbinding neoliberal dream: their worn-out physique, crude comportment and demeanor, and ill-advised and -selected style and clothing mark them as irredeemable outcasts in the entrancing cityscape that they have built with these outcomes. In shuffling and reshuffling the polarized differences, the scathing identification of "who you are" for locating cheap labor for industrial capital and the manipulation of "who you might become" for warranting speculative proliferation of financial capital are linked into a fantasized Ponzi economy that serves to benefit everyone but the workers.

Undoubtedly, in fostering and furthering the binaristic relationships that feed competing needs of entities implicated in neoliberal relationships, the difference-making machinery re-creates contradictions, conflicts, and clashes that pave the way for internal fissures and fractures that in turn create the necessary conditions for transformative change. Following the daily running and grounded effects of the machinery, I suggest that we can identify and access these spaces to lay the foundation for better futures.

First, the difference-making machinery has produced multiple mighty state-market subjects vying to expand their discretionary territories to gain more advantages, having escalated global competition to unsustainable levels so that it unfolds as knee-jerk antiglobalist or nationalist mobilizations. As chapter 4 shows, decades-old neoliberal practices have transformed China from a monolithic politico-economic amalgam into a matrix of rivaling state-market competitors that wield total power in their own sphere. To facilitate China's marketization and avoid a Soviet-style political overhaul, the party-state instituted the GDP growth rate as the first and foremost criterion to use in evaluating its multitiered subdivisions. This has turned local Chinese governments into bona fide entrepreneurial subjects, emboldening them to use any resources and means at their disposal to maximize economic and political outcomes. The central government also keeps drawing and redrawing gendered, classed, sexualized, and racial/ethnic lines to recategorize the population—both citizens and noncitizens—to create new biopolitical edges that attract an influx of capital and facilitate state-controlled outbound investments. These investments rescale China's national boundaries by augmenting the party-state's totalizing power to push through its expansionist agenda. Heavily reliant on predatory circulations of sovereign power, these aggressive acts have resulted in backlash from other sovereign states seeking to reclaim and revitalize their own nationalist leverage. Having created notable cracks in the World Trade Organization–based free trade system as the ground of the global neoliberal order, these responses reverberate in the form of demagogic authoritarianism, virulent mobilizations, and trade protectionism rendered as overdue economic nationalism that will sharpen their competitiveness.

Second, the multidirectional and multidimensional machinery is inherently full of crevices and openings. Thus, marginalized groups, navigating along and across its interconnected vectors, partitions, and connections, can map out subversive interstices, enclaves, and disjunctures. As Wanning Sun notes, new communication technologies such as the internet and social media have contributed to "digital political literacy" that enables subaltern groups to regenerate inventive cultural practices and "insert themselves into the symbolic order and make moral and political interventions in the field of public culture" in China.[107] Focusing on *danmei*, a queer fandom online community that consists mainly of well-educated, professional, urban, single women deemed unlovable and unable to love, chapter 5 illustrates how this group takes a nonconfrontational strategy to make room for resistance under the belly of the beast. Tiptoeing around the draconian gendered biopolitics and focusing on the sexual vector (which is relatively less monitored by the Chinese state), *danmei* fans build a utopian world of same-sex intimacy about gay men and articulate their ideal of love. Having successfully popularized a soft and effeminate version of masculinity that challenges the state-endorsed hypermasculinity and heteropatriarchal norm of love, they contribute to a more inclusive and diversified space for sexual minorities and women.

Last but not least, despite the universal rationality that is trumpeted as its epistemic and ideological foundation, neoliberal governance incessantly appeals to and recreates emotive attachments and integrates rationalized biopolitical control with preemptive conditioning of affect. These deployments make use of independent, contingent, and multiplex material and discursive practices that might converge but often contradict one another. As chapter 4 shows, rural youths leave high-paying construction and manufacturing jobs in droves for work in service industries that yields lower monetary returns but carries more affective weight by promising to improve their love capabilities. Driven by such irrational feelings, the exodus of rural laborers disrupts their biopolitically predetermined path to a slow death, leading to a thorny labor crisis that compels the state-capital alliance to mitigate its grim exploitation, although only momentarily. This love-filled fantasy has also informed a new residential pattern that shakes the patrilocal basis of sexism in rural areas, creating new room for Chinese women's subsistence and resistance. Women's growing awareness of independence has become a direct threat to Xi's rule, which has turned to masculinist, patriarchal, and paternalistic decrees as the source of legitimacy—resulting in more violent and stringent control by the state.[108]

I have divided the book into two parts. Part I, "Mapping the Edgeless Land-scape of Love," probes the prismatic temporal (chapter 1) and sociospatial (chapter 2) registers of the Loveland and explores the ways in which love is orchestrated as a public sentiment that serves the shifting needs of the party-state and capital. Part II, "Tracing the Machinery That Both Integrates China into and Separates It from the World," examines how affectively reg-istered love and biopolitical calculus, coordinated by the difference-making machinery, complement (chapter 3) and contradict (chapter 4) each other to facilitate China's neoliberal transition and neocolonial expansion, while spawning contradictions as possibilities of subsistence and survival for sub-altern groups (chapter 5).

Part I examines public culture as its major object of analysis, attending to the intertextual and extratextual modalities of transnational discursive ex-changes as they circulate between China and other parts of the world, plotting the genealogies and topologies of love as created out of the phantasmagoric vectors of gender, class, sexuality, and race/ethnicity. I do not accept these categories of difference as given but use them to develop an inquiry into how categorized relationships become established as part of the regulatory biopo-litical regime that effects neoliberalization in China. Taking a queer of color critique approach, I also work against these categories to foreground power relationships and engage the becoming aspects of the machinery to interro-gate its speculative manipulation of affective ecologies.[109] Using the category of queer as a diagnostic instrument, I develop "an analysis of geopolitically reproduced relations of power" through polarized differentiations.[110] I also re-visit the nationalist mobilizations that reconfigure "historical relations among political economies, the geopolitics of war and terror, and national manifes-tations of sexual, racial, and gendered hierarchies."[111] This approach allows me to identify the invisible heteronormative linchpin that anchors the seem-ingly impossible affiliation between socialism and neoliberalism in China (chapter 1) and tease out the "ambivalence, theoretical openness, and inde-terminacy" of "Asia" and "Asianness," exposing them as processual histories enfolded and unfolding in sync with China's neoliberalization (chapter 2).[112]

Part II draws upon formal interviews, informal conversations, focus group discussions, and participant observation, while supplementing and cross-referencing the empirical data with a pointed discursive analysis. The analyses of chapters 3 and 4 are mainly built upon ethnographic work that I conducted between May and August 2012 in Hai'an and Wuxi. Two friends of mine, Xiao Li and Dan Li, provided accommodation and other help to facilitate my fieldwork. I interviewed over a hundred rural migrants and local farmers or workers. Roughly half of them were men working in construction or related industries, such as home decorating and gardening, and the others were women working in various export-oriented manufacturing industries, ranging from clothing, textile, and silk weaving to electronics. Additionally, I interviewed about twenty people related to these workers in certain ways, including owners of factories and small businesses, housing developers, salespeople in international trade, media professionals, labor agents acting as intermediaries between Chinese workers and foreign employers, and government officials. In 2016, I revisited some of my informants in Hai'an to follow up with them.

Hai'an and Wuxi have a unique position in China's transitioning process. Bordering Shanghai on each side of the Yangtze River, the two regions are divided not only by a physical gap but also by profound disparities that have varied with the vicissitude of China's modernization since its forced opening up to the West after the First Opium War (1839–42). When Shanghai emerged as a commercial and industrial powerhouse in the mid-nineteenth century, countless laborers, merchants, and entrepreneurs flooded the city from Guangdong, Jiangnan (in the southern Yangtze Delta), and Subei (now northern Jiangsu).[113] Part of the impoverished Subei area, Hai'an has supplied labor for Shanghai and other affluent areas while building its national reputation for having reserves of skilled construction workers and making high-quality silk products. By contrast, Wuxi is located at the heart of Jiangnan—China's most prosperous region since the middle of the Tang dynasty (around 780 BC). It witnessed the burgeoning westernization movement in the 1860s and has been at the forefront of China's industrialization ever since. Like other coastal metropolises, it has attracted numerous migrant workers and gone through dazzling urbanization and gentrification since the 1990s. As labor-sending and labor-receiving regions, respectively, Hai'an and Wuxi serve as ideal locations to investigate labor-capital dynamics involved in China's marketization and global expansion. During my fieldwork, I spent considerable time in the homes and dormitories of my informants and engaged in observation and informal conversations. I also spent much of my fieldwork at various locations of production, such as construction sites, factories, small workshops, family mills, and farms. More than an outside observer of capital's faceless exploitation of labor through calculated biopolitical management, I immersed myself in the daily tempo of the Loveland in nonproductive activities such as family dinners, birthday parties, weddings, festival celebrations, and mundane chores, probing how affectively oriented (or disoriented) subjects are produced as the voluntary servants of China's neoliberal regime. My goal is to develop insights into the modus operandi of China's two economic pillars: export-oriented manufacturing and real estate industries. The chronological hiatus between my two periods of fieldwork allowed me to deepen my understanding of how the state has intensified gendered, classed, and sexualized disparities to extract biopolitical value as a means of maintaining China's competitiveness when confronted with the challenges from its Southeast Asian neighbors that offer cheaper labor and material resources.

The last chapter turns to a group of female *danmei* fans and examines how they navigate the multilayered difference-making system for survival and subsistence. Between 2009 and 2013 I conducted in-person, telephone, and online interviews with sixteen fans who were introduced to me by friends and recruited through snowball sampling. Ranging in age from eighteen to their early thirties, all of the fans were single urbanites except for one, who is from a rural region in southern China. Three identified themselves as bisexual (one was in a same-sex relationship), with the others being heterosexual. At the time of the interviews, two were students in senior high school, four were attending college, and three were working on a PhD. The others had all earned a bachelor's or master's degree and had full-time jobs in a college, foreign corporation, or government (one had just been laid off). After the interviews, I kept in touch with them by email or text messages to ask follow-up questions. My analysis is supplemented by my survey reading of popular online *danmei* fictions, interspersed by a critical reading of *Beijing Comrades: A Novel*, arguably one of China's "earliest, best known, and most influential contemporary" *danmei* works.[114]

Working against the performative lineage of desire and intimacy in the sixtieth-anniversary celebration of the People's Republic of China in 2009, chapter 1 untangles the mechanism that orders the temporal lines of the Loveland in tune with biopolitical regulation to reshape the republic's sharply polarized historiography into a coherent timeline. As my analysis reveals, gender, class, and sexuality constitute the basics of the difference-making machinery that stabilizes China's transition, foreshadowing an increasingly oppressive China under Xi's hypermasculine and patriarchal leadership. The gingerly framed and represented family love between the first couple is a recent demonstration of the fantasmatic working of love to harden and broaden China's global neocolonial thrust.

Turning to the mass-mediated body and using as an example one of the most popular entertainment TV programs in Chinese history, *If You Are the One*, chapter 2 probes the spatialized (or despatialized) topologies of love. I explore how the unbounded Loveland changes its ambience to facilitate China's neoliberal transition and rescale its national boundaries to garner new biopolitical and affective momentum for expansion. In promulgating love as the trophy for winners, the show valorizes a self-serving rationality to further neoliberalism's dominance in China and beyond. In specifying the means of winning, it delimits the scope of lovabilities and love-abilities to interject a property-based fantasy of family love into people's mundane lives and bar rural migrants from its affective orbit. Endorsing and echoing the transnational discourse of Asia and Asianness, it also builds an ethno-racial linkage to reinforce the Chinese diaspora's affective tie to the so-called homeland—a major source of foreign investments that invigorated China's marketization in the first place—and prompts an exodus of middle-class people and capital in pursuit of the dream of a good life projected onto the as-yet-uncharted West.

Tracing the life trajectories of a group of rural migrants, chapter 3 unpacks the ways in which love-spawned collective fantasies prescribe the migrants' path to a slow death with almost no outlets. Throughout their love-impelled dream-pursuing journeys, these workers have traveled along divergent and disparate routes but with identically preordained destinations. No matter how hard they try, their love-imbued dreams remain a mirage that leads them to perform still more self-defeating striving. Via the mesmerizing Loveland, they entrap themselves within a willful dream to work for the well-being of everyone but themselves, contradicting the "serving yourself, therefore benefiting all" mantra of neoliberal economics.

Chapter 4 explores the fissures arising within the difference-making system for possibilities of changes. The rationality-based neoliberal truth claim runs counter to the reality that disillusioned working subjects are constantly reproduced through fanciful and erratic feelings in support of the neoliberal matrix. Meanwhile, spurred on by the dreams of a good life modeled on the Western nuclear family, new residential patterns emerge in rural China, creating new room for gender equality for women. Last but not least, intensified competition between entrepreneurialized state-market players has revealed the brutal nature of the laissez-faire economy and motivated resistance among marginalized groups.

The last chapter shows that in building a love-only fictional world of gay men, well-educated single women have created an outlet for their own frustrated and suppressed love and project their ideal of love free of market logic onto an ethereal homoromanticism embodied by feminized gay men who are constructed, paradoxically enough, as their mirror image. This allows the women to disrupt gender polarity and heteronormative conjugal relationships objectified for market transactions and subjected to the state's pronatal initiatives. However, following a men-only logic that resonates with transnational homonormative story lines of queer gentrification, the women also create what I call a "homopatriarchal form of love" that furthers neoliberal supremacy.

In the following pages, we will see that in charging and recharging love's hallucinogenic traction to keep alive rural migrants' aspirational dreams as the key driving force of the world's factory, the borderless Loveland is indeed where China meets the world. Demarcating its boundless borders in binaristic terms that support the polarizing mechanism of the difference-making machinery, this fantasmatic lovescape is also precisely where China departs from the world.

Part I

Mapping the Edgeless Landscape of Love

Love of the Zeitgeist

Temporalized Desire in the PRC's Sixtieth-Anniversary Ceremony

The year 2009 was a milestone for the People's Republic of China (PRC). It marked the sixtieth anniversary of the regime's founding in 1949 and the thirty-first anniversary of the country's 1978 reform and opening up. More importantly, according to the official narrative, it witnessed the nation's rejuvenation after years of torture and subordination by foreigners. In April 2009, when many countries were still grappling with the shock waves of the financial meltdown, the state announced China's recovery as the first in the world, making explicit its ambition to lead the global recuperation.[1] Later that year, to elevate its image as an aspiring leader, Beijing lavished bountiful resources in both financial and personnel terms to distill and recapitulate the PRC's decades-long transformation into a one-day spectacle, fed live to the world by China Central Television (CCTV), which has a monopoly on the media industry in the country. For the military parade alone, Beijing apportioned roughly $44 million to bring the troops armed with the most advanced and awe-provoking technologies on site for the commemoration. Sharing both an office building and staff with the 2008 Beijing Olympics organizing committee (for example, Yimou Zhang, the director of the opening and closing ceremonies of the Olympics, orchestrated this celebratory extravaganza), the team of the PRC's sixtieth-anniversary ceremony assembled a group of top-notch professionals to stage another media blitz and send a clear message to the world—that "a modernized, cosmopolitan, and future-oriented China is resurging toweringly in the Eastern quarter of the globe."[2]

Undoubtedly, the ceremonial event carried paramount weight for the Chinese state not simply because of the timing of the ritualized decennial celebration, but also because of its designated historiographical positioning as a milestone of the reform, one that effectively reunified the PRC's disrupted temporal lines. Since its inception, the party-state has frequently mobilized the public to look backward and memorialize the past to create the standpoint of a new China, exhorting the people to escape the legacy of its past to give meaning to the nascent regime.[3] The posturing of rubbing against the bitter past to account for socialist China, which Xin Huang calls "*suku*" (or "speaking bitterness"), was performed to cultivate people's identification with the new China and consolidate the newly established politico-ideological system.[4] Admittedly, it is not uncommon for modern nation-states to strengthen social control through unifying administration of the temporal regime.[5] Yet the historiography became a particularly pressing issue for the PRC, since the 1978 reform divided its official timeline into two "thirty years."[6] The tension between the supporters of these two periods, marked by divergent modes of governance, had nearly reached a flash point by 2009. In March 2012, Bo Xilai, the former secretary of the Chongqing branch of the Chinese Communist Party (CCP) and the most prominent follower of the Maoist line characterizing the first thirty years and champion of the Chinese New Left, was removed from his position and charged with corruption and sentenced to life imprisonment a year later.[7] Bo's abrupt downfall is a footnote to the cutthroat struggles brewing within the CCP and the acutely polarized Chinese society writ large. In remaking and staging the synchronicity of the regime's past, present, and future through the ritualistic performance staging of what Mark Rifkin calls "inherently shared time," the 2009 festivities played a critical role in restructuring the PRC's ruptured timeline into a consequential sequence that moved forward into the imagined future.[8] More importantly, laden with such pivotal investments, the festivities were expected to mitigate the tension between the Chinese society and the party-state that kept emanating from the relentless use of neoliberal practices.

Tracing how the party-state staged the affective apparatus of desire and intimacy with the historiographic representation in its sixtieth-anniversary ceremony, this chapter probes the temporal register of the Loveland as it enfolded in the processual backdrop of China's social transformation and global expansion. Keeping a critical eye on the discursive repertoire deployed through the performers, I detect and dissect the chronobiopolitical techniques of gender, class, and sexuality that the state has used to fashion the cultural contour and resculpt the organic texture of these national bodies to straighten its fractured historiography. Taking a feminist intersectional approach, my exploration shows that, following the performative timeline, the gender difference of the performers is weakened and replaced by class disparity in the Maoist period and then reemerges as a way "to conceal the new class structure and class differentiation" in the wake of the reform era, revealing the tripartite relationship between gender, class, and the state that is shaped by and shifts with sociopolitical and economic agendas.[9] As the culmination of the event, the feminine dancers paying tribute to the PRC's sixtieth anniversary reproduced all the Chinese people as subordinate subjects and simultaneously incarnated the state as the people's hypermasculine antithesis. The gendered performance, on this account, rejoined the Chinese society and state through patriarchal bonding as the pathway into the regime's futurity.[10] Via a queer lens, my scrutiny further untangles how "the gaze of desire . . . and the narrative of desire [were] gradually wiped away" in the regime's first thirty years and intimate attractions resurfaced as the timeline proceeded into the second thirty years—unearthing the hidden heteronormative linchpin of the seemingly impossible affiliation between socialist and neoliberal China.[11] Therefore, the performers' bodies are "bound into socially meaningful embodiment through temporal regulation" and re-created from impoverished revolutionaries who subordinated their intimate lives to collective socialist causes, becoming classless gendered and sexualized subjects who freely pursue their own desire to stabilize China's neoliberal transition.[12]

Furthermore, my inquiry echoes Elizabeth Freeman's call to "think against the dominant arrangement of time and history" used to iron out unruly creases of historical inexplicability and curate an ornate historiography.[13] It also echoes Xiaomei Chen's "antipropaganda" reading of contemporary CCP pageantries to reveal "contradictions, inconsistencies, and deconstructive clues with which to question the conventional wisdom that propaganda purports to advance."[14] This critical engagement captures the misplaced components, unassimilable remnants, and excessive spillovers flickering beneath and beyond the ordered temporal register of desire and intimacy so as to discern the difference-making machinery that underwrites the anachronistic manifestation of the heteronormative gender relationship and punctuates the ritualistic performance. In dismantling the ways in which the gendered, classed, and sexualized boundaries of the Loveland are modulated in alignment with calculated biopolitical control to anchor China's marketization and global expansion, my scrutiny exposes details about the hidden interstices, unassimilable residues, and temporal dissonances within the neoliberal system to identify transformative potentials.

Situating the Spectacle in Intersectional Biopolitics

At 9:00 AM on October 1, 2009, the PRC's sixtieth-anniversary celebration began with spectacular aerial views of an array of cultural and geophysical landmarks, including the Great Wall, Yellow River, Forbidden City, and Three Gorges. Following a view of Tian'anmen Square, decorated with forty million potted plants, the TV camera focused on the 180,000 participants in the square, creating an enthralling mise-en-scène that lent audiences around the world real-time festive sensibilities. At 10:00 AM, shortly after a flag-raising ceremony, Liu Qi, then secretary of Beijing's Communist Party, announced the start of the event. With a sixty-gun salute, a military parade began along Chang'an Avenue, reviewed by the top-ranking CCP leaders gathering on the top of the monumental gate, Tian'anmen (the gate of heavenly peace). The sixty-six-minute parade featured "around 50 new and sophisticated weapons systems never before shown in public including the J-10 jet fighter, and the latest road-mobile inter-continental ballistic missiles with a range of more than 11,000km," intended to show off China's militant prowess in the face of the escalating territorial disputes with its neighbors and to increase people's patriotic attachment amid surging antagonism toward the state's neoliberal practices.[15] In contrast to the bellicose mood that permeated the morning events, at 8:00 PM, Tian'anmen Square was lit up gleefully with sixty firework displays shaped like birthday candles. With the 42,000 shells shot into the air (double the number fired at the 2008 Olympics opening ceremony), the fireworks show enlivened the ambience, setting the stage for a grand gala that turned the square into the site of an exultant night carnival.

The eighty-minute civilian parade between the military parade and the gala acted as the centerpiece of the state's temporal regimentation. Directed by Wei Chen, a renowned professor at the China Conservatory of Music, the show was designed as a time travel that invented new possibilities "for moving through and with time" for the audiences, compelling them to reencounter the past and engage with the present to interweave the two for a collective imagining of the PRC's future.[16] As the CCTV anchors remarked, "over a hundred thousand representatives from all walks of Chinese society and other countries make up thirty-six marching groups, sixty lavishly ornamented floats, and six minishows" in the parade to offer "a panorama of the glamorous history of China."[17] Under the theme of "Striving Forward with Motherland," the parade was broken into three parts: "Thoughts," "Accomplishments," and "Prospects," which spotlighted the PRC's politico-ideological accomplishments, sociocultural transformations, and idealized future, respectively. In accordance, the direction team prepared seven marching groups—called "Foundational Struggling Efforts," "Reform and Opening Up," "Centennial Leap Forward," and "Scientific Development" for the "Thoughts" part; "Dazzling Achievements" and "Splendid China" for the "Accomplishments" part; and "Brighter Future" for the "Prospects" part. Their performance was broadcast live, as were four minishows programmed as a footnote for the "Thoughts" section, to epitomize the contributions of the four leaders of the CCP—that is, Mao Zedong, Deng Xiaoping, Jiang Zemin, and Hu Jintao. To better understand the temporal logic underpinning the spectacle, we need to situate it in its historical and transnational background, which allows us to disentangle the links between China's social upheaval and the intersectional biopolitical techniques that the state developed for engineering it.

The Maoist state used class as a central biopolitical tool to substantiate the parameters of the new China.[18] Drawing upon Marxist-Leninist orthodoxy, the party-state hailed the eradication of class differences as the sine qua non that freed China from exploitation and oppression. In the early 1950s, modeled on the Stalinist paradigm, the state established a centralized structure called "circular resource allocation system" to bring social production under its control, attempting to eradicate capitalism at its core.[19] In the new system, the urban-concentrated industrialization garnered momentum from rural areas as the source of subsistence and raw materials and supplied rural areas with materials and other goods produced in due course.[20] Yet these policies imposed new forms of class disparities between urban workers and farmers, contradicting the discourse of worker-peasant solidarity that the state promulgated to valorize the socialist cause of building a classless society.[21]

The Maoist state also evoked gendered biopolitics to sponsor and strengthen the centralized economy and classless ideology. Starting in the 1950s, the regime followed the guide of its Eastern European allies to implement Friedrich Engels's ideal of proletarian gender egalitarianism as the quintessential foundation of socialism.[22] The state revamped the conjugal system to grant women more agency and independence and integrated them into public labor en masse as part of an endeavor to eradicate class inequalities and justify the socialist cause.[23] On the discursive level, the state invoked revolutionary male norms to popularize a plethora of images of gender egalitarianism that distinguished the new China from its feudal past and capitalist foes, and it used cultural icons such as the Red Detachment of Women to showcase women's equality with men.[24] On the policy level, the state incorporated biopolitical techniques targeting women's reproductive capacities into its macro planning to consolidate the economic system and implemented a set of pronatal policies that continued into the late 1970s.[25] As Zheng Wang notes, these state-sponsored feminist initiatives also created room for women—particularly rural women—to have their voices heard, and "their strong determination and their remarkable ability to endure hardship" won compliments that inspired the popular image "Iron Girls."[26]

As the marketization initiated in the 1980s spread across the country in the early 1990s, the media switched their focus from working-class people and peasants to the newly formed middle class.[27] As a result, in a change from the Maoist discourse of building the classless society, public discussions of class inequalities and social injustice have become topics that are not presented in the media. In 2009, *Dwelling Narrowness*, a TV soap opera that touched only the tip of the iceberg of the egregious class disparities in China, was promptly banned by the state after it spawned nationwide discussions of these issues. In academia, discussions of class inequalities are stringently controlled by the state, and as an analytical category, class has been replaced by social stratification—an innocuous term purged of political connotations that were central to the Maoist doctrine of class and class struggles.[28] In brief, China's middle classification of media discourses is part and parcel of the gentrifying rhetorical shift that is in sync with global neoliberal expansion.[29]

Along with China's economic reform, monolithic gender egalitarianism gave way to miscellaneous gender discourses, and the gender essentialism held at bay by the socialist state resurfaced to shore up the middle-class ideology.[30] Entrepreneurship, in particular, is heralded as the hallmark of normative manliness, echoing R. W. Connell and Julia Wood's observation that business manhood has become the hegemonic form of masculinity in the age of globalization.[31] For Chinese women, a contradictory role is prescribed to redefine their femininity. To become socially recognized subjects in China's neoliberal society, they are instructed to pursue more education and professional skills to be independent, competitive, and successful, like their male counterparts.[32] But women's traditional role as caretakers and homemakers for bourgeois families is also emphasized, to "compensate for state retreat, or for state failure to provide social infrastructure and support."[33] This self-contradictory rhetoric dovetails with the new global pattern of gender and labor: while neoliberalism disrupts the public-private divide by recruiting more women into the global labor market, those women are often confronted at the micro level with contradictory and essentialist gender ideologies.[34]

In contrast to the long-standing use of class and gender, sexuality emerged as a new biopolitical vector only with the recent intensified attempts at reform. In the 1990s, Mao's heavy-handed punitive policies to suppress homoeroticism and homosexual behavior were gradually replaced by discourses of pathological and perverse sexual behavior to assemble a new segment of the Chinese population.[35] In the new millennium—with networking made possible by digital technologies and internet-based queer cultures and communities—homosexuals, partly voluntarily and partly forced, entered the public space and people's vernacular conversations as a social group.[36] Today, it would be almost impossible not to encounter such neologisms as *jiyou* (or "gay friendship"), *gong* (or "top"), and *shou* (or "bottom"), which have been popularized by the emerging queer fandom culture and netizens.[37] Building upon the newly constructed identity of homosexuality, heteronormativity and dimorphic gender configuration constitute and reinforce each other to secure the position of the bourgeois familial matrix as the impeccable anchor for neoliberal society.

Revisiting Temporalized Desire with Critical Eyes

As a snapshot of the PRC's decades-long transformation, the civilian parade surged into the audiences' view, using chronological order and starting with "Foundational Struggling Efforts." It took the audiences back to the regime's revolutionary and reconstructive inception with an image of Mao Zedong, the PRC's founder, first, followed by three parading squads called "Fighting Fearlessly," "Creating the New China," and "Painstaking Pioneering Efforts." The parade also set the tone of the ritual, which was designed to galvanize nationalist fervor, by echoing the time-managing strategy that Heather Love calls "feeling backward"—which both harnesses and denounces emotive reactions related to the past to buttress the present and future to mitigate the escalating pressure on the state.[38] Since the 1920s, as Andrew Jones notes, public music and dancing have served as a crucial instrument for the state to use in re-creating a public sphere that involves both harmonized movements of bodies and highly gendered presentations.[39]

Reminiscent of what Jinhua Dai notes about the dominant symbolic regime during Mao's era, the opening section of the parade highlighted class (in terms of the classless ideal) to fuse gendered tropes (gender egalitarianism) with the statist agenda (socialist construction). "The image of Woman, as contained inherently in the spectral structure of male desire" as it is what she sees in other cultural products, gradually disappears with the gaze of desire and the narrative of intimate attraction.[40] In "Foundational Struggling Efforts," for example, the parade organizers applied the color codes of blue and white (the emblem of working-class identity that enjoyed its full swing in the 1960s and 1970s) to the men's bodies to accentuate their resilient proletarianism and to stylize the women by leaving ostensibly masculinized traces on their torsos. All the performers' hair was cut short to give them an identically sharp look, further blurring their gender difference and tingeing them with the revolutionary ethos hailed by the Maoist state as the proletarian essence. Even their mannerisms and comportment—including gaits, postures, and facial expressions—were reconfigured via stringent military training to minimize their embodied gender differences and foreground their revolutionary camaraderie, erasing any traces that would remind the audiences of mutual attractions and desire.

"Ansai Folk Waist-Drum Performance," dedicated to Mao's leadership during the minishow, rendered the centralized position of class even clearer. According to CCP rhetoric, Mao distinguished himself from other Communist leaders by tailoring the Marxist canon to China's historical specificity and cultural contingency and by rallying peasants, as the proletarians' staunchest allies, to secure the ultimate victory over the Japanese invaders and Nationalists.[41] In contrast to the Soviet-style realism that embraced workers as the ultimate emblem of socialist nation-states, the Maoist regime placed images of burly and hard-edged peasants side by side with superhuman workers as its ubiquitous poster children.[42] Ostensibly, the choreographic tapestry of "Ansai Folk Waist-Drum Performance" embraced this visual narrative tenet. Staged as the highlight of a harvesting season in rural northern China, this performance brought a group of male drummers clad in costumes and headdresses akin to ancient military costumes into the limelight. The dancers hit the drums attached to their waists spiritedly, producing rhythmic drumbeats and heart-throbbing folk music. As they bounded and leaped to change positions, the performers shouted at a high pitch to express their gratitude for another bountiful year. These dance pieces knitted together a montage of the PRC's stirring days of reconstruction. By showcasing the gleeful rurality and triumphant mood while ignoring miserable episodes, this sequence helped produce the collective amnesia of the state-imposed urban-rural disparity. Building on the deliberate recodification of rural life and identity, this dance boosted the revolutionary momentum set in motion by the preceding proletarian performers and represented a return to class-based socialist China.

As the parade proceeded into the reform era, the visual and narrative focus switched from class to gender—from the worker-peasant solidarity fortified by gender egalitarianism to the reappearance of gender dimorphism to dilute the class hues and reenact the flow of desiring energies.[43] The organizers employed the engendering trope to refashion the parading subjects on the surface level, as well as to redeploy their corporeality and organicity in sync with the vicissitude of the PRC's staged temporality. "Youthful China," the mini-show to glorify Deng Xiaoping, "the architect of China's economic reforms," is a good case in point.[44] A sharp departure from the preceding (and following) squads that arrayed all the parading subjects into gender-undifferentiated groups, this performance featured a pairing of all the performers as partners in ballroom-style dancing. Reminiscent of the heteronormative prom, an important coming-of-age ritual in the West,[45] the sixtieth-anniversary celebration presented the rearticulation of China's modern transformation in ostensibly gendered and sexed terms. Clad in exotic costumes that adequately defined their bodily shapes but left almost no traces of class, the dancers constituted an enclosed signifying space founded on their sexed gender polarity (see figure 1.1). In particular, with their hair in ponytails, "elongated bodies, and open easy smiles," and staged self-determinacy over personal desire and intimacy, the female performers resembled the images of the "Model Girl" and "New Woman" that had emerged in between the two world wars as the epitome of the bourgeois lifestyle, Western civilization, and modernity around the world.[46] Appearing together with the rise of modern nationalisms, both gendered icons were delicately controlled by the state as historical agents and images to serve varying manifestations of hegemonic nationalism.[47] In short, the parade directed the audiences' attention away from the PRC's fierce foundational moments to peaceful postsocialist development by moving from "Hua Mulan's masculinized women to the humanist trope of the post-revolutionary subject to the feminine object under the patriarchal male gaze."[48] Trafficking femininity "in the double bind of new exploitation and compromised freedom" secured the smooth transition.[49] Between the gender-linked socialist past and the neoliberal present, a liminal realm of heteronormative intimate encounters loomed, calling for more in-depth deconstruction in the later section of the anniversary celebration.

The gendered chronobiopolitical articulation of intimacy in the rest of the parade further erased the traces of class disparities in the neoliberal China depicted. In the minishow "Crossing the Century" (extolling Deng's successor, Jiang Zemin), a team of ebullient and robust young men waved colorful fans and pranced forward into the wind. Like the ballroom-style dance, their exotic dress code obliterated class cues. Sparing no complimentary comments about the virile young men and the robust spirit that they embody, the CCTV anchors made the masculinist connotation of the performance still clearer. Hailing the young men's masculinity as the epitome of the powerful Yangtze River, the source of China's vitality that had safeguarded the country through thick and thin into the new century, the anchors acclaimed the performers for clearing one obstacle after another and encapsulating the masculine essence that defines the PRC's centennial transformation.

However, the dancers' bodies should not be treated at face value as a mere palette to use in the coordinated applications of gender- or class-tinged hues and strokes to paint a flattering portrait of the PRC. Just as their color spectrums and cultural morphs varied during the televised parade, their organic and fleshly qualities altered in concert with the PRC's restaged timeline. One year before, fiery controversies had enveloped the efforts by Zhang to manipulate the performing bodies at the opening ceremony of the Beijing

Fig. 1.1. Dancers performing in pairs in the civilian parade at the celebration of China's sixtieth anniversary.

Olympics in the "national interests."[50] Zhang's attempt to use the photogenic nine-year-old Miaoke Lin to perform while the seven-year-old Peiyi Yang (whose crooked baby teeth were deemed potentially damaging to China's public image) dubbed her voice prompted a deluge of criticism from both domestic and international media.[51] Composed of almost the same members of the Olympic organizing committee, the ceremony's direction team held a similar belief that the bodies of parading subjects should be closely watched to ensure China's interests. Yet if it is comparatively easy to substitute one flawless body for a defective one on small-scale occasions like lip-synching, it is even more feasible to reconstitute the organic textures of bodies available for massive events like parades. Critics heralded the women performers in both the military and civilian parades for their highly unified performance as well as nearly identical bodily shapes and sizes (see figure 1.2).[52] But to achieve precision and unison on such levels, potential participants first had to go through a rigorous screening process, and those few who passed had to complete an egregiously laborious training, sculpting their bodies to meet the state's exacting requirements.[53]

The parade's temporal rhythm, which proceeded with and through these methodically reconstituted national bodies by switching the focus from class to gender, was nonetheless punctuated by incongruous staccatos. The classless socialist China that built its symbolic coherence on minimized gender differences continues to be haunted by their dogged persistence and untimely reemergence. In the first section of the parade, for instance, the bourgeois feminine skirts belied the gender-neutral dressing code, leaving the

Fig. 1.2. Female soldiers noted for their nearly identical bodily shapes and sizes in the military parade at the celebration of China's sixtieth anniversary.

female proletarians at odds with the masculinized revolutionary ethos. By comparison, Bolshevik moralists repeatedly called out women in the Soviet state who adopted Western lifestyles and fashions to get them to stop contaminating the communist spirit.[54]

Likewise, in the waist-drum show that followed, the anchors' comments pushed the gender line to the other side of the dichotomy, thwarting its equalizing tenet and destabilizing the classed pivot of socialist China. To quote their gender-steeped remarks: "With a history of over two thousand years, Ansai waist-drum was a wartime product. With no traces of conflicts left in China's peace-and-development-blessed new era, it has now turned into an expression of the peasants' visceral jubilation over another harvesting season and their bountiful life. The intensive drumbeats, robust steps, varying patterns, and macho shouts combine to instill the masculine beauty of men from the Loess Plateau, whose confident moves and beaming smiles fully index the Chinese people's elation about their emancipation and democratic political participation."[55]

Instead of the ghostly matter that impedes smooth temporal progression, the anachronistically gendered bodies in practice cast light on the underlying chrononormative pattern.[56] As Freeman suggests, chrononormativity is "a mode of implantation, a technology by which institutional forces come to see like somatic facts" that primes our lived realities as the rhythms that align our embodied being closely with chronobiopolitical techniques.[57] Our lived embodiment, as Walter Benjamin contends, is "thoroughly colored by the time to which the course of our existence has assigned us."[58] In this regard, the disordered gender residues and flashbacks surrounding the national bodies index how the zeitgeist of contemporary China has shifted from using class to using gender as a powerful lever for its neoliberal transition.

When seen against the broader backdrop of state-ordained social upheavals, the gendered zeitgeist becomes more obvious as the vital chrononormative tool used to neutralize the social anxieties and antagonisms inflicted by restructuring. Contrary to the self-congratulatory tone of the rurality and proletarianism replayed in the parade, peasants and workers (as the de jure masters of the country) have borne the major brunt of China's neoliberal transition: "The beleaguered peasants, who comprise 70 percent of the national population and 50 percent of the labor force, have found their income in dramatic decline since 1997."[59] This polarization has continued to widen since China joined the World Trade Organization in 2001. As of 2010, 1 percent of households (mostly urban ones) owned 41.4 percent of the national wealth.[60] In addition, in 2012 almost ninety million Chinese people still lived on less than $2 a day, an indicator of extreme poverty used by the World Bank.[61] Simultaneously, the income ratio between urbanites and rural residents increased from 2.57:1.0 in 1978 to 2.90:1.00 in 2019.[62] Neoliberalization has also increased class disparities in other postsocialist societies like Russia.[63] However, China has developed its economy by deliberately using classed and gendered biopolitics to turn impoverished Chinese workers and peasants into a precarious and hyperexploitable segment of the population.[64] As they are used to drive China's dizzying industrialization and urbanization, the state curtails their physical presence to guarantee that it will not contaminate the presumably evolving urban skyline and life.[65]

No doubt, the state's egregious exploitations have also met unrelenting resistances that have taken various forms of recalcitrance and come from different disenfranchised groups. In 2010, a suicide epidemic erupted at the workers' camp for a Guangdong-based factory of Foxconn, the major contractor for Apple products, and the world was appalled when eighteen rural migrant workers attempted suicide.[66] Besides the individual suicides, the anxiety, hostility, and despair of the indentured Foxconn workers (a combination that Jack Qiu calls "iSlaves") led to intermittent confrontations with the management.[67] In January 2012, after a fruitless negotiation marathon, over a hundred Foxconn workers in Wuhan threatened to commit suicide collectively as the last means of resistance to relentless exploiters.[68] In the midst of the increasingly acrimonious labor-capital relationship, the state disavowed its commitment to social equality and took a custodial role to secure uninterrupted capital reproduction, resulting in a larger share of budget being devoted to preempting resistance from civilians than to improving the country's defensive military capacity.[69] Open discussions of class disparities and even the Marxist canon are monitored by police and can have harsh punitive consequences.[70] Gender is seen as a new ground to be used to mitigate disgruntlement, concealing the escalating tension between the Chinese state and society.[71]

Part and parcel of the zeitgeist of neoliberal China, gender dualism pervaded the theatrical recounting of the country's Maoist and socialist past in the parade, and that dualism even haunted its original construction decades earlier. As Xiaomei Chen notes, in the magnificent show *The East Is Red*, "an early attempt to construct a Mao cult [in 1966] . . . reached its apex during the Cultural Revolution." This spectacular ritual "begins with a prologue titled 'Sunflower Turning Toward the Sun,' in which seventy female dancers in long, blue silk dresses wave silk sunflowers props in time to [its] theme song."[72] "With grace and tenderness," the dancers "walk toward the radiant sun rising from the ocean (which is projected on the rear-stage screen, symbolizing 'the vivid image of sunflowers growing toward the sun while the masses are guided by the CCP's leadership')."[73] On the surface level, this symbolic technique hyperfeminizes all the performers through its floral analogy, contradicting the Maoist zeitgeist that celebrates the eradication of gender differences through women's masculinization.[74] However, the heteropatriarchal relationship that the technique creates also justifies the subordination of personal desire to the collective statist cause, and that cause is key to the construction of the socialist regime of intimacy that Haiyan Lee calls "revolutionary romanticism."[75] To disentangle the recurrent disordered gender representations and understand how the relationships among gender, class, and the state shift with varying social climates, we need to contextualize this gender paradigm in a broader historical background. The next part of the chapter offers a brief review of gender and the state in Chinese history that helps us home in on the difference-making mechanism to see how it modulates the regime of intimacy to uphold the PRC's social transformation.

Rebuilding the Timeless Nation-State in Subordinate Intimacy

The state-imposed urban-rural class disparities are recent. In contrast, gender has long been central to the organization and management of family, political bureaucracy, and other social apparatuses in China.[76] "The prominent role of the government in defining gender relations and sexuality," Susan Mann argues, "is a unique, enduring feature of Chinese history that sets the Chinese experience apart from other modern industrial nations."[77] As early as the Han dynasty (206 BC–220 CE), the feminine behavior prescribed in the Confucian classic *Three Obediences and Four Virtues for Women*, by the female Confucian guru Ban Zhao, laid the cornerstone for managing the politico-ideological order of the Chinese Empire. The title refers to the social norms that stipulated women's duties and subordinate role in the family, and the state recursively referenced the book to justify the submission of subjects to the monarch and validate the bureaucratic hierarchy.[78] In the Song dynasty (960–1279 CE), a group of male Confucian pundits developed the gendered doctrine into a compendium of instructions that view "the family as the microcosm of civic virtues and skills," arguing that political elites need to learn to "govern the state by managing one's own family."[79] As a repository of discursive and administrative tools, gender was instrumental for the monarchs in managing the feudalist apparatus.

As the Middle Kingdom started to crumble in the sixteenth century under the combination of external colonialist impingement and internal grassroots revolts, the imperative to build a modern political system surfaced and intensified. Because of its entanglement with the imperial structure, gender became a convenient and crucial resource for such an undertaking.[80] For instance, in the late nineteenth century, male intellectual and political leaders such as Kang Youwei and Liang Qichao centralized women to articulate and promulgate their nation-building vision. The only way to lift China out of the chaos and re-create a modern state, they asserted, was based on the enlightenment and emancipation of the uneducated and backward Chinese women.[81] In the early twentieth century, as Shanghai started its urban sprawl, varied discursive efforts surrounding female sex workers competed to gain moral advantage and control the narrative about China's future.[82] Women's gender and sexuality became, as Gail Hershatter puts it, the embattled site that "embraced populations from various nations, regions, and classes, and harbored political agitators ranging from Christian moral reformers to Marxist revolutionaries."[83]

Since the 1920s, both the Nationalist and Communist intelligentsia have used gender to elaborate and promote their rival agendas for building a modern China. While the Communists defined "women's status as equal citizens as a marker of China's arrival at modernity," the Nationalist Party incorporated the emancipation of women into its master plan for a national revolution.[84] After the PRC's foundation in 1949, the CCP used gender consistently as a way to facilitate the massive project of class-branded socialist constructions. In comparison with life-and-death class struggles, gender vectors were deemed much safer, and gender inequalities were understood as nonantagonistic contradictions within frenzied political mobilizations.[85] As China's neoliberal practices have rescaled class structure and resulted in tenacious resistance on various fronts, gender has replaced class as the way to reorganize the gender-class-state triangulation for social stability. To deepen our understanding of how gender works in China's recently minted neoliberal conditions, I will further interrogate the difference-making mechanism that has fused gender with the Chinese nation-state.

Feminist theories are helpful for disentangling the intricate relationship between gender and nation-state, proffering a plenitude of incisive tools to dislodge the gendered facade of nation building.[86] Scholars note that political authorities in places other than China also constantly draw upon families and patriarchal relationships to substantiate their politico-ideological propositions.[87] Women in particular are frequently co-opted as an empty signifier for exigent symbolic investments and used to patrol the imaginary boundaries of nation-state.[88] For instance, Shawn Michelle Smith finds that Americanness was first construed as a national identity through the angelic, ethereal, and sacrosanct moral ideal embodied by true middle-class white women that was distinct from the British one built on aristocratic conception.[89] Uma Narayan shows how women in postcolonial India were assigned varying roles to facilitate divergent nationalist movements and anticolonial mobilizations.[90] Similarly, in reviewing the history of Afrikaaner and African nationalisms in South Africa, Anne McClintock elucidates how competing nationalist projects built their universal appeal through the gendered accounts projected onto different imaginaries of women.[91] In the spirit of these feminist insights, I now proceed to tease out the nationalist covering of China's ceremony to unpack how the gendered fabrics morph to contrive the PRC's forward-moving temporality.

As the grand finale of the convivial homage, the last minishow (dedicated to Hu Jintao, then the PRC's president) is of particular import. Titled "Blessing China," this show was designed to complete the tribute-giving ritual and commemorate the PRC's accomplished past, glamorize its trailblazing present, and envision an even more spellbinding future. To drive home this temporal triplet, a group of female dancers took over the stage and used their entrancingly blithe performances as an invitation to all Chinese nationals to join in the blessing of their homeland. The show's title deliberately left the subject of the blessing unclear, but the show itself clarified that the Chinese people were the subject. Its theme song "Today Is Your Birthday" makes this clear:

Today is your birthday, my China.
In the morning I released a flock of white doves.
The doves fly through mountain ridges,
bringing back an olive leaf to you.
We are celebrating your birthday, my China.
Wishing that you would have suffering no more and remain serene
forever.
The doves fly across the sky and ocean,
bringing back your children's nostalgic call from afar to you.
A wish from your children is recounted to you that the moon would
always be at its fullest and your children would always be happy.
The doves fly through the wind and rain,
bringing back a golden wheat ear to you.
A wish from your children is chanted to you wholeheartedly that you
would persevere through the bad weather and always thrive.[92]

First composed for the PRC's fortieth-anniversary ceremony, in 1989, this song is a key part of the urgent endeavor to salvage the party-state's damaged public image.[93] The gendered rhetoric attempts to soften the antipathy toward the murderous state and heal the wounded relationship between the state and nation. In the months that followed the crackdown on the Tian'anmen Square movement, "the CCP embarked on the task of 'raising morale,' of winning back the hearts and minds of the Chinese people through ideological persuasion," and popular music played a vital role in the relevant propaganda.[94] Switching among the pronouns *my*, *I*, and *we*, the song eulogizes the relationship between the Chinese nation or people (or "us") and the state and compares it to that between children and mother, attempting to sweep the state-sanctioned massacre under the carpet and whitewash the clearly savage CCP authorities as a loving and nurturing maternal figure.

As Lynne Segal reminds us, the metaphorical use of gender "is always intensified in times of crisis, or in the consolidation of new regimes of power."[95] Gendered crisis management has long-standing historical and cross-cultural precedents that take various forms. For instance, in the United States after 9/11, the administration of President George W. Bush presented the federal government as a paternal protector, reasserting its sovereign power that had been challenged and diminished by the terrorist intrusion. This rhetoric also exhorted US citizens to relinquish facets of their civil rights in support of the administration's War on Terror at home and abroad.[96] In contrast to the US state, which was viewed as a hypermasculine fatherly guardian, the Chinese government, after the calculated killing of its own citizens, presented itself as a caressing maternal figure, yearning to embrace all her children with unconditional love to dampen the raging fire burning within.

Recycled two decades later, the gendered focus of "Today Is Your Birthday" shifted with China's sociopolitical climate and rising status in the global community, as the country evolved from a novice laissez-faire economy to a seasoned leader of global neoliberalism. The symbolic transition in the use of the song functions through an array of discursive and visual tropes deployed via the bodies of the dancers to inject a new life into the song with their mesmerizing gendered performance. At the center of the televisual view, the performers tweaked and twisted their lithe choreographic moves to push the nationalistic ceremony to its acme. The camera turned these national bodies into pliable and subordinate feminized subjects by focusing on the dancers' ample and shapely torsos, agile and delicate postures, and subservient and ecstatic countenances through a medley of long shots and close-ups. Thus, the dance simultaneously expunged all the cues that

Love of the Zeitgeist   51 would remind the audiences of their other identities, especially those based on class or ethnicity. As the dancing team swung along with the love-defined song, they ushered into focus a giant peony-shaped floral float that, following the melodious music, unfolded into a full blossom that revealed a female dancer rising from its pistil. Waving their delicate sleeves breezily with the song, the dancers captivated the audiences with their floral embodiment of femininity. Working through the feminized dancers and subjects of blessing as the referential point, the gender trope concretized the ambivalent imagery of China that had been troubled by intensified internecine struggles stemming from class and ethnic disparities as the hypermasculine antithesis of these feminine dancers and legitimized the presence of a masculinized image of China for collective admiration and commemorative rejuvenation. For those viewers who had weathered the stormy Cultural Revolution, this happy ending surely brought a sense of déjà vu, because the floral gender trope had been deployed as the central technique of Mao's cult of personality in *The East Is Red*.[97] This gendered futuristic beckoning, in my view, is also an imposing harbinger of an increasingly aggressive global China in the paternalistic and patriarchal reign of Xi Jinping.

It is worth noting that in specifying China rather than the PRC as the object of the blessing, the show replaced the sovereign entity of the state with the imagined community of the nation as the recipient of the ritualistic performance. However, as Benedict Anderson reminds us, nation and state are not always a priori wedded.[98] Instead, their contested relationship calls for persistent labor to correct the slippages and slides emanating from between them.[99] As a leading player in the global network of capital that is ruled oxymoronically by Communists, China is an appropriate example of this fraught relationship. Having fully embraced neoliberalism in governance and the ensconced market as the primary mechanism for managing Chinese society, the party-state has disavowed its early commitment to leading the Chinese nation and people toward social justice and equality and has morphed into a sturdy ally of capital. The neoliberalizing practices have fundamentally reconfigured the social structures, and the Marxist-Leninist-Maoist mantra of building a classless socialist China has lost its appeal as the state's ideological basis, pressuring the state to find new resources for remedying its antagonistic relationship with the Chinese people and nation and reclaim its legitimacy.[100] Nationalism is a convenient resource that is constantly mobilized for such purposes. If not handled appropriately, however, it can entail new threats to thwart the state from within. While seeking ways to create a nationalist fervor for its legitimation in the public eye, the CCP leadership has been wary of the volatile nature of nationalism, especially that of the populist form—which "might detour or even endanger the state's other policy interests and, worse yet, could turn inwards against the regime itself."[101] Since the mid-1990s, the state has cultivated and circulated anti-Japanese sentiment to garner nationalist support for its policies.[102] In 2012, state-organized anti-Japanese rallies quickly escalated into nationwide demonstrations that in turn became violent manifestations and altercations. The patriotic energies fomented and mobilized by the state crossed the line, exploding into wide-ranging anticorruption protests advocating democracy.[103] Trapped in this dilemma, the Communist authorities use nationalist affectivities to serve their agenda while endeavoring to keep the concomitant emotive eruptions under control.

The integration of individuals into a collective body as the people is at the heart of building modern nation-states, and the inclusion of "bare life"—human lives as purely biological organisms external to and beyond the jurisdiction of state power—in a sovereign state as citizens is the ultimate source of the state's sovereign power.[104] Put simply, the right to define who is included in and who is excluded from the people valorizes the state as a coherent politico-juristic unity. However, as Aihwa Ong contends, citizenship should be treated not merely as a political entitlement defined and granted by the state, but as an ongoing process of subject making, embedded in complex dynamics that involve "the cultural practice and beliefs produced out of negotiating the often ambivalent and contested relations with the state and its hegemonic forms that establish the criteria of belonging within a national population and territory."[105] Throughout human history, because of their naturalized relationship to the body, categories such as race, gender, and sexuality have repeatedly been invoked as ways to ground political propositions that are otherwise arbitrary and subjected to external challenges.[106]

As surging subversive forces and resistances confront the Chinese state, gender provides a way to address public anger over skyrocketing class inequalities and fierce ethnic tensions, and it helps reformulate the cultural norm of citizenship so as to rejoin the people and nation with the state. In the final minishow at the anniversary celebration, the female dancers serve both as the surrogates for all Chinese nationals and as an on-site liaison, creating a dialogue between the absent interlocutors (namely, the people and the party-state). Representing all the Chinese people and dedicating the blessings to the state through the ethereal gendered performance, the dancers not only feminize the former as citizens subordinate to the all-encompassing sovereign power of the latter, but they also legitimize the latter as the masculine authority to protect and control the former as its citizens. Through this gendered polarity, all other

disparities and differences were erased and absorbed into the manicured imagery of China, and the Chinese nation (as all the effeminate citizens) and the party-state (as the masculinized sovereignty) were joined as a buttressed construction (see figure 1.3). Through the ceremony, gender has a prominent presence in reconstructing the image of China in the passing socialist time, magnifying its appearing in neoliberal time, and highlighting its rising status in the global community through the staged synchronization of the PRC's past and present to reintegrate a fragmented Chinese nation-state into a timeless given.[107] Using an array of chronobiopolitical techniques—such as rewinding in the class-based revolutionary festivities, spotlighting by the gendered ballroom dancing, and fast-forwarding through the floral performance that brings the future into the awareness of the audiences—the eventful performance compresses a multitude of disconnected and uneven temporalities into a single whole to complete the PRC's undisturbed and creaseless timeline.

As what Chen calls the "incubator of future political leaders," the CCP pageantries were orchestrated to secure a stable transition between different leaderships and governing modalities.[108] A performer in *The East Is Red*, President Hu developed his own gendered sensibilities by participating directly in the staging of the revolutionary intimacy between the subordinate

Fig. 1.3. Female dancers representing all the Chinese people dedicate blessings to the party-state in the civilian parade at the celebration of China's sixtieth anniversary.

Chinese people and the patriarchal Communist leader in the 1960s that was encapsulated in the vivid images of sunflower dancing as discussed earlier. Four decades later, this legacy was rearticulated as the comparable peony floral trope to glorify Hu's leadership and repair the splintered relationship between the Chinese people and the state. Likewise, China's first lady, Peng Liyuan—a household name that dominated the grand finale of multiple high-profile propaganda performances—has developed a firsthand gendered knowledge that has been integrated into her husband's ruling style. And that style, to no small extent, is based upon the manipulation of public intimacy.

For the rest of this chapter, I revisit the liminal realm of heteronormative desires in the parade that marks and reconnects the PRC's periodization, and I unravel the hidden sexual foundation of China's stabilized neoliberal transition. I expose how the staged performance foreshadows the rise of a more assertive China supercharged by the heteropatriarchal and paternal love of Hu's successor, Xi Jinping.

The Hidden Sexual Pivot of the Impossible Affiliation

As the foregoing analysis lays bare, the proliferative realm of desire and intimacy enacted by the ballroom-style dancing performance divided and bridged the gap between the PRC's socialist past and neoliberal present. The paired mutually referencing male and female bodies constitute the site that restarts the flow of desiring energies and attaches these affectivities to a diametrically gendered and sexed corporeality. For a long time, personal desire and romantic attachment were subjected to draconian policing and severe punishment, due to their supposed connection to individualistic indulgence and bourgeois hedonism, and were subordinated to the statist cause as "revolutionary romanticism."[109] The liberalization of private intimacy offered a sensory index of China's social transformation.[110] Since the 1990s, a mélange of cultural formations that differentiate desires into the hetero- and homosexual desiring duo has replaced the blanket repression of individual intimacies.[111] Heterosexuality has been further valorized as the norm to gauge and evaluate all other (supposedly perverse) desires to reshape the Chinese population in accordance with scaled-up marketization.

In the PRC's synchronized temporalities, the performative heteronormative encounter creates a self-referential vantage point that serves to ground the repolarization of gender so as to facilitate the symbolic periodization and reconnection of the timeline. Judith Butler has offered a useful heuristic to explicate this complicated relationship. Suggesting that gender is "performative," she explains how heterosexuality, once established as an imperative premise, lays the foundation both for repetitive practices over the corporeal body that reproduce the gender of quotidian performance and for gender and anatomical sex in unison so as to perpetuate the dualistic gender system.[112] For example, in the romantic pairing, the dancers' anatomical sex (rendered self-evident by their starkly contrasted and reshaped bodily contours), their gender (codified as different but complementary by the cultural protocols inscribed into their embodiment), and the gender of their performance (read as masculine or feminine through the dancing styles, which were loaded with the heteronormative cues) coalesced, replicating and sustaining the gender dichotomy. Thus, the show efficaciously re-created and contained the intimate dynamics between the differently gendered dancers by naturalizing heterosexual desire as a priori—which, in turn, buttresses the gender dimorphism that grounds the undisrupted timeline of the PRC.

This hidden sexual linkage enables the pivotal emulation of the heteroromantic encounter, which serves to link socialist and neoliberal China. As the fulcrum of China's temporalized transformation, the public staging of personal intimacy is not just symbolic but also biopolitically consequential. In light of this counterintuitive impossible affiliation, Roderick Ferguson cites Chicago's dazzling urbanization at the dawn of the twentieth century as an example of how to unlock the overlapping relationship between socialist and capitalist systems through the lens of gender and sexuality.[113] As capital investments created new jobs, dominant groups of residents became increasingly concerned that the countless poor and working-class migrants flooding into the city in search of work could unsettle the social order. To reshape the working class and limit its disruptive potential, liberal ideologues suggested that members of the working class be assimilated into the middle class, with its familial model, and hence become decent subjects who fit into urban life. Contrary to the liberal view of the bourgeois nuclear family as the bedrock of capitalistic societies, Marxist gurus touted the gender-egalitarian family of the proletariat as the antidote to capitalism, plagued by gender inequality, and as the quintessential characteristic of socialist societies.[114] Despite their different idealized social orders, the rival capitalist and socialist camps nevertheless found a rare common ground in their shared endorsement of heterosexuality as the foundation for human and societal development. Therefore, according to Ferguson, both "took normative heterosexuality as the emblem of order, nature, and universality, making that which deviated from heteropatriarchal ideals the sign of disorder."[115]

The shared heteronormative script of Marxism and liberalism translates into an array of social policies, legal systems, cultural norms, and popular discourses, as well as other structural arrangements that underpin China's drastic changes.[116] Following Karl Marx's proposition of the production of material goods as the basis for human development, Engels added that the social reproduction of human subjects turbocharges societal growth.[117] Hegemonic construction thus naturalizes heterosexuality as an unspecified imperative guideline for all socialist regimes. The Maoist state implemented a series of policies to incorporate women's reproductive capacities into the comprehensive planning system as what it referred to as birth planning—which, Mao insisted, should be under the control of the state for building a new China.[118] Emboldened by Mao's projection of China's exponential growth and industrial productivity that should be accommodated by a growing supply of laboring bodies, the state took a steadfast pronatal stance from the 1950s through 1978.[119] Correspondingly, the regime took the radical move of criminalizing homosexuality, together with all other forms of sexual conduct and desire deemed nonconducive to reproduction and the creation of laborers.[120] These polices ended a long tradition that had created a relatively tolerant, if not fully welcoming, social environment for homoerotic intimacies and same-sex relationships.[121]

In 1979, in tandem with the marketizing shift, Deng Xiaoping announced the infamous one-child policy, the master plan to restructure the Chinese population, as a modified version of Mao's birth planning, and he consolidated it through constitutional amendments in 1982. Yet Deng's plan should not be denounced simply as a series of cold-blooded necropolitical maneuvers designed to slash the birth rate by forced abortion and sterilization. Rather, it should be seen as a cluster of calculated biopolitical stratagems to manage both the size and quality of the Chinese population and render it better suited for long-term development. In other words, if socialist China was mainly interested in controlling the quantity of the population in accordance with a planned economy, neoliberal China is more interested in maintaining a population of high enough quality to be suitable for increasing its competitive edge in the global market. Calling these seemingly contradictory biopolitical policies "Leninist" and "neoliberal" respectively, Susan Greenhalgh and Edwin Winckler argue that the PRC has repaired the rupture between its socialist past and its neoliberal present by continuing to invest in the calculated management of the population.[122]

Fusing rationalized biopolitical management of the population with intimacy-enabled conditioning of subject making, sexualized differentiation is especially vital to China's neoliberal transition. In tandem with escalated marketization, biopolitical regulation has evolved from totalizing punitive control to a more relaxed modus operandi that centers on the valorization and normalization of personhood to reproduce self-reliant and free subjects who will respond to and be governed by market mechanisms. The proliferation and circulation of cultural norms that embrace the self-determinate desiring subject, such as the public staging and celebration of the heteroromantic encounters in the parade, is the critical stratagem par excellence that realigns subject making with the biopolitical restructuring of the population to engineer the marketizing transition.[123]

In contrast to malleable gendered and classed metrics that alter their contour and outlook to fit into and facilitate changing governing modalities and sociocultural climate, sexuality has held its heteronormative ground in spite of mutating gender and class norms and continues to constitute the foundation of the difference-making machinery. The amorphous boundaries of the Loveland are concretized by the gendered, classed, and sexualized parameters of the machinery in binaristic terms and are integrated into the biopolitical calculus that serves China's neoliberal restructuring. Shifting its temporalized register of the affectsphere, the kaleidoscopic lovescape recreates the idealized image of Chinese citizens—from masculinized revolutionary proletarians (who subordinate their personal desires and intimacies to collectivized socialist constructions) to the dualistically gendered sovereign self striving for love in its own right in neoliberal China. As I show in the following chapters, to become loveable and love-able, either desiring subjects have to take the decorative and submissive feminine role and succumb to an all-encompassing paternalistic state power, or they must identify with an iron-fisted patriarchal state and act as domineering manly men.

Conclusion

In mapping the volatile temporal register of China's Loveland, this chapter has dissected how intimacy and desire were publicly staged with the reconstructed historiography of the PRC. As the analysis shows, the gendered, classed, and sexualized metrics of the difference-making machinery enables a nonlinear, exigent articulation of the heteronormative relationship to help address the social and ideological crisis that stems from China's neoliberal restructuring and stabilize the country's transition from socialism to neoliberalism. Overlapping with each other, gender and class create a flexible mechanism that enables the state to project and maintain the socialist doctrine of a classless society epitomized by gender-equal proletariat couples. As neoliberal reform intensifies and entails spiraling inequalities and antagonisms, the overlapping relationship between gender and class is reconfigured to address the emerging discord and ensure a smooth transition: gender replaces class as the linchpin to combine the nation and the state by moving to a feminine and submissive citizenry that is subordinate to a masculine and paternalistic state. However, as my queered reading reveals, underlying the ever-shifting symbiosis between gender, class, and the Chinese nation-state is the hidden heteronormativity that has stabilized their fraught relationship and anchored the otherwise impossible smooth transition.

As China seeks to further expand its transnational influence and global clout, love takes a more daunting paternalistic and heteropatriarchal form, foreshadowing the overdetermined rise of Xi as the strong leader. Embraced as a loving father who oversees China's sustained ascent in the new millennium, he is idealized as the person who will, against all odds, help China achieve its ultimate comeback with his embodied love for the family-nation. Chapter 2 continues to chart the expansive sociospatial edges of the Loveland and delineate how the heteronormative love exemplified by Xi is concretized in Chinese people's daily life through what I call homepatriarchal love. Focusing on the popular dating game show *If You Are the One*, I interrogate the sensory ambience of the borderless Loveland and develop a broad view of its sprawling affectsphere to explicate how the difference-making machinery informs and enables both the spatialized and the despatialized articulation of love to rescale China's physical and imaginary boundaries and integrate it into the global network of capital.

2

Only If You Are
the One!

The Expansive Neoliberal Universe
through Love Competitors' Eyes

"Can you feel it?" Following the French singer Jean-Roch Pédri's upbeat vocal, an elevator decorated with neon lights slides down into the TV camera's view. The flashy elevator stops and reveals the eager face of a young man. Stepping out of the elevator, the man prances to the center of the stage as the excitement and gleeful curiosity of the audiences quickly heat up to the pounding music. Reveling in the halo bestowed on him by the high technology, he must also endure the intense scrutiny of the twenty-four women lined up behind podiums across the stage (figure 2.1). According to the rules, he has twenty minutes to impress these women and bond with as many of them as possible, after which he takes one off the stage as his date. If he cannot convince any of the women to say yes to him, he must leave alone in a stinging debacle, accompanied by the sound of the Malaysian Mandarin pop diva Fish Leong's sentimental ballad "Sorry, You Are Not the One." Indeed, in these highly dramatized and colorful exchanges, the male participants in the globally relayed competition must demonstrate their sincere desire and capacity for love, which in turn becomes a litmus test of the lovabilities and love-abilities of thousands of millions more people in front of the TV.

This Chinese reality show is known widely across the Sinophone world as *Feicheng wurao* (meaning "if you are not sincere, please do not bother me"), or *If You Are the One* (hereafter, *IF*), and watching it has become a routine weekend pastime for many Chinese households and a visual evocation of the nostalgic fantasies of the place called homeland for countless people in the diaspora. In March 2010, barely three months after its debut, *IF* had already become the most popular entertainment program on Chinese TV. Since then, each episode has attracted around fifty million viewers on average, breaking a string of rating records.[1] Consider, for example, that this weekend night dating game show on a regional TV station (shown at 9:10-10:50 PM on Saturday and Sunday) appeared for a long time on the viewing chart behind only *Network News Broadcast*, a program of China Central Television (CCTV) mandated to be shown on local stations during evening prime time, and the program following it, *Weather Forecast*.[2] As a result of *IF*'s phenomenal success, its producer and distributor, Jiangsu Television (JSTV), increased its market share from 2.3 percent in 2009 to 7.9 percent in 2010 and reached over 10.0 percent in 2011-12.[3] Via digital technology and social media, *IF*'s influence has extended to Chinese-speaking communities around the world. Addressing love-related anxieties and worries, as well as the general uneasiness of people of marrying age, the show amplifies the tension related to people's intimate lives and therefore has attracted a deluge of criticism from both academics and Chinese Communist Party (CCP) censors.[4]

Focusing on China's mass-mediated ecologies of love and using the dating game show *IF* as a window, this chapter continues my exploration of the

Fig. 2.1. In the opening session of *If You Are the One*, a male participant faces twenty-four female participants.

expansive Loveland and identifies how its affective tendrils extend in the milieu and service of China's neoliberal transformation. Through a critical review of the historiographic reconstruction of the People's Republic of China (PRC) waged through national bodies, chapter 1 mapped the ways in which the chrononormative construction of intimacy has been wrought out of the overlapping vectors of the difference-making machinery to suit the changing politico-economic agenda as China switches from socialism to neoliberalism. This chapter moves from the temporal to the sociospatial register and from the metabolic to the mass-mediated body to examine the role of love in the Chinese reality TV and cross-cultural media exchange. I aim to throw into relief the Loveland's edgeless affectsphere and delineate how it is enfolded and unfolding in contemporary China to profile and undo the gendered, sexualized, classed, and ethno-racialized differentiations that cast and recast our lived scenes in profound neoliberal terms. The mass media have broadened the affective ambience of the Loveland far beyond nation-state borders, exposed its haptic tentacles to unprecedented cross-cultural influences, and endowed it with near-ubiquitous capacities to modulate people's love capabilities that "confound [our] assumptions about propinquity and distance, physicality and virtuality."[5] Thus, the borderless Loveland is the pivot of our quotidian rhythms and structural changes in the age of globalization. As the embedded anchor of time and space that we coinhabit, it also primes our emotions, cognition, and actions into a conjoined process in line with transnational neoliberal restructuring.

Instead of adding more evidentiary munitions to the already overflowing critical arsenal to liberate love from the manipulative shackles and allow for its free articulation and unencumbered pursuit, this chapter uses the reality show as a critical optic to paint a broad picture of the paradigmatic shift of love that cleared the way for China's neoliberalization and global expansion. As the crystallized manifestation of divergent social forces marked with historical specificities and sociocultural contingencies, love can be heavy. As the tool that equips us to unlock the process through which these social forces, specificities, and contingencies are integrated into a particular manifestation, love can be light, too. I push the inquiry of *IF* from questions focused on the TV program (such as "what are the major themes of love?" and "how is love represented?") to broader concerns (like "what is love rendered to do?" and "what can this rendering of love do for China's social transformation?"). My analysis thus travels both the light and the heavy avenues that love has been pushed along in the midst of China's current social upheavals. I do not use this transnational media spectacle as another case for exploring

"Sinitic-language cultures on the margins of geopolitical nation-states and their hegemonic productions."[6] Instead, I take a feminist and queer approach to dismantle the state's love-enabled spatializing and despatializing practices to rescale "the very cultural parameters of China and Chineseness" and "Asia/Asianness" for sponsoring its imperialist outreach.[7] Tracing the deterritorialization and reterritorialization of the expansive Loveland across regional, national, and transnational sociospaces, my inquiry also unearths the obscured and tangled relationship between the generic shift of love and China's meteoric ascendency in the global network of capital to unpack the difference-making machinery that undergirds their symbiotic genesis.

Integrating National and Transnational Interests by the Mediated Industry of Love

The dazzling popularity of *IF* throughout the Sinophone world, at least at its start, was orchestrated using the sensationalizing strategy that the direction team adopted to foment and fortify controversies over intimacy, marriage, family relationships, class mobility, gender and sexual norms, and so forth. Gang Wang, the program's director, acknowledged that *IF* was not conceived "to be a pure dating or entertainment program, but to concern itself with various hot-button topics, including housing issues, children, in-law relationships, income, careers, and DINKS [double-income no-kid households], all the social issues that emerge during the dating process."[8] In the third episode, a freelance writer named Chen Zhao invited Nuo Ma, an attractive female participant, on a date, asking, "Are you willing to go out for a ride on my bicycle?" Apparently unimpressed by this classic dating offer, Ma giggled and blurted out an impulsive and blunt reply to her suitor: "I would rather be crying in a BMW car!" Ma's inflammatory comment and thinly veiled money-driven telos of intimate relationships went viral immediately, precipitating a deluge of criticisms from netizens and prompting a nationwide debate about the ethics of love that lasted for years.[9] It also forwarded the misogynist narrative that conceals drastic class inequalities by claiming that they are problems only about women.[10] Other topics, such as the representation of well-educated women as invariably unlovable or the nouveaux riches flaunting their wealth to tout their superb love capacities in the televisual competition, have touched a nerve among the public, turning the show into a lightning rod for debates that have had far-reaching effects in circles broader and deeper than those of simple love affairs.

Unlike the sensations and sentiments that the show produces on individual levels, sociocultural phenomena like the show itself rarely occur in isolation.

Instead, they are part of a generic formulation of intimacy and desire through a complex array of books, films, TV programs, websites, advertisements, editorials, photographs, and illustrations in newspapers and magazines, as well as other items of public culture. As chapter 1 demonstrated, the pursuit of self-centered desire replaced the statist mandate of self-restraint or even self-denial to espouse the socialist cause as China moved into its reform era, profoundly reconfiguring its affective ecologies to charge its marketizing energies with new paragons of self-serving subjectivities.[11] By placing personal romantic encounters under the public's scrutinizing eyes, *IF* is central to this individualizing paradigmatic shift. Opening up private courtship for public discussion and debate, it animates a new genre of love "whose conventions emerge from the personal and public filtering of the situations and events [of intimacy] that are happening in an extended now whose very parameters are also always there for debate."[12]

Although showing only the tip of China's bustling landscape of love, *IF* adequately indexes the commercialized scope and depth of the borderless Loveland with its immense popularity. As Shuyu Kong notes, in 2009, JSTV's major competitor, Hunan Satellite TV, outbid it; obtained the copyright for the British dating game show *Take Me Out* from Bertelsmann's RTL Group, a transnational media megacorporation; and turned the show into a Chinese version named *Women yuehui ba* (or "Let's date"). In early 2010, JSTV responded by launching a slight adaptation of *Take Me Out*, that is, *IF*. Both clones of the British program soon achieved remarkable success, but the unlicensed version, *IF*, secured a bigger audience share and increase in advertising revenue.[13] Competitors of these two major provincial media agglomerates quickly imitated their profitable initiatives: over fifteen dating game shows suddenly appeared on regional TV stations across China, constituting a nationwide spectacle of love. Of course, the success of these programs created other business opportunities and market segments. The dating website jiayuan.com (*shiji jiayuan*) struck gold when it sponsored the show. On May 12, 2011, the website—building on the exponential increase in traffic and membership following the TV exposure—completed its initial public offering (IPO) on the Global Select Market of the National Association of Securities Dealers Automated Quotations (NASDAQ) and earned over $70 million in the stock market almost overnight. By offering China's bubbling lovescape for cross-border financial speculation, the website transformed itself into a transnational corporate matchmaker with a total value of $329 million.[14]

China's entrepreneurial groundswell of love, as intuitive and spontaneous as it might appear, is the cumulative result of a momentum that has taken years to build. For Chinese born in the 1950s and 1960s, Teresa Teng is a memorable name. The most renowned and respected artist in Cantonese and Mandarin pop music history, the songs of the Taiwan-based singer were banned in the PRC for most of the 1980s. The CCP condemned her "*mimi zhiyin* (or "decadent sounds"), considered to be capable of eliciting and perpetuating people's self-indulgent desires and "seducing citizens from the pressing tasks of nation-building and anti-imperialist resistance" that "took shape in the years before the Communist victory in 1949."[15] Teng's immensely popular romantic ballads could be found only via piracy. The state did not let these individual romantic reveries loose until the early 1990s, when they became available as a by-product of its full embrace of the laissez-faire economy. Subsequently, private intimate emotions and behaviors, such as those related to love and sexual desire, became not only topics that could have public articulation, but also vital conduits to demonstrate one's individuated identities. For example, Chinese men's major concern about their sexual well-being, as Everett Zhang elaborates in *The Impotence Epidemic*, shifted away from overflowing libidinal potency to the lack of it in China's free market.[16] As in other Asian cultures, sexual prowess became a hallmark of independence and a currency for men to use as they developed mutual trust for business collaborations through their complicit manipulation of women's bodies and sexuality.[17]

The landmark success in 1991 of the soap opera *Kewang* (or "Yearnings"), based on family relationships, was an eventful incident that germinated the paradigmatic shift in China's romantic scenes.[18] The Loveland was removed from the state-ordained homogeneity of revolutionizing red love and pluralized into a kaleidoscopic mélange with unbounded hues and patterns, and the alterations in its contour, texture, and fabric opened the floodgates of the long-subdued personal desire that had been labeled as a noxious and illegitimate topic in Chinese media representations. Thereafter, the mediated public culture has been flooded by proliferations of love in audio, visual, print, and electronic formats, and personal romance has become one of the most (if not the most) lucrative subjects. For instance, the Chinese film industry has witnessed a remarkable 19 percent annual growth in the past decade. Its revenues soared from less than 1 percent of the share in the world box office in 2005 to 17.5 percent in 2016, second only to the revenues of the US film industry.[19] Out of the $8.48 billion that the Chinese film industry made in 2016, *The Mermaid*—a film that combined the genres of fantasy, romantic comedy, and drama and that was made by the Hong Kong actor and director Stephen Chow—earned over half a billion dollars, becoming the highest-grossing film of all time in China by that year.[20] Consider a few other glamorous numbers: in 2013, although the romance genre trailed behind action movies in terms of its share of box office revenue (18 percent versus 33 percent), it dominated the domestic market (29 percent versus 26 percent).[21] Amid the commercializing craze for love, transnational media, especially those based in Hong Kong and Taiwan, play a particularly important role. They ramified China's romantic milieu into hybrid imaginaries of modernity that are both Western inflected and regionally specific.[22] In so doing, the film industry integrated China's Loveland into the global traffic in images, texts, and videos that Purnima Mankekar and Louisa Schein call "mediated erotics."[23] More recently, the success of reality shows like *IF* has reshuffled power dynamics and transformed China from a net importer of popular media by a wide margin to an emerging cultural powerhouse with mounting clout.

What is worth the most attention, however, is not the glocalized outlook but the hybridized texture of China's mediated love industry. In the infrastructural and discursive layers of the Loveland, the coupling of a licensed (or even unlicensed) Western platform with locally produced content is the rule of the game. While closely following and adopting almost every programmatic step of *Take Me Out*, JSTV set the pace of its editing and producing process to ensure that the final product should fully abide by the CCP's rules. Many other popular reality shows—including *China's Got Talent* (owned by Fremantle Media in the British market and Sony Music Entertainment in the American market), *The Voice of China* (owned by Talpa Productions in the Dutch market), *Strictly Come Dancing* (owned by British Broadcasting Corporation [BBC] in the British market), and *I Am a Singer* (owned by Munhwa Broadcasting Corporation in the South Korean market)—also use the coupling of global and local. In these programs, the state maintains control over the editorial and production procedures but outsources other duties (such as branding, marketing, and advertising) to private and transnational capital. As Yuezhi Zhao argues, the party-state has learned this lesson from the swiftly derailed trajectory of the liberalization of mass media that was initiated in the late 1970s as part of the marketizing experiment.[24] For example, the 1988 documentary *Heshang* (or "River Elegy") played a crucial role in precipitating the outcry for Western-style democracy that culminated in the tragic Tian'anmen Square massacre. The horrendous crackdown by the state on public discussion of democracy was followed by the reimposition of draconian control over media, and the marketizing process was then halted and not resumed until Deng Xiaoping's 1992 Southern Tour—which rekindled China's neoliberalization.[25] Ever since then, media reform has been full of "ambiguities and contradictions," resulting in the mixture of CCP guidance and market logic.[26]

The hybridization model is not as much an ad hoc attempt by the state to retain its diminishing power by taking a hard-core ideological stance vis-à-vis the liberalizing market forces as it is an ingenious stratagem employed to realign the state's interests with those of national and transnational market stakeholders. The state launched marketization in the top-ranking government-run media as a business-oriented experiment in the 1980s. As a central part of the neoliberalizing attempt to streamline governmental functionalities, the state sought to reduce its financial responsibilities for the media and "used the core and affluent Party press as a sponge to absorb the unprofitable, chaotic, and disobedient small papers and magazines."[27] Meanwhile, in the mid-1990s, the state introduced recentralization campaigns under the mandate of increasing China's soft power around the globe. A number of regional media conglomerates—as well as national broadcasting giants such as CCTV—were created to boost competition and increase Chinese media's market shares on the provincial, national, and transnational levels.[28] According to the plan, the market would not just optimize the reallocation of media resources and reduce the financial burden on the state, but it would also sharpen the overall competitiveness of the Chinese media system. Against this backdrop, the Jiangsu Broadcasting Corporation (JSBC), the de jure owner of JSTV, established a goal in 2001 of becoming centered in Jiangsu, excelling in eastern China, taking the lead in the country, and building global influence.[29] As a regional multimedia conglomerate, JSBC's businesses include television and radio stations, film studios, newspapers, and websites, as well as the distribution of audiovisual products.[30]

The restructuring of the media system soon led to a spate of problems, including those related to budget plans, personnel regulations, the allocation of resources, and the distribution of profits. As the state-engineered recentralization and conglomeration did not fully accomplish the marketizing goal, after the sixteenth CCP National Congress the state initiated a new project (referred to as a cultural system reform) to promote the media's commercialization through a strategy called divestment. As Zhao points out, "by spinning off market-oriented operations from existing party-state media conglomerates and turning these operations into relatively autonomous market entities that are free to absorb outside capital and pursue market-oriented expansion," the state advanced the marketization of media while simultaneously fortifying itself.[31] The business part of media operations, such as advertising, printing, and distribution, was severed from the hard-core editorial duties, and "by allowing the media to internally differentiate into an editorial, non-business section and a business section, it embolden[ed] the media to pursue profits in a more unabashed and effective manner."[32] *IF* is part of this divestment initiative. As mentioned above, while JSTV has control over the editing and producing processes to guarantee its productions' correct political contours, it outsources the marketing and advertising functions to private capital, efficiently aligning programs with both the appetite of the audiences and the needs of the advertising market.

More broadly, this cultural system reform is also a response to the intensified demand for more market share by transnational media capital following China's joining the World Trade Organization (WTO) in 2001. The fiercely protected Chinese media constituted one of the last lucrative industries in China to be privatized, and it had long been coveted by transnational capital.[33] China's entry into the WTO further consolidated the opportunities for transnational media corporations to penetrate the Chinese market, both through and beyond the formal provisions of the WTO accession agreement.[34] For instance, its membership required China to increase the annual number of films imported from Western countries from ten to fifty.[35] Meanwhile, Chinese political elites used the WTO entry as both a material and a symbolic opportunity to further the divestment agenda in such a way as to retain their power. Within the new structure, foreign investment in nonessential components, including information infrastructure, service provision, and technological knowledge, can be compatible with the state's agenda. However, under no circumstances would the government relinquish its authority over the essential parts, such as editorial rights.[36]

To sidestep the party-state's still stringent control over the editorial core of the media system, transnational corporations employ an array of flexible and eclectic strategies—including market entry and share expansion through copyright licensing rather than direct participation in production. This gives the Chinese media much-needed experience that allows them to create shortcuts to market success, pushing the business boundaries of entertainment and maximizing the satisfaction of market interests without transgressing the Party line. As Zhao puts it succinctly, "if the vulgar [such as individual intimacy] was once denounced by both state socialist and liberal cultural elites, 'kowtowing to the vulgar' is now the mantra of the Chinese media industry."[37] In this sense, capital and the party-state pursue love as an economically conducive and politically safe zone wherein to serve their collective interests.

The strategy of subjecting the media system to the needs of the state and market forces simultaneously situates the Chinese media in a position that is neither external to global neoliberalizing influences nor completely subordinate to the liberalizing effects unleashed by the opening up of the domestic market. As Anthony Fung suggests, the transnational exchanges of mediated images, discourses, and ideas in an increasingly marketized and globalized Chinese media system will not inevitably undermine the CCP's authoritarian control and lead to liberal democracy, as many critics hope. Rather, the hybridization model allows the interests of transnational media corporations, capital, and the state to be interwoven, "and the move of one party will also impinge on the subsequent strategies of the other."[38] The state is not a passive receptor or self-reliant agent, and it mobilizes and reshapes transnational media capital and culture to serve its own agenda and interests. By incorporating global capital needs into the Party line, the state successfully transformed the Chinese media system from a propagandist apparatus to "Party Publicity Inc."[39] As Jing Wang notes, "the state's rediscovery of culture as a site where new ruling technologies can be deployed and converted simultaneously into economic capital constitutes one of its most innovative strategies of statecraft since the founding of the People's Republic."[40]

This knowledge creates a vantage point to further untangle the significance of the Chinse media ecology in general, and the dating program *IF* in particular. It also provides a critical lens to gauge China's public culture and sui generis modality of neoliberalization and, more importantly, the modus operandi of the difference-making machinery that is vital to global neoliberal restructuring. Using *IF* as a magnifying tool, the remainder of this chapter will zoom in on the daily tempos of the kaleidoscopic Loveland to tease out the specificities and singularities of China's neoliberal transition. I will give depth and shape to the gendered, sexualized, classed, and ethno-racialized links that constitute the global network of capital connecting the newly neoliberal China with the liberal West.

Instrumentalized Love as a Neoliberalizing Tool

At best, *IF* is a modified appropriation of *Take Me Out*, and at worst, it is an outright copy of the Western program.[41] In its original design, *IF* copied each part of the British archetype with two exceptions: in each episode of the Chinese version, five (instead of four) male participants, one at a time, complete a three-round game and compete for the particular attention of twenty-four (rather than thirty) female participants, who are lined up behind lecterns. As in the British model, they use three prerecorded videos to start each round of the game. These videos, called "The First Impression of Love,"

"The Second Thought on Love," and "The Final Decision about Love," respectively, are used to introduce the man's personal background, describe his ideal date, share comments about him by family members and friends, and help him bond with as many of the women as possible. After finishing their game—either winning or losing—the male participants have a question-and-answer session to further substantiate their lovabilities and love-abilities off the stage for the TV audiences. The women can turn off their lights to signal rejection at any time during the course of the game. If no lights are left on, the man has to leave. Male contestants also have the right to choose—at the beginning, a first-sight "attraction lady" (figure 2.2), and at the end (if more than one light is still on), the final pick.

The formatting, not just the sensational content, matters for the show. In the original design, female participants were granted nearly unlimited time and space to secure a Mr. Right, unless they opted to withdraw voluntarily. Hailed by some media critics as a "feminist" move, this arrangement is said to subvert "the traditional gender paradigm for promoting women to the domineering and judging position usually occupied by men."[42] Although its unsettling feminist potential remains debatable, this format breathes some fresh air into the dating shows that are banally centered on men and the male gaze, and it is unarguably a major contributing factor in *IF*'s rating success. In 2016, pressured by the audiences' decreasing attention and the faltering market share, the show's team reversed the gender rule and placed male participants on the judging podiums instead. However, the public backlash

Fig. 2.2. A male participant selects his first-sight "attraction lady" on *If You Are the One*.

compelled the show to switch back to its women-leaning power structure after only four trial episodes. In April 2017, the producers reformatted the show again. This time, instead of remaining behind the podiums, female participants reappear on the stage at the start of every game so the male contestant can decide to put them into either the "interested" or "uninterested" group. After that, the power to choose goes back to the female side, returning the show to its original and familiar format—except that each male guest can now choose two "attraction ladies," one at the beginning of the game and the other at the end of it.

Despite its oscillations regarding who chooses whom, IF has adhered to the one versus multiple format shared by many other dating shows that characterizes the generic departure from previous programs. Taiwan- and Hong Kong–based media introduced China to TV dating programs in the mid-1990s. A new genre at the time, these shows arranged for participants to "meet on a one-on-one basis, such as on *The Rose Date* (*Meigui zhiyue*, Hunan Satellite TV) and *Saturday Rendezvous* (*Xiangyue xingqiliu*, Shanghai TV), two of the most popular programs at the time."[43] Featuring an equal number of male and female participants, these programs offered ample opportunities for paired interactions and thus less competition, to create feelings similar to those that might arise in real-life dating. In the one versus multiple format, however, participants are always mindful of their limited possibilities of walking triumphantly away from the stage as "the one" and are constantly reminded of the probability that they will be disqualified. In a staged battle of love watched by millions of viewers (who might be their future rivals), the participants are fully motivated warriors who are ready to maneuver and deploy the armaments at their disposal to survive and become "the one." The winners' experiences are collected into an array of self-help guidelines widely circulated online, which can be easily found by any would-be warriors willing to push their love capacities to the limit via the TV's amplifying camera.

For the men, IF might not be a head-to-head battlefield, but the fight is no less intense. Instead of engaging one another directly, they need to defeat their rivals by flexing their love muscles and getting the most lights kept on to the end: the more lights, the merrier. In the original setup, if any man could keep all twenty-four lights (reduced to twenty-two later) on after his initial appearance and secure a match at the end, he and his date would win a free trip to a romantic destination provided by the show's sponsors. When retreating into the background, the newly matched-up pair was also showered with flower petals as festive music played—a triumphant ending reminiscent of

the high point at numerous Western-style wedding ceremonies. The number of lights serves as a measure of each man's heteronormative masculine prowess to the women; the audiences; and, most importantly, their competitors. As Michael Kimmel argues, homosocial settings largely construct masculinity.[44] To testify to and prove one's masculinity requires both virtual and symbolic control of women either with or (as in this case) without the presence of one's male peers or rivals.[45] The women's attentive and affective responses, signaled by the lights and spotlighted by the camera, function as this symbolic control.

In contrast to their male counterparts, the female participants have a far more confrontational battle, which can be as explicit as an open fight for a commonly desired man or as subtle as the undercurrents of competition for the title of "attraction lady." Granted enough space and time, the women can maneuver in the arena to attract the bachelors on-site or in front of the TV. Many stories circulate about how a participant failed on the spot but ultimately found a soul mate through the televisual matchmaker. If a woman either leaves the stage happily with a perfect match or withdraws in remorse, a substitute will be brought up. The new woman's stage life often starts with a well-crafted self-introduction purported to leave a long-lasting impression on the bachelor participants and viewers. In the show's most recent format, female participants turn the opening session of each game into a short fashion show, trying to upstage one another by using delicate makeup and wearing an elegant dress, having graceful and captivating bodily comportment, and sometimes having an eerie or outlandish demeanor (figure 2.3). In short,

Fig. 2.3. All of the female participants enter the stage on *If You Are the One*, in a way reminiscent of a fashion show.

the battle between the women starts with their first appearance and intensifies as the show unfolds into new warring scenarios.

In my view, with the focus shifting from one-on-one interaction to intense competition for attention, this Western-based generic change in dating shows has repercussions that extend far beyond representational politics and aesthetic standardizations.[46] In fact, its epistemic and political implications are legion. Framed as the trophy calculable in advance and attainable by strategized endeavors, love becomes a teleological end point in itself, exemplifying what Alain Badiou and Peter Bush call "love under threat."[47] Love, they argue, is an innate quest for truth, and any cost-benefit calculations and approximations would be a threat to its fruition into universality and transcendence. According to Herbert Marcuse, love's seeding impulse for truth is a bodily instinct for pleasure that has been subdued by our alienating working relationships and the ubiquitous commercializing logic represented by TV shows like *IF*.[48] To read through affect, love is the biologically ingrained and complex "formations of embodied sensation that have coalesced through the advance of ancient evolutionary processes operating in deep time."[49] It is our "varied, surging capacities to [love] and to be [loved] that give everyday life the quality of a continual motion of relations, scenes, contingencies, and emergencies."[50] In addition, love is rooted in our shared embodied histories that set the ground for coconstitutive dependence, collective responsibilities, and reciprocal caring. It cannot be calculated and obtained through rationalized reasoning toward, against, or in relation to a teleological end point. Instead, love is our body's "hopeful opening, a speculative opening not wedded to the dialectic of hope and hopelessness, but rather a porous affirmation of what could or might be."[51] Indeed, modulating our phenomenological experiences of feeling intimate and molding our ever-expanding bodily capacities to become more intimate, love concretizes its affectsphere in its own ongoingness and reclaims its affective forces through visceral properties that are sedimented in our becoming selves and worlding process.

Rearticulating love as the telos, the paradigmatic reformulation as encapsulated by *IF* constitutes the instrumentalization of love: an epistemic shift fundamental to the making of neoliberal subjects. Instead of an array of historically accumulated and culturally marinated bodily capacities for mutual respect and reciprocating care, love is reframed as a manageable and obtainable item that is either within our reach or thousands of miles away, depending on how we deploy our calculus. According to this logic, love is the ultimate trophy of the televisual game that beckons participants to chronicle, calculate, and strategize how to use their prowess. Even outrageous comments made by participants like Ma and the wealth-buoyed haughty and condescending attitudes embodied by the nouveaux riches can get a green light as long as they serve to boost the subjects' capacity to win the love. The ends justify the means. This logic endorses the subjectivistic turn to reason that has ensconced self-interests as the universal and exclusive criterion of rationality since the Enlightenment.[52] Subjectivistic reason, as I have elaborated elsewhere, is the epistemic basis for the construal of a self-serving homo economicus as the neoliberal paragon.[53] Just imagine: if love can be warped for such an instrumental end, then what cannot?

As an ensemble of divergent and emergent energies, the borderless Loveland takes its shape and depth through the remaking of the polarized relationships of gender, sexuality, class, and race/ethnicity. In the remainder of this chapter, I further unpack the ways in which the instrumentalizing logic of love has been transplanted from the West to China through spatializing and despatializing practices. I show how love, under the directives of both the party-state and capital, develops new patterns along specific biopolitical metrics to delimit the culturally and sociopolitically charged affective forces to reassemble Chinese citizens and diasporas for implementing neoliberal governmentality.

Projecting the Neoliberal Fantasy through the Spatialized and Despatialized Loveland

According to a Chinese student who was pursuing his PhD degree in Britain, it was shocking to learn that in *Take Me Out*, the male participants never discuss their income and the women do not ask about it—though income is a topic frequently brought up and nearly routinized in the show's Chinese clone.[54] Likewise, as Rachel Dubrofsky notes about the US dating game show *The Bachelor*, although only men with an established professional profile qualify to be bachelors, each episode centralizes the participants' intimate interactions rather than focusing on their material possessions.[55] Conversely, *IF* manifests a materializing tendency writ large in the case of its male contestants. For instance, in the opening session of each game, "The First Impression of Love," the men highlight the most important aspects of their (supposedly) disparate life stories and personalities. However, most have followed an identical path by delivering a statement of personal accomplishments defined in marketable value and monetary terms—including educational background; job, with its location often specified; salary; amount of savings in the bank; ownership of property and cars; and so forth. Since

IF's 2010 inception until its reformatting in April 2017, at least a third of the men decided to film their introduction while driving a car. As the car moves through rapidly changing views, the camera that is set up to provide lateral full-face close-ups and medium-range body shots of the protagonist "accidentally" captures the logo (naturally of a luxury brand) on the steering wheel. This allegedly inadvertent move is choreographed to provide a tantalizing glimpse into the man's commodities-certified lavish lifestyle that cross-references his self-laudatory narrative. In an episode from 2010, a rich young man caught the audiences off guard by his well-chosen irony. As usual, the account of his life began with a prerecorded narration specifying his persistent yet fruitless search for a soul mate. As his opening statement moved many in the audiences to tears, the narrative focus, with no hints or transitions, suddenly swerved into parading his wealth and private properties. For the audiences, this rhetorical hijacking might be an unsavory appetizer they had to swallow. However, for the women on the stage, it was the palatable main course that distilled the man's merits and best skills efficaciously to knock his opponents out. He kept five lights on to the end, a record that took months to break.

Entrepreneurial aspiration and business adventurism prove to be another set of essential skills to establish the men's prowess. As the show's host, Fei Meng, complained at one point, *IF* is replete with self-acclaimed business geniuses about to transform the world with their grand plans (figure 2.4). Like Meng, other members in the program's host team minced no words in their criticisms of participants who keep boasting of their Fortune 500 enterprise in the making yet provide no clues about how they plan to achieve the goal. In a 2011 episode, a man slightly changed his entrepreneurializing profile to differentiate it from others: in the introductory video, the man (who was only in his early twenties) stated that he had a plan to salvage his parents' bankrupt business and rebuild it into a transnational corporate empire. But his plan was punctuated with a montage of his everyday life cramped between home and a farmers market, showing his small vegetable vending business as a modest yet grounded start for achieving his ultimate goal. Notably, this approach not only moved to tears Meng's partner, Jia Le—the so-called emotion mentor who has earned a reputation for his scathing on-site comments and bulging pectoral and tight abdominal muscles. The video also motivated Meng to break a rule for the first time and provide the man and his date with a free trip to Hawaii, the supreme honor otherwise reserved for only the most popular contestants. Like this fortunate man, the love contenders who seek self-made entrepreneurial success usually receive the acclaim of the host

team. More importantly, they remain among the most favored ones by the women on the stage and many more watching attentively at home.

As mentioned above, fans of the show curate strategies as effective as the ones mentioned here into a series of online instructions for future contenders. Although the guidelines they provide vary and even contradict one another regarding the tangential parts (dress, rhetoric, posture, and so on), these love lexicons have a common core in their most essential recipe for success: having a good job or lucrative business, possessing monetary and other forms of assets, and demonstrating resilient entrepreneurship and business acumen. Consequently, as the plot of the game advances and becomes more complicated, the imagery of the most popular men becomes clear, measuring what it means to be lovable and detailing how to become love-able for all Chinese men.

Without a doubt, the women on the stage are the people who most directly define the profile of *IF*'s love winners and, as a corollary, what a very attractive man would look like in contemporary China. In a 2010 episode, Fangzhen Zhu emerged as another controversial figure for declaring that it would cost a man 200,000 yuan (around $30,000) to shake her hand. Inflaming the already boiling controversy ignited by Ma, Zhu's comments involved the program in a critical maelstrom that further boosted its ratings and market share. Many viewers even suspected that the comment was a planted gimmick, compelling Meng to use *Network News Broadcasting*, the party-state's

Fig. 2.4. Fei Meng, a Chinese TV personality who has built his popularity as the host of *If You Are the One*.

most authoritative voice, to defend the untampered nature of the game.[56] But what is at stake here is not finding a way to verify the authenticity of the individuals' love-seeking experiences. Instead, we might ask in what ways and to what ends has a motley array of heterogeneous and unbounded love capacities been condensed into such an alarmingly oversimplified pattern of homogeneity and conformity?

Ironically, the very neutrality and objectivity that the host team sought to establish in its self-defense reaped the most criticism and precipitated a punitive response from the state. According to *IF*'s official website, any interested individual can complete a questionnaire that asks for basic demographic information and sign up for the game online, or by telephone or text message, and the program will choose participants from the pool.[57] Given the controversial participants who have appeared on the show, outcries have centered on their money-driven pursuit of courtship and unfiltered materialism. This pattern was said to exacerbate rampant consumerism and bourgeois decadence, further undermining the socialist principles of justice and equality, and therefore should be stringently censored. Pressured by the public's raging anger, the State Administration of Radio, Film, and Television of China (SARFT), a governmental agency in charge of all media-related issues, released two official documents that introduced a draconian rule regarding all TV programs and radio shows about dating and intimacy. The new regulations mandated diversity of participants and reasserted the socialist value of equality as the inviolable bottom line.[58]

The nebulous socialist value superimposed onto the straightforward market rule by the state needs to be examined through both epistemological and practical lenses to better understand how neoliberal governmentality works in China's mass-mediated landscape of love. The state, as Michel Foucault posits, is never fixed or static: instead, it is both the target and the product of specific governing practices and represents a dynamic opening that is always being made and remade.[59] Introduced in response to the sociopolitical crisis stemming from the application of the Maoist mantra of class struggle and as an attempt to salvage the CCP's legitimacy by experimenting with the market mechanism, neoliberal governmentality has basically created two factions within the bureaucratic monopoly of the CCP—neoliberal and Maoist (or New Left).[60] As the neoliberalizing process advanced, the tensions between the two camps increased and rose to the surface, and their internecine fights pushed the political regime to the brink of a militant face-off between the adversary groups in 2012, one that implicated multiple top-ranking officials and ended up with their incarceration or death.[61] As chapter 1 showed, to repair

看来黄老师没有做到 韩束 白BB霜

the temporal, ideological, and governmental split between China's socialist past and its neoliberal status quo, the state created its sixtieth-anniversary celebration as a spellbinding spectacle to increase the people's nationalist identification—which could help reunify the splintered historiography. The tripartite structure of gender, class, and sexuality underwrote the state's temporal management that helped resolidify the Chinese nation-state from a polarized disarray to a love-blessed, unified entity.

In the case of *IF*, the triangulation of gender, sexuality, and class also undergirds the difference-making machinery instrumental for the party-state to burnish its de jure socialist brand without tarnishing its de facto governing decree of market rule. The state's call for diversification resulted in the reshuffling of the TV show's host team. Han Huang, a female social psychologist, joined as the second emotion mentor, to redress the blatant gender imbalance of the gatekeepers of this heteroromantic game (figure 2.5). As a faculty member at the Jiangsu Party School, she also embodies the visible hand of the state that is intended to neutralize the deleterious and polarizing effects of marketized media. The new regulations also ordered the show to diversify along class lines. As a consequence, participants from a variety of segments of the population—such as teachers, graduate students, bus drivers, and workers—are selected to compete against wealthy businessmen and members of professional elites, thereby giving the show a more equitable and inclusive veneer. The production team, as instructed by the state, strenuously eliminates the participants' financial information to ensure that the transactional telos should not dominate the game or disturb its pluralistic

Fig. 2.5. Han Huang, widely known for her role as the emotion mentor for participants on *If You Are the One.*

and impartial tenor—at least on the surface. In short, by using its sovereign power to create an open arena that allows people from different class segments to compete, the state exerted the sort of neoliberal governance that, according to Foucault, hinges on the creation of a level ground for competition and the guarantee of everyone's ability to enter it, but nothing more.[62]

Under the new rules, the dominant form of masculinity defined by financial possessions such as private property ownership gained more traction through the fabrics of gender, sexuality, and class of the competitive Loveland rather than losing ground in the game. Despite the mounting challenges from a more diversified pool of rivals, the men equipped with a good education, a high-paying job, private property, luxury cars, entrepreneurial ambition, and acumen—as well as those who are tall and attractive—continue to win. As the result of the allegedly open and unbiased competition rather than the preferences of certain eccentric individuals, these winners are embraced as the norm rather than scrutinized as anomalies according to socialist principles. This normalized masculinity, when contrasted to the losing Others, becomes more acceptable as a given. In 2010, after one man expressed his preference for a financially reliable date, he found himself swiftly engulfed by firework-like pops and flashes triggered by the extinguishing of lights, which resulted in an embarrassing moment of speechlessness before the next candidate was introduced. In 2012, when a male participant informed the women that he lived in a dormitory with his coworkers, all the women on the stage switched off their lights and sent him home alone and still single. Likewise, in 2013, after a sincere yet ill-advised confession by a callow contender that he would rather be a stay-at-home father than a breadwinner, all the lights went off, shredding the hapless man's already diminished self-esteem and troubled conception of manliness. Rather than criticizing these scenarios as contradicting socialist values, people laugh the episodes off and accept the sure loss of those undeserving of love and unable to love. As these hard-learned lessons are curated alongside jubilant moments of victory into pedagogic resources, they re-create and consolidate the market-rule-codified masculinity as a self-fulfilling prophecy that limits and redefines Chinese men's love capacities.

Indeed, as the self-generated and -replicating internet love instructions indicate, our emerging capacities to love and be loved and our world-building processes are joined through the Loveland that takes varying shapes via the overlapping vectors of the difference-making machinery. Our love-seeking sensorium captures a porous ensemble of sociohistorically situated and politico-economically charged forces, energies, and power and translates them into tangible forms of gender, class, and sexuality. Simultaneously, the re-created structures and systems of gender, class, and sexuality reorganize our bodily capacities to be loved in ways to attune our very mode of being with ongoing broad changes. In the 1960s, as the United States entered its prime after World War II and during the full-blown Cold War with the Soviet Union, men's desirability was recoded as the three bulges—that of wallet, muscles, and crotch—goading American men to engage in profiteering, bullying, and sexual exploration.[63] As globalization proceeded at an accelerated pace in the 1990s, well-dressed globe-trotting men jetting through airports across countries and continents on packed business trips became the dreamed-of mates for many women, a new epitome of masculinity that incites and reifies marketizing momentums.[64] In the new millennium, many Asian men find their newly established business profile and financial power to be potent resources to supplement their gender and sexual appeal, which were previously overshadowed by those of their Western white counterparts, and to lay a homosocial ground for more commercial collaborations.[65] Amid the battling encounters re-created by *IF*, the mediated Loveland instills a self-serving ethos of neoliberal episteme into the depth of people's sovereign selves—one that incentivizes them to love solely by outperforming and defeating other contenders and that reconstitutes their sensibilities to receive reciprocating love in flagrant market forms.

In addition to these love-impelled men, the contentious Loveland re-creates the women on the show's stage as the object of neoliberal governmentality. Instead of creating more space for self-determination, these women's presumably agential subjectivities—specifically, their ability to judge—are subjected to a pervasive male gaze and compromised by the attendant self-censoring. Despite *IF*'s shifting format, one setting has remained consistent: all the games begin with the selection of attractive women. This is a high point for many men, but the process of being differentiated, classified, and judged is embarrassing and awkward for the women. With no other information available and interactions barely initiated at the time, most men make decisions on purely physiological terms, and unsurprisingly they both reflect and reinforce the predominant social norms about women's bodies. Compared to the materialization of the men, which frequently comes under fire, the blatant and deliberate objectification of women is barely questioned, let alone censured or disciplined by the state. Just as the love capacities of the most competitive men are steeped in marketable values and qualities, so the most popular women seldom fail the test of corporeal measurements, with their unimpeachably attractive porcelain faces and curvaceous yet slim bodies. Aware but not critical of the dehumanizing codification of their personhood, many women succumb to, and sometimes even endorse, these objectifying terms for their own benefit. If the heavy, pancake-type makeup and the exotically intricate falbala dresses might be arguably justified as necessities for the theatrical purposes of broadcasting, the open bragging about anatomical features such as breast size by some women to inflate their love capacities is a definitive indication of the female subjectivities inflected by the heteronormative and androcentric gaze. This deforming gaze, via the men's deciding fingers and the TV's amplifying eye, permeates and remolds China's Loveland. And in turn, it substantively reconfigures women's capabilities of receiving and returning intimacy. As China moves from socialism to neoliberalism, the default position of Chinese women has also shifted from revolutionaries with independent characteristics and personalities back to decorative and supportive figures for their husbands and the patriarchal state, as delineated in chapter 1. However, these love battles in which the body is a vital weapon provide another lens for us to closely reexamine how women's capacities to love and be loved wobble with the ups and downs of the sociocultural tidal waves. We can also chart the fuzzy affectsphere and boundless ambience of the Loveland to identify how it constantly changes its contours and textures in tune with neoliberalization in China and beyond.

The reessentialized feminine ideal is not just a retrograde version of Chinese women's traditional roles as submissive housewife and sacrificial mother. Instead, the ideal is imbued with new features as desired in these neoliberal times. In one episode, after a man stated that he had come on the show to find a virtuous housewife and devoted mother to carry on his family's patrilineal line, the female participants immediately protested to Huang, the emotion mentor. Women, as they made clear, are not merely men's reproductive machines but individuals enjoying full independence and agency. In actuality, this man's undisguisedly condescending view of women's reproductive and supportive roles does not reflect the mainstream of the show. For most male contenders, women with superlative physical attractions but subpar intellects like Ma might be someone they would date for fun, but surely not the one they will bring home to meet their parents. Rather, the ideal date in the eyes of the male competitors combines a set of contradictory attributes: someone who is simultaneously a pliant and coy Barbie girl, whose persistent dependence on them for attention and care can appeal to their male chauvinist egos, and a smart and reliable partner, who can lend a hand when and if needed. Tingting Liu, an immensely popular IF-manufactured TV personality, provides a useful example. Coming from a wealthy family, Liu has a stunning track record of academic and professional accomplishments that makes her a competitive market subject par excellence. She also embodies the idealized virtues of sensibility, conscientiousness, and docility required of today's Chinese women. Taken together, these qualities and attributes have earned her the catchy moniker *sanhao nüsheng* (or "three good girl" or "merit girl"), a play on merit student—the honor that recognizes Chinese students who excel in virtuous behavior, intellectual accomplishment, and physical activities. This moniker places her among the most celebrated and liked female participants in *IF*'s history.

This contradictory ideal of femininity is not unique to China but is, rather, an internal element in the re-creation of surplus labor through the making of gender differences in tandem with and wrought by neoliberal globalization. As a group that was historically relegated to the private sector along the sexual division of labor as extra-market subjects, women constitute a seemingly limitless reservoir of untapped labor to be exploited by capital.[66] Since the 1980s, gender has played a vital role in creating surplus labor to release the overaccumulated capital in the West and abet its transnational reproduction. In India, for example, the state and international nongovernmental organizations (NGOs) sponsored a microcredit program called Mahila Samakhya that provides financial resources for low-caste rural women to achieve their entrepreneurial dreams—a women-targeted gender biopolitics to re-create market subjects and wage laborers for Western capital.[67] The states of the Four Asian Dragons, such as Singapore and Hong Kong, have introduced an array of policies since the 1980s, including reforms of higher education and the welfare system, that transformed native middle-class housewives into an educated, skilled, and self-reliant labor force. This facilitated the industrial upgrade plan for promoting both city-states' profiles as hubs that anchored capital migration from Europe and America to the Asia-Pacific region.[68] Since the PRC's founding in 1949, women have taken jobs outside the home to make an equal contribution with men to socialist construction. Women are now overconcentrated in sweatshops, manufacturing export goods and pressured to be subservient and obedient to their male supervisors and capital interests and imperatives that the men serve. Otherwise, their femininity would be irrevocably undermined and they would be disqualified from having romantic relationships—the gendered and heteronormative biopolitics of reassembling docile labor for capital.[69]

In addition to women's re-created self-sufficient and competitive subjectivity in public, their gendered roles in the private space have also proliferated to "compensate for state retreat, or for the state's failure to provide social infrastructure and support" stemming from neoliberal restructuring.[70]

As neoliberal globalization fundamentally destabilizes and reconfigures the public-private divide by recruiting more women into the transnational network of labor supply, women often confront contradicting gender ideologies at the local level.[71] The gendered biopolitics exhorts and pushes women to redouble their productive and reproductive roles to better serve the politico-economic agenda stipulated by the neoliberal playbook, which expands the market rule to all societal sectors. As a result, in the United States "women are caught between neoliberal rhetoric which casts women as the 'new entrepreneurs' by devaluing women's traditional family roles, and neoconservative views which emphasize 'family values' and cast women as selfish and irresponsible if they do not fulfill their mothering roles."[72] In China, the dating spectacle of *IF* crystallizes and animates the contradictory double roles of womanhood and, more broadly, normalizes the commonsensical conceptions of women's desirabilities and potential for intimate relationships, which rest on their capabilities to carry out these expanded market and family duties.

The most important thing we have learned from China's fantasmatic Loveland so far is that love is not just an assemblage of sedimented bodily capacities that orient our phenomenological experiences of receiving and returning enamoring feelings. Rather, it is also something integral to a situated and embedded cluster of principles, procedures, inclinations, and orientations that give shape, direction, and meaning to these experiences. In our collectively inhabited global era, women's conflicted love formulas are reconfigured across borders in forms that, though disparate, converge toward the same end. In Japan, the formulas take shape as the term *Christmas cake*, which coerces ambitious professional women into conjugal relationships by alleging that their love capacity is evanescent. Women must fulfill the conflicting ideal of love before their shelf life expires when they turn twenty-five.[73] In Singapore, the conflict comes directly from the state authorities' exhorting female PhDs to slow down or halt their academic pursuits so they can fulfill their socially expected marital and reproductive responsibilities.[74] In China, a far sterner political tone delivers the same message: the state labels professional women who are still single at twenty-seven as leftover women and singles them out as the primary source of social instability and problems. These women are told that they must give up their unrealistic romantic dreams and enter a relationship that can yield an enduring family life, thus restoring the propriety of the society.[75]

Via the unbounded vectors and overlapping layers of gender, sexuality, and class of the metamorphic Loveland, the heteroromantic relationship and possession of financial goods—private property, in particular—are further combined into a normative form of intimacy that I call homepatriarchal love, which anchors the neoliberal expansion in China. In North America, the entanglement between private property and the heteropatriarchal system, as Mishuana Goeman suggests, can be traced back to the inception of settler colonialism and capitalist nation-states. As the colonies consolidated private property as the legal basis for citizenship, the heteropatriarchal system was institutionalized as the primary means of safeguarding and transferring property. Additionally, the universalization of the heteropatriarchal system and its imposition onto indigenous populations justified and expedited land grabbing by colonial settlers, extending the territories of the capitalist nation-states that we know as Canada and the United States.[76] The monogamous heterosexual relationship, as Friedrich Engels explains, erects a conjugal linchpin to secure the patrilineal transfer of private property for the capitalist system.[77] Since the 1970s, the promulgation of owning private property as a universal human value by international organizations has become a new hegemonic instrument for the United States to use in extending its global neoliberal outreach and dominance.[78] Across Europe and the United States, as Lauren Berlant argues, neoliberalism has been cherished as a set of aspiring dreams about a good life. Building upon the life-changing and -affirming promise of "upward mobility, job security, political and social equality . . . durable intimacy . . . [and] meritocracy" that it offers, the neoliberal dream pulls people toward it repeatedly, often with cruel and deadly consequences.[79] As noted in the dating show, the Western neoliberal dream was transferred to China and rearticulated in comparable gender, sexuality, and class tropes, but it also was aligned with Chinese characteristics: upward social mobility, intimate heteropatriarchal stability, and complementary gender dualism, all of which are interwoven through the possession of material and financial goods.

A fiery and vehement encounter in a 2017 episode of *IF* illustrates the dense links between the sticky homepatriarchal love and China's expansive neoliberal dream life. The game started with a lighthearted conversation. Zhaosong Gao, a self-described backpacker, used the legendary love story of the Taiwanese novelist and translator Sanmao for a manifesto of his liberal lovestyle.[80] Since the 1970s, the wildly popular author had turned herself into an epitome of the cultivated, liberated woman, "not just because of her many books, newspaper columns, song lyrics, and public lectures, but also because of her free, cosmopolitan, and 'legendary' life that captured the imagination of many Chinese eager to look beyond their own borders" for true love.[81] This

helped Gao strike a chord that resonated with quite a few women. The san-
guine and agreeable mood, however, did not last long: one woman pressed
Gao on whether this nomadic lifestyle was anchored in a perpetual home—
read here as a privately owned property. His equivocal answer that "I don't
want to be confined by it" and his dodging the question did little to appease
the women, inviting more questioning and kindling grueling exchanges.
Zhengyu Jiang, the newly instated emotion mentor, intervened. There is a
categorical difference, Jiang concluded, between Gao's liberal style and that
of the women. Enabled by stable income and financial security, the latter
enjoy the freedom to choose their preferred way of loving. Conversely, shun-
ning family-associated responsibilities, the former's self-construed love ideal
was a clumsy attempt to cover up his poverty—or at best a form of escapism.
Emboldened by Jiang's comment, more women levied scathing criticisms
and launched into strident condemnations of Gao's irresponsibility to his parents and future spouse, forcing the man to try to defend himself with a litany
of alternative understandings about love and family. Among the women who
shared Gao's love philosophy, Rong Ma, a successful businesswoman, chose
to leave the light on for him until the end. Yet this decision, as she made clear,
was only to show her support of Gao's—and her own—irrepressible quest
for love beyond its omnipresent homepatriarchal affective tendrils. It was
not to indicate that she was willing to be his girlfriend. Although financially
equipped to continue the pilgrimage to her romantic ideal, Ma chose a different path and let her capacities conform to the ingrained homepatriarchal
mandate of love. At the close of this dramatic and intense encounter, Meng
(the supposed voice of equity and inclusion) suggested that despite their
peripheral status, alternative contenders like Gao should be respected or at
least tolerated—a neutralizing comment that further normalized the homepatriarchal registers of the good life in neoliberal China.

This example indicates that as a cluster of good-life promises, homepatriarchal love works through a futuristic and other-place-oriented logic. As
repetitively verified in the love contest, the attributes of ownership of private property and consumer goods—as well as polarized complementary
gender roles, ambitions, and resolutions for upward mobility—could substantiate one's enamoring abilities to lay the groundwork for an enviable
and durable family relationship. In showing that a love-drenched good life
can be achieved by the subjects, the Loveland regenerates these objects and
attributes as the source of the good-life dream. As Sara Ahmed puts it, "to
experience an object as being affective or sensational is to be directed not
only toward an object, but to 'whatever' is around that object, which includes

what is behind the object, the conditions of its arrival."[82] Following this logic, the correlation between the much-longed-for love life and the attributes and objects surrounding it is displaced into a relationship of causality: to become lovable and love-able, people must prepare for, cultivate, and defend these attributes and objects, as doing so is the condition that will bring the anticipated good life in the foreseeable future or other places. Put differently, what draws us toward these things is the hope for love, a commonly coveted emotion, and the desirable family life that will follow in its wake. Love thus re-creates inseverable affective tethering that works with the calculative logic of biopolitics to reproduce human beings as both the subjects and objects of neoliberalism to fortify and further its global dominance, a topic that I discuss further in chapter 3.

By virtue of its futuristic and other-place-oriented projection, homepatriarchal love hardly ever fails—and when it does, the failure is deferred elsewhen and will be addressed elsewhere to keep the hope open. As human divergences are ceaselessly re-created in oppositional forms, the difference-making machinery grounds the polarizing mechanism that in turn anchors and engineers the rejuvenated projection of the good-life dream for sustaining neoliberalism. In the next part of this chapter, I will unravel how the polarization through ethno-race rescales the national boundaries to energize China's marketizing experiment and uses the West as an uncharted territory of the liberal future to retain people's unfulfilled love aspiration, which has prompted the knee-jerk exodus of people and capital from China.

Ethno-Racializing Neoliberal Dream Making

While the state wields its newly amassed financial clout to expand China's global footprint, it also looks to inflate its hegemonic forces to match the imperial outreach. In 2007, the seventeenth CCP National Congress announced a strategic plan to revitalize China's soft power and waged a series of initiatives to increase China's overseas cultural influence. In 2011, the state-owned Xinhua News Agency leased two giant billboards in New York City's Times Square, "the so-called crossroads of the world," to run a months-long publicity campaign for the PRC—a move viewed as the mark of China's arrival and expansion in Western markets.[83] However, international media outlets viewed endeavors like this as barefaced propaganda intrusions.[84]

Compared to such ham-handed self-promotion that met with massive challenges outside China's borders, a less obtrusive approach that Jing Wang calls "indoctriment" has proved more effectual.[85] By packaging ideologically inflected messages into frivolous and pleasurable cultural products for fun and enjoyment (especially in formats familiar to Westerners), this strategy gives the state's propaganda regime an innocuous cover and finds a smoother road into international markets. The recent breakthrough of the foreign-inspired Chinese reality shows such as *The Voice of China* and *I Am a Singer* in the global media market is a notable example. With its synthetic remaking of the Western genre with Chinese characteristics, IF has extended its popularity beyond the Sinophone world and attracted a broad swath of audiences in the West. Since 2013, SBS2, a youth-oriented national channel in Australia, has been broadcasting the program with English subtitles.[86] To increase its global impact, JSTV has produced and aired dozens of special episodes of IF with overseas Chinese participants from the United States, Canada, Australia, New Zealand, Germany, Italy, Spain, Britain, France, and South Korea, among other countries. Via long shots zooming in on the intimate lives of diasporic youth, IF provides a window into the daily existence of diasporic Chinese to build an affective bridge between them and the so-called homeland.

The targeted places and audience groups dovetail neatly with the new pattern of Chinese emigration—which, after being suspended for over three decades, has surged exponentially since 1980 with a disproportionate flow to North America, Europe, and other developed countries in the Asia-Pacific area rather than Southeast Asia, the primary destination of previous generations of migrants.[87] The rerouted exodus contributes to the reproduction of surplus labor to release the overaccumulated capital in the West. In the 1960s, to address the labor shortage deriving from the surging demand of capital, major industrialized countries such as Australia and Canada rescinded their restrictive policies to attract more immigrants, and Asia, a continent they had turned their backs on for years, became a prime target.[88] The Immigration and Nationality Act of 1965 repealed such US laws as the Immigration Act of 1921, which capped the number of newcomers allowed into the country based on their national origins and restricted the flow of migrants from Asia. Since 1965, Asia has been a major source of new immigrants to the United States.[89] Since the late 1970s, neoliberal restructuring has accelerated this process in the name of re-creating the global free market—not just for capital, but also for labor. Accordingly, the number of China-born immigrants soared from 299,000 in 1980 to 2.1 million in 2016, a growth of over 700 percent.[90]

However, a closer look reveals how IF's special episodes profoundly distort, or at least misrepresent, the demographics of diasporic Chinese. Obviously, the mandatory diversity rule does not apply outside the PRC. The show's diasporic participants, most of whom are not Chinese citizens, come from identical middle- or upper-class backgrounds and are highly paid professionals in medical, financial, legal, or technological industries; graduates of Ivy League schools; or successful business owners. In the first episode featuring Chinese Americans, for example, seventeen of the twenty-four female participants had earned or were working toward a college degree, and more than half of them had received at least a master's degree from famous graduate schools. The men's profiles were even more glamorous: the male participants included the builder and owner of a prosperous start-up, a PhD student at Columbia University, a high-ranking employee of one of the world's top hundred corporations, and a financial professional working on Wall Street. These homogenizing representations belie the heterogeneous Chinese diasporas that have grown in four different ways: by students turning into immigrants, emigrating professionals, chains of immigrants, and immigrants who arrive by illegal means.[91] Collectively, the members of these four groups can also be divided into two categories: those with "portable skills" (students and professionals who overstay their visas) and menial laborers (the majority of migrants who come in chains and almost all "illegal" immigrants).[92] Despite their obliteration by *IF*'s romanticizing camera, the groups in the second category nonetheless account for a huge segment of the Chinese diasporas. Every year around 30,000–40,000 Chinese immigrants enter the United States and Europe illegally, ending up with jobs that pay minimum wages or less.[93] In contradiction to the common view presented in the media, even a large percentage of those who arrive through legal channels have entered low-paying industries with dead-end jobs. As a survey of migrants from Qingtian County in Zhejiang province shows, workers and peasants accounted for over 75 percent of the roughly 40,000 residents who left China legally between 1979 and 1995. With limited education and work-related skills, they could find jobs only through their connections with other members of their ethnic group, and they worked mostly in restaurants and garment factories for low wages.[94] In contrast to the spectacular picture painted by *IF*, due to the enormous economic inequalities among groups of Chinese Americans, the poverty rate among that population is shockingly high: 13 percent compared to 10 percent for US households overall.[95] With the influx of Chinese students from wealthy families and of investors turned immigrants into North America, Europe, and developed countries elsewhere in the world, these inequalities are expected to continue growing.

To facilitate capital's transnational reproduction, absolute additions to the labor force through migration works in tandem with reproduction of relative surplus populations through polarized difference making. For instance, the intersectional biopolitics of gender, class, and race ramified the post-1965 immigration to the United States to serve the varying politico-economic agendas and contingent needs of capital.[96] The state designed policies to re-produce a populace segment with the skills to sponsor and perpetuate the country's projected position in the upper echelon of the global division of labor, otherwise known as the knowledge economy. Accordingly, legions of students in the sciences, technology, engineering, and mathematics (most of whom are male) and who come from affluent families in Asia head to the United States for education and job opportunities. Compared to the maximum of twelve months that their peers majoring in the humanities or social sciences have to stay in the United States for optional practical training after they earn their degree, these students have up to twenty-nine months to find a job that will enable them to become permanent residents or US citizens. Consequently, as of 2010, technological professionals from Asia—including India, China, Taiwan, Hong Kong, and Macau—account for 53.9 percent of the high-tech labor in California's Silicon Valley.[97] This creates an enormous brain drain for these Asian regions.[98] In the meantime, lower-class immigrants from Latin America and Mexico come to the United States in droves to replace the so-called unruly Blacks as docile laborers in low-value-added industries such as garment and textile making and agribusiness, as well as service jobs that cannot be outsourced, including domestic work and nursing.[99] Through these different biopolitical practices, immigrant groups from different places are pulled in to satisfy the divergent needs of capital. Meanwhile, they are re-created as distinct racial groups and surplus populations for the industries that they are labelled as unfit for: for example, Asian students are alleged to be good at math and sciences and thus marked for engineering work, while Mexicans are seen as fit only for farming jobs. The racialized difference making regenerates and maintains competition among these groups to thwart their solidarity for collective negotiation and reduce labor costs.

Certainly, as a biopolitical vector rooted in the Western history of colonialism and imperialism, race plays a vital role in facilitating global neoliberal restructuring.[100] Not simply a taxonomic label to stratify human populations, race intersects with gender, class, and sexuality to re-create infinitely devalued labor groups to sustain the day-to-day reproduction of capital.[101] For instance, Asian is a relatively new racial category in the United States and was first formulated in the late nineteenth and early twentieth centuries to lump Chinese and Japanese immigrants into one racial group reserved for low-paying menial work and ensure the sustained supply of cheap labor for boosting the imperialist expansion in the West.[102] When the United States shifted its developmental focus in the 1970s, the racial valence of the term *Asian* changed accordingly. Despite the diverse cultural, class, and gender backgrounds of the new immigrants from Asia, a geopolitical category first informed by Western colonialism, successful and well-educated male professionals are cherry-picked to define the whole group as the so-called model minority.[103] According to this homogenizing racial discourse, the accomplishments of Asians are grounded in their shared values of loyalty, respect for authority, and a focus on family and education. These traits are often attributed to the "Confucian values," and the failure of other minorities such as Blacks and Hispanics is imputed to their lack of such traditions.[104] Refueling the culture-based color-blind racism in the United States, the racialized myth of the Asian model minority reinforces the pejorative narrative about Blacks and Hispanics as lazy, system-milking, and uninterested in education and unworthy of success in the free and competitive market, and it irons out the systemic disparities stemming from and wrought for neoliberal restructuring.[105] Racialized polarization disrupts the coalition forged during the civil rights movements between Asian immigrants and Blacks and clears the way for more deleterious policies.[106] More insidiously, these racialized myths reinforce the stereotype of Asians that provides the US neoliberal economy with continuous supplies of skilled immigrant workers from Asian countries and regions.[107]

As its affective ambience expands beyond the nation-state borders via the mass-mediated tendrils, the Loveland becomes more susceptible to cross-cultural exchanges and discursive formations. By selecting the participants and defining who are the most competitive contenders, *IF* incorporates the racialized neoliberal norm into China's phantasmagoric Loveland. The program aired three episodes about Chinese Americans in 2011, in the midst of the Occupy Wall Street Movement—one of the largest protests against global neoliberalism. Hailing the success stories of a select group of new immigrants, these episodes turned a deaf ear to the thunderous outcries from a broad social coalition against the intensified inequalities stemming from neoliberal globalization. In one of these globally relayed love competitions, a financial professional working on Wall Street received unanimous endorsement by the host team. Quite strikingly, outside this TV-created heteroromantic bubble, infuriated activists from across the United States and around the world were swarming into the heart of the financial industry and expressing their anger about its scavenging speculation that had turned the globe into a casino for profits and triggered the 2008 financial tsunami.

As a biopolitical vector deeply entangled with Western colonial history and capitalist praxes, race also reshapes China's Loveland and further integrates it into the neoliberal universe.[108] In addition to overseas Chinese, *IF* has invited a number of foreigners to participate. Among them, the contenders from the West are uniformly white, while those from other countries are all of other racial groups, echoing and replicating the predominant narrative in Euro-American societies that all the Westerners are white, and all the other races are from other places. Just like in their home countries, on the show the whites are foregrounded to be among the most attractive people. In 2017, *IF* aired an episode about the most popular male contenders, who were selected by the production team. Seven of the top ten were foreign nationals (from Russia, Taiwan, Britain, the United States, Japan, and Canada), and of them, three were of Chinese descent, three were white, and one was half-white and half-Asian. A British entrepreneur and NGO volunteer with the Chinese name Rui Gao became the all-time favorite man, and he embodies the attributes of other popular Chinese men, except for his racial identity (figure 2.6). Throughout the elaborated love scenarios, Western societies are also romanticized as purely white, with all Chinese who live there enjoying successful lives and having nearly as much affective attention as their white compatriots. When further scrutinized, these racialized tropes reveal a two-pronged exceptional logic of difference making that undergirds the Loveland's affective macrocosm. By virtue of their well-calculated investment in self-optimization through education and hard work, the Chinese immigrants

Fig. 2.6. Rui Gao, the all-time most popular male contender selected by the production team of *If You Are the One*, in an interview.

have achieved an exceptional status that is almost white. Yet their mobility reinforces the racial hierarchy that perpetuates other minority groups' status as unmeritorious and thus not worthy objects of love and intimacy.[109]

The mass-mediated Loveland is not simply passive in regard to the difference-making machinery. Rather, the Chinese state has altered the Loveland's contours and textures through racialized polarization for its own benefit. As David Harvey notes, China has taken a unique road to neoliberalization, differing from the industrialized Western countries and the Four Asian Dragons with its heavy reliance on foreign investment.[110] And the ethno-racial network has played a vital role here.[111] Because the phenotypically and phenogenetically grounded racial formation is not as relevant in China and the Sinosphere as in the West, the state instead uses the culture-based ethnic tie as its primary biopolitical tool. Since the mid-1990s, ethnic Chinese in Hong Kong, Taiwan, Singapore, and other regions have contributed to approximately 60 percent of China's foreign direct investment, and their companies account for over 70 percent of China's foreign enterprises.[112] More recently, the state has identified overseas Chinese and Chinese citizens studying and working abroad as important extrajurisdictional biopolitical resources in that they "are not only serving China from abroad or by returning, but after they return they play a leading role in many aspects of China's 'going out' strategy."[113] To garner their support, the party-state has changed its antagonistic stance toward the Chinese cultural tradition and, in particular, Confucianism—which had been deemed alien to the Maoist and Communist doctrine—turning it into a crucial discursive repertoire to naturalize the ethnic linkage with diasporic Chinese.[114] In this light, the state uses *IF*'s overseas special episodes as a source of ethnicized leverage to rescale the national boundaries, with the hope of getting more overseas Chinese to jump on its development bandwagon.[115] On July 1, 2016, the state implemented a policy that mandates more stringent censorship and direct control of foreign-inspired entertainment programs like *IF*.[116] Subsequently, more ethnic Chinese on these shows have praised the statist agenda, extolling their emotive connection to the homeland and performing their allegiance to the PRC. They tout their plan to better serve the country through the highlighted cultural-ethnic linkage. The state's aggressive recruitment of overseas Chinese and students to forward its "going-out" scheme has raised the eyebrows of Western politicians.[117] And the naturalized ethno-racial distinction marks China as racially different and "preparing for a clash of civilizations" that intensifies the nationalist frenzy among Western right-wingers.[118]

The ethno-racial differentiation informed by the exceptional logic is a two-pronged process. Via the ethno-racialized prism, Chinese immigrants are homogeneously romanticized as an exceptional group relishing the fully achieved good life in the fantastic West. Simultaneously, their exceptional overseas life further magnifies the problems plaguing the failed homepatri-archal dream at home: soaring housing prices, perpetuated inabilities to love and dangling impossibilities of being lovable, and the increasingly intrusive patriarchal state, to name just a few. Via these diametrically different life prospects revealed through this polarizing ethno-racial lens, the fading neo-liberal dream of countless Chinese citizens is projected onto the uncharted liberal West and rejuvenated in the liberating future there. Although its affec-tive connection is infinitely deferred to there and then, the homepatriarchal love has already reconstituted our lived realities here and now. In the 2016 US presidential election, many Chinese immigrants who are usually wary of public displays of political views flocked to Donald Trump and took dramatic measures such as chartering airplanes to fly banners bearing the words "Chi-nese Americans for Trump" to show their support—creating a spectacle that even media in China vied to cover.[119] Trump's racist and populist pledge to "make America great again" has galvanized new immigrants perturbed by rising economic disparities and the diversified gender, sexual, and racial demographics that collectively represent an imminent threat to the neolib-eral dream that they expect to realize in a racially purified and prosperous United States. The irony is that the annual number of new "undocumented immigrants" from Asia increased by 202 percent from 2000 to 2013, mark-edly outpacing the much-maligned immigration from Mexico and Latin America, and the three countries with the fastest rates of increase were India (306 percent), South Korea (249 percent), and China (148 percent).[120] Of the eleven million "undocumented" immigrants in the United States, China has sent 268,000, trailing only Mexico, Guatemala, El Salvador, and Honduras.[121]

Still more Chinese enthralled by prospects of the good life are on their way. According to *The 2012 Report about Chinese Transnational Migration* published by the *Global Times*, a major mouthpiece of the party-state, more than 70 percent of the Chinese individuals with net wealth of over 100 million yuan (approximately $1.7 million) have emigrated to other countries or are considering doing so.[122] In other words, the sticky attachment to homepa-triarchal love has spawned and maintained the massive outflow of capital and the Chinese middle class that has driven up property prices in Western societies and re-created Asians as the new racialized source of transnational financial capital.[123] In the face of mounting pressure stemming from the capi-tal flight and brain drain, the party-state has implemented far more stringent regulations of transnational financial transactions.[124] It has also established policies to govern the migration of the CCP cadres who are the major beneficiaries of China's marketization: they can either migrate and withdraw from the system that enables them to accumulate capital, or they need to stay in China and continue benefiting from the deepening neoliberalizing process.[125]

Conclusion

As this chapter demonstrates, by conveying a gladiator-like feeling of competition through the generic reformulation of love, the reality TV show *If You Are the One* valorizes self-serving rationality as the dominant way to justify market fundamentalism and facilitate China's neoliberal transition. In constricting the scope of lovabilities and love-abilities, the show builds transnational leverage to integrate Western neoliberal terms of gender, sexuality, and class with Chinese characteristics into the norm of homepatriarchal love and makes that love the idealized way of living in China. The show also rebuilds the ethno-racialized bridge to rescale the national boundaries and remake the homeland for the Chinese diaspora, playing an integral role in facilitating China's neoliberalization and furthering its global expansion. However, the polarizing racial difference making not only further disenfranchises a huge segment of the population in terms of their lovabilities and love-abilities, but it also further alienates China from the rest of world.

I end this chapter with a perplexing love scenario as a preview of chapter 3. Under pressure from the state's diversity directive, in July and August 2010, *IF* aired three special episodes featuring rural migrant workers. I have two questions about this programmatic setup: First, why would the move to open an equal arena for love have to be delimited in such a way that it actually curtails the love capacities of the subaltern groups? Second, if the bracketed love sphere for the overseas Chinese is justified by their alien status and the state's expansionist scheme, then why would the rural migrant workers—as fully legal Chinese citizens—be cordoned off to participate in this glamorous love competition? As I will make clear in chapter 3, the preconditioning of love potential as such is critical to the regeneration of the willing servitude of the rural migrants to the state and capital that is key to China's social transformation.

Part II

Tracing the Machinery
That Both Integrates
China into and Separates
It from the World

The Woeful Landscape
of Love

Work Hard, Dream Big,
and Die Slowly

RETURNING HOME BACKWARDS

Returning from Beijing to Shenzhen, from Dongguan
to Hangzhou, from Changshu to Ningbo
from Wenzhou to Chengdu, returning to the earth and plants
to the fragrance of grain, home is still
very far away, it's a pair of lost straw sandals
return and return, return from the factories
return from machines, return from tears,
return from forty back to thirty
to twenty, to ten . . . home is still
very far, it's a pair of lost straw sandals
return and return, facing the future
return to your mother's body—and there
there's no glory or dishonor, no difference between rich and poor
no separation between city and country. There are no tears
and everyone you meet is family.

IT SEEMS I'M REALLY HIS FATHER

When I went home one time, my son
was playing with the neighbor's kid
when he saw me he hid behind my mother's body
sticking his fingers in his mouth, sucking on them
as he peeked out, quietly, timidly
sizing me up, as though I weren't his father
but the neighbor's kid was excited
not knowing what to do with himself, singing for a bit
then dancing, then riding a kitchen stool
flying about shouting, circling my courtyard
running one lap then another, wanting to get close to me
until it was dark and he still didn't want to go home
so it seems I'm really his father.

—Yihong Tang

The sentimental verses above by Yihong Tang—a migrant worker-poet born in 1970 in Yilong, Sichuan province—speak directly to the ambivalent feelings about home held by many rural migrants. Like Tang, they trudge across varied urban terrains in the hope of making a better home for those they leave behind, only to be rejected by the place they temporarily inhabit and the nostalgic space they always long to return to. Even worse, the harder they try, the more they are alienated from their homes, both the real and the ideal ones. When all the potentialities of homecoming are foreclosed, these migrants have no place other than the maternal body to regress into if they do not want their last hope to be overwhelmed and assimilated by regulatory biopolitics, estranging identifications, and discriminatory systems. For dislocated migrants, their love-fabricated home dream is an infinitely enticing but perpetually out-of-reach mirage characterized by loss, remembrance, displacement, boundless melancholia, and profound cynicism. The love that they deem sacrosanct can be truly woeful. Yet love is not firmly set in such ways: it becomes so only when the love "that draws your attachment actively impedes the aim that brought you to it" and leaves no room for exit.[1]

Building upon the broad view of China's Loveland that the first part of this book brought into focus, this part continues to interrogate the lethal arrangements through which love is integrated into unjust biopolitics and dissect how these prejudiced setups create conditions of hospitability and hostility within which certain lives are more livable and others are not even worth pursuing in neoliberal times. By parsing multifarious transnational and intertextual exchanges, the first part mapped out the affective edges of China's unbounded lovescape. The second part spells out more details about the mechanism that advances the operation of the apparatus of love, using ethnographic engagement with a group of migrant workers whose everyday lives reveal the embedded effects of that apparatus. Paying close attention to the groups rendered unlovable and love-unable by the neoliberal logic of intimacy, it also explores disenfranchised subjects' unceasing efforts to carve out alternative ways to survive and resist in the ruinous Loveland to identify room for change within the global neoliberal system.

This chapter traces the rural workers' migrant route that was established as a result of China's phenomenal development from the mid-1990s to the dawn of the new millennium, investigating the ways that the country's neoliberal transition and neocolonial expansion combine the calculative biopolitics and the speculative apparatus of affect to function. In delineating the woeful stories of these love-impelled migrants, this chapter reveals how neoliberal economies appeal to and re-create emotions, desires, and sentiments to reproduce willful subjects. As a cluster of desirable potentialities to be actualized by the emerging dichotomies of heteronormative encounters, complementary gender engagements, upward social mobility, and other oppositional relationships, love orients the unknowable futures of migrant bodies toward manageable probabilities to secure the profit-making circulation of financial capital, based on the translation of sheer uncertainty into probabilistic forecasts.[2] My analysis also lays out the uneven distributions of livabilities, precarities, and vulnerabilities through the establishment of gendered, classed, and sexualized biopolitical forces, illuminating how migrant bodies are disparately identified and marked for varying productive uses by industrial capital. Taken together, these analytical lines shed light on the links between the retrospective management of biopolitics and the futuristic preregistering of affective tendencies, unmasking the difference-making machinery that underlies and coordinates their divergent implementation to shore up transnational neoliberal domination.

The Chinese Market That Is Moved by Love

In the middle of 2017, with the publication of an investigative report titled "Chinese-Style Blind Date: My Son Is Only 33 and Won't Consider Any Girls without Beijing *Hukou* [the official registration system of residency]," the *Phoenix Weekly* threw a bombshell into China's already hyper-strained lovescape. In the article, the state-owned magazine described in detail the dynamics pervading the weekend marriage market in Beijing, which is packed with anxious parents trying to find their children a date, and thus presented the boundless ambience of the Loveland. In particular, "The Snobbism Chain of the Chinese-Style Blind Date" (a graphic from the article that has been widely circulated) sarcastically qualified a person's nebulous love capabilities into a set of identifiable attributes, including residential status, academic and professional background, income and personal assets, and so forth.[3] Using this graphic, parents can easily spot a top-notch husband candidate for their daughter with Beijing *hukou* and a graduate degree, an apartment in a downtown area and a luxury car, and a monthly income of at least 50,000 yuan (roughly $7,400).[4] Such a man's best match "would be a physically attractive woman born and bred in Beijing with a flat in downtown Dongcheng or Xicheng districts—at a pinch she could own property in the northern university district. She must have a mid- or high-end car, a month[ly] salary of 20,000 yuan and at least a bachelor's degree to her name."[5] Building upon the qualities laid out by these ultrarealistic specifications, anyone can find a perfect match through their parents' watchful eyes, even without their physical presence. Within days, this article had already been reprinted by a number of major print and internet media, making a stir with its poignant yet lighthearted satire and unveiling the stretched landscape of love that has turned into a hunting ground for the haves and the have-nots.

The article's message did not surprise me. By studying China's phantasmagoric lovescape, I had already been exposed to its excessively commercialized status quo. Back in 2012, when I was starting my fieldwork, I learned firsthand about the scale of market penetration into the private spheres of love, dating, and marriage. For instance, although Hai'an was the only county in its area that was not one of the top hundred most affluent counties in China at the time, its bustling marriage market was second to none. Any man of rural background should own at least one property—either a countryside villa or, preferably, a condo in a township—to qualify for dating. As of 2019, an apartment in the county of a hundred square meters (slightly over a thousand square feet) could easily cost over 750,000 yuan (roughly $115,000). In addition, to transform a dating relationship into a conjugal one, a man would need to pay his future parents-in-law at least 120,000 yuan as the betrothal gift and buy his would-be wife the so-called four golds (a gold ring, earrings, necklace, and bracelet), which would cost another 20,000 yuan. Considering that the local medium monthly income is around 3,500 yuan, the price of becoming a groom is unsettlingly high. The cost on the bride's side is much less: her parents can simply purchase a car as a wedding gift, and even that isn't required.

Hai'an's fiercely competitive conjugal market offers us a glimpse into China's ultracommercialized lovescape. Although a long-standing tradition, locals had kept the cash and gift exchange between the conjugal families to a minimum level just for the purpose of expressing courtesy and gratitude to each other. Only recently have the amounts of the cash and gifts increased to such an extent that they can result in lifelong debt for the average working family. As the barometer and incubator of China's marketization, the Loveland—as shown in *If You Are the One*, discussed in chapter 2—has morphed into the homepatriarchal apparatus grounded in private property. The pioneer feminist intellectual He-Yin Zhen argues that as far back as the late Qing dynasty, property relations have been the key to social life in China. The legal institution of private property justified women's subordinate status as property and constituted the origin of uneven accumulation of capital that spawned other forms of social inequalities.[6] In this regard, feminist scholars call for "a total social revolution that would abolish state and private property to bring about true social equality and the end to all social hierarchies."[7] During the Maoist era, the state dismantled the private space of the family to clear the way for collectivized living and a socialist economy. As China moves into neoliberalism, the institution of the privatized nuclear family has reappeared along with the rise of economic liberalization and dichotomized gender inequalities.[8] Previously in Hai'an, as a woman working in a garment factory told me, "girls would send a matchmaker over to inquire about the financial situation of their suitor. Now they will directly ask themselves: 'Do you have a flat? Where is it located? Do you have a car? What brand is it? How much do you make a month?'" Any inappropriate answer to these questions, especially the one regarding housing, could immediately remove the man from the candidate pool.[9] For women, this is a screening process to identify the right candidate who can deliver on the good-life promise. For men, it is the price they have to pay to enjoy the dividends from gender privilege and patriarchal power. To avoid replicating the misogynistic neoliberal rhetoric that blames women for soaring class inequalities, we need to delve further into the gendered and classed layers of the Loveland to unpack its underlying logic of marketization.[10]

By reinstating private property as the primary means of achieving the good life in the neoliberal condition, homepatriarchal love contributes to China's marketization. When the transition process resumed in the early 1990s, land "whose monetary value had been neglected since 1949, suddenly assume[d] a very important role in the overall Chinese economy."[11] By reclaiming the socialist principle of collective ownership, the state reasserts its monopoly over land and simultaneously sells the right to use the land to developers and buyers for a limited period (50–70 years), reinventing private property in a format that best suits its interest. In the early 2000s, the state consolidated real estate as a new growth area.[12] Thereafter, "real estate investment grew rapidly from about 4 percent of GDP in 1997 to the peak of 15 percent of GDP in 2014, with residential investment accounting for over two thirds of the total real estate investment."[13] This does not even include the upstream and downstream industries that the sector feeds, such as those producing steel, concrete, decorations, furniture, and other consumer goods. Moreover, with the 1994 tax assignment reform, the state introduced fiscal decentralization to incentivize local governments to deal with economic affairs in ways favorable to the marketized economy. Thus, "fiscal reform, especially the separation between central and local taxes, has defined the boundary of local revenue, and given a greater incentive for the local government to mobilize the revenue, leading eventually to local corporatism."[14] Land sales became a key source of local public finance and accounted for about 18 percent of local governments' total revenues, while property and land-related tax made another 12 percent contribution in 2017.[15] Tying private property and the heteropatriarchal apparatus of intimacy and desire together, the Loveland substantively boosts the real estate market as a key developmental motor.

People's engineered attachment to homepatriarchal love that defines the normative way of living in neoliberal China is further naturalized as the so-called *gangxu* (or "rigid demand") and used to promote consumerist demands. One day when I was conducting fieldwork in a garment factory, I started to chat with a worker in her early twenties about her dating experience. Unlike most of her peers, she said that she would not use property ownership as a strict requirement if the man was her "true love." Overhearing our talk, another worker interrupted her abruptly: "Your parents wouldn't think that way!"[16] Having a daughter of the same age as the first woman, the second felt compelled to intervene and share some real-life wisdom with her young coworker. Other (mostly senior) workers echoed her comment, pushing the young woman into awkward silence. Exchanges like this frequently occurred in my interviews, especially with people having one or more daughters. Denouncing the transactional telos of marriage in general, these interviewees nonetheless all made an exception for their own daughters. They intimated to me that their daughters should find someone with financial security so they could be spared from having as harsh a life as their mothers. Witnessing China's dramatically changing landscape of love, these workers have developed a coping strategy to navigate the turbulent shifts without challenging the dominant narrative promoted by the state. Versed in the gendered, classed, and sexual terms of homepatriarchal love they learn from media products such as *If You Are the One*, they feel qualified to guide their daughters through the tumultuous dating scene and find ways to displace hefty financial burden and anxiety inflicted by the cutthroat market economy onto the daughters' future spouses. Noticing the intergenerational dynamics of love, savvy businesspeople have incorporated into their marketing playbooks what they refer to as mother-in-law economics. As a billboard that I saw by the highway from Hai'an to Wuxi proposes, "the difference between mother-in-law and aunt is just an apartment."[17] In addition to their role in housing, the love-afforded anxieties have become a crucial driving force of China's consumer market. In 2012, mother-in-law economics was responsible for 2 percent of the annual growth in China's GDP (the total growth rate was 7.8 percent).[18] As we can see, market needs are driven as much by hope and despair as by rational reasoning.

Compared with young women, young men have less leeway in the ferocious marriage market, and love-agitated yearning for the good life has ensnared myriad Chinese men in capital's profiteering cycle. The single male workers I interviewed dreamed about saving enough money to purchase an apartment of their own. For them, love is an enticing set of potentials to which owning private property holds the key. In the eyes of married men, moving their wife and children from dingy rural cottages into a sleek urban home is the ultimate driver of self-destroying toil. For these men, love is making an unswerving commitment to the homepatriarchal promise. Despite the differing threads of their home-building love stories, one thing is clear: the wealth they may accumulate at the cost of their physical and mental well-being can never satisfy capital's ever-expanding appetite. In Wuxi, a construction worker's daily pay rose from around 100 yuan in 2007 to 160 yuan in 2012, a 60 percent increase not commonly seen in other sectors. During the same time, the average price of urban housing in China soared 68 percent from 3,445 to 5,791 yuan.[19] Minor as this numerical difference might appear to be, it reveals one grave rule: payments to labor should never outpace the gains by capital, because otherwise the latter would face a crisis of reproduction. Confronted with the frothy market and an imminent crisis for capital, in 2016 the Chinese state took blunt measures as part of its *gongjice gaige* (or "supply-side structural reforms") to reduce the oversupply of property. By the end of that year, sales of commercial property, including residential housing, had spiraled nationally by 22.5 percent, with prices spiking in the first-tier cities (such as Beijing, Shanghai, and Shenzhen) with many second-tier ones following suit.[20] Instead of solving the crisis of capital reproduction, the state displaced the burden onto new buyers and thus deferred the problem to the near future. Driven by their inseparable attachment to homepatriarchal love, more male workers are mired in this crisis, with debilitating consequences in sight. As a construction worker complained, he once took an eighteen-hour daily shift from 3:30 AM to 11:30 PM for extra earnings to help his son find a date. "If I had not quit, I would have already died," he told me.[21]

Through the Loveland, the reinstated patriarchal system is further integrated into China's market economy, using children as a way to rejuvenate the promise of a deferred good life and thus perpetuating the reproduction of working subjects willingly enslaved by capital. In the West, as Friedrich Engels noted, the monogamous marriage is a congealed form of the patriarchal and patrilineal systems central to capitalistic relationships: by its control of women's reproduction, the capitalistic state establishes and secures a patrilineal line for the transfer of private property and wealth and thus consolidates the market mechanism.[22] In neoliberal China, through its normalized homepatriarchal layers, the Loveland remakes not only working-class men but also their parents as affectively enmeshed subjects serving the collective interests of the state and capital. A Hai'an native with twenty-five years of experience in the apparel industry told me that she planned to quit her management job in a local factory and go back to Mauritius for a job on the shop floor that would pay her more. Noticing my surprised expression, she sighed: "I have no choice. I have a son."[23] Her son owned a home décor business and was doing well financially. Still, the mounting pressure imposed by the homepatriarchal norm compelled her to contribute to the realization of her son's love-dream just like other anxious parents. According to a popular saying, "having a son is like starting a China Construction Bank (*jianshe yinhang*) and getting ready for more work, but having a daughter is running a China Merchants Bank (*zhaoshang yinhang*) and just waiting for investment" (in Chinese, *zhaoshang* means "business solicitation"). As capital reconfigures adult sons as its leverage to access more laboring bodies, family-focused love creates new minors to orient their parents' future life in a direction demanded by capital. A discussion I had with a group of female workers in a family mill clarified this point. Curious about my work, they wondered in which direction it would lead my future life. After I told them of my plan to get the work published and find an academic job, I redirected the question to them: "So what is the plan for your future?" "Me?" said one woman, who was apparently taken aback by my question. After pondering for a few minutes, she said, "I don't really have any plan for myself." Her co-worker quickly jumped in: "Yes! Children are all her hope. Children are her sky." Taking a deep breath, the first woman seemed to finally find her answer, saying, "As long as my children are okay, I will be fine."[24]

As a former migrant, this woman had worked in multiple cities for over fifteen years before joining the mill. When her children reached school age, she had decided to quit her job in the city and move back home with her children so they could receive a better education and more support. Offering a flexible schedule and convenient location, the mill job allowed her to balance her work and life, which revolved around her two children. In the West, as Lee Edelman contends, reproductive futurism inherently suppresses and precludes queer subjects from participating in a heteronormative social life.[25] Yet in China, imperative participation in a reproductive future could become no less oppressive if the trajectory of these workers' lives was bent to reflect the combined interests of the party-state and capital.

Unsurprisingly, after years of separation from their children with sparse communication, many migrants find their family relationships in trouble and sometimes irremediably damaged, contradicting the promissory prospect anchored in heteronormative reproductive futurism. In Hai'an, one construction worker kept coming back to talk to me after I interviewed him. In me, a stranger who would stay for only a short time, he found a much-needed ear for his sorrow at having lost his son's love—a problem common among and normalized by his local peers. As the breadwinner of the family, he traveled between his home and different construction sites in the hope of fulfilling first his own and then his son's homepatriarchal dream. Love had motivated him to take lethal risks (such as working eighteen-hour shifts), and he was anguished to find that his sacrifice was met only with nonchalance from his son. Compelled by his masculine ego, which was hardened by the life he had led, he kept these tearful stories to himself, only sharing them with visitors like me as a rare cathartic outlet.

As these examples show, the apparatus of love is the publicly tempered sentiment that instigates and primes our emerging feelings and emotions, and it shapes our process of world building to pave the ground for China's marketization. I next show that as the embedded structure that orients and registers our affective tendencies, the fluid boundary of love is also textured by the gendered, sexualized, and classed vectors of the difference-making machinery to enmesh countless rural migrants as disposable subjects serving capital's productive needs—and, more importantly, to shrink the horizon of their emerging selves to accommodate its speculative circulation for refueling global neoliberal economies.

The Classed Roadblocks on Tearful Migrant Routes

As Tang's sentimental lines at the beginning of the chapter articulate, beneath rural migrants' love-inspired and spellbinding dream of home are the bleak realities that keep limiting the dream's promissory horizon. As 2017 drew to the close, a fire broke out in a crammed apartment building in an industrial neighborhood in southern Beijing. The flames quickly devoured the building before the firefighters arrived, claiming the lives of nineteen people, seventeen of whom were rural migrants. But it was the state's reaction that rendered the fire truly lethal to these urban outcasts, who had refused to relinquish the home dream they had built in the city. Using the fire as a justification for eradicating all illegal structures housing unregistered residents to prevent future incidents, the Beijing municipal government attacked the migrant enclaves through egregiously bad measures such as cutting off the supply of water and electricity with no notice and enforcing evictions by bulldozing buildings. As the pressure from the public and media mounted, the state defended its reckless actions as part of its plan to purge the "low-end populations" and to "modernize, beautify and gentrify the Chinese capital as a showcase for the Communist Party," concealing its manipulation of the population and intrusive regulation of individual lives.[26] Driven into the merciless cold from the place they had called home, millions of migrants became homeless overnight, forced into exile in the displaced futurescape of their aspirational family dream.

Compared with the unmoored migrants in the cities, whose home-building future was under ceaseless attack by the state, the children they had left behind at home were trapped in the yoke of negligence and oblivion, spending their youth in endless waiting and seeing no better future. On the morning of November 19, 2012, in Bijie—the most populous city of Guizhou, the province that is the source of more migrants than any other—five boys about ten years old were found dead in a dusty dumpster. The children, who came from three related families, suffocated on the fumes from the charcoal they had burned while cuddling together to keep warm through the wintry night as their parents worked thousands of miles away to give them a better life.[27] On June 9, 2015, also in Bijie, four siblings ages five to fourteen committed suicide together at home in a village, leaving a note for their parents that said: "Thanks for your kindness. I know you mean well for us, but we should go now." They swallowed pesticide and ended their young lives.[28] Caused by the barefaced biopolitics that had created and driven the massive rural migration to energize China's urbanization and industrialization, these premature deaths are the direct consequence of the state-sponsored production and exploitation of class-differentiated vulnerabilities for the welfare of the government and capital.

Unlike the outright deaths that have attracted much critical attention, the slow deaths hovering over the roughly two hundred million rural migrants and more than sixty million children they leave behind (together accounting for roughly 20 percent of the Chinese population) have been normalized, if not fully accepted, as part of the quotidian scenes in contemporary China.[29] Instead of direct victimization, this slow death is the physical wearing out of migrant bodies in a way that "points to deterioration as a defining condition of [their] experience and historical existence."[30] Driven by the love-infused yearning for a good life, many migrant laborers are recast as caring parents, loyal spouses, and filial children, willingly sacrificing their own well-being and prosperity for the families' benefits and contradicting a universalized self-serving neoliberal subjectivity. Thus, sacrificial love keeps the migrants attached to the objects, fantasies, and worlds that promise a gleaming good life but in actuality deepen and perpetuate their bodies' destruction, leading to the dead end of debilitation, enervation, and incapacitation. As the coda of *The Last Train Home*, an award-winning documentary about a migrant worker's family, unfolds, the couple's love-motivated hard work to help their family break out of the migration cycle leads only to trauma.[31] Xiao Li, their teenage daughter who grew up with her grandparents and younger brother, has quit school after a heated argument with them and joined the migrant army despite her parents' persistent opposition. Although at first sight her decision appears to be impulsive, in fact, it is the result of the combination of the managerial biopolitical system and the affective Loveland that has incorporated itself into the Chinese people's sensory habitus and daily lives.

Indeed, by altering the classed parameter of the difference-making machinery, the Chinese state has developed and implemented an array of legislative and administrative policies regarding residency, education, insurance, medical care, housing, and other livelihood issues. It intends to reproduce and maintain dispossessed migrants "as floaters, as impermanent outsiders for whom the state [is] not responsible, in order to serve the state's own fiscal and modernization needs."[32] In the early 1950s, following the Stalinist model that prioritized industrialization as the sine qua non for communist modernization, the Maoist state legislated a dichotomized urban-rural structure to brace the "circular resource allocation system" used for socialist constructions.[33] In this system, rural supplies of food and raw materials bolstered the urban-based industrialization, and farmers got part of the produced values and materials to support themselves and their work.[34] After World War II the Soviet state had a labor shortage, but China's problem was the oversupply of labor. In 1953, the state created the *hukou* registration system to stratify citizens by their birthplace, attempting to force surplus peasant laborers to return to their rural homes. As Mao Zedong's Great Leap Forward ended up in catastrophe in 1958, the state decided to enforce the *hukou* system to prevent hunger-stricken rural residents from flooding into cities and thus forestall social tumult and political chaos. By providing certain types of welfare—such as food, free housing, and low-cost education and medical care—to urbanites only, the *hukou* system not only made rural migration into cities almost impossible in Maoist China, but it also imposed egregious class inequalities onto the polarized social structure.[35] Since the initiation of urban reform in the 1980s, building on the *hukou* system, the state has reformulated the class inequalities between urbanites and peasants to help cultivate and consolidate the market mechanism. In 1984, the state lifted the grim restriction on rural migration and allowed farmers to move to cities. Starting in 1992, it first permitted and then encouraged massive rural migration to increase the labor supply to meet the explosive needs of unleashed capital. Henceforth, "instead of only being allowed to operate in the nearest free-market pocket, individuals have increasingly been able to move long distances and dramatically change their status and occupation."[36]

Notably, the state embeds a string of push and pull factors in the residential asymmetries regulated by the *hukou* system to stimulate and sustain the exodus of the rural population to urban and coastal areas. Simultaneously, it redraws the biopolitical setting to facilitate the extraction of their labor values to boost the developmental agenda. The biased policies of the state have generated compounded effects that sharply restrict the scope of options for the supposedly freed farmers, including a sharp decrease in the amount of farmland, soaring living expenses, and growing income disparities between rural and urban residents—as well as a robust demand for labor in construction industries and other nonstate sectors in cities. In Wuxi, for example, a construction worker told me that although the government had reduced the crop tax in the early 2000s, other farming expenses, such as the costs of fertilizers, pesticides, and equipment, have risen strikingly as a result of marketization. "After deducting the expenses of fertilizers and labor, you will only make several hundred yuan per square acre. My family can only make a couple of thousand yuan a year. You know, it is far from enough to support my family," the farmer told me in an interview.[37] Migrants like him, who have been pushed out of their homes by bleak job prospects and mounting pressure to support their families, populate construction sites across China's cities. While legitimizing the right of Chinese peasants to move freely across the country, through other insidious techniques the state has sharply narrowed migrants' choices of paths to align their life trajectory with capital's oscillating needs.

In addition to the invisible hand of the free market that works through disciplinary biopower, the Chinese state uses a visible hand to wield its totalizing sovereign power by legislative and administrative means, undermining the negotiating capacities of migrants to maximize its and capital's benefits. Disenfranchised as the disposable "floating populations" in cities, innumerable rural migrants are deprived of legal protection and turned into hypervulnerable and exploitable subjects despite their full legal citizenship.[38] Unlike urbanites, they have minimal to no access to medical care distributed through the *hukou* system, and it is common to see construction workers ignoring illnesses and injuries and continuing to work until their health collapses and they have to stop. In the meantime, they suffer from job fluidity and insecurity stemming from constant changes in their work schedules and locations, and their bosses refuse to provide them with basic life insurance. Of course, the workers are not eligible for any *hukou*-based pension, either. The escalating worry about their future has turned many migrants into working machines, or indentured laborers who toil without stopping. In my fieldwork, I saw many workers in their sixties or even seventies who were still performing the precarious tasks of high-rise construction at formidable heights—such as welding and wiring scaffolds and wood frames without harnesses—to earn a meager livelihood, while their urban peers were basking in sunlit city parks and relishing retirement. In one extreme case, a woman told me that for nearly twenty years she had worked in a silk factory for twelve hours a day, with only one day off a year.[39] On top of this enslaved labor, the state directly abuses rural migrants, treating them as cash cows. To remain eligible to stay in cities for jobs, the migrants "are required to pay for the temporary resident permit and the work permit in one lump sum," and their families also have to pay "security fees" at home.[40]

Hukou-allotted educational resources change the horizon of rural migrants' future in favor of capital, and thus they have a strong impact on the migrants. Since the mid-1990s, the streamlining of public education in the name of budgetary reform and fiscal austerity has considerably reduced both the quantity and the quality of schools in rural areas.[41] As a result, despite the steadily growing number of college graduates in the wake of higher education reform in the late 1990s, the percentage of rural students in universities in China continues to decline. Between 1978 and 1998, for instance, about 30 percent of the students at Peking University, known as China's Harvard, were from rural areas, but in 2010, this number dropped sharply to only 10 percent.[42] Similar changes can also be identified at Tsinghua, the Chinese equivalent of the Massachusetts Institute of Technology.[43] Blaming themselves for the purposively distributed and retained inequalities in educational resources, many migrants buy into the rhetoric of meritocracy and self-accountability, perpetuating the state-imposed disparities in the service of the market. After the neoliberal rule solidified its reign, education became another item for sale, ironically marketed to migrants' children via the *hukou* system. In Hai'an, for instance, property ownership would grant urban residential status to a rural family, which, in turn, would give its children access to lavish educational resources.

In brief, akin to the racialized prison-industrial complex in the United States, set up to undermine the life expectancy of Blacks and subdue their resistance, in China class is the basis for the extralegal production and calculated exploitation of residency-differentiated precarities intended to limit the biological and biopolitical vitality of rural migrants for the welfare of the market and government.[44] While migrant bodies' biopolitical values are tapped for profits, their biophysical viabilities are worn out as they move toward their fateful demise. Many construction workers develop serious problems with their waist, lungs, and stomach from the heavy-duty and dirty work they do, while many apparel workers struggle with neck, shoulder, and waist pain for sitting too long, and nearly all silk workers' hearing becomes impaired by the noisy machines that they run all day long. As a woman joked with me, an experienced doctor can easily figure out her identity as an apparel worker from her doddering gait and curled-up sitting posture. With that in mind, the doctor could effortlessly identify her problem and decide her treatment without performing any exams or tests. If making clothes leaves marks of physical harm and chronic pain on the laboring body, construction work is far more consequential and can reduce a person's life expectancy by five years at least, as many workers mentioned to me. Deprived of educational opportunities to improve their chance of avoiding the slow death cycle, these workers are preordained to wither prematurely, sacrificing their buoyancies for the benefits of the state and capital. In this regard, China's residency-based biopolitical stratification is comparable to the race-induced apartheid system in South Africa.[45] Furthermore, the systematic re-creation of precarious conditions and discriminatory barricades within its sovereign territory by the Chinese state to disaggregate and reaggregate its citizens to reproduce graded subjects in capital's interests is no less insidious than the nationalist thrust that right-wing Western politicians use to reclaim nation-state borders for restratifying human lives and biopolitical valences to facilitate capital's boundless profit making.[46]

The Gendered Biopolitical Engine of Marketization

Certainly, gender is another differentiating vector used by the state to cull and cultivate the population in concert with its marketizing tenet. In 1978, Deng Xiaoping introduced the one-child policy in tandem with his reform plan. In 1980, constitutional amendments incorporated eugenics, packaged as a policy needed to regulate women's reproductive agency to meet market needs. Subsequently, stringent birth control policies were introduced to restructure China's demographics and markedly increased the young adult share of the population. With the median age of only thirty-two and few elderly people and children to support, the reshaped Chinese workforce was "well positioned to cope with the dramatic social and economic changes occurring all around" in the 1980s and 1990s.[47] Gendered technologies accommodated the state's withdrawal from welfare provisions as well. Government-sponsored care for aging groups that Mao had pledged to provide as basic welfare and that Deng had also endorsed to justify the one-child policy was transferred back to the private family as the reform deepened. Anchored by the dichotomized gender discourse that celebrates men's and women's complementary family roles, the shifting of responsibility for welfare functions to the family was put into effect without stirring up much resistance. Unlike the patrilineal tradition destabilized by Mao for its close relationship to private property, the patrilocal system remained nearly intact throughout his reign, laying the foundation for the resurrection of the private family. Nursing the elderly was reinstated as men's filial responsibility, especially in rural areas where state-provided care had been minimal. Since the private family has also turned into the primary actor in the farming system, men's preferential status is reinforced by their bodily advantages in physical labor. Taken together, these factors further reduce women's biopolitical value and give rise to rampant female infanticide across rural China in the aftermath of draconian birth control.[48]

Needless to say, rural women's devaluation by gendered biopolitics is also critical to China's reintegration with the global economy. With the opening up of the Pudong area in 1992, Shanghai—China's former center of textile and apparel production—started to dispatch these labor-intensive sunset industries to adjacent areas that had less costly labor resources, clearing the way for the development of high-value-added industries, such as finance and information technology, across its urban sprawl.[49] With a rural population of over half a million, Hai'an was an ideal destination for labor-intensive manufacturing industries. In 2012, Hai'an was home to over a thousand medium-size factories (those employing at least fifteen workers) and taking and fulfilling orders from Japan, the United States, members of the European Union, and other industrialized countries every day. By the time of my second visit in 2016, more than half of these factories had been shut down, and only a few had reopened in neighboring countries with lower wages, such as Vietnam and Bangladesh. The dramatic cross-regional and transnational shuffling and reshuffling of capital investment—which has all taken place within the short span of three decades—provides a telling footnote to China's meteoric rise among the global neoliberal economies and the insolvable confliction that has emerged during this process: the inrush of capital drawn by China's bountiful labor resources that sustained its stunning development versus capital's impulse for nonstop relocation in search of an ever-cheaper labor force. As in other developing countries, in China the rural female workforce provided a major attraction to labor-craving capital. Of the sixty-eight apparel and textile workers I interviewed, only four were men, and of all the workers in China's export-manufacturing industries, over 80 percent are women from rural areas.[50] Determining the conspicuously female character of China's industrializing engine is the gendered difference-making machinery, which runs unceasingly to produce cheaper labor from within to retain footloose capital. In Hai'an's women-dominated apparel factories, for instance, the higher the position, the more likely it is to be held by a man with higher pay than a woman. When I hinted at the flagrant inequality of labor division and income, some women sprang to the system's defense, evoking an essentialist conception of gender. Work on the factory floor, they contended, is women's "natural" job because they are more attentive to details, and men usually receive more education that qualifies them for more senior positions. In addition, men can sell their greater capacity for physical labor and get higher-paying jobs, such as in construction and decoration, to provide good lives for their wives and children. Evidently, the gendered machinery has made these women willing subjects, subordinated to capital's unevenly configured exploitation. Against the backdrop of neoliberal globalization, the gendered biopolitical devaluation has unfurled its scope beyond the nation-state's boundaries to accommodate capital's cross-border traffic. Not surprisingly, China has to compete with its Southeast Asian neighbors for foreign investment by offering more disenfranchised workers, who have been modified through gendered differentiation for exploitative purposes. To partake in the planetary sharing of dividends, China also sends its national capital abroad to exploit subjects devalued by gender elsewhere, as seen in its recent Belt and Road Initiative (BRI).

To that end, the party-state uses its sovereign and disciplinary powers to maintain the gendered axis of the difference-making machinery and thus fortify the complicit alliance that it has forged with capital. In 2015, right before International Women's Day on March 8, two principal mouthpieces of the Chinese state, Xinhua News Agency and the *People's Daily*, released reports hailing women's contributions to the economy.[51] A group of female construction workers, as these propaganda organs claim, put on delicate gowns and heavy makeup for their first professional portrait, and through sophisticated photogenic techniques, these coarse "female men" (*nühanzi*), hardened by menial labor, were transformed into graceful "goddesses" (*nüshen*) with exquisite beauty and breathtaking auras. Purporting to celebrate women's contribution by twisting the female workers' gender embodiment to fit within the boundaries of normative femininity, the pieces endorse the masculinist perception of the construction industry and relegate women to a lesser position by rationalizing their biopolitical devaluation that is at the heart of capital reproduction. Though this glaring example created only a tiny ripple on the tidal waves, it shows how the totalizing sovereign power sanctions and cultivates the immensely polarized gender system in conjunction with other disciplinary means such as scientific discourses, cultural representations, and institutionalized education. To perpetuate the gender dichotomy and serve market needs, Chinese women are repeatedly told that they should pursue subjects and professions fitting their scientifically verified gender roles.[52] Thus when the time comes to start their careers, many of them find that their odds of getting a job are remarkably lower than those of their male peers. Worse still, the terms of women's jobs are often written in unapologetically biased ways regarding their duties, income, benefits, and so forth. If anyone dared to challenge these unequal rules, their disobedience would entail dire consequences—including losing the chances of being hit by Cupid's arrow and realizing the dream of a good family life, as media pundits preach tirelessly through popular platforms like *If You Are the One*.[53]

Contrary to the homogenizing representation of construction as predominantly men's territory, women have become common in the industry, which operates under an incrementally entrepreneurial modality. Developers divide a project into specialized parts—such as designing, foundation laying, walling, and ceiling and roofing—and outsource the work to different contractors. To enhance their efficiency and productivity, the contractors subcontract the jobs to workers who, rather than receiving daily wages, get paid only after completing their individual contracts. A prevalent modus operandi in China's labor-intensive industries such as manufacturing and construction, the multicontractual and pay-by-the-piece model turns workers into self-reliant market subjects, motivated to optimize their limited resources (namely, physical labor) to maximize monetary returns. For this reason, as I noted in Wuxi, many migrants chose to work as couples, with the husband putting his physical labor to maximum use and the wife performing the supportive role of *xiaogong* (or "junior worker"). The wife focused on less physically challenging and technically rigorous parts while also performing household duties to ensure their rejuvenation for more work. Women's underpaid productive labor and unpaid reproductive labor thus ensure the uninterrupted reproduction of laborers, which, in turn, enables the unending reproduction of capital in a double exploitation through women's biopolitical devaluation.

Xiao Wang, a brave intruder into the masculine territory of scaffold building, is an intriguing example of capital's often unrecognized subsidization by gender. Like other couples working on the site, Xiao Wang and her husband left their home in Guizhou and came to Wuxi. She had worked there for several years when I met her. As one of only two female scaffold builders at this construction site, she embodied a defiant presence in this ultramanly realm characterized by excessive requirements of endurance, energy, and stamina. In spite of all the odds and her bodily disadvantage, Xiao Wang won recognition and respect from all her supervisors for her outstanding performance. But she was subject to constant derision, baseless questioning, and direct harassment from her coworkers: "How can a woman be a scaffold builder?" "Are you really a woman?" "Can't your husband support you?" Gender-oriented slurs of this ilk were levied against her almost every day, throwing her relationship with her husband into deep trouble. Fearing his masculinity was being eclipsed and subdued by Xiao Wang's financial contribution, her husband tried to find fault with her, repeatedly pressuring her to quit her job.

She never yielded, though, saying: "I am willing to do this. Don't belittle us [women]. We can do an equally good job [as men]!"[54]

Despite the pride in herself and enjoyment of her capacity to work like a man, Xiao Wang accepted less pay than what men doing the same job got. "You know," she told me, "this is a man's job after all. It is normal that they pay me less."[55] Her persistent challenge to the gendered division of labor was neutralized by her internalized subordination to the devaluating and undervaluing logic of women at the core of capital's biopolitically energized reproduction by gender difference. As Ngai Pun puts it, "the biopower . . . is not only interested in molding a general [proletarian] body but also a particular sexed body, a feminine body to fit the factory discipline."[56] Indeed, Xiao Wang's experience encapsulates how the difference-making machinery regenerates antagonistic gender relationships to re-create competition from within, with the goal of better serving the concrete needs of capital while helping reduce its labor costs.

Moving into a Debilitating Future through the Difference-Making Machinery

To be sure, the classed and gendered axes of the difference-making machinery reinforce each other to cement rural migrants' contrived vulnerability and docility in support of neoliberal economies. As Liu's woeful experience discussed at the beginning of the book demonstrates, the story lines that many women workers shared with me include the common thread of sacrificial love. After finishing junior high school, when they were about fifteen, these women left their homes to find jobs in cities to help with the familial finances. Without much educational training, they had little choice but to squeeze into packed sweatshops that did not require much professional skill, but only obedience and compliance. Keeping only enough of their meager incomes for subsistence, they sent the bulk back home to sponsor their brothers' schooling to preserve family members' hope of improving their lives. Unlike their urban compatriots who enjoyed state-sponsored welfare, they had nobody but their families to fall back on. To absorb the consequences of the one-child policy and keep the family's patrilocal line intact for future care and support, many of these women left home to escape forced abortions and stringent punishment by the local government to give birth elsewhere, constituting a key source of the dislocated floating populations for compound exploitation by the state and capital to maximize their financial returns.

Rural Chinese women's fateful migrant routes that converge through the intersectional biopolitical setup reveal the difference-making mechanism that is key to neoliberal restructuring in China and globally. For instance, Hong Kong and Singapore, once major destinations for transnational reshuffling of labor-intensive industries, launched their plans of industrial upgrading that focused on the promotion of their citizens' biopolitical values after losing their competitive edge to other Asian countries with lower wages. The reform of higher education lies at the core of this upgrading, which aims to incorporate more local housewives into the labor market to transform the cities into hubs that broker the cross-border migration of capital with high-quality service in the sectors of management, finance, and health. Female immigrants from less developed nearby countries such as the Philippines and Indonesia are brought in to perform the domestic work shed by the local women.[57] Likewise, as China seeks to upgrade Shanghai into another hub city in the Asia-Pacific area, the state funnels many urban and local women into more lucrative sectors such as finance and information technology, while less profitable jobs (including domestic work and manufacturing) are transferred to their biopolitical others—that is, migrants and rural women from underdeveloped regions.[58]

Coordinated through the difference-making machinery, biopolitical promotion often accommodates biopolitical dispossession in line with politico-economic agendas. The fashioning of the worldly Singaporean hub city, as Aimee Bahng notes, "involves the figurative disavowal as well as the actual evacuation of undesirable populations in Singapore, both of which have occurred since the turn toward neoliberalism."[59] The aggressive recruitment of foreign academics by the Singaporean government accompanies glaring acts of dislocation and displacement as numerous people are forced out to make room for biotech campuses filled with industry professionals and international experts.[60] In China, while first-tier cities such as Beijing, aiming to perfect their gentrified skylines, try to purge the unregistered "low-end populations," other aspiring second-tier cities—including Tianjin, Xi'an, Wuhan, and Chengdu—compete with one another to attract more college graduates as major biopolitical investments in improving their futures.[61]

To buttress the functioning of the biopolitical managerial system, the difference-making machinery alters its dichotomized layers to change the affective boundary of the Loveland, refueling the promissory good-life dream to recast the migrants' futures for present manipulation by the state and capital. Pregnant migrant women who have no access to state-sponsored medical care and nursing must move back home for delivery and then return with their newborns to the city for work. When their children reach school age, the women have a problem: public education resources in the city are limited and costly for those without urban *hukou*, and schools for migrant children are poorly funded and frequently targeted for elimination and urban gentrification. Impelled by their family-centered love, many women quit their jobs and move back home to fulfill their maternal and filial responsibilities. The vacancies they leave are soon filled by love-motivated newcomers, and only very few lucky returnees can find jobs at home that allow them to meet their double obligations to family and the market. In Hai'an, many factories and family mills serve as makeshift after-school centers, where children can finish their homework while their mothers run the sewing machines to meet their piece quota of the day. As the ending of *The Last Train Home* attests, if a woman tries to avoid her family duties and focus on her market role by leaving her children with their grandparents, she not only risks losing the children's trust and love, but she also jeopardizes the family's children-anchored future by perpetuating the migration-death cycle.[62] In the West, beginning in the 1970s, manufacturing industries instituted strategies "of recruiting mostly young, unmarried women without children and firing them when they married, gave birth, or simply reached a certain age."[63] In contrast, in China the neoliberal matrix produces out of homepatriarchal love an inexhaustible "young, docile [female] labor force that can be worked hard with minimal health problems."[64]

Innumerable male migrants are also forced into enslaved labor by the delusory love. Homepatriarchal in essence and scope, this love impels married male workers to endure loneliness and estrangement from their families to realize the family dream in spite of the alienating and hostile urban milieu. It also condemns single male workers to unending travail in the hope of accruing their market-defined love capacities, which have become what determines not just their gender normativity but also their basic humanity. As a single worker older than forty told me, his poverty-induced celibacy made him a regular target of ostracization and attack by coworkers. The hapless man's incapacities of love reveal the frigid reality for many rural men. The intersection of *hukou*-imposed class inequalities and binaristic gender norms has starkly restricted their lovabilities and love-abilities, rendering marrying within the group or the less privileged group almost their only option. The severe gender imbalance exacerbated by rural female infanticides further reduces their chances, resulting in approximately thirty million men across rural China who might not be marriageable at all.[65] Many unfortunate bachelors are motivated to seek harder, longer, and overburdening work to improve their financialized terms of love so they will be able to find a bride from a poorer area of China or a less-developed country such as Vietnam or Cambodia.[66]

Married men unanimously project the hope of a good life onto their children, propelled to endure enervating and dehumanizing enslavement as well. Affected by the reproductive futuristic dream, many migrant families are willing to spend half to two-thirds of their annual income on their children's education, which they believe is probably the only means of upward mobility for the family. As a construction worker admitted, he could make around 50,000–60,000 yuan a year, and he spent 35,000 yuan on his two sons' schooling. The narrative of self-made success has been vastly discredited in the West after the 2008 financial crisis, but the meritocratic rhetoric of social mobility has found a new audience that, ironically, is a primary target for exploitation in the reshuffled neoliberal economic landscape. But unlike the neoliberal maxim's ultra-individualist quality in the West, in China it has developed a new texture with local characteristics. It is the well-being and prosperity of the family that incentivize poor migrants to undergo cruel exploitation and unabashed discrimination rather than pursuing personal interests only.

Again, at the heart of the male migrants' dream is their unswerving home-patriarchal love. Having built glamorous urban architectural complexes with their blood and sweat, they ask for nothing but a roof over their head in return to anchor their homely love. Yet their persistent endeavor to break down biopolitical shackles that undermine their existence rescripts their biophysical contours and textures in ways that leave marks which further keep them from their original goal. Because of their uncouth dress and unrefined gait and gestures, migrants are constantly ridiculed and scorned by their urban compatriots, asked to pay extra fees for taking a bus, or barred from shopping in department stores. The embodied stigma (etched so deeply into their flesh and bone), habituated demeanor, and collective memory of enormous daily toil appear almost impossible to conceal even by the most elaborate grooming and painstaking learning, placing them on the margin of the cityscape as the perpetual outcasts. As Tang puts it,

> *The uniform is gray*
> *and I want to hide it*
> *the gray of tearstains and sweat-stains*
> *glue odor, machine oil odor, the odor of grievances*
> *homesickness in the seams*
> *I want to hide all that too*

it's twenty years old, the time I've spent in the factory
I'll hide those twenty years
they're so big, they once bound me
like binding a soundless cicada
that's trembling all over
I'll hide the trembling
hide it, hide it all
take its gray color, and
all the diligent work and my mute self
the others who made me mute
and hide it all away in the deepest place
hide it where no one can find it
I'm afraid I'll drag it out
from deep in my memory
so it can make me suffer again
so it can wound me.[67]

Titled "Hide That Uniform Away," this poetic narrative details how the difference-making machinery fixes Tang's body in an outlandish position through the identification of his embodied existence and simultaneously preregisters his future suffering by infiltrating his sensory and sentient becoming-being. Like Tang, many rural migrants are subject to this kind of double haunting. Unlike his fellow workers, Lao Wang comes from Chaohu, a medium-size city in Anhui province, and was relatively new to the construction industry when I met him in Wuxi. After spending about one week on the site, I became acquainted with Lao Wang and other workers, but I could still feel the distance they tried to keep from me. One morning when I walked by his dorm, I found that Lao Wang had not gone to work and was lying on his bed, sick. I stopped to ask if he needed help. My offer disarmed him, and after a relaxed conversation, he started to tell me his story as an urbanite who had become a migrant worker. Lao Wang used to have a coveted job in a state-owned enterprise. But, like many other hapless urban workers, he was laid off from his position amid the rampant privatization of the public sector in the late 1990s. To make a living, he started a street vending business with his wife. But in 2010, when his older son started high school, he closed the business to join the army of construction workers and make more money to cover the increasing tuition. At first, he took only jobs close to his home so that he could take care of his family. In early 2012, Chaohu merged with Hefei, the capital city of Anhui, and thereafter most of the local construction projects were suspended, forcing him to leave home for other jobs. After re-locating to bigger cities like Wuxi, Lao Wang felt almost as if he had arrived in a different world, where life was especially difficult for woodworkers and bricklayers like him. "They despise us," he told me. "For those working in the factories, it is not as this bad." "Is it because of your job?" I asked. "Yes," he replied quickly, as if he had been waiting for this question. "They can tell that we are woodworkers and bricklayers at the first sight!"[68]

Two years of work in the field had proved long enough to resculpt Lao Wang's corporeality and put him on the other side of the state-imposed boundary between urbanites and rural migrants, making him join them in an obsolete and abhorred corner of the cityscape to conceal their unwel-come existence. "Dark! You are too dark! When you get off work and go to the street in clean clothes with coworkers," Lao Wang lamented, raising his voice, "they [urbanites] can immediately tell our [construction workers'] identity from the way we talk and behave." "No matter how nicely you are dressed?" I asked lightly. He shook his head and poured out his long-subdued anger: "No. It won't work at all. We are so dark, and they look at us very differently. When we want to buy clothes in the department store, the shop assistants just despise us, especially when the clothes are expensive. If we ask about the price, they usually ignore us. Or they tell us 'You migrant workers could never afford them, so why bother?'"[69] Whenever this happened, Lao Wang and his fellow workers would produce a pile of cash and throw it on the counter to provoke and relish the urban snobs' awe and speechlessness.

Undoubtedly, capital has significantly extended its means of reproduc-tion by intertwining the retroactive differentiation of laboring bodies with the projective registering of their futures. China's rapid financialization of the real estate market offers probably the best example to show how these integrative tactics work. From the eastern coast to the western hinterland, through the hands of migrant workers like Lao Wang, uninhabited ghost towns are springing up across China at a miraculous speed and scale. As Roderick Ferguson noted about Chicago's urbanization in the early twenti-eth century, these workers are marked through their classed, gendered, and sexualized identities and are subordinated as disposable groups that com-pete with one another to push their exploitable values to ever-higher levels for maximizing capital's gains.[70] At the same time, despite Xi Jinping's com-ment that "houses are built to be inhabited, not for speculation," China's real estate market has been let off the regulatory hook, with the average housing price galloping to break one record after another and moving far beyond what most people can afford.[71] Instead of meeting people's need for shelter, the love-drenched aspiration of a better life affectively attached to urban properties drives the insane market. Taking the homepatriarchal form, love sustains the migrants' self-defeating hard labor by rescripting their bodies in ways that debilitate them for the urban life. As we have seen in the special episodes of *If You Are the One* with migrant workers, their love prospects are cordoned off and their existence limited to prevent contamination of the urban futurity. Turning the city's future from "profoundly unknowable states [threatened by indecent migrant bodies] into probabilistic forecasts" by precluding these bodies from its becoming existence, the biopolitically modulated Loveland helps complete the translation that is key to capital's financialization, which in turn hinges upon undisturbed profit-making circulation anchored in what is expected to be an ever-improving cityscape.[72]

In brief, capital's retrospective and projective manipulation of laboring bodies is integrated by the difference-making machinery into a coordinated setup to subjugate the rural migrants as discrete competitors to reduce its labor costs and to create new urban imaginaries to project the never-to-be-fulfilled, property-anchored love aspiration that fuels its speculative circulation. The resultant bodily debilitation, psychophysical erosion, and other harms of the disenfranchised subjects are "not just an unfortunate by-product of the exploitative workings of capitalism . . . but required for and constitutive of the expansion of profit."[73] That said, I do not mean to treat the difference-making machinery simply as an apparatus that functions at the direction of the state and capital. In the next section of this chapter, I show how the difference-making machinery also informs and enables new patterns of disparities that lay the foundation for China's imperialist global outreach.

China's Differentiation-Buttressed Global Expansion

In July 2018, the premier Russian newspaper *Nezavisimaya Gazeta* published an opinion piece criticizing China's BRI. As the essay highlights, despite the exponentially growing loans provided by the Chinese government that have boosted infrastructure construction in Africa and Eurasia, the BRI fails to create jobs for the local populations because most of the projects are contracted behind closed doors to China's state-owned enterprises (SOEs), which often bring in their own workers rather than hiring local people.[74] Although not the first criticism of the BRI from the international media, the tirade that came from China's major geostrategic ally shows the mounting resistance to China's labor-export plan to support the widespread BRI projects.

Admittedly, in contrast to other industrialized countries—which can capitalize on their technological advantages, capital, and/or militant prowess for imperialist expansion—China has its primary competitive edge in its huge labor force, and it has expedited its labor exportation as its integration into the world economy increases.[75] After China's entry into the World Trade Organization in 2001, hundreds of thousands of Hai'an women go to Japan each year, filling jobs in apparel and textile factories that only Japanese women older than fifty who have financial difficulties would take. To be eligible for the required work permit, Chinese applicants have to be under thirty-five (according to a friend in Hai'an, under thirty before the 2011 Fukushima earthquake), as specified in the recruitment fliers that I saw there. Many young Chinese men also leave their homes to find jobs in Japan, but their jobs are mostly in agribusiness, leaving farm work at home to older family members. These Chinese migrants offset their biopolitical disadvantages of nationality, citizenship, and class with their advantage of age, giving them an equal footing to compete with Japanese nationals for the attention of capital that has redoubled its capacities of profit making in the transnational terrain of labor valuation and devaluation. Like the people recruited through so-called guest worker programs in North America and Europe (such as the Mexicans working temporarily in the United States through the Bracero program and Turkish people working in Germany through the Gastarbeiter program), the young able-bodied Chinese can work in Japan for no more than one year.[76] The earnings that they send back home are used by the Chinese state to fuel its own development, contributing to the local economy without adding to the public welfare burden.

Just as Southeast Asian diasporas have built close-knit ethnic networks facilitating labor migration to the United States and Europe, so Chinese migrants create place-of-origin-based linkages that connect China's rural workforce with capital's surging needs elsewhere, setting the stage for a lucrative industry in labor trafficking.[77] Lao Qiu, a construction worker from Sichuan province with decades of overseas experience, is a good example. After working for a high-ranking general in the Angolan army for eight years, he was promoted to a management position overseeing Chinese workers for his boss. Building upon this experience, Lao Qiu honed his language skills and developed a network as well as other social and cultural capital that have enabled him to bring eighteen relatives, friends, and acquaintances from his hometown to work in Angola. Having made "a good sum of money," Lao Qiu planned to further tap this business opportunity and start a labor agency specializing in jobs in Angola and nearby countries.[78] In China, the place-of-origin-based means of sharing information about jobs like this has turned into a major channel for transnational labor migration that has the enticing potential of profit making. In 2012 in Hai'an alone, the service of connecting local workers with overseas employers was offered by around twenty agencies, whose owners were all former transnational migrants who relied on local networks for clients. To help a person find a job in a foreign country, they charged a fee of 20,000–180,000 yuan depending on the destination— the more developed the destination country, the higher the cost.

Locally formulated origin-based differences create a new area in which the party-state can extend and fortify its sovereign power transnationally, and private networks of labor recruitment turn into a vital venue to facilitate its imperialist expansion. Domestically, the state usually exerts its totalizing power through stringent surveillance and deceptive propaganda. As Anita Chan notes, many migrants are enticed to isolated areas with the promise of a good job and then forced to work in conditions like slavery and risk being physically tortured if they attempt to escape.[79] In foreign contexts, the totalizing power of the state is wielded through SOEs—its corporate incarnations and extensions that are operated like independent kingdoms enjoying partial, if not full, sovereign power over their territories. As Lao Qiu told me, with the permission of the local government, many Chinese SOEs hire security guards to patrol their semisovereign realms. In the name of security, they confiscate the workers' passports, thus trapping them within their domains and turning them into "labor camps" that resemble concentration camps.[80] Attracted by the good-life promise projected onto the uncharted soil, many rural Chinese move across nation-state borders to revitalize their aspirational dream, only to find that its odds of materialization get even slimmer there. Their wages are commonly lower than offered, and sometimes even less than their earnings in China. Stuck in the alien environment and subdued by the sovereign power through punitive means such as pecuniary penalties, starvation, and physical abuse, they are once again entrapped in the service of the national capital's exported transnational reproduction.

The reductive view sees places of origin as merely natural ways to distribute populations, but sovereign power structures these geophysical localities as biopolitical inequalities. In an alien environment, places of origin are "most often invoked as grounds for affiliation and assistance by men who left their homes to work."[81] Geographical markings and physical features not only define the people but also shape the biopolitically administered bodies that inhabit them.[82] In China, regional differences constitute a particularly important parameter of difference making to classify and manage populations, shaping people's identities as Latinx, Polish, and Italian identities have become ethnic labels in the United States.[83] Through case studies of the Subei people working and living in Shanghai, Emily Honig shows how people's origins intersect with their social class to create an ethnicity-like identity. Class, she suggests, "was constituted through native place identities, and the construction of native place identities was part of a discourse about class. Furthermore, it was precisely because those identities were so inextricably linked to class that they assumed ethnic dimensions."[84] She demonstrates how since the late nineteenth century social class and places of origin have worked together to formulate and reformulate migrant laborers to meet varying economic needs in China.

Honig's deft unpacking of the origin-induced differences offers a critical lens to explore the embedded working of the difference-making machinery that disciplines and configures labor migration both within and beyond nation-states. Migrants from less developed areas, such as Anhui, Sichuan, and Guizhou, populate the construction fields of Hai'an, which has earned a national reputation for its reserve of local construction workers who would normally work in more developed regions such as Shanghai and Nanjing. Regional differences have also become an index of the typology of the construction industry, which can easily be mapped onto the geographic origin of the laborers: woodworking is usually done by workers from Anhui, for example, and scaffold building and bricklaying by those from Guizhou. In general, workers from affluent areas are concentrated in higher-paying fields that require more skills. In transnational settings, through the origin-based network of labor migration, Chinese workers often end up working for a Chinese boss who comes from the same area and find their exploitation no less devastating than it was at home. Many interviewees are thus more willing to work for foreigners who would treat them better, feeling that Chinese bosses are usually much harsher and shrewder because "they are so familiar with Chinese people, and they know how to manipulate us in a much worse way than foreigners."[85] In the late nineteenth and early twentieth centuries, North America attracted hundreds of thousands of migrants from Asia with the promise of settler family life. However, the migrants found that they were reduced to less valued subjects by the racialized, gendered, and sexualized disparities reformulated along their moving trails.[86] Similarly, in their cross-border pursuit of the love-drenched home dream, many Chinese rural migrants are subordinated into devalued working subjects by the barricades regenerated through the difference-making machinery.

The original differences, of course, also intersect with other vectors of the difference-making machinery to shape transnational labor migration and build connections for collective negotiation, as workers' unions are banned and brutally suppressed in China.[87] As many Chinese workers with foreign experiences told me, men from poor rural areas most likely end up working in the Middle East or Africa on one of the infrastructure construction projects whose numbers are spiraling with China's expansionist outreach. According to Lao Qiu, about 95 percent of Chinese working in Angola are men from rural areas, and they are concentrated in the construction industry. By contrast, it is more common for rural women to find jobs in developed countries such as Japan and members of the European Union in the sunset industries avoided by local people. China's gendered and classed pattern of transnational labor migration thus fits neatly into the global trend in which male workers "constitute a higher proportion of migrants to 'developing countries' whereas women comprise a majority of migrants to many 'developed' countries."[88] Luckily, in addition to allowing workers to connect with each other, origin-based connections also enable them to negotiate with management for better treatment and working conditions. As a worker in Wuxi put it, "it does not matter how skillful a worker is. The key is the number. The more people you have, the better price you can get."[89]

Conclusion

To sum up, as the sociohistorically embedded apparatus that conditions and primes our feeling and sensing, the Loveland creates concrete affective elements "with a distinct power to compose not only our near spheres, but also horizons of future promises."[90] In neoliberal China, along the gendered, classed, and sexualized vectors of the difference-making machinery, love becomes an end point in itself as a cluster of capacities attainable through private property ownership, polarized gender relationships, and upward mobility. Infinitely projected onto the future and other places, people's presumably accruing lovabilities and love-abilities regenerate "the felt reality of the nonexistent, loomingly present as the *affective fact* of the matter," preordaining the futures of yearning migrants to ensnare them as yoked subjects.[91] The pleasures of being inside this love-induced relationship, as this chapter demonstrates, "have become sustaining regardless of the content of [the] relationship."[92] Via the difference-making machinery, the fantasmatic texture of the Loveland concretizes and is aligned with the gendered, classed, and sexualized biopolitical calculus to advance the exploitation of disenfranchised migrants and maximize the benefits of the state and capital. The retroactive biopolitical calculation and the speculative projection of affective tendencies fuse through the dichotomizing operation of the difference-making machinery, which plays a nexus role and both anchors and advances China's marketization and integration into the global network of capital.

Working through the polarizing logic as the central tenor of neoliberal governance, the difference-making machinery also regenerates oppositional relationships, relentless rivalries, and interminable fractures that converge into emerging crises. Despite their accommodated functioning, the divergent operational modalities of the biopolitical system and the affective Loveland have prompted persistent contradictions and frictions that create prominent ruptures and fissures within the neoliberal apparatus. In chapter 4, I show how the difference-making machinery recharges anticommunist sentiments and re-creates China as the major threat to the capitalist world in ways that undermine the post–Cold War neoliberal global order and produce concrete change.

Lessons from the Polarizing Love

Mapping Contradictions for Social Change

This chapter shifts the focus from the neoliberal regime's daily operation to recurrent malfunctioning, to probe the regime's self-contradictory logic and identify the root cause of persistent capitalistic crisis. As discussed in chapter 3, the affective apparatus of love and the biopolitical calculus are coordinated through the difference-making machinery so the transnational neoliberal system can function, and they have generated legions of delusional migrants to energize China's marketization. Yet these two systems, as this chapter demonstrates, can never be fully fused because of their antithetical modus operandi, and in regenerating contradictory relationships to accommodate their divergent ways of working, the polarizing machinery opens the door to enduring crisis. Thus, the emerging contradictions can be viewed as traces that we need to follow to find a space where the subalterns can survive and to help lay a foundation for long-run transformation.

In this chapter, I trace how the capitalistic crisis takes root in the competing tendencies of deterritorialization and reterritorialization inherent to the process of capital reproduction. On the one hand, capital must constantly be released from its "spatio-temporal fixes" to take advantage of physically bounded material and labor resources and avoid overaccumulation, creating and extending intricate spatial networks of transactional activities that run independently of sovereign power.[1] On the other hand, the sovereign power that is institutionalized in the form of state apparatuses ensures that "market institutions and rules of contract (including those of labor) are legally guaranteed, and . . . frameworks of regulation are constructed to contain class conflicts and to arbitrate between the claims of different factions of capital," which redraws and consolidates boundaries to hamper capital's freewheeling movement.[2] As the central governing mechanism of the neoliberal system, the difference-making machinery changes its interconnected vectors and its shapes and textures to produce a balance between border-crossing capital and border-re-creating state apparatuses to prevent contradictions from imploding. However, its exigent techniques can only displace and postpone the self-regenerating capitalistic crisis—they cannot offer a master plan to eradicate its contradictory core. These polarizing operations engender even more contradictions, which advance the crisis on new fronts.

Building upon my ethnographic engagement with the migrant communities in Hai'an and Wuxi, my investigation identifies how contradictions proliferate on functional, structural, and categorical levels to untangle the genesis of the capitalistic crisis and its implication for concrete change. In contrast to the prevalent narrative that hails the laissez-faire market as the primary, if not the exclusive, instrument for managing human and societal relationships, I argue that the difference-making machinery conjoins pervasive biopower and totalizing sovereign power to exercise neoliberal governing praxes. As a result of decades-long polarizing neoliberal governance, different levels of the Chinese government have been restructured into a string of self-serving entrepreneurial subjects vying to expand their discretionary domains in search of more competitive edges and benefits. As a whole, the Chinese party-state has switched to a confrontational approach to solidify and expand its territories of forceful sovereign power and maximize its financial returns in the global market. Its aggressive stance has escalated tension with other sovereignties to an extent that has eroded the international trading system based on the World Trade Organization (wto) and sparked grave crises within the neoliberal order, such as the rampant nationalist backlash that has kindled economic disintegration on global levels.

Additionally, neoliberal systems work through the difference-making machinery to develop an array of contingent techniques for optimizing the market mechanism's ability to manage and extend our societal life. But instead of concerted initiatives neatly ordered by a centralized directive, these governing techniques are loosely clustered around the layered machinery as independent, heterogeneous, and often contradictory discourses, policies, legal practices, and institutional establishments. Thus, the multidirectional and multidimensional structure of the machinery gives subaltern groups possibilities of navigating its interconnected parameters and in doing so, of finding crevices and inconsistencies within the system that can be used to create spaces of survival and subversion. For instance, the liberalist discourse of human rights and freedom instrumental for neoliberal restructuring in Western democracies is frequently invoked by disenfranchised migrants to challenge the party-state's brutal exploitation. Many poor Chinese male workers use the hypermasculine ethos promulgated by the state to cultivate market subjectivities as a critical way to bring their plight to the attention of the public and Chinese Communist Party (CCP) leaders. Furthermore, through its repeated appeal to private property ownership for recharging its affective traction, homepatriarchal love shakes the patrilocal foundation of sexism in ways that have disrupted the gendered biopolitics designed to subjugate Chinese women—particularly rural ones—for the benefit of the state and global capital.

Finally, grounded in retroactive calculation and speculative manipulation, respectively, the regulatory biopolitical matrix and the affective Loveland use categorically different operational modalities that have resulted in marked cracks in the supply chain of labor central to China's developmental agenda. Many rural youths are motivated by the desire to be lovable and love-able and are leaving higher-paying construction and manufacturing jobs in droves for work in service industries that has a lower monetary return but more promissory features of the good life. This love-impelled departure enables the youths to break away from the foreshortened life path scripted to uphold capital's profit-seeking circulation. Their allegedly irrational decisions have contributed to what I call the relative labor shortage in China's manufacturing and housing industries, compelling the state-capital alliance to relax its grim grip over the subaltern groups momentarily and prompting a seismic shift in the global industrial network.

Sifting through these scattered sites of contradictions, my analysis identifies and spotlights the root cause of the capitalistic crisis to deepen our critical understanding of the transnational neoliberal system. Paying close attention to the ruptures opened up by the functioning (and malfunctioning) of the difference-making machinery, this investigation also provides a deeper view of neoliberal control, which is crucial for constructing a common ground to lead us to a more just world.

The Overpowering State-Market Players

In September 2018, after months of open- and closed-door meetings and debates, the rhetorical battles between the United States and China turned into a full-blown trade war, marking a historic breakdown of economic integration between the two largest economies in the world as well as the inception of the so-called new Cold War that could profoundly reshape the world.[3] The administration of President Donald J. Trump lambasted China as a "trade cheat" that had rigged the free market for its own benefits and sabotaged the global economy.[4] According to Trump, China had not only failed to "enact promised economic reforms [in its bid for WTO membership] and backtracked on others," but it also had taken state-sponsored measures to undercut the advantages of US corporations around the world.[5] In response, Trump positioned himself as a champion of economic globalization, vowing to force Beijing to make structural changes to restore free trade and allow US corporations, investors, and commodities more access to the Chinese market.[6] By blending a procapital globalist stance into his nationalist pledge to put US interests first, this strategy helped Trump consolidate his electoral base, providing him with more power to press his neoliberalizing agenda even further both at home and abroad.[7] In essence, this salvo epitomizes the simmering tension at the heart of the neoliberal system, between capital's innate quest for unobstructed movement for profits and state power that both supports and deters its profit-seeking circulation.

My personal encounter with the contradictory logic of capital reproduction can be traced back to mid-May 2012, when I first arrived in Hai'an. Unlike other peasants occupied with harvesting at the time, many local farmers had an extra list of chores on top of their routine schedule: collecting cocoons before the pupas inside hatched into moths. Thankfully, based on its auspicious climatic and geophysical conditions, Hai'an is known as China's hometown of cocoon silk for its highly developed sericulture. The locals thus lead a better life than farmers in many other parts of China who rely on crops as their sole source of income. During my stay in the home of a local friend, Xiao Li, I found that his parents were eager to share exciting changes in their lives with the guest from the United States. Breeding silkworms twice a year, they can make about 12,000 yuan (depending on the purchase price offered at the time by the local government), which covers nearly all their basic household expenses throughout the year. Since each cycle takes only a month, they have plenty of time for other jobs. As in many local families, Xiao Li's mother stays at home doing farm work, and his father, Lao Li, travels regularly to big cities for construction jobs to make extra money. As Lao Li proudly claimed, the newly implemented market emancipated people from austere state control and allowed them to optimize their talents and stamina for financial returns. As a result, the family now lives in a modestly furnished two-story brick house that contrasts sharply with their old home—a small thatched-roof cottage shown in a picture that hangs on their new wall.

The Lis' case is not unique in Hai'an, where rows upon rows of grandly decorated houses radiating pride and affluence impress many first-time visitors like me. From 2002 to 2012, the local gross domestic product (GDP) soared from 87.00 billion yuan to 480.14 billion yuan—more than half of the GDP of Xining, the capital of Qinghai province.[8] Hai'an's spectacular look speaks volumes about the market's transformative spell. As one of China's regions first opened to the global market, its success encapsulates the country's mind-blowing changes during its so-called golden age, the first decade after its WTO entry under the leadership of President Hu Jintao (2002–2012), and reaffirms the neoliberal saying that the rising tide lifts all boats.[9] According to the state, the double-digit growth rate magnified the GDP from 364.5 billion yuan in 1978 to 51,932.2 billion yuan in 2012, reducing the number of Chinese with incomes below the poverty line from 250 million in 1978 to 15 million in 2008.[10] As the size of the economy has quadrupled, "the country's roads, railways and skyscrapers [have become] the envy of the world, and the standard of life in the Chinese countryside has radically improved."[11]

However, the free running of the magical market is repeatedly interrupted by the overpowering state. One evening, the Li couple returned home very upset and speechless. After I calmed them down, they recounted their experience during the day. With a high yield of cocoons as a result of good weather, they had expected to make some extra money in that cycle, but to their dismay, the price offered by the government was so low that they had made even less than in the prior year. The price in Dongtai, a neighboring town, was much higher, though. When I asked why they had not taken the items for sale to Dongtai, the answer shocked me: the local government would not allow them to sell their produce to any private parties or outside Hai'an and had ordered the police to patrol highways and roads at the border day and night. Any disobedient farmers would face exorbitant fines and have their cocoons confiscated. What most infuriated the Lis, however, was the state-appointed vendor—who had stolen part of their produce, alleging that he "needs to deduct the weight of the soaked cocoons." The forced transaction, in Lao Li's words, violated the free market rule and "farmers' human rights." He asked for my assistance, since he felt that my US identity had "the power that local officials have to pay attention to."[12] It was the first time that I had ever heard any negative comment, let alone the one about the government, from Lao Li, a humble, genial, and happy man who was always smiling at others. Although having received little formal education, he was nonetheless versed in the Western discourse of freedom and personal liberty and invoked it to substantiate and corroborate his criticism adeptly. I fully understood his point. Throughout the previous week, his family had worked almost nonstop from 4:00 AM to 1:00 AM of the next morning every day, with no time for adequate sleeping and eating. But their hard-earned produce was arbitrarily expropriated by the state, whose representatives did not even show them basic respect. After countless protests in vain, many local farmers submitted to the abusive government, but when I—a US-trained academic— arrived, that seemed to rekindle their hope.

My experience in Wuxi further pinpointed how the state used its visible hand to maximize market benefits. Thanks to my friend Dan Li, who hosted my stay, I received several invitations for lunch or dinner from local businesspeople and state employees hoping to "make friends with the educated people from the United States."[13] To learn more about China's social changes, I met a few of these people with Dan. One day, after several rounds of greeting and toasting during a lunch with a group of housing developers and government employees, they got drunk and began to speak more freely. Ignoring their own complicit roles, they complained bitterly about the government's numerous violations of human rights for farmers and workers. They attributed all of these social abuses to corrupt CCP cadres, and they hoped that my research project could generate some repercussions to challenge unconstrained state power. To help with my fieldwork, they introduced me to Xiao Yuan, a labor contractor with over twenty years of experience in the housing industry. As a liaison between capital and labor, Xiao Yuan believed that there were many problematic outcomes that weakened the Chinese developmental engine. Having worked his way up from laying bricks and welding scaffolds, he had built a strong solidarity with workers and was committed to making their censored stories available to a wider audience. Xiao Yuan shared with me many instances of horrendous wrongdoing by the state—including multitiered nepotistic outsourcing of construction projects by government officials, bulldozing of civilians' properties by state-hired thugs, and police-enforced grabs of farmers' land—which reaffirmed the deep-seated imbrication of the state and capital. Yet like Lao Li, he understood these issues to be a matter of specific CCP leaders and believed that finding ways to curb these bad people's power, particularly with assistance from the West, would be sufficient to solve current problems.

Contrary to Lao Li's and Xiao Yuan's blaming individual maleficence, the antimarket dealings by the state are innate to the neoliberal machinery rather than epiphenomenal digressions from its regular agenda. To exercise neoliberal governmentality, various self-serving subjects need to be created to establish and sustain market competition as active participants. In the former Soviet Union, the market was built externally in the wake of an overhauled politico-economic structure. In China, however, the bureaucratic system was retained as the platform used to remake players from within and set the stage for market competition. The 1994 tax assignment reform allowed local governments to keep a certain portion of tax revenues to cover the expenses of running the public-sector organizations in their jurisdiction (such as governmental agencies, police departments, and public schools) and to fund their own developmental projects.[14] This fiscal decentralization turned local governments into entrepreneurial states that sought ways to optimize their revenues.[15] To boost and sustain competition, the central government introduced economic metrics as the primary criteria to evaluate the performance of local leaders—metrics that in practice are simplified to the GDP growth rate. Subsequently, the foremost item on the agenda for government officials shifted to the cultivation and maintenance of a favorable environment to improve the profiteering capacities of local businesses, and the sovereign power they held became a convenient instrument for achieving the goal with minimal cost.[16] Many businesses were directly developed from local, state-run collectivistic township and village enterprises (TVES) through privatization, which have retained tight connections to their former supervisors.[17] The police-enforced appropriation of cocoons in Hai'an is a prime example. All the major silk manufacturers were formerly local TVES that monopolized the access to raw materials such as cocoons that were appropriated by the state at a remarkably low price unavailable to their competitors.

On top of their logistic role, local governments also directly participate in market competition by restructuring extramarket relationships within their jurisdiction (such as kinship networks, familial and household arrangements, and farming systems) and creating new opportunities of profit making out of these relationships.[18] In China, as in other developing countries, land became the most important and convenient resource to use in inflating GDP numbers in the short term.[19] Local governments use their sovereign power to grab land from farmers, often by force, and monopolize its supplies and sales. Building upon close-knit relationships formed with developers, they can manipulate the market to maximize their financial returns. This circuit of appropriation of sovereign power for maximizing profits is not merely a matter of individual corruption as Xiao Yuan believed, but rather an integral part of neoliberal governance in contemporary China. Using their totalizing power to the fullest capacity, entrepreneurialized states push market competition to unbearable levels, dismantling the self-righteous neoliberal narrative of equalizing, freeing, and benefiting all and revealing the truly brutal nature of the laissez-faire economy. State-sponsored exploitation of this kind has precipitated resistance across China, including labor strikes, local electoral challenges, anticorruption protests, prodemocracy demonstrations, and mass suicides.[20]

These powerful state-market players' boundary remaking via sovereign power is crucial to facilitating capital's unstoppable transborder traffic. For instance, by rescaling their sovereign territories, several Southeast Asian countries—including Malaysia, Thailand, Indonesia, and Vietnam—have established special economic zones similar to the ones in China, where favorable tax policies, free use of land, and even partial sovereign power are provided to increase their competitiveness and attract foreign investors.[21] More recently, under escalating pressure from the West over its state-sponsored developmentalism and exodus of capital, the Chinese government announced a new plan to turn the island of Hainan into a new free trade zone, allowing transnational capital full entry into sectors that are protected elsewhere, such as medical care, telecommunication, and finance.[22] Using the apparel industry as an example, Janet Collins deftly shows how the neoliberal apparatus fuses physical mobility and immobility to increase capital's capability to pit its spatial flexibility against the geographic affinity of labor and raw materials for the profiteering use of borders and disparities. According to this logic, apparel corporations that originated in industrialized countries have been broadly redistributed around the globe by outsourcing different aspects of production to regions with low-cost labor and materials.[23] Liz Claiborne, a marketer of clothing headquartered in New York, controls the marketing and branding of its products while outsourcing other aspects of production such as designing, sewing, and packaging to a variety of countries, thus creating a global business empire built upon its creativity and promotion capacity.[24] With a portfolio of over twenty-six brand names, Liz Claiborne integrates capital's deterritorialized movability with reterritorialized manufacturing built upon established and newly remade borders of labor, materials, and facilities, which enables the company to re-create room for profits within the so-called low-value-added sunset industries.

Through the integrated deterritorializing and reterritorializing tactics of capital reproduction, the physically bounded market players in manufacturing attempt to navigate the shifting terrains of planetary profit making and sharing for survival and growth. Relying on its low-cost materials and workforce as well as its convenient location, Hai'an has built highly reputable export-processing apparel and textile industries that have provided plentiful job opportunities for locals and migrants, making key contributions to the local economy. After the 2008 crisis, the global market has been unpredictably volatile, and "foreign customers become much harder to deal with than before," as several business owners complained to me.[25] The unmatched movability of capital has turned the globe into a gigantic buyer's market, allowing multinational companies to pit vendors located across the world against one another to maximize monetary returns. The new business climate makes it costly and precarious for local manufacturers to keep a regular working team on hand, as market demands vary from day to day and even hour to hour. To minimize their cost and reduce their risk, many large and medium-size manufacturers outsource certain parts of their jobs to smaller factories, workshops, or family mills that have more flexibility to cope with capricious foreign clients without the financial burden stemming from maintaining large quantities of equipment, giant factory buildings, and other expensive facilities. These workshops and mills usually focus on one aspect of the production, such as cutting, sewing, or adding buttons. In Dagong, a small town in Hai'an County with fewer than a hundred thousand residents, there are over a thousand small businesses of this kind struggling to survive with their specialized workforces and ill-equipped sites. In this context, oppositional differences re-created through gendered, classed, and other interconnected lines become their major venues to reduce labor costs, setting up new boundaries to differentiate and devalue working subjects to squeeze the most surplus labor values needed for survival.

The advocacy of national corporate interests by sovereign power on international and transnational scales is not a new phenomenon.[26] However, with the advent of the 2008 crisis, it has escalated to an unsustainable level. To increase Walmart's market share in the global South, for example, the US government has provided considerable subsidies to help the company reduce costs and become more competitive.[27] Amid the recession following the financial meltdowns, radical right-wing politicians in Europe and the United States appropriated the nationalistic furor of many people to fortify their power. Turning the presumably pluralist identity politics and multiculturalism popularized by the left on their heads, far-right Western politicians reinforced the nationalist hysteria by redefining who to include and who to exclude in imagined nation-state communities and intensified their political control in ways that allowed them to further shrink the state's regulatory power over capital, to the detriment of the working majorities. For instance, the Trump administration significantly cut the corporate tax, claiming that doing so would bring jobs back to the United States.[28] Concurrently, by framing China as the imminent external threat, Trump developed a fervent group of followers to support his agenda. Ironically, the competitiveness and profiteering capacities of US corporations—high-tech or not—are predicated upon the re-creation of a precarious and willing labor force across the globe. In 2012, Foxconn, a major contractor for Apple, announced that it would replace workers with robots in certain jobs on the factory floor, as a labor shortage in China hampered the quality and production of Apple's flagship product Iphone 5, substantially dragging down the high-tech company's stock price.[29] The so-called labor shortage that plagues multinational corporations and the Chinese state, as I show below, stems from the inherent contradiction within the global neoliberal system that the difference-making machinery is able to defer but not to resolve.

Mapping Ruptures within and between Entrepreneurial States for Resistance

Indeed, the neoliberal regime is fraught with contradictions that subaltern Chinese can use to make concrete changes in their lives. Yet if the neoliberal system hinges upon the metamorphic abilities of the layered machinery for working, the result of its operation would be the re-creation of groups of heterogeneous identities and competing interests rather than a universal resistance force—the "multitude" that Michael Hardt believes is required for revolution.[30] The neoliberal apparatus has attempted to pit different groups against one another and make it hard to understand its multidirectional and multidimensional functioning and ever-shifting contour and metrics. This makes it difficult to see beyond the chaotic status quo and identify possible ways to achieve substantive change.[31] Therefore, it is crucial to develop a fine-grained account of the protean governing machinery to build solidarity for resistance.

As discussed above, the increasingly oppositional relationship between the United States and China has exposed remarkable cracks in the neoliberal system. In the recent exchanges of geopolitical blows by the two major state-market players to extend their sovereign power and improve their competitive edges, many Chinese workers have found ways to subvert the dominant narrative advocated by the party-state and fight for social recognition and equal treatment. In the eyes of many migrants I interviewed, as someone from the United States, I embodied the rivaling sovereign power and was seen as being able to help detect and expose the corrupt dealings by the state and help them realize their aspirational dream. In 2012, anti-US sentiment was already widespread in China, which made me worry that people might shun conversations about sensitive topics with me. To build rapport, Xiao Li introduced me to his family members and friends as a patriotic Chinese student returning from the United States who was curious about China's development. In spite of my concerns, many farmers and workers turned out to be very outspoken with me, sharing their opinions of the state and corrupt government officials with almost no reservation. However, they usually did not tell their most woeful stories until I had revealed my US identity. Seeing my corporeal body as a vehicle that could transport the compelling US sovereign power— and, as a corollary, sympathetic Western political forces—across geographic limits to discipline the ruthless Chinese authorities, many interviewees projected their life-improving hope on me, someone who actually had no bearing on it (as defined in the legal terms of citizenship). When they learned that my research project might be published when it was completed, they all urged me to do so in the United States because "it is no use publishing it in China."[32] Many of the migrants believed that even given my work's tenuous linkage to the United States, it had transformative potential that many of them thought could be actualized into palpable changes in their daily lives.

In my exchanges with migrant workers, the liberalist discourse of personal freedom that proves instrumental to the construction of the neoliberal regime (for example, think of the persistent legislative efforts to allow corporate entities the ability to have rights as humans do) at Western geopolitical junctures was frequently invoked by them as a tool to resist the neoliberal mandate in China. As the party-state bolsters its biopolitical control to further devalue them and advance China's economic restructuring and global expansion, they learn to deploy and embrace the liberalist notion of human rights as the rhetorical stakeholder of the Chinese state's sovereign rivals to hold it accountable for their designated debilitation and enervation. Citing the West as China's opposite, many interviewees, especially those with overseas working experience, found a way to pin down the state's brutal exploitation of their biopolitical values. Da Liu, a Hai'an native, told me that while working in the Middle East, he followed the news on Western TV and online news platforms almost every day to keep track of critical reports about the

CCP to better understand its abusive nature. After he returned home, short-wave international radio stations such as German Wave and the Voice of America became his major sources of information. He told me: "People can enjoy human rights and freedom in other places, but there are no human rights and freedom in China. There is no election. I want to select the leadership, but the government will not give me the opportunity. I want to elect a government that is really concerned about the people!" He also urged me not to move back to China.[33] Like him, many other workers harnessed the liberalist ideal of individual freedom to re-create a contingent space within the transnational market to challenge the state-capital alliance and demonstrate their desire for change.

It should be noted that the notion of personal freedom has long been co-opted by Western state-market players to maximize their own advantages. Before the Beijing Consensus came onto the critical radar recently, its prototype, the so-called Asian model, had received much censure for its heavy reliance on state support for development and its violation of human rights.[34] As Laura Hyun Yi Kang suggests, "by the 1990s Asian miracle and its variant of East Asian miracle became highly charged and contested designations in a debate about two contrasting models of development, an 'Asian model' distinguished by strategic state planning and intervention and a 'Washington Consensus' paradigm of a greatly reduced state that mainly facilitates the international flow of goods and capital."[35] Western politicians frequently lecture countries considered to be the major advocates of this model, such as Singapore and Malaysia, for their bad human rights records. However, these politicians are often driven by statist interests rather than real concerns about the citizens of these countries.[36] With China's growing involvement in the global market, it has emerged as the major human rights abuser. I want to be clear here: I have no intention of trying to justify the CCP's exploitative biopolitical control of the Chinese people. Instead, I use the sensationalized exchanges over human rights as a lens to look further into the intricate layers of the transnational neoliberal regime and to track the ruptures re-created in the belly of the beast that might benefit the precarious working majorities. However, in romanticizing Western sovereignties as monolithic rivals of the Chinese state rather than as assemblages containing multiplicities and conflicts and having only loose connections to China, many workers accept the fractionalizing techniques central to the playbook of the neoliberal machinery that perpetuates its global dominance. Viewing the political forces implicated in the transnational network of capital as oppositional rather than relational and complicit, they will likely be disappointed again, since these polarizing practices also project their aspirations elsewhere and elsewhen and thereby support the neoliberal apparatus.

Certainly, China's state-sponsored contradictory neoliberal governance has faced sharp criticisms from within as well. As Lao Wu, a migrant worker I met in Wuxi, put it, over three decades of neoliberal practices have turned China into "a capitalistic society in terms of administration, fiscal system, and social structure . . . but socialist in terms of political bureaucracy." He further stated that "Though it is called 'harmonious,' it is not harmonious at all. It is only a rhetorical device to mitigate social antagonism and tell the general people not to revolt. The income gap between the rich and the poor is over hundreds of times. Bosses are having banquets in luxurious hotels while migrant workers are eating pickled vegetables. How could it be a harmonious society?"[37]

Echoing the Maoist discourse, he posited that China's status quo is the result of "the restoration of capitalism." He compared the enormous income gap between the rich and the poor to "the slave-master relationship characterizing capitalist society" and argued that it is far worse than the exploitation of farmhands by landlords in old China. But unlike radical Maoists who call for another Cultural Revolution and political purges to restore the socialist tradition of the dictatorship of the proletariat, Lao Wu was wary of the statist form of socialism that focuses on collectivized living and sharing responsibilities, which cripples people's agency and creativity and ultimately hampers economic development. Acknowledging the liberalizing benefits of the market economy, he suggested that its polarizing effects need to be neutralized by systematic state regulation. Instead of turning back to the Maoist state monopoly, he contended that China should use the socialist legacy to redistribute the benefits generated by economic restructuring to help more working-class people, and the state should focus on the interests of the general public rather than those of capital.[38]

Lao Wu's sophisticated understanding of neoliberal governance is built upon his unique lived experience as an outside insider in China's state-run neoliberal machinery. He had served for several years in the Central Guard Bureau, the military unit responsible for the security of top CCP leaders, and he was very close to the heart of China's totalizing sovereign power, seeing clearly how it is imbricated with the pervasive disciplinary biopower to activate and actuate marketizing momentum. Yet unlike his veteran colleagues, who have benefited from their positions within the system by having coveted job opportunities, handsome pensions, and social networks they can continue to capitalize on for the rest of their life, Lao Wu fell victim to the system's unprincipled Machiavellian operation. Due to the rampant nepotism in political bureaucracies, he did not get a job promised to him by the state after he retired from the bureau, and he also lost the farm allotted to him at home while he had served in the military. At the time of our meeting, he had just turned fifty-eight and had been drifting between dozens of construction sites for almost three decades to eke out a meager living. His imperturbable tranquility, composure, welcoming demeanor, and sage comments revealed his many insights about the harsh realities under the neoliberal juggernaut. Our conversation lasted for nearly three hours, ending only when it was time for lights out in the workers' living area.

In contrast to Lao Wu, who believed in adjusting governing styles to make prudent and methodic changes possible, other workers I met in Wuxi and Hai'an were fighting for immediate transformation. Invoking the Maoist discourse of class struggle to make their case, these workers, albeit fewer than those embracing the liberalist notion of human rights and freedom, pose a more direct threat to the state. In the summer of 2018, a group of workers at Jasic Technology, a privately owned manufacturer of industrial welding equipment located in Shenzhen, sought to set up a workers' union to counter abuses by the management. After their request was rejected and the company fired them, the labor activists staged protests outside the company's gates for days. Thwarted by police intervention and detentions, the protests quickly resumed and spiraled into a general movement for social justice and equality. Various leftist groups and university students from across the country joined them, rallying around Marxist and Maoist doctrines.[39] At first, for fear of destabilizing its legitimacy, the state balked at crushing the protests in the way it had treated other dissident groups. Before long, it found a new reason to justify draconian suppression, asserting that the activists were Western-influenced liberals who had been organized by hostile foreign powers to disrupt China's social stability. Despite the activists' persistent repudiation of liberalism and the West, the state ordered police to storm their rented apartments in riot gear and to incarcerate a number of them in detention centers.[40] In sum, the uncritical embrace or rejection of Western sovereign powers and liberalist discourses without a holistic overview of how the neoliberal machinery functions through the polarizing operation could ultimately lead to defeat rather than salvation.

Reshuffling the Gender Dynamics for Feasible Changes

For other workers, the masculinist ideal promulgated by the state became their major conduit of resistance. Indexed by bodily virility and patriarchal control, hypermasculinity is important to China's neoliberal governmentality for a number of reasons: it is the disciplinary technique used to foster the market subjectivity of reasoning and rationality, the symbol that legitimizes China's shift from socialism to the market economy and its ascendancy in the global network of capital, and the unifying tool used to neutralize disparities and dissonances surrounding other identities for stabilizing upheavals.[41] But for many male workers, it provides a way to turn their work-hardened physique into an empowering device and make their voices heard in the settings designed to suppress them. Their exploitation-alloyed somatic beings become a marker of masculine prowess, enabling them to reclaim their ground in the hostile Loveland and dismantle the contrived incapacities of love that render them unfit for a promised family life. Although subaltern Chinese have generally been silenced in the media in the age of neoliberalism, rural migrants find the internet and social media particularly useful, putting these technologies to various creative uses.[42] As Wanning Sun notes, this allows them to "insert themselves into the symbolic order and make moral and political interventions in the field of public culture."[43] While I was conducting fieldwork in Hai'an and Wuxi in the summer of 2012, Xuri Yanggang, a migrant worker vocal duo, was at the zenith of its popularity. Two years before, Xu Wang and Gang Liu (the members of the duo) had uploaded a homemade video onto Youku (the Chinese version of YouTube) in which they sang the ballad "In the Spring" in a messy apartment. Written and first performed by the rock musician Feng Wang, the song did not cause much stir at its debut. But the genuine rendition by the workers gave it a new life. Using spring as a familiar metaphor of fleeting happiness and perpetual nostalgic longing, the song captures the mixed feelings that characterize countless rural migrants' unwavering search for a love-filled home:

> I still remember the spring of many years ago.
> At that time, I had not yet chopped off my long hair.
> I didn't have credit cards and didn't have her, either.
> I did not have a home with hot water running for twenty-four hours.
> Yet back then I was still happy,
> though I only had a broken wooden guitar with me.
> On the street, under the bridge, and in the wilderness, I sang a song that
>   no one cared about.[44]

In this song, the home is lost the moment their search begins. Calling upon audiences to remember their short-lived existence, the two workers turn the music into a celebration of themselves as unsung heroes refusing to be erased from the cityscape and banished to their fateful end. The chorus says: "If one day I am old with no one to rely on, please keep me in that time of happiness. If one day I quietly leave this world, please bury me in this spring." Their undying dream of home finds a timeless harbor in the cyclical spring.

If the lyrics faithfully portray the precarious realities and sentiments of the migrant life, the earnest and masculine performance of the migrant workers turned musicians has had fervent echoes. "Operating outside the strictures of 'mainstream' popular music," rock music has been a critical venue for subaltern Chinese to articulate their oppositional ideologies of individualism and antifeudalism.[45] Weaving a defiant spirit into their hypermasculine performance, the band unleashed an emotive storm online and created marked fissures within the seemingly impregnable state-capital alliance. In the unrefined video, the camera switches between Liu, who is seated and plays the guitar, and Wang, who stands with a cigarette in his hand, as they alternate singing. Following the rhythmic flow, the camera flashes lightly across their devoted countenances as they engage in making indulgent gestures and adopting provocative stances. When their voices are combined in the chorus, the camera stays on Wang's shirtless and sweating sinewy body to spotlight his tight abdominal, bulging pectoral, and etched triceps muscles. This alternation, when coupled with their band's name (meaning "masculine energies in the rising sun"), becomes the central register of the song's affective valences to disrupt the ominous lovescape set up to disqualify them for love—as shown in the discussion of *If You Are the One* in chapter 2. It turned out to be very effective. The video quickly went viral, and within three months it had garnered tens of millions of viewings and comments that often focus on the musicians' raw masculinity.[46] The repercussions then spilled from the virtual to the real world. After viewing the video, Qiang Zhou, a rising political star and then secretary of the CCP's Hunan Provincial Committee, commented that the performance demonstrated the working-class spirit and recommended that all CCP cadres should watch it and pay more attention to poor migrants, which created a rupture in the state-capital relationship.[47]

Significantly, in Xuri Yanggang's masculine rendition, many construction workers find their long-lost voices and retrieve their hope of love. On a stormy summer day that I spent in a dormitory for construction workers in Wuxi, a group of shirtless men sat on the floor, playing mah-jongg in the sparsely furnished room while the smells of perspiration and spicy stir-fries filled the air. Onlookers gathered around them, giving advice to the losing players and taking jealous jabs at the gleeful winners. Rain pounded outside the room, and the deafening thunder and suffocating dark clouds pushed those inside to retreat farther into the makeshift shelter. Gambling is the only means the workers have of relaxing in the dreary routines of life in the field and dormitories. Even small games such as this are impossible without bad weather, since the prevalent pay-by-the-piece model has turned them into working machines that run unceasingly to maximize monetary returns. During a break from their game, one man turned on his MP3 player, releasing the guttural and heart-rending voices of Xuri Yanggang. Mesmerized by the lugubrious tune and the singers' raw rendition of "In the Spring," several workers started to swing their bodies and sing along, and slowly the others got lost in the melancholic nostalgia saturating the music and the room. Then someone broke the silence, shouting: "Ah, they are so manly!" As a dislocated emigrant incentivized by my challenged masculinity to move out of China and pursue my dream of home on the other side of the Pacific, I, too, was moved by the musicians' hypermasculine shouting and singing.[48] I shared the nostalgic family love of the workers. Gradually, my vision blurred, taking me back to that windy morning in late spring when I parted from my beloved mother at the Shuangliu international airport in Chengdu City and strode in tears off on my no-return journey to a daunting new world.

In fact, the regulation of family life has been integral to China's managerial biopolitical system since 1949. As Yunxiang Yan notes, collectivizing initiatives in rural areas such as the People's Commune brought an end to most of the public functions of the family during the Maoist era, and with these functions centralized by the state, the family ceased to be the pivot of rural public life.[49] Unlike the consolidated state control in other societal sectors, Mao's policies, Yan argues, did not create a new familial pattern.[50] And despite these drastic changes, the family has continued to be grounded as a privatized space through the patrilocal tradition.[51] Between 1950 and 1976, this pattern was cemented and continued despite a paradoxical environment: "the often repressive egalitarianism of communism permitted more Chinese parents and children than ever before to realize core ideals of traditional Chinese familism, while at the same time the revolution eliminated many of the original incentives for wanting to realize those ideals."[52] In other words, notwithstanding the state's pronatalist policies, rural families were reluctant to have more children to accrue and pass on their private property since wealth was fundamentally demonized during Mao's reign.

Under the nascent socialist regime, family reform broadened and deepened through the restructured gender paradigm. In the 1950s and 1960s, in addition to a series of pronatalist stratagems informed by Friedrich Engels's articulation of gender egalitarianism, the state also sought to push all citizens into socialist construction and share the output equally regardless of their gender identity, thereby incorporating thousands of millions of women into public work.[53] However, as the family's restructuring left its private functions mostly intact, their mandatory relocation to their husband's kin group cut many women off from their social network and reduced them to a vulnerable position in the emerging contexts. This paradox added to women's responsibilities as both caring mothers and wives and men-like workers, farmers, and soldiers in Mao's era.

My women interviewees echoed this observation, dismissing the myth that Chinese women enjoyed more freedom and equality during the Maoist era as propaganda. As they recalled, when they got home bone-weary after having spent a whole day in the field, they had to finish all the housework before they could rest. Compared to women's marriage-induced relocation, matrilocal change of residency for men—*daochamen* (or "marrying into one's wife's family")—was rarely heard of in Maoist China. The unequal conjugal setup of residency survived the tempestuous construction of socialism and continues into China's reform era. Not surprisingly, matrilocal residency was unanimously disavowed by the male workers I interviewed, who stressed that they would never move into their wife's kin network: doing so in their eyes would be the ultimate blow to their masculine ego. Ostensibly, patrilocality not only serves to leverage men's unearned dividends in the conjugal system, but it also shores up their unchallengeable superiority in heteronormative gender relationships.

Liu's woefully registered love, discussed at the beginning of this book, illuminates how the conjugal rule of residency restricts one's love prospect. Mutual attraction initiated the dating relationship of Liu and her husband, but the seed of their antagonism was planted soon after the new husband moved in with the wife's family, and that antagonism exploded with the birth of their first son—who inherited the family name from Liu. "Every time when my husband hears other people calling his son by the last name," Liu told me (pausing at the painful memory), "the smile on his face would immediately freeze into an angry look. He feels that he has no face at all." As her husband saw it, losing the right to carry on his family line, the first and foremost patrilineal privilege, removed his imprint from the family altogether, forcing him to surrender his patriarchal power over family issues as important as finance and decision making and as minor as daily menus. During our conversation, he kept ranting that he really hated the fact that "nowadays more and more women are taking control of their familial finance."[54] Given his defeated heteropatriarchal ego, his wounded feelings have congealed into a misogynist stance that goads him to constantly intervene in his wife's personal life, which in turn has led to unending arguments, shoves, and brawls. As witnesses and victims of the polarized gender politics, Liu's two sons have grown into avid supporters of women's rights, as she proudly claimed. However, there are limits to their feminist identification, especially when it comes to their own dating relationships. Regarding residential issues, the feminist young men remain very stubborn and conservative. In fact, one of them had just broken up with his girlfriend over a dispute on this matter at the time of my interview.

Liu's sons grew up during China's neoliberal transition that was driven by the intersectional biopolitics of gender, class, and sexuality, which in turn produced profound changes in family life. In the late 1970s, to experiment with the market mechanism in rural areas, the state reinstalled the family as the basic unit for agricultural work and transactional activities. Following the patrilocal rule, this family-based marketizing initiative reproduced the socioeconomic foundation of gender inequality by propping up men's naturalized role for hefty physical labor and their default access to familial wealth. In contrast, "rural women married 'out' of their natal villages, and daughters could not easily substitute for a son either economically or in rituals of honor or mourning."[55] The state's unwillingness to sponsor welfare provisions in rural areas further confirmed men's preferential status in the patrilocal structure as major care providers for parents. China's neoliberalization, at least at its early stage, buttressed the patrilocal ground of the heteropatriarchal system to increase sexism against rural women in particular. It also condoned the widening gender disparities in general, a fractionalizing and fractioning technique that is pivotal for biopolitical devaluation by the difference-making machinery to facilitate marketization.

The patrilocal rule also had ramifications for the state's biopolitical plots to realign the population through socioeconomic transitions and reshaped gender relations across China. As Deborah Davis notes, the consequence of the one-child policy and having only a daughter was much harder to swallow for rural families than for urbanites, spawning rampant sonogram-guided selective abortions in rural areas that significantly changed gender ratios.[56] At the time of my fieldwork in 2012, roughly 122 boys were born for every 100 girls, while in environments with no meddling this ratio should be 105–106 to 100.[57] In 2020, there were approximately thirty-five million unmarriageable bachelors, mainly from rural regions.[58] As mentioned in chapter 3, male migrants seen as miserable outcasts in China's outrageously commercialized Loveland often endorse the market logic by paying to find a wife from less developed regions or countries. This helps pave the way for a massive transregional and transnational industry of mail-order brides at the expense of dislocated women struggling with untold emotional and psychic trauma.[59] Although some people argue that the severely skewed gender balance has shifted the dating game in women's favor, the competitive Loveland has reset the bar of men's love capacities so high that it has generated a huge group of well-educated urban women who are unable to find a suitor. These new gender dynamics, as chapter 5 shows, have created a group of fiercely independent women who refuse to be bounded by the Loveland and seek to project their love ideal beyond its far-reaching affective edges to subvert the neoliberal machinery from within.

As I discussed in previous chapters, out of the interconnected vectors of the difference-making machinery, love is crystalized in the homepatriarchal form as a vital register of the collective sensorium surrounding family life and intimacy. Compounded by shifting demographics, this normative form of love also sets the stage for a new familial pattern—namely, the neolocal residence.[60] Compelled by the quasi-mandatory ownership of private property, many men are pushed into the real estate market to seal a deal and achieve their dream of owning a home. At the same time, as the one-child-policy generation comes of marital age, the son-reliant filial support system has gradually lost its demographic basis. Taken together, the love-induced property frenzy and biopolitically restructured demographics produce a neolocal model that features couples' equal sharing of nursing responsibilities for the elderly. In Hai'an, this trend had been in place for a few years when I arrived there in 2012, and it has become more pronounced as increasing numbers of rural couples strive to emulate their urban peers by moving out of their parents' home to their own, ideally located in a town or bigger city. The neolocal trend not only restructures the residence pattern but also, and more importantly, shakes the patrilocal basis of women's biopolitical devaluation and thus leads to a more equitable gender environment.

The immensely commercialized Loveland also elevates women's market value to such an extent that new trends have emerged that subvert the state's restrictive gendered biopolitical control. Given the intense competition for men in the marriage market, it is not surprising to see that many parents now prefer to have not sons but daughters who would not add to their economic burdens. It is also intriguing to observe how people justified this calculative logic by framing the normalized family-centered love in essentialist gender terms: "women are naturally better caretakers [for the elderly] than men."[61] As Chinese women are incorporated into the neoliberal system en masse, many interviewees were motivated to increase their daughters' market values, which could eventually benefit the family—a marked departure from the earlier generation, when almost no rural families were interested in investing in their daughters' future. During my first visit in Hai'an, when the harvesting hustle was underway, *gaokao* (the national college entrance exam, often called the world's toughest exam) was also taking place.[62] While waiting anxiously for the results, some parents solicited suggestions from me about school choices to prepare for different possibilities. They told me that they were willing to send their daughters to private schools if the test results were not satisfactory. In the United States, private universities that charge higher tuition and fees are normally the top-rated schools that would increase students' marketable values. Private schools in China are much more affordable, but they are invariably worse than public ones in terms of educational quality and future employment prospects and thus are less likely to increase students' market values. Workers' commitment to their daughters' education could be perceived as a sign of the increasingly gender-neutral reproductive futurism that could benefit Chinese women writ large. Additionally, the shifting attitude toward abortion among Hai'an and Wuxi people offers another marker of the increased market values of girls and women. Although many people would still like to have a sonogram (which has been banned by the state) before their child's birth, that desire is now mostly driven by curiosity rather than an intention to abort a fetus based on its gender.

To be sure, China's social landscape of gender is not progressing teleologically into a bright future with greater biopolitical potential for women under the auspices of the newly minted neolocal model. Instead, it is rife with regressive digressions. Overt sexism remains entrenched among the older generations and in less developed regions, while the younger generations are more likely to be committed to gender equality. In a lighthearted and derisive tone, one of my interviewees tried to downplay her eventful reproductive experience, which could have changed her life trajectory utterly: "When my child was born, it was lying on its stomach. My mother-in-law turned it over and found it was a boy, and then she grinned from ear to ear."[63] Her coworker was not as lucky. Under the pressure from her mother-in-law, this woman's husband filed for divorce right after their daughter was born. Compared with coastal and eastern regions like Hai'an and Wuxi, unapologetic gender discrimination is still salient and pervasive in hinterland China. For instance, a female worker from Guizhou told me that in her hometown "if you have a son, others will respect you. If you don't, other people will look down upon you and think you don't have descendants of your own."[64]

Through its multidimensional running, the difference-making machinery produces an array of tactical governing practices to sponsor the neoliberal apparatus. Developed for contingent needs of the state and capital and loosely linked through the machinery rather than neatly aligned by a master plan, these practices can converge. However, more often than not, they contradict one another, generating frictional subversions from within. In the next section of this chapter, I focus on China's so-called labor shortage to explicate how the self-replicating crisis of the neoliberal apparatus is fueled by the antithesis between rationality and affect that are intermingled at the core of the apparatus's daily operation.

Dissecting the Labor Shortage to Locate the Crisis Root

China's so-called labor crisis can be traced back to 2008, when the country sometimes referred to as the world's factory had to send millions of rural migrants back home after many Western clients cancelled orders amid the financial crisis. Despite the market's eventual comeback, many workers decided to stay home rather than returning to their previous jobs, creating a labor shortage that severely affected the export-processing and construction industries across coastal regions and cities.[65] With the relocation of most production lines to China's interior—where local governments took aggressive measures to help with labor recruitment, including implementing controversial enforced internship programs for college students—the unfeasibility of sustaining a stabilized workforce in the face of volatile global markets was apparent.[66] During my first visit to Hai'an, the owners of many local apparel and textile factories were struggling to recruit, let alone retain, enough skilled workers and had to turn down some international clients to avoid penalties for failing to fulfill orders on time. When I revisited these factories in 2016, many of them had shut down and relocated to neighboring countries such as Vietnam, Bangladesh, and Pakistan. The factories that had managed to stay open had replaced many manual laborers with machines that need only periodic checking and cleaning by human hands.

In 2012, widespread anxieties over the labor crisis were rampant, as many observers thought that China would reach its Lewis turning point in 2013—a watershed point marking the end of the population dividend and decades-long spectacular development. Popularized by Arthur Lewis, winner of the Nobel Prize in economics, this concept posits that in the early stages of industrialization an economy grows fast, with the support of foreign technologies and capital as well as plentiful, cheap, and unskilled laborers from rural areas. After the extra value of agricultural labor has been depleted, wages start to rise, which reduces the profit margins of labor-intensive industries. When this occurs, development should focus on technology-intensive industries instead, to retain its momentum.[67] Invoking Lewis's concept, many scholars, media professionals, and public intellectuals joined the chorus of critics, asserting that China's labor pool would reach its apogee in 2013, a year deemed to be the turning point of the national economy.[68] The hypothesis was also endorsed by the National Informatics Center and Chinese Academy of Social Sciences, whose statistics suggested that the number of laborers would reach its peak of over one billion in 2013 and gradually decline thereafter.[69] There was extensive coverage of this public apprehension by foreign media, although many of these press accounts expected the shift to occur between 2020 and 2025.[70]

As anxieties continued to rise, a full-scale pronatalist turn appeared to be the only available option for the state to prime the biopolitical pump in the nation's favor, especially after the universal two-child policy put into effect in October 2015 failed to increase the birth rate.[71] In September 2018, the National Health Commission announced that its three family planning units had shut down, and a new department called the Division of Population Monitoring and Family Development would replace them and take responsibility for "establishing and perfecting a specialised system for supporting families," sending a signal that the government plans to scrap its long-standing birth control policies.[72] Unlike the reversion to the two-child policy, this restructuring of governmental agencies received little publicity. However, it was far more consequential because it foreshadowed a fundamental change that could allow Chinese families to have unlimited numbers of children for the first time in decades. This pronatalist backtracking was in response to mounting pressure from the aging population whose members were expected to widen the pension shortfall; the urge to generate more customers to boost the slackening market; and—most important—the shrinking labor pool that had once been considered inexhaustible. The state tried to minimize public attention to this shift to mitigate criticisms of its miscalculated biopolitical stratagems.

If we look further into China's labor crisis, it is not hard to see its hidden side. The population aged sixteen to sixty dropped slightly, from 921.98 million in 2012 to 919.54 million in 2013.[73] However, only around 35 percent of college graduates and 26 percent of those receiving graduate degrees had found a job by June 2013, the lowest shares since the data had been tracked by the state.[74] The employment rate for job seekers with college and graduate degrees has improved since, but the imbalance between the low-skilled labor supply and the high-end job demand has grown into a structural conflict that has become more acute in recent years.[75] Seen in this light, with the increasing oversupply of workforce in other sectors, China's labor crisis is relative and pertains only to the lower echelon of the job market, thus demanding a more in-depth critical analysis.

The relative labor crisis has generated minor but palpable changes for those at the lower end of the workforce, however. My interviewees told me that after 2007, many bosses started to make the best offers possible to attract and retain experienced workers, as opposed to the old days when rural migrants competed desperately with one another and would take any job offer. As a result, in Wuxi, a skilled construction worker could make over 8,000 yuan a month in 2012, an amount double that of a new college graduate. Likewise, pressured by the labor exodus, many employers offered different benefits to incentivize workers to take more and longer shifts to keep their machines fully running. For instance, although the labor law that stipulates overtime payment passed in 1994, employers did not comply with its provisions until 2012. With the support of businesses by local governments, complaints and protests by workers had remained futile, sometimes even incurring forceful suppression by the police. In contrast, apparel workers in Hai'an told me that they could make two yuan per hour in addition to their regular pay-by-piece wage after a ten-hour shift. Although still underpaid according to the law, many workers accepted the increase as better than nothing. Moreover, with their negotiating capacity growing along with the labor gap, construction workers could request a monthly paycheck. That was completely unimaginable ten years earlier, when they had to wait until the end of the year to get their wages and had to engage in extreme acts such as threatening suicide to have their bosses pay them in full. Entering the pension system is another new benefit for rural migrants. To retain skilled workers, many large factories have been compelled to sponsor their pension plan if they become formal employees, which requires them to sign a contract specifying a mandatory work schedule (at least eleven hours a day and twenty-eight days a month). In other words, capitalists continue to use mandatory benefits for Chinese citizens as a leverage to get workers' docility and loyalty—a situation that is nonetheless seen as an improvement by many precarious rural migrants.

The acknowledged improvements notwithstanding, the labor exodus persists among rural youth. In the factories and construction sites that I visited, it was very rare to see people younger than thirty. My observation was confirmed by the interviewees, who noted that very few young people were willing to take these jobs now, preferring others that provide them with more leisure time, albeit much less pay—including jobs such as supermarket or department store salesperson, accountant, receptionist, office clerk, or engine assembler. In Hai'an, a saleswoman working in a supermarket for eight hours a day promoting the purchases of consumer goods from international companies such as P&G and Unilever can earn around 2,000 yuan a month, about half the wage she would get working in an apparel factory for twelve hours a day. Those willing to take heavy-duty jobs such as construction and decoration can make even more. In spite of the neoliberal rhetoric of universal self-serving market subjectivity, members of the younger generation do not make their decisions solely to maximize their monetary gains. In the neoliberal environment, they are not willing to *chiku* (or "eat bitter") as previous generations were, as Lao Li suggested. Because of new digital technologies, they know much more and are far shrewder than their parents. He added, "it is difficult for people to discipline their children now."[76] Simple and straightforward as they are, his comments raise a basic but crucial question about the neoliberal regime: in an environment replete with free-flowing information deemed to be ideal for market subjects to fully act upon their reasoning capacities and optimize personal gains, what else directs their decisions and actions if the calculative drive to maximize their benefits is not the only determining factor?

In essence, rationality and affectivity are imbricated with each other in the day-to-day running of the market. Any decision made to maximize one's benefits needs to be judged by its future actualization to determine whether it is rational or not. The deferral of the realization of the expected results, as Brian Massumi posits, "is an expression of the paradox that neoliberalism's promise of satisfaction unnerves the rationality it extols, giving it the affective shakes that cannot be cured."[77] As the scope and intensity of transactional deeds escalate in the expansive market relationship, "the rational risk calculations of the subject of interest become more and more affectively overdetermined by the tension between fear of the future and hope for success, and between satisfaction and its uncertain deferral."[78] According to this account, although the standard quantitative measures of success are celebrated as the only criteria by neoliberal ideologues, "the surplus value of life that makes each pulse of life feel that it was worth living for itself, above and beyond the increasingly impressive achievement of just getting by," is often what makes a decision "rational."[79] In the Euro-American context, life's surplus value is measured as the desired good life defined by meritocratic class mobility, gendered bourgeois normativity, and heteronormative intimacy in the neoliberal condition.[80] In China, it has developed different layers and is projected as the private-property-pivoted heteronormative conjugal relationship that is blessed by meritocratically afforded social mobility.

As chapter 3 suggests, the difference-making machinery plays the integral role in fusing quantifiable profit making with qualitative differences that increase our life value to pave the ground of the market system. Sara Ahmed's "economic model of emotions" is crucial to expounding this relationship, showing us how the workings of capital and affect are both differentiated and linked through the common thread of circulation.[81] Drawing upon the Marxist critique of the logic of capital, Ahmed views affect as a different form of capital, which "does not reside positively in the sign or commodity, but is produced only as an effect of its circulation."[82] As she suggests, the circulation of capital is driven by the passion to "accumulate [benefits] (whether it be value, power, or meaning)" by absorbing more resources and adding surplus value in the process. In contrast, affect moves continuously to increase itself "as that which is accumulated over time [in its circulation]."[83] The accumulated affect is manifested as feelings attached to certain "objects, or indeed as objects with a life of their own, only by the concealment of how they are shaped by histories, including histories of production (labor and labor time), as well as circulation or exchange."[84] In practice, the biopolitical devaluation—infinitely reproduced through the difference-making machinery—creates the foundation for capital's profiteering reproduction by offering a renewable inventory of oppositional differences for capital's utilitarian re-creation of surplus labor value. In the meantime, the machinery regenerates various polarized items, relationships, discourses, and imaginations to rejuvenate and anchor people's affective tethering to the ever-expanding qualitative surplus value of life, and modulate their way of living. As the manifestation of the accumulated affective forces, these items, relationships, discourses, and imaginations are vital to conceal capital's exploitative circulation and sustain the exploited subjects' habituated mode of living.

By finding and maintaining a middle ground to balance the antithetical relationship between rationality and affectivity, the difference-making machinery postpones the innate crisis of the market economy rather than eradicating its contradictory root. In China, the affective attachment to the surplus life value takes shape as homepatriarchal love, building a hermeneutic horizon that Ahmed calls "orientations" to direct people's feeling, sensing, perceiving, and decision making.[85] Working toward an ensemble of items, relationships, discourses, and imaginations that anchors the affective attachment

rather than the rational end point to maximize one's benefits, homepatriarchal love orients many rural youths to jobs that might bring them fewer
monetary returns but bring them closer to realizing the good-life dream.
In this sense, homepatriarchal love is the key factor contributing to China's
emerging labor shortage that profoundly affects the country's manufacturing and housing industries, and it deepens the crisis of overaccumulation
of capital. Due to its aggressive plan to find overseas outlets for its products
and resolve the domestic crisis, China has intensified its search for more
international markets and resources in a drastic manner that further alienates it from the liberal democracies and identifies it as an emerging threat
to them. In response, Trump intensified the antagonistic policies to thwart
China's state-sponsored attempts to overtake the United States.[86] He also
doubled US funding for infrastructure projects around the world to counter
the expansion of the major adversary of the United States.[87] In addition to
this external threat, he spoke directly to the unfulfilled good-life dream of
the working poor in the United States victimized by the flights of capital
and job opportunities, and reframed other disenfranchised groups, such as
Mexicans and Muslims, as unlawful subjects who pose direct threats to the
surplus life value of the American people. Pledging to take radical measures
to purge them, Trump packaged himself as the one who could realize their
deferred dream by making America great again.[88] In so doing, he created a
sticky affective attachment that drew more good-life pursuers around him to
secure his electoral success in 2016.[89] Trump's affectively driven ascendancy
in the electoral ecosystem reshaped the US neoliberal system, which is now
presumably engineered by the calculated assimilation of oppositional differences and labor devaluation enacted through these differences.[90] More
right-wing politicians around the world have followed suit and stoked hate-
ful nationalist frenzies to push their neoliberal agendas, posing challenges to
the global neoliberal order that is about to rewrite our future.

Conclusion

As this chapter has shown, instead of a recent phase of capitalism that combines an unbridled laissez-faire economy, liberalist ideology, and bourgeois
state structure, the global neoliberal system is the compound result of divergent practices and discourses that serve capital's innate reproductive
need for profits. Confronted with incessant crises stemming from the contradictory deterritorializing and reterritorializing tendencies in capital reproduction, neoliberalism is not preordained to progress linearly into its final

version. Instead, it alters the interconnected parameters of the difference-making machinery to reproduce multiscalar governing practices that enable its metamorphosis for self-preservation and continuation. However, the regenerated oppositional differences also expand the scope and intensity of crises that call for more paradoxical enactments, laying the ground for devastating occurrences on broader and deeper scales.

In delineating the ways in which contradictions emanate out of the difference-making machinery on operational, structural, and categorical levels, this chapter unravels the neoliberal regime as a self-regenerating system that is open to challenges and disruptions. Tracing its endemic dysfunction, my analysis also identifies emerging possibilities for change from within the neoliberal system. Chapter 5 shifts the focus to another marginalized group generated by the malfunctioning machinery: well-educated professional urban Chinese women rendered excessive for homepatriarchal love.[91] That chapter also explores how the women mobilize their internet-induced "digital political literacy" to create a space of resistance and survival in the alienating affectsphere.[92] Using these women as an example, I show how marginalized groups are able to navigate the borderless Loveland to redefine love in their own terms for concrete change.

Love with an Unspeakable Name

The Exceptional *Danmei* World as the Escape Route

As 2018 drew to its end, a legal case sparked outcries across China over the state's "flagrant disregard for fundamental human rights."[1] On October 31, a writer known by her pseudonym, Tianyi, was sentenced to over ten years in prison for writing and circulating homoerotic fictions, precipitating a shock wave in the *danmei* community—a women-driven fandom culture that centers on fictional same-sex male relationships. Since its introduction from Japan in the 1990s, *danmei* (or "indulgence in beauty") has attracted countless followers identifying as *funü* (or "rotten women"). As both writers and readers, they have turned the community into a sacrosanct realm to twist male celebrities and fictive icons into discursive forms they can play with to imagine, foster, and regenerate queerness.[2] In this collectively built fairyland, fans are committed to the imaginary men they create to love each other, contributing to a paradox of "their (homosexual) love for us" versus "our (oftentimes heterosexual) love for them."[3] Building upon internet-based grassroots distribution networks, *danmei* has emerged "with a diverse range of local and global media and celerity cultures" and "developed into a transnational, all-inclusive, and female-dominated meta-fan culture" that "subverts heterosexual normativity, fosters alternative social and economic networks, and generates a convergence of cultural and media flows from both the East and the West."[4] Mobilizing the technological capabilities afforded by the internet and social media, many female fans, like the male migrant workers discussed in chapter 4, develop a collective identity for political socialization.[5] As *danmei*'s influence grows, the state has subjected it to tightening censorship and begun arresting fan-writers "on the charge of disseminating obscene articles."[6] Still, the severity of Tianyi's sentence exasperated many netizens. Citing a 2010 case in which a man was jailed for only eighteen months for imprisoning children, an internet user commented, "I don't understand the law, but there have been people who did things as inhuman as this and only get a year and a half."[7]

For many Chinese, Tianyi's case indicates not just the end of the short period of welcome changes within the heteronormative biopolitical system, but also the increasingly heavy-handed stance of the state against dissidents daring to challenge its heteropatriarchal reign.[8] On March 5, 2015, the Beijing police arrested five activists who had planned to wage a campaign to raise the awareness of sexual harassment on public transportation on International Women's Day. The month-long detention of the young feminists, as the respected feminist scholar-activist Zheng Wang pointed out, "has changed the landscape of Chinese feminism" and prompted a vast transnational mobilization in support that unfolded into "a fascinating example of a successful feminist response to authoritarianism" in China and around the world.[9] Outspoken activists pose a direct threat to the state by "challenging government edicts that marriage and families are the foundation of the country's political stability" and "celebrating single, queer, and often childfree women."[10] In contrast, *danmei* fans take a sideways strategic step in the direction of gender and sexuality diversification and avoid using clear signs of homosexual and transgender identities in everyday life to provoke confrontation.[11] Given that the Chinese state bases its legitimacy upon the patriarchal and masculinist rule now more than ever, it is not surprising that the authorities moved toward preemptive securitization to eliminate any subversive potentials before they can be actualized.

The major demographic group of *danmei*'s members—urban young heterosexual women with good educations and decent jobs—also constitutes the subgroup of Chinese women with the highest rate of singlehood, a group that has become the primary target of the state's pronatal initiative to address the emerging labor crisis discussed in chapter 4.[12] If thousands of millions of rural men are disenfranchised by their embodied debility and impoverishment and seen as outcasts in China's deeply commercialized Loveland, numerous well-educated urban women refuse to get on the state-directed romantic bandwagon and conform to the deleterious homepatriarchal form of love.[13] According to the neoliberal ethos, they ought to improve their market values through calculated personal optimization. Because the overinvestment in market activities makes it hard for them to perform their familial duties, such as getting married, they are also seen by the state as responsible for surging social instabilities. As the biopolitical setups and the affective Loveland are joined through the polarizing machinery to harness women's market productivities and household reproductivities to better serve China's economic liberalization, many *danmei* fans have received a good education as a benefit of the process and developed acute awareness of civil rights, the need for reciprocal care, and communitarian responsibilities, as well as a fervent yearning for self-determination and social recognition. Having grown up in the midst of the state-controlled neoliberal transition, they epitomize the generation indoctrinated in the mixture of the socialist legacy of equalities and justice and the trending Western ideal of individual freedom and liberty. Just like the feminist activists, they repudiate their gendered regenerative responsibilities and as a result are targeted by the state to shore up its developmental agenda, as the birth spike following the introduction of the two-child policy has not materialized as expected.[14] Yet in contrast to the activists' call for systemic changes, *danmei* fans rely on the fictional platform of male same-sex desire to articulate more diverse and flexible paradigms of gender and masculinity.[15] They have created pockets within the expansive lovescape to make cathartic ventriloquism and reformulate and circulate ideal love among themselves, which has attracted much attention from academics.[16]

This chapter examines how a group of female *danmei* fans find an escape route from the alien Loveland through collective efforts of creating an alternative space of love. It uses my ethnographic engagement with the community between 2009 and 2013, as well as a survey of popular online *danmei* works and a critical reading of one of the best known *danmei* novels, *Beijing Comrades: A Novel*, by Bei Tong.[17] My analysis details how the fan-writers create contingent space in which they have adventures, foster solidarities, and continue making dreams to recast the conditions for extending their love potentialities. For a large number of *funü*, the women-driven cyber community is their most important means of developing an intersubjective consciousness and empathic connectivity beyond the reach of the expansive Loveland.[18] As its name (borrowed from the Japanese *tanbi*) indicates, *danmei* is rooted in the Japanese *tanbi* aesthetical tradition of a female-focused artistic niche, which differs from the androcentric Western norm centered on the voyeuristic male gaze at women.[19] Enlightened by this tradition, Japanese women have carved out a unique, although marginalized, space to reconfigure the male body by building on female psychology and physiology. For example, Japanese manga are noted for often depicting "men as beautiful, powerful, and erotic."[20] In addition, the women-oriented genre (known as *shōjo manga* in Japanese and Boys' Love in English [hereafter, BL])—the origin of *danmei*—portrays gay men almost universally as "androgynous, tall, slim, elfin figures with big eyes, long hair, high cheekbones, and pointed chins."[21] BL views same-sex male relationships as a site of "a beautiful and pure form of romance" that is distinguished from adulterated heterosexual desire.[22] Exceptionalizing the homoromantic world as a site of true love, *danmei* fans provide "particularly valuable spaces for women—as well as others—to exercise agency, public communication, and creativity."[23] In fact, many of the *danmei* fans I interviewed identified themselves as feminist. In the words of one interviewee, all *funü* are "equalists" who advocate the unbiased treatment of all human beings.[24]

That said, I do not mean to uncritically celebrate *danmei* as liberatory and progressive or its fans' unflinching pursuit of queer love as another example of Chinese feminist and LGBTQ activists' rights-focused efforts to bring about inclusive changes. Fran Martin has identified a unique "backward" mode of the female homoerotic imaginary in contemporary Chinese culture—namely, depictions of women's mutual attraction as "a universal female" love during the evanescent period of adolescence and youth.[25] Setting this specific form of love in the past as an unfulfilled schoolgirl romance, the memorial mode of representation creates a safe zone within the dominant heteromarital system to articulate marginalized female same-sex desire in ways that simultaneously bolster and undermine the traditional discourse on homosexuality. Like Martin, I interpret *danmei* as a creative site where fans can manifest their ideal love, which carries an unspeakable name in the omnipresent homepatriarchal Loveland, and explore how it both shapes and is reshaped by the overlapping vectors of the difference-making neoliberal machinery.

Taking an alternative avenue to liberal pluralist analysis, this chapter follows what Petrus Liu calls a "queer Marxist approach" that rejects "inclusion as a mode of social redress," and it opts instead to unpack geopolitically and socioeconomically reproduced relations of power through situated investigations of varying configurations of queerness.[26] Seeing the fandom-driven cultural praxes of same-sex male desire as both tangled up in and exceeding the kaleidoscopic lovescape, I intend to unravel the social forces that subtend these creative expressions, chart the transformative potentials they inspire, and identify confrontations emerging from the dynamic exchanges between these forces and potential ends. My analysis is also informed by Howard Chiang's call for denaturalization to interrogate "Chineseness and queerness as cultural constructions that are more mutually generative than different, as open processes that are more historically co-produced than additive."[27] I take a historically sensitive approach to situating the intercultural queer formation in the fantasmatic terrains of love to unpack how China redefines its boundaries in the neoliberal world. I ask the following questions: How is love formed and formulated in *danmei*? How do we interpret these specific forms and formulations of love in the context of neoliberalization in China and transnationally? How can we account for the political values and social consequences of these forms and formulations for *danmei* communities in particular, and marginal groups in general? As the difference-making machinery keeps doubling its fractioning and factionalizing prowess through the parameters of gender, sexuality, class, and ethno-race to perpetuate the neoliberal apparatus, what can we learn from the queerness reproduced by self-described feminists to dissect the embedded functioning of the machinery? Centered on these questions, this chapter looks for ways to plumb the crevices within the boundless landscape of love that may lead to substantive changes in the neoliberal system in the long run.

The Gendered Love of [Homo]Sexual Desire

"I would rather see two beautiful boys fall in love with each other than with a girl!"[28] For most fans, this is the first and foremost reason why they were drawn to *danmei*.[29] Seeing other women as inevitable rivals, they would rather lose the battle of love to a man than to another woman. As one interviewee commented, "as far as I know, most *funü* are not lesbians. They are attracted by *danmei* because they like cute boys. They don't want to see a cute boy fall in love with an unattractive girl, so they would rather see two handsome men in love with each other."[30] To elaborate and substantiate their espousal of same-sex romance, some of the fans invoked the Platonic conception of love to extol it as fundamentally spiritual and transcendent. As another *funü* remarked, "I think *danmei* is about the pure love between beautiful boys. I can strongly feel that. Maybe I cannot say it is a fantasy, but I can say it is more like empathy. It is better for us to preserve this sacred and universal emotion between two men rather than seeing a handsome man with another woman."[31]

In contrast to the fans with this sublimated perception of queer love, other fans have garnered more sensual satisfaction from reading about and viewing beautiful men engaging with each other sexually. *Danmei*'s major attraction, in their eyes, lies in the pleasure accrued by the multiplied number of the objects subjected to their voyeuristic indulgence, allowing them to take an upper hand as the reader-producer to shape, maneuver, and direct men's bodies and libidinal energies in ways that best satisfy their own desire. With little to no sexual experience, they admitted that in their writing practice, they constantly had to use their imaginations to project their heterosexual fantasies onto the penetrated figure(s) to push the plotted man-man intimacy beyond the limits of their knowledge. "To enrich their understanding of homosexuality," some *funü* "would befriend gay male classmates and a few daring ones would even visit gay bars, but most could only resort to gay websites and gay porn circulated on the Internet."[32] Imaginatively using men's bodies and sex for their enjoyment, female fans reverse the power relationship in the androcentrism that Laura Mulvey has identified in the Western aesthetic tradition.[33] Yet the fans contradict their own equalist claim by upending the dichotomy but leaving its imbued power inequalities intact. Hence, they diverge from the feminist standpoint that, as Patricia Collins formidably sums up, embraces and fights for equalities for all marginalized groups.[34] Their feminist championship of queer love, in this regard, should be further scrutinized rather than taken at face value.

Regardless of its purified or hypersexualized manifestation, the fans' embrace of queer love is mediated by gender difference, as evinced in their overt aversion to lesbianism—for which almost all of my heterosexual interviewees expressed a clear distaste. The reinscribed gender line between gay men and lesbians belies the fans' claim that they espouse transcendent love, laying bare the fact that their celebration of queer love is more about gender than sexuality: for them, queer love is delivered as the straight female desire to explore the gay male sexuality and challenge the patriarchal gender norm. Homosexuality, as Yukari Fujimoto puts it, is thus a trope that serves to purify love, removing it from "the tarnished male-female framework of heterosexual love."[35] In my survey of popular online *danmei* texts, I found that underneath the divergent story lines of the homoerotic entanglements lies a marked commonality: the fan-writers romanticize the love between their gay characters while sparing them from real issues such as institutionalized discrimination, subtle unequal treatment, and blatant harassment that routinely plague the members of sexual minority groups.

Beijing Comrades is renowned for its "realistically rendered romance, its explicit sexual encounters, and the elaborate, heartbreaking power-plays between the characters."[36] The book is a prime example of the same-sex love utopia. The story starts when Chen Handong, an arrogant, wealthy business-man from an elite political family, hires Lan Yu, an innocent and hardworking college freshman who is struggling to pay his tuition, for a late-night assign-ment. Despite its playful and transactional start, the random encounter con-tinues with an "emotional roller-coaster ride of the on-off relationship" and develops into an enduring love affair for Lan Yu, "who falls for Handong, not because of, but in spite of, the latter's money."[37] In contrast, Handong leaves Lan Yu "again and again for different reasons: his intimacy issues after he and Lan Yu get too close, boredom with a monogamous relationship, social and family pressures to get married, the intervention of medical experts, a plot hatched by Handong's wife and mother to ruin Lan Yu's reputation, and Handong's bouts of internalized homophobia."[38]

Lan Yu's unwavering love persists against all the odds and culminates with a posthumous revelation after his death in a car accident: Handong learns that when he was jailed for "bribery, smuggling, [and the] illegal pooling of funds,"[39] "his family and his ex-wife Lin Ping declare[d] him a lost cause, but Lan Yu [came] to his rescue by paying an obscenely large sum of money to someone who can pull strings" to save him from imprisonment.[40] The story ends with Handong's sentimental memorialization of the love of his life at his new home in Canada three years later, which casts a long-lasting empathetic spell over its readers.

Posted first onto the now defunct website Chinese Men's and Boys' Par-adise in 1998, when the burgeoning *danmei* culture had just started to boom in China, *Beijing Comrades* "quickly gained cult fame in China's gay commu-nity."[41] It spawned divergent ideas about the identity of Bei Tong, "an untrace-able username-turned-pseudonym that doesn't reveal any gender identity."[42] For the English version published in 2016, Scott Myers, the translator, used three independent original texts, "the 1998 Chinese text published online, a cleaned-up 2002 adaptation published in Taiwan, and the rewritten edition Bei Tong attempted to publish in China shortly thereafter," cutting these nar-ratives and integrating them into the final version.[43] As Liu suggests in the af-terword, the "Internet made it possible for the author not only to publish the novel but also to incorporate netizens' feedback with complete anonymity, rendering the story an 'authorless' text"—like many *danmei* productions.[44] Heralding "Lan Yu as the embodiment of values and emotions found in our 'natural' state of being prior to, or at least untainted by, the complications of economics," Liu argues that the novel romanticizes "the conceptual dichot-omy between love and money."[45] It offers a compelling anticapitalist narra-tive that has been used for multiple feminist purposes to rewrite the scope of human sexuality in terms of what is speakable, thinkable, and doable in China.[46] Conversely, Ling Yang, a scholar who has studied and written extensively about *funü*, is doubtful about the story's place in *danmei* culture for three reasons: the relationship between Handong and Lan Yu is not monogamous; Handong maintains relationships with women, including having two heterosexual marriages; and the author could not be a woman because "there is a streak of male chauvinism . . . that will definitely upset hardcore *funü*, as many of them have a strong feminist consciousness."[47] But as Liu sees it, what matters the most is "not who the author was, or the politics of the text itself, but the place it holds in Chinese society," as well as the fact that the novel has "a candid description and a reflection on human sexuality makes it a feminist work."[48] Quoting Liu's comments, Hongwei Bao also defends the critical value of the text, positing that through the juxtaposition of the "noncommercial" and "pure" gay love with commercialized heterosexual love and marriage, it serves "as a critique to the commercialization of social relations and affective terrains in the postsocialist era."[49]

To me, what is missing in these debates is the fact that "pure" gay love is made possible only by a double salvation (a struggling rural student is saved from losing his educational opportunity, and an ill-fated businessman is saved from incarceration and the resulting suspension of his life), which is predicated on the lavish financial resources unavailable to most members of sexual minority groups. Indeed, in *danmei* fans' imaginary, all gay men are born with lots of money, and they are created to love and love only—a pointed appropriation that has invited a plethora of criticisms from many gay men. For them, *funü's* hallucination of the "pure" gay love is deliberatively manipulative, or at least too naive to be realistic.[50] In China's deeply commercialized landscape of love, the laudable style of love characterized by Lan Yu and Handong's relationship has become extremely scarce, if not utterly extinct. Noting the rampant market intrusion into human emotions and affect, Alain Badiou and Peter Bush insist that love should move "beyond seduction and, through the serious mediation of marriage, [become] a way to accede to the super-human in the original."[51] A conjugal relationship can lead our love-searching free will to its final destination. Many *danmei* fans would agree, and they attempt to create male same-sex relationships to demonstrate, in our ordinary world ruled by money, how to unshackle love from the heteromarital system ordered by the materialist doctrines and retain its ultimate truth. In the eyes of female fans, gay men's brave transgression of the gendered barricade is such a feat.

In stark contrast to the dreamland of love that they build together, many *funü* find their own intimate lives distressing and despairing. As chapter 3 shows, when China moved away from socialism and to neoliberalism, numerous women faced increasing pressure from their hefty financial burdens and thwarted class mobility and had to give up their love dream for a more realistic plan to find a financially reliable partner. *Danmei* fans are especially frustrated by the fact that marriage has degenerated into an apparatus to subjugate rather than free their souls for love, echoing Friedrich Engels's argument that bourgeois monogamous marriage creates private property on the backs of women to perpetuate the capitalistic system.[52] Contrary to Engels's conclusion that socialist proletarian marriage is truly freeing and egalitarian, the Maoist state strengthened the regulative biopolitical function of marriage and incorporated the conjugal system into its developmental plan, in which "socialist civilizing agendas have been formulated, contested, and in some cases transformed through the bodies and practices of local women."[53] As a vital part of the socialist construction, ethnic minority groups were forced to discontinue their use of alternative conjugal forms and practices and conform to proletarian doctrine. When the state adopted neoliberalism as its central governing rationale in the late 1970s, the marriage scripts shifted again correspondingly. In 2007, the party-state initiated a nationwide campaign about *shengnü* (or "leftover women") to disparage women who remained single after the age of twenty-seven. In an extremely condescending tone, in the name of love the propaganda attempts to coerce these women into marriage for "a happy family life" to build "the harmonious Chinese society."[54] Soon enough, the state-sanctioned rhetoric crept into vernacular discourses, and neighboring countries have also adopted it to sponsor their own coercive biopolitical agendas that target single women. In Singapore, the late senior leader Lee Kuan Yew once commented, "A PhD's fine, but what about love and babies?"[55] Lee's pressure on well-educated women to increase their fertility rates for reproducing high-quality population for economic development immediately provoked a massive backlash.[56] Disgruntled by the materialized and manipulative heterosexual conjugal relationship, many "leftover" *danmei* fans see same-sex romance as their last hope of carrying the torch of transcendent love.

The shifting gender norms underlying the love-disguised statist decree of marriage are in sync with China's neoliberal transition, in which the essentialist conceptions held at bay earlier have started to proliferate again.[57] Contradicting the state's pronounced commitment to gender egalitarianism that is still included in its official parlance, the new norm instead prescribes a contradictory role for women, as shown in the discussion of *If You Are the One* in chapter 2. While women are encouraged to pursue educational opportunities for individual optimization and strive for professional success like their male counterparts, their naturalized roles as caretaker and homemaker are also promoted to "compensate for state retreat, or for state failure to provide social infrastructure and support" to facilitate neoliberal restructuring.[58] In brief, if you are overeducated, preoccupied with your professional career, and not fulfilling the reproductive role nature establishes for you by joining the marriage system in time, you might lose your love capacities for good. During our conversations, several fans repeatedly asked me and themselves the same questions: "Why do I need protection and support from men? Why aren't there other social roles for us women?"[59] Yet anyone daring to challenge the gender disciplines enforced by sovereign power could face formidable castigation and even punitive consequences, as seen in the horrendous detention of the five feminist activists.

Championing men's same-sex love as the ideal, *danmei* fans seek to create an alternative space in which to tiptoe around the egregious patriarchal rule and expand a diversified gender spectrum that disrupts the phallocentric foundation of gender dimorphism through collective storytelling, which allows them to project themselves onto the receptive character of *shou* (or "bottom," meaning "reception") to explore multiple possibilities.[60] As for the insertive-receptive dyad, Judith Butler suggests that within the compulsory heterosexual system, the phallus or penis lays the symbolic foundation for the polarized complementary gender relationship.[61] While surveying the online *danmei* stories, I was delighted to see how the fans, building on terms borrowed from Japanese BL stories, found creative ways to unsettle the unequal gender-sexual relationship by expanding the social positions and values for both the penetrators and the penetrated. For example, the roles of *shou* (or "the penetrated") include *aojiao* (or "haughty") *shou*, *nüwang* (or "queenly") *shou*, and *qiang* (or "dominant") *shou*. Likewise, *gong* (or "the penetrator") is not always the domineering party in the relationship but takes varying roles such as *jianqi* (or "athletic") *gong*, *zhongquan* (or "dog-like loyal") *gong*, or *yinü* (or "feminine") *gong*.

Even so, among the kaleidoscopic *gong-shou* genres promoted by the fan-writers, the paradigm of the domineering penetrator and the docile penetrated remains the most popular, anchoring many *funü*'s self-fantasization of their intimate relationship. In this genre, the power differentials involved in the sexual positions are ephemeral, resonating only in affective and sexual exchanges and not translating into systemic disparities as is the case in the heteronormative gender relationship. Despite the *shou*'s role being represented by those who are caressed in private moments of intimate and sexual exchanges, many fan-writers included their educational background, professional qualities, and access to resources in their public profiles, and according to that information, they enjoy equal social status with their insertive partners. Lan Yu clearly embodies such a position. Introduced as the one who is dependent on Handong, both sexually and financially, Lan Yu becomes an all-around equal to his lover-patron, with an equivalent educational background (one is an architecture major with a degree from a leading university; the other is a Chinese literature major with a degree from a rival school), a successful career (a self-made architectural professional versus a shrewd businessman, who was born into a rich family), and above all, a comparable self-confidence despite their disparate rural and urban backgrounds. Using the monetary gifts from Handong to save him from being incarcerated and turn his patronage into his salvation, Lan Yu sweeps away the last traces of inferiority attached to his family heritage that initiated their commercialized encounter in the first place. Reverberating with Hoang Tan Nguyen's call for a reconception of bottomhood to disrupt the sexualizing economy and hierarchy, these narratives embrace strategies that are critical for destabilizing gender and sexual norms, for example, using arousal, receptiveness, and recognition instead of domination and mastery.[62]

Despite the flexible social roles of the penetrator and the penetrated and the relaxed power dynamics between them, the physiological and corporeal standard for who counts as a legitimate *danmei* gay remains consistent: he must have soft and delicate facial features, a lanky and elegant figure, and a well-groomed and stylized dress code. The *funü* frequently apply their queer sensibilities, cultivated by *danmei*, to gauge the sexual orientation of men around them. I asked my interviewees whether they did this to every man and got an unequivocal "no." Instead, they provided with me a short and rigid list of qualities: only beautiful, androgynous, and stylish young men—those they call *huameinan* (or "floral men")—could attract their attention. *My Hero*, a reality show on Shanghai Dragon TV, triggered a nationwide debate over the two prevalent versions of manhood that were in stark contrast in 2006: "the soft and fragile men (floral men) versus the muscular and rough men (macho men)."[63] Kam Louie suggests that throughout premodern Chinese history, the former had always been the object of desire for women, "unlike the Anglo-American image that until recently has been singularly dominated by the macho man."[64] Ostensibly, *danmei* men are the reincarnation of this soft masculine code in modern neoliberal China.

To excavate the present meaning of androgynous *danmei* men without naturalizing certain forms of queerness as distinctively Chinese and some

Chinese cultural aspects as "distinctively queer yet not in any Western sense of the word," we need to broaden our vision to see how gender and sexuality intersect to propel the biopolitical engine for the development of human societies.[65] The category of heterosexuality, as Michel Foucault suggests, is a modern construction crucial to capitalistic systems. In Europe in the eighteenth and nineteenth centuries, burgeoning market economies garnered no small amount of momentum from the sexualized disciplines of individual bodies and biopolitical managements of populations. Through discursive formations, scientific studies, and medical practices—and with the support of juridical protocols, legal practices, and the social institutions of state, family, and school—homosexuality was created and promulgated as a categorical antithesis to concretize an otherwise nebulous notion of heterosexuality. Meanwhile, via crisscrossing maneuvers of biopower and biopolitics, other supposedly abnormal sexual categories, such as child sex, adolescent masturbation, and extramarital relationships, were generated along with the demonized homosexuality to delimit the human sexual spectrum in ways that valorized the heterosexual conjugal relationship as the normative way of being. Normalized selfhood channels people's heterogeneous libidinal energies into reproductive activities and consolidates the nuclear family as the way to inculcate subjects that best suit capital's needs.[66] Building upon Foucault's observation, Butler argues that imperative heterosexuality lays the Western foundation of the gender dichotomy that positions masculinity and femininity as relentlessly oppositional to each other.[67] For instance, as massive production became the dominant mode of the market economy in the wake of the industrial revolution in the United States, the term *heterosexual* appeared in an article that Dr. James G. Kiernan published in 1892.[68] Despite their naturalized attraction to people of the other gender, heterosexuals were seen as comparable to homosexuals for their association with "nonprocreative perversion."[69] This not only affirmed the superiority of different-sex eroticism, but also reinforced the pathologizing of homosexuals as a degenerative group troubled by gender inversion.

Unlike the pathologized Other in the West, same-sex desire and intimacy characterize a gender system that embraces rather than demonizes the soft and feminine version of masculinity in premodern East Asia.[70] For instance, in precapitalist Japan, "monasterial male-male homosexuality was acceptable, if not normative—something that horrified Christian missionaries" in their evangelical pursuits.[71] In a relatively amiable social climate, the rule of Bushido highlights the loyalty among handsome young samurais that was translated into a celebrated form of same-sex love. This legacy also informed the prevalent images of effeminate and beautiful gay men that characterize Japanese BL manga. As Japan entered the Meiji era and initiated its modernizing project in the 1860s, the binaristic Western gender norm was introduced to legitimize the sociopolitical upheavals and facilitate change.[72] In China, since the full-scale market economy has developed only with the recent transition to neoliberalism, the pathologization of homosexuality and the polarization of gender were absent for a long time.[73] This left ample room for creative expressions of same-sex desire and intimacy as well as transgender and androgynous performances in literary works, folklore, and other cultural forms.[74] In everyday life, the eroticization of effeminate men was also common among wealthy elite men and emperors during premodern times.[75]

With all that said, the construction of soft beautiful men by *danmei* fans should not simply be reduced to a women-led revamping of China's legacy of effeminate queer masculinity. As a response to the ever-tightening patriarchal and masculinist governance in neoliberal China, *funü*'s collective working with queerness needs to be parsed with theoretical tools to excavate its embedded meanings and nuanced political significance. As I explicate in the next section, by rewriting the bodily economy of masculinity and power, the fans seek not only to redefine what is lovable and who is love-able but also dislodge the reified foundation of identities and create a queering space to remake differences as sites of voluntary affiliation rather than biopolitical parameters for polarization by the neoliberal machinery.

Reworking the Bodily Economy of Love for Equalities

Almost all the *funü* fans I interviewed expressed a preference for macho men as their ideal partner, contradicting the unanimously embraced *danmei* imageries of floral men. If that is so, I asked, "why are the images of men created by you identically fragile, delicate, and effeminate?" In response to this question, one interviewee suggested that the popularization of such kinds of masculinity could fundamentally shift the power dynamics between men and women. As she contended, "those guys think they are very attractive, but I think now we girls can be lovelier!"[76] In other words, in redefining the aesthetic of the male body by modeling it on female physiology, *funü* are able to unsettle men's corporeal access to the privileged symbolic position so that women can seize hold of it and become "lovelier." Oblivious to the power disparities involved in gender polarity, this unconcealed self-serving rhetoric caught me off guard and spurred me to delve into *funü*'s self-claimed and self-righteous feminist stance.

Although biological determinism lost its appeal in academia long ago, particularly in the humanities and social sciences, masculinity, as Jack Halberstam argues, is still treated as composed of a priori characteristics that reside innately with or in men's bodies by many scholars, including some feminist scholars.[77] This approach centralizes the critical barrage on the body's cultural and discursive facade but leaves its organic and fleshy qualities off the radar. The reductive paradigm, seen in this light, is impervious to the surging academic interests in the body, and the resulting oblivion sets the stage for subtle but concrete political consequences with far-reaching effects beyond scholarly endeavors.[78] Assuming that men's corporeality gives them a defaulted access to masculinity, scholarly work following this avenue accepts bodily organisms as the primary, if not exclusive, index of the unequal gendered social structure and biopolitical parameters, further naturalizing women's subordination and devaluation and benefiting the state and capital, as shown in chapter 3. The correlation between body and gender thus needs to be complicated rather than taken for granted. Butler argues that as both a corporeal style and an act, gender is intentional and performative. The internalized heterosexual construction of gender is signified and stabilized through its repeated and sustained externalization and performance on our bodies. Specifically, the gender and anatomical sex of the performer and the gender of the performance constitute the three body-anchored dimensions at play in the signification and operation of the gender system, which is "falsely naturalized as a unity through the regulatory fiction of heterosexual coherence."[79] Our daily lives led through and by our organic bodies as the performing interface are evaluated through the binarized social values invested in gender (including the polarities of aggressive and docile, self-contained and emotional, and strong and feeble) for the verification or falsification of their attunement with the other two corporeal dimensions of gender—namely, anatomical sex and socially defined gender role. Only unification of these three dimensions would make the performer a socially recognized subject, which is a process of becoming ordered by and simultaneously reproducing the heterosexual gender paradigm.[80] Butler sees that by mocking how gender functions in such a tenuous way, drag reveals the imitative nature and contingency of the gender system.[81] She thus calls for a strategy of parody to subvert the heteronormative gender system: "if the anatomy of the performer is already distinct from the gender of the performer, and both of those are distinct from the gender of the performance, then the performance suggests a dissonance not only between sex and performance, but sex and gender, and gender and performance."[82]

Predating Butler's proposition, performances of impersonating the opposite sex have a history in Chinese culture that dates back to the thirteenth century and include various artistic forms of cross-dressing.[83] One example is *The Ballad of Mulan*, a world-famous story about "a young Chinese heroine who disguises herself as a male warrior and joins the army and goes off to war in her old father's stead."[84] Beginning as an anonymous and undated work, this story was first written down in the *Musical Records of Old and New* between 500 and 600. As "one of the earliest texts that challenge the oppressive patriarchal constraints on Chinese women," it has been translated into multiple artistic forms with far-reaching transnational appeals.[85] *The Butterfly Lovers*, a love story about another legendary female cross-dresser, Zhu Yingtai, is often regarded as "China's *Romeo and Juliet*" and has been turned into an orchestral adaptation (*Butterfly Lovers' Violin Concerto*) that has become a common feature in concert halls worldwide.[86] As a plot device, cross-dressing generates "unruly delight that breaks free from the discipline of formally well-behaved narrativity and staid, coherent points of view," and it has also been adopted in a wide range of musical, theatrical, literary, and cinematic productions that have informed award-winning films such as *Farewell My Concubine* and the performances of iconic figures such as Mei Lanfang and Yam Kim-Fei.[87]

As a charged site of gender politics and resistance to cultural hegemony embedded in Chinese history, gender transgression carries varying meanings and implications different from those of contemporary drag performances in the West. For instance, although female impersonators in Beijing opera—the male *dan* (or "female roles") of subversive gender and sexual ambiguities— have become its defining feature (and well known to Western audiences), both men and women were involved with cross-dressing performance when the opera originated in the Yuan dynasty (1271–1368).[88] A prime effect of the cultural operations of Chinese opera, as Siu-Leung Li suggests, is to provide an unsettling inquiry into the question posed by Foucault, "Do we truly need a true sex?"[89] To neutralize these subversive potentials, the Mongolian authorities stringently controlled performers' on- and offstage conduct, which had disparate impacts on male and female performers when compounded by the gender hierarchy and reinforced "the social segregation between the classes and sexes, further degrading the [female] Yuan performers' social status."[90] In the late eighteenth century, in the midst of intensified anxiety over the untamed bodies of transgressive women performers, the Manchurian rulers of the Qing dynasty banned women from publicly performing in Beijing opera.[91] Against this backdrop, during the anti-imperialist May Fourth Movement in the 1920s, young intellectual leaders called for a reform of drama, inviting "women to perform on the modern stage" and challenging the prejudice against actresses and allowing women to "speak in their own voices and strike their own poses."[92] Yet the reform of having all female roles performed exclusively by women resonated with the newly introduced Western medical notion of sexual difference at the time and, ironically, reinforced the essentialist understanding of gender despite its allegedly feminist call.[93] In the meantime, the rise of Yue opera (a women's opera) in the Shanghai area in the early twentieth century, as Jin Jiang argues, makes "the 'feminine' concerns of the everyday equally as important as the 'masculine' public discourse of nationalism and modernity."[94]

Given the complicated background of gender transgression and cross-dressing in Chinese history, *funü*'s alternative praxes over men's bodies should not be embraced uncritically but vetted closely to excavate the embedded meanings. Regardless of their effeminate stylish grooming, dressing styles, comportment, and bodily attributes, floral men are imbued by fan-writers with a wide range of qualities and characteristics that do not conform to the polarized sociocultural constructions of heteronormativity. As one interviewee told me, the most popular story line features effeminate gay men with such supposedly masculine qualities as independence, ambition, and confidence. In my survey of *danmei* websites, I also noted that this story line has considerably more hits and positive responses and nearly dominates the online communities. In these stories, the beautiful men's feminized embodiment constantly runs counter to their male anatomical sex and their masculinized dispositions and personalities, reproducing the discordances to unsettle the socially prescribed unification of the three corporeal dimensions as the only recognized way of living and being for humans. These persistent praxes have created ruptures in the rigid heteronormative gender system, as seen in China's increasingly LGBTQ-friendly social climate, particularly among the younger generations, and evidenced by the widely circulated imageries of floral men that eclipse the state-backed hypermasculine symbols, including President Xi himself.[95]

Furthermore, the women-centered parodic rearticulation of the male body and its symbolic relationship to masculinity can be seen as a queering endeavor to disrupt identity-grounded difference making and power structuring. Unlike the person mentioned above who advocated a "lovelier" position for girls, other *funü* I interviewed did not intend to re-create a whole new fictive world in which women can take control of the reins from their male peers by removing their sole corporeal access to masculinity and associated privileges. Instead of making women "lovelier" and thus giving them more unearned privileges than men, these *funü* would rather see a democratic environment open to all. The images of floral men not only appear less threatening than those of muscular and aggressive macho men, but they also index an emerging territory of flexibility, mutation, and contingencies. As one *funü* put it, "when redefining the male body, you are also redefining the female body. I really like the gray area [between men's and women's bodies], and it blurs the bodily basis of masculinity and power so people can have equal access to the things they want."[96] In Eve Sedgwick's words, this "gray area" is the quintessential imprint of "queer," as it involves "the open mess of possibilities, gaps, overlaps, dissonances, and resonances, lapses and excess of meaning [that occur] when the constituent elements of anyone's gender, of anyone's sexuality aren't made or can't be made to signify monolithically."[97] Building on tenacious efforts to disrupt the homogenizing connection among one's body, identities, and access to social power and resources, *danmei* fans multiply and reimagine differences as queering spaces for voluntary affiliation and sociality rather than monolithic and fixed biopolitical vectors for differentiation and calculation of individual and collective lives under the neoliberal directive. Resisting "queerness-as-sexual-identity (or anti-identity) . . . in favor of spatial, temporal, and corporeal convergences, implosions, and rearrangement," their love-enabled praxes retain "queerness exclusively as dissenting, resistant, and alternative" and have the potential to lead us beyond the neoliberal control that is based upon polarization and opposition through the identity-anchored difference-making machinery.[98]

As Aihwa Ong and Pheng Cheah remind us, transformative endeavors are embedded in and always constricted by living realities.[99] All of my heterosexual and some of my bisexual interviewees limited same-sex love and homoerotic desire to the period of adolescence and youth, which as Martin argues, is the "recuperative de-realization of present or future [homosexual] possibility on the part of a dominant, patriarchal sex-gender system."[100] Entangled in neoliberal restructuring in the Chinese and global context, *danmei* is by no means impervious to the normative remaking of queerness that takes shape along with this restructuring process. Thus, we need to broaden our horizon to do justice to the transnational repercussion generated by *danmei* in the context of fundamental socioeconomic transformations.

Unpacking the Love In Between

In light of their steadfast love of *danmei* and beautiful gay men, it is ironic to see many fans struggling to maintain a distance from the wonderland they have created. Their unfaltering love can be easily determined by their unreserved investment of time, money, and energies in that world. In an online discussion group that I was involved with, members organized several long-distance or even transnational trips to show support of their "gay" idols such as Wallace Chung, Ge Hu, Leehom Wang, and Wallace Huo (none of them identifies as gay). However, they also strove to draw a clear line between their everyday life and the *danmei* world. One seasoned *funü* told me emotionally: "As I have said, I read *danmei* just to kill time. In my real life, it is hard for me to recall what I have read in *danmei*. It is hard to connect this experience with my life."[101] These fans disavow any connection between their real lives and *danmei* not so much to mask its impact on their life, but rather to foreclose potential criticisms stemming from *danmei*'s so-called problematic contents. The fans share a concern about being socially punished or ostracized because of their fandom—a concern that reflects their ambivalence toward *danmei*. Trapped between the promissory futurities of substantive changes and the pressing actualities of alienation and subjugation, many *funü* struggle with a state of in-betweenness that, to borrow José Esteban Muñoz's words, casts light on a liminal space of transition between a utopian world of "then and there" replete with possibilities, messiness, mutations, and plurality and a prison house of "here and now" fraught with monolithicity, orderliness, singularity, and totality.[102]

Nevertheless, the otherworldly love in between has had concrete effects on the fans' intimate life as a dueling conception of their own relationship to gender. For both heterosexual and bisexual interviewees, the perception of their gender role in their intimate relationships was relational, volatile, and sometimes self-contradictory, depending upon their engagement with *danmei* works. For instance, although nearly all of the interviewees insisted that for their ideal lover, such virtues as being masculine, mature, reliable, caring, and responsible are essential, they are not opposed to taking care of or even financially supporting a beautiful young man. "I want to marry a macho man, but I can also take care of a beautiful man," one of them claimed.[103] As for their own position in the relationship, most interviewees endorsed such values as self-reliance and equality, but they also deemed finding *changqi fanpiao* (or "securing a long-term breadwinner") the ultimate goal for all women. One of the doctoral students I interviewed encapsulates this paradoxical interpretation of the heteronormative conjugal relationship. Contrary to the assumption that education increases women's independence and gender equality, this woman considered "becoming a housewife upon graduation" her highest life goal. She added, "but I don't want to be too dependent on men, so I would like to be that kind of housewife who can go to work outside home whenever I want to."[104] Despite her preference for a macho man, she stated that she would not mind supporting a boyish and beautiful *danmei*-style man—not as a wife, but like an elder sister or mother.

Many *funü* frequently invoke the rhetoric of mother's love for beautiful *danmei* boys to explain their nonnormative approach to the heterosexual relationship and simultaneously rebut potential censure deriving from threatening men's role as the primary provider of financial and emotional support, as stipulated by the heteropatriarchal system. Their active engagement with *danmei* culture develops this discourse. Fans traditionally take a follower role, but *funü* take a stance as both controlling and dedicated figures in the interaction with their "gay" idols. As many interviewees highlighted, impelled by their motherly instinct, they are committed to providing unconditional support and care to help innocent young men grow, mature, and excel in their careers. *Danmei* provides a convenient way to channel such devoted love. Even if this love, in others' eyes, seems to be misplaced on someone with a presumably different sexual orientation, it has influenced the fans' daily lives as the ambivalent conception of the heterosexual relationship stretched between the craze for a strong and reliable macho man mandated by the heteromarital system and the faithful love for the effeminate, beautiful boys idealized in the *danmei* world.

In addition to its homoromantic focus and mostly straight fan base, *danmei* culture is also essentially urban—not only because of its urbanite fandom groups, but also because of its urban-centered story lines. This cultural imprint was also reflected in my interviewee pool. Only one of the sixteen interviewees came from the rural area. As she told me, compared with their city-born peers, very few rural children and adolescents can afford to have their own computer to freely browse the cyberspace-based *danmei* texts. Needless to say, the state-imposed rural-urban inequality is incorporated into *danmei*'s cultural texture, as shown by the title and content of *Beijing Comrades*. Although that work's author does not produce a distinct narrative about China's capital city, "references to Beijing's unique colloquialism (*zan ma*, 'our Ma'), political events (Tian'anmen), fictive venues (Lan Yu as a student at 'Huada'), and urban problems (traffic, inflation, corruption, income disparity, real estate development, and the influx of migrant workers)" suffice to define for readers its predominantly urban mise-en-scène.[105]

Danmei's urbanized cultural provincialism is informed by and indexes the broad sociocultural upheavals in which the focus on workers and peasants in socialist China shifted swiftly to one on the middle class in neoliberal times—making the growth of the latter population segment a national project that signifies China's membership in the developed world.[106] *Danmei* is part of this macro discursive transformation. As suggested above, across *danmei's* visual and narrative registers, beautiful men almost unfailingly avoid real issues that members of sexual minority groups have to grapple with on a daily basis, such as homophobia, hate speech, and other forms of blatant discrimination. One interviewee said: "They (*funü*) assume that *xiaogong* (young top) already possesses many material properties. So the story rarely touches upon the poor people's life and other social problems."[107] That is, the class privileges of the fictive figures in *danmei* equip them with the social mobility to transcend the gender, sexual, and social barricades to love in ways unavailable to the majority of Chinese LGBTQ people. This gentrified form of queerness is only plausible and laudable for its fans on the ground that it is aligned with their own escapist projections of love-afforded privileges, anxieties, dissatisfactions, and desire in the milieu of China's neoliberalization.

Setting its narrative in the context of the Tian'anmen Square movement, a milestone in the neoliberalizing process in both Chinese and transnational contexts, *Beijing Comrades*, as Chiang suggests, "registers an unruly tension of cultural and visual (dis)identification that transcends the ideological and even geopolitical contours of (post)-socialist China" and enables us to delve further into the global transformation through the intricate layers of *danmei*.[108] In addition, David Eng suggests that *Lan Yu*, the cinematic adaption of the novel directed by Stanley Kwan, is a cultural landmark showing that self-identified Chinese gays and lesbians position themselves as new subjects by embracing their desires that were long suppressed by the state. They embody a new modernity that offers a critical tool to organize and evaluate not only nonnormative sexualities and desires, but also historical continuities and ruptures among China's semicolonial past, revolutionary aspirations for a socialist modernity, and contemporary investments in global neoliberalism.[109] Similarly, Bao argues that the gentrifying formation of queer desire is both enabled by and marks China's integration into the global neoliberal system, noting that the utopianized pure gay love is not only enabled by the reinforced class disparities but also comes to fruition in the wake of the Tian'anmen Square massacre that marked the end of China's socialist revolution and the inauguration of neoliberal times.[110]

The gentrification of queerness by neoliberal logic is not endemic to *dan-mei*, though. Instead, it indexes the prevalent urbanization and commercialization of queer cultures and queerness that take the form of the dominant "global gayness."[111] In Japanese BL manga, same-sex relationships often have plots involving seduction, blackmail, and desire within professional contexts and urban settings, with the economically powerful young top taking the upper hand and assuming the savior's role in the relationship.[112] In the Philippines, the long tradition of *bakla* that conflates homosexuality, transvestism, and lower-class status is "being disappeared" as a result of the coordinated strategies of invisibilization and discipline by local markets and the state. Its ordered death is necessitated by the bid for a form of sexual modernity grounded in whiteness, musculature, hypermasculinity, and class mobility that is vital for signifying and warranting the country's membership in modernity.[113] In the United States, by altering its racial, gender, and classed cultural layers, queerness is being reformulated, with its subversive potential for collective justice seriously tamed by attaching new conservative valences to it. Consequently, masculine middle- and upper-class white men with stunning muscularity have become the poster children of the normalized queerness that Lisa Duggan calls "homonormativity."[114] This particularized form of queerness constitutes an affective foundation for making the bourgeois lifestyle, leisurely flexibility, and individualist pursuits the hallmarks of the normative neoliberal subject and global citizen.[115] Via the normatively queered formation, hypermasculinity and whiteness are further disseminated and re-created to legitimize the self-serving instrumental reason and calculative rationality—the epistemic foundation of neoliberalism—to fortify and further its global reign.[116] Building on the transnational discourses of normative queerness and the raw materials from other gentrified queer cultures afforded by the digitalization of communication, fans have integrated *danmei* culture into the globalized planetary gay scenes.[117] The use of male homoromantic relationships as a transcendent escape route from China's imminently marketized Loveland thus reproduces an overdetermining and homogenizing stereotype of gay men and tightens neoliberal control by proclaiming the wealthy, consumerist lifestyle as the only viable way of living and being in the neoliberal condition. As a result, *danmei* is embroidered into the transnational tapestry of normative queerness and partially, if not completely, incorporated into the identity-ordinated neoliberal difference-making machinery to forward its expansion and domination on new levels.

Conclusion

In this chapter, I revisited the strategies and praxes that *danmei* fans use to survive and endure within the Loveland that—in support of the neoliberalizing agenda—alienates them, both deceptively and coercively, from the kind of intimate relationship they strive to pursue. Centering on the newly formulated and relatively less administered sexual vector of the difference-making machinery that enjoys more leeway in the face of the ruling heteropatriarchy, the fans develop and deliver unsettling forces that have spilled into the interconnected gender parameter more stringently controlled by the state's managerial biopolitical regulation. In so doing, they produce new spots of and trends in contradictions within the neoliberal apparatus that have led to concrete changes. As a result, it is now safe to say that the queerness-focused *danmei* praxes have contributed to a more inclusive public climate for alternative gender and sexual articulations, and that with the increasing visibility of those articulations, *funü* have popularized the discourses of homosexuality and inserted them into vernacular rhetoric. In today's China, it would be difficult for people not to encounter in daily conversations or online communications such *danmei*-informed terms as *haojiyou* (or "gay friends"), *gong* (or "top"), *shou* (or "bottom"), and *gaipian* (or "gay pornography"). Even dominant media such as China Central Television have to bow to these changes for the sake of their market shares.[118] The popularized androgynous masculinity has also become a robust rival to the state-backed hegemonic hypermasculinity, compelling the Chinese Communist Party to take measures to stem the radiating influences of the effeminate soft men and tackle the "masculinity crisis."[119]

Meanwhile, the difference-making machinery alters its own contours and elements to tackle emerging insurgencies and adapts with the shifting sociopolitical and economic climate to be spared from fundamental changes. Within the limits set by the neoliberal machinery, progressive and subversive endeavors often follow an exceptionalizing route that Jasbir Puar calls "piecing" to sort out certain subgroups within a marginalized group for recognition and incorporation at the cost of other subgroups' further marginalization and subordination.[120] As the case of *danmei* indicates, following the men-only logic and echoing the transnational normative lines of queer gentrification, homepatriarchal love is disassembled and reassembled into a homopatriarchal version that reinforces the neoliberal reign by endorsing its masculinist and bourgeois metrics. In the conclusion I offer a holistic understanding of the difference-making machinery that I hope could help us envision a more robust future for transformative changes.

Envisioning a Love-Enabled Future

Early on the morning of January 23, 2020, the Chinese government made public a stunning decision: Wuhan, a metropolis with over eleven million residents, would be locked down later that day to quarantine the epicenter of an outbreak of COVID-19, a potentially lethal disease caused by a novel coronavirus. Within weeks, this virus had stormed the world, morphing into a pandemic that has taken millions of lives and torn countless families apart. As the battle to contain viral transmission escalates and compels more states to shut down their borders to forestall disastrous consequences, the governments' measures also reinstate barriers that profoundly restrict the mobility of people and goods, causing severe shortages of critical protective gear and medical materials in many nation-states. Having thrown the world into disarray, this public health crisis exposes the downside of the neoliberal model of globalization, a model that has created both "extraordinary efficiencies" through "an ever-increasing specialization of labor across countries" and "extraordinary vulnerabilities" for fragmented international supply chains that depend on certain overreaching market players, such as the so-called world's factory controlled by the Chinese state.[1]

By calling a sudden halt to our ordinary life, the global pandemic has ushered in a devastating economic crisis unlike any other. With all the lives that it has cost, the chaos shows how recurrent capitalistic crises take root at the heart of the neoliberal system in such a dreadful way that we can no longer turn a blind eye. As one of the central arguments of this book makes clear, repeated economic crises like this are inherent in the tug of war between border-crossing capital and sovereignties that maintain and remake borders to both facilitate and hinder capital's movement. To ensure the uninterrupted running of the neoliberal regime, the difference-making machinery revises existing polarities and furnishes new ones to defer the occurrence of crises but cannot eradicate their genesis and, thereby, set the stage for the eruption of disasters and chaos on deeper and broader scales. Sadly, the pandemic has been co-opted by the Chinese state to advance its sui generis neoliberal governance that is characterized by draconian control.[2] This has enabled the authorities to consolidate more state-owned enterprises into corporate giants, so as to outcompete Euro-American rivals and achieve global dominance.[3] Similarly, the crisis provides "political fodder for [Western] nationalists who favor greater protectionism and immigration controls."[4] In turn, this solidifies the nationalists' power base and allows them to advance relentless privatizing agendas at home and rally more supporters to strike back at their new common enemy abroad.[5] In short, despite their disparate approaches, the Chinese Communist Party (CCP) and Western right-wing politicians share a polarizing doctrine and stir up confrontational sentiments to fortify their alliance with capital, opening the door to more calamities on domestic and international fronts.

Certainly, the current crisis has widened the rift between China and the West, fueling the full-blown new cold war that could put an end to global economic integration.[6] More alarmingly, it is pushing the world to the brink of direct military confrontation.[7] It is more urgent than ever to find a route to radical changes without replicating the ruinous terms of the neoliberal regime that have contributed to our present turmoil. Chela Sandoval proposes that love could be a key instrument that permits us to reduce opposition and embrace each other, find understanding and community beyond polarities, and revive hope and faith in the potential goodness of a peaceful world.[8] Love, as she puts it, "can access and guide our theoretical and political 'movidas'— revolutionary maneuvers" toward a more humanitarian future.[9] Yet as I have laid bare in this book, love itself is entrapped in the polarizing machinery, and we need to find ways to release it from the neoliberal mandate to create a more peaceful future. Generally speaking, macropolitical transformations require the conditioning and modulating of tendencies and momentums on micropolitical levels for transformative energies and relational engagement, and only when tendencies and momentums pass the threshold and make eventful changes possible can far-flung upheavals ensue in the form of revolutions and regime changes.[10] As Brian Massumi reminds us, "if the germinal conditions are not tended counter to the [dominant regime of power], the exclusions and hierarchies are apt to return in what can be an even more virulent form."[11] In other words, the conditioning might not be the direct cause of revolutionary changes, but it is decidedly a prerequisite as it primes the scope of potentialities and propensities and paves the way for the shifts.

Taking off from where Sandoval's hermeneutics of love stops and lingers, this book has developed a novel theoretical and methodological approach that, I argue, is the first step we need to take to build a love-enabled peaceful future. My engagement with China's bustling public sentiment of love offers details of the polarizing neoliberal machinery and illuminates how it modulates our desire-induced affectivities, sensibilities, and socialities in varying ways to uphold and forward limitless capital reproduction in global times. My diagnosis accounts for the ways in which the neoliberal machinery integrates the borderless Loveland into the regulatory biopolitical system to drive and sustain China's marketization and reintegration into the global economy. Showing how the difference-making machinery fuses emerging affective tendencies with rationalized being to align our becoming individualities with structural changes, I foreground the integral role that the machinery plays in the making of our selves and the world to engineer neoliberal restructuring around the globe. Through an embedded analysis of the cases in which it fails to perform this role, I also identify the trails of fragments, contradictory scraps, and awkwardly assembled segments that the machinery leaves to find possibilities of concrete change, and I explicate how these trails that lead to ruptures are crucial for subaltern groups to create their own spaces of resistance and survival. Taken together, these analytical lines drive my query to its conclusion: if the polarizing machinery continues to hold the reins as the central mechanism used to organize and manage the global order, the disaster that we are wrestling with will surely persist and plunge us into more calamitous tragedies. There are three reasons why this is the case.

First, the difference-making machinery has been altering its gendered, classed, sexualized, and ethno-racialized layers to reproduce oppositional relationships, thereby constraining our affective potentials and undercutting our will to preserve the status quo. In contemporary China, by linking love's actualization with an ensemble of bifurcated objects, social groups, and relationships, the machinery defines the expansive boundaries of the Loveland and prevents us from fully discerning and dissecting the links between structural changes and our individualization to find a way toward substantive changes. By projecting our never-to-be-fulfilled love potentials infinitely onto something and somewhere else, it enforces our affective attachment that entraps us in oppressive biopolitical control with almost no exit, while strengthening the conditions for more manipulative practices by the state and capital to advance their complicit exploitation. As this deepening crisis manifests itself, the polarizing machinery has been put into full gear by despotic rulers like Xi Jinping to redefine meanings of such virtuous human emotions as love and reconfigure our collective and individual lives to advance their pernicious agendas. It has also enabled brazen politicians like Donald Trump to manipulate people's allegiance to their community and nation-state and construct and burnish their brand so as to tighten capital's rule over those who are already struggling and suffering.[12]

Second, the machinery has created an intricate network that both extends beyond and reinforces nation-state boundaries to ensure the unfettered working of the global neoliberal apparatus. The network maintains the balance between pervasive biopower that runs horizontally, on the one hand, and totalizing sovereign power that functions in a vertical, top-down fashion, on the other hand. In so doing, it maintains a middle ground in the regenerative deterritorializing and reterritorializing tension that is inherent in the process of capital's accumulation and reproduction. As we have seen in Hai'an's export-oriented clothing and silk industries and Wuxi's construction sites, biopower is distributed through gendered, sexualized, classed, and ethno-racialized dichotomies through this network to remake barriers across regional and national borders for capital to turn into new profiteering opportunities. Through the barricades that it enforces on local levels, this network also alienates laboring groups from one another to thwart solidarities of resistance and perpetuate the uneven distributions of benefits and opportunities that subjugate those groups for further exploitation. Moreover, the reinstated asymmetrical differences of gender, class, ethno-race, and sexuality provide new resources for politicians to redraw and enforce nation-state boundaries that buttress their control of sovereign power to maximize benefits of capital. If we continue to be ruled by the neoliberal machinery in polarizing terms, we will surely be stuck in a deadlock: while the market is further released from the regulatory power of state, it aggravates the ordeal of the working majorities by separating and pitting them against one another to make them accept even worse deals. Under the market-centered governing rationale, centralized state power is continually abused to reorder and fortify polarized social control, concretizing slow death as the subalterns' only viable way of living to better serve the combined interests of the state and capital.

Last but not least, the metamorphic network of power ensconced in the difference-making machinery is the most important, if not the only, instrument the dominant groups can use to retain and advance their planetary control. As the example of *danmei* indicates, through the polarizing operation of the machinery, urban Chinese women's praxes of gender and sexual diversification to resist and challenge the statist heteropatriarchal rule are neutralized and transformed into new tools of gentrification and exploitation that can be used by privileged groups to reinforce economic inequalities and neoliberal principles on broader scales. Just as the coronavirus evolves and mutates to spread and survive, so the network of power, by actively morphing its eclectic parameters, can alter its shape and texture to retain its basic structure and survive shifting sociocultural climates. Building upon its elasticity and flexibility, the network leaves ample room for the dominant groups to find ways to secure and further their domination. Just as spiders bounce up and down along woven threads in cobwebs to pursue their resisting prey, so privileged groups are able to dodge and offset subalterns' challenges by moving across and through the layered network of power to reinforce their control.

Through a critical engagement with China's fantasmatic landscape of love, this book casts new light on the difference-making machinery and identifies its essential role in the transnational neoliberal system by pinpointing how it reintegrated the long-isolated Middle Kingdom into the global market yet simultaneously keeps it separate from the world as the emerging threat. The book traces the ways in which the public sentiment of love fuses with the biopolitical calculus through various polarizing practices to drive neoliberalization in China and beyond, and it unmasks the obscured chronological and epistemological connections between China's transformation and massive restructuring around the world. In so doing, the book dismantles the reductive discourse that heralds China's developmental model as the alternative to the Western neoliberal paradigm, unpacks the Cold War legacy that sees China as never having changed under communist rule, and disrupts the oppositional mentality that has sustained this legacy. Having walked readers through China's love-anchored tumultuous transition from socialism to neoliberalism, this book also provides detailed documentation of the unresolved conflicts emanating from the process that have converged into torrential forces setting China apart from the world again. In this regard, my analysis not only refutes the claim of calculative rationality to legitimize universal neoliberal rule but, more importantly, expands our horizon and allows us to better understand the polarizing mechanism that both undergirds and threatens to overturn the global neoliberal apparatus. In the last part of this conclusion, I focus on emerging dystopian scenes to articulate why, without this broadened utopian horizon, the catastrophe will likely persist and evolve into more dreadful disasters even in a projected postglobal era.

The Difference-Making Machinery in the
Postglobal Era

Following several beeping sounds and a muffled dialogue, a bird's-eye view of a sparkling urban sprawl is revealed in front of my eyes as I watch a video. Guiding viewers over and across blocks of cramped high-rises, bustling streets, and a river that flows serenely, the drone's camera zooms in on a uniformed policewoman who is talking intently into a walkie-talkie. A roomful of policemen sit behind her, poring over their computer screens, and a wall-size monitor at the back has a futuristic look usually featured in science-fiction movies. It shows an eerie image: live feeds of various city scenes are juxtaposed with a Gaode map (the Chinese equivalent of Google Maps) that displays real-time traffic and the head shot of a man whose personal information appears to the side. The camera's eye stays focused on the center of this room, offering viewers a panorama of its whole setting and providing a voyeur's paradise—or, in Michel Foucault's characterization, a panopticon that epitomizes the modern carceral system.[13]

Titled *In Your Face: China's All-Seeing State*, this video was produced by the BBC News in 2017, and it captures the daily routine of officers at the Guiyang police station as they run a massive surveillance system to keep in order the five million residents in the capital city of Guizhou province.[14] Cameras loaded with state-of-the-art facial- and gait-recognition software have been installed in over ten thousand public areas, overseeing every corner across the city. They are connected to an expansive network through a giant database, leaving no place out of reach.[15] With the help of artificial intelligence, these high-powered cameras are able to identify any subjects within seconds, providing detailed information about their age, gender, ethnicity, occupation, family members, and where they were the week before, and then feed footage back to the monitoring center in real time. If the police spot something, they zoom in. "For ordinary people," the policewoman explains to the BBC correspondent, "we will only extract their data when they need our help. . . . We only use it when needed." But what she means by "when needed," as the correspondent explains, is when needed "not only to prevent criminal behavior. But to predict it, too."[16]

The correspondent is correct. In the face of unfolding crises both at home and abroad, the Chinese government aims to revolutionize its security capabilities to capture and eliminate any subversive potentialities before they are actualized. The CCP first piloted these intrusive technologies in Xinjiang province to tighten its grip over the Uyghur minority, "a Turkic ethnic group of some 10 million Sunni Muslims considered by Beijing to be a hindrance to the development of a 'harmonious society.'"[17] Iris scanners and Wi-Fi sniffers are in wide use in bus stations, airports, marketplaces, the ubiquitous checkpoints, and even residential areas, and their data are collected by an "integrated joint operations platform" that stores more information about the populace under surveillance—"from consumer habits to banking activity, health status and indeed the DNA profile of every single inhabitant of Xinjiang."[18] Equipped with such sophisticated panoptic systems, the Chinese government has built hundreds of so-called reeducation centers to detain individuals with a potentially suspicious data trail and separate them from other Chinese people. Seeing each body not as an organic entity marked by ready-made labels such as ethno-race and gender but as "composites of information that splay the body across registers of disciplinary space and time," the system targets data, instead of "identity or the subject or its representation," to detect emerging oppositional differences and stem unsettling forces.[19]

As right-wing politicians in the West hark back to the feedback modality to rekindle gendered, classed, ethno-racialized, and sexualized antagonisms and lay the ground for their electoral successes, the Chinese state weaponizes and escalates its high-technology feedforward engagement to modulate people's affectivities and foreclose potentials of crisis. Under this Orwellian surveillance mode, the difference-making machinery blurs the boundaries between the past, present, and future as well as actualities, potentialities, and certainties in ways that have extended the state's control over people's becoming selves and worlding processes so that it is almost limitless. As I have delineated in this book, the party-state repeatedly resorts to the established dichotomies of gender, class, sexuality, and ethno-race to refine its retrospective calculations and projected devaluation of bodies and populations to facilitate China's neoliberal transition. In the midst of a string of profound challenges, the state strives to upgrade the unblinking gaze of its electronic eyes to follow the winding trails of people's affective tendencies, as well as to preregister people's emerging potentialities and recast them into new antagonistic relationships for preemptive purposes. With its biomolecular and organic qualities and textures opened up for unencumbered access and ceaseless processing by the state, the human body "no longer inhabits disciplinary spaces, but is inhabited by them."[20] Put succinctly, the bodily habitation of the established categories of gender, class, sexuality, and ethno-race gives way to full-scale inhabitation of the body to mine granular variations and infinite mutations for the future use of emerging differences. By 2017, 176 million cameras had been put in place to keep watch on over 1.4 billion Chinese citizens, turning them into new oppositions when needed.[21] The number is expected to soar to 2.76 billion cameras in 2022—two per capita—to oversee China's transformation into a "moderately well-off society" by the time Xi finishes his second term as president.[22]

The coronavirus's ubiquitous proliferation turned into another opportunity for the CCP to upscale and expand its technocratic skills, with the goal of bringing people's potentialities under its polarizing control and extending its crisis-foreclosing capacities by increasing surveillance to a new level of intrusion. Upgraded facial recognition technology is able to "detect elevated temperatures in a crowd or flag citizens not wearing a face mask," and data gathered through individuals' smartphones would automatically send details about their daily traces to surveillance centers.[23] Meanwhile, Chinese residents have to report their own and each other's health condition through cell phone apps to pass technologically administered health tests. All the collected and prepared data will then be collated into identifiers such as QR codes that determine where you can go, what you can do, and even who you are. For example, under the watchful eye of the state, people from Wuhan found that they had acquired a new identity that sharply distinguished them from their compatriots. With this new Wuhan identity, officially recognized with a *hukou* or not, they are singled out as unwanted in hotels and guesthouses, for jobs, and even in their own neighborhoods—they become outcasts in their own country when needed.[24] Through the imagined Wuhan body as the presumed vehicle of mobility and mutability, the coronavirus cultivates new affective attachments that cut across tangible and imaginary boundaries to impact biopolitical measures and biomedical discourses. Conversely, the physical Wuhan body is simultaneously made viral by its contagious capacity and affects state policies to contain its mobility. In brief, by turning viral affectivities into a concrete label that it prepares to separate the identified from the unidentified, the state seeks to preempt pathological potentialities by locking down the vessel of viral transmission that it has produced through polarization.

Building upon this radically proactive difference-making strategy, the CCP claimed that it had successfully defeated the virus and reaffirmed its status as the global capital of surveillance, which further sets it apart from the rest of the world. For instance, the telecom giant Huawei, the major architect and exporter of China's surveillance network, found itself at the center of a global tussle as the trade dispute started by the Trump administration continued and escalated. With its help, "18 countries—including Zimbabwe, Uzbekistan, Pakistan, Kenya, the United Arab Emirates, and Germany—are using

Chinese-made intelligent monitoring systems, and 36 have received training in topics like 'public opinion guidance.'" As technological innovations are increasingly being harnessed to monitor the lives and activities of China's 1.4 billion people and as the country's surveillance know-how and equipment are being exported to the world, the Chinese regime could further divide the world and "help underpin a future of tech-driven authoritarianism, potentially leading to a loss of privacy on an industrial scale."[25] Concerns like this are shared around the world, converging into another rallying point to accelerate the economic decoupling process that is under way. In the face of mounting pressure, the party-state seems to have found one answer. With its sophisticated and unparalleled surveillance skills, its leaders aim to achieve real-time control of Chinese society in a way that the Maoist state was never able to do. Thus, it is poised to retreat from the market-oriented neoliberal model and revert to the autarkic system of a centralized and planned economy.[26] Putting the difference-making machinery to wider and more invasive use, the future that the CCP envisions will definitely be starkly different from the more equal and peaceful future that people dedicated to social justice and positive social change all desire and strive for. Unless there are shifts in the polarizing doctrine of the extensively revamped and upscaled machinery that switch its tendencies toward and momentum for fundamental changes, the future of the planet will be considerably bleaker. I hope that the love-informed new horizon this book has portrayed will help pave a path through the turbulence and build an alternative and better future.

Notes

Introduction

1   Interview by the author, May 29, 2012, Hai'an, China. Pseudonyms are used through-out the book to protect my interviewees.

2   Tiantian Zheng, *Red Lights: The Lives of Sex Workers in Postsocialist China* (Minne-apolis: University of Minnesota Press, 2009). Also see Everett Yuehong Zhang, *The Impotence Epidemic: Men's Medicine and Sexual Desire in Contemporary China* (Durham, NC: Duke University Press, 2015); Julia F. Andrews and Kuiyi Shen, "The New Chinese Woman and Lifestyle Magazines in the Late 1990s," in *Popular China: Unofficial Culture in a Globalizing Society*, ed. Perry Link, Richard P. Madsen, and Paul G. Pickowicz (Lanham, MD: Rowman and Littlefield, 2002), 137–61.

3   Lauren Berlant, *Cruel Optimism* (Durham, NC: Duke University Press, 2012), 2.

4   Kathleen Stewart, "Atmospheric Attunements," *Environment and Planning D* 29, no. 3 (2011): 452.

5   Kathleen Stewart, "Weak Theory in an Unfinished World," *Journal of Folklore Re-search* 45, no. 1 (2008): 74.

6   Michel Serres, *The Parasite*, trans. Lawrence R. Schehr (Baltimore, MD: Johns Hopkins University Press, 1982), 224–25; Kathleen Stewart, "Arresting Images," in *Aesthetic Subjects*, ed. Pamela R. Mathews and David McWhirter (Minneapolis: University of Minnesota Press, 2003), 431.

7   Derek McCormack, "Remotely Sensing Affective Afterlives: The Spectral Geographies of Material Remains," *Annals of the Association of American Geographers* 100, no. 3 (2010): 643.

8   Lauren Berlant and Kathleen Stewart, *The Hundreds* (Durham, NC: Duke University Press, 2019), 5.

9   Jasbir Puar, *The Right to Maim: Debility, Capacity, Disability* (Durham, NC: Duke University Press, 2017), xvi. Also see Berlant, *Cruel Optimism*.

10   Charlie Yi Zhang, "Mapping the Will for Otherwise: Towards an Intersectional Critique of the Biopolitical System of Neoliberal Governmentality," in *Biopolitical Governance:*

Gender, Race and Economy, ed. Hannah Richter (Lanham, MD: Rowman and Little-field, 2018), 139-59.

11 C. Zhang, "Mapping the Will for Otherwise."

12 See Melissa Gregg and Gregory J. Seigwoth, *The Affect Theory Reader* (Durham, NC: Duke University Press, 2010). Also see Patricia Ticineto Clough, *The Affective Turn: Theorizing the Social* (Durham, NC: Duke University Press, 2007); Brian Massumi, *Parables for the Virtual: Movement, Affect, Sensation* (Durham, NC: Duke University Press, 2002); Berlant, *Cruel Optimism*; Kathleen Stewart, *Ordinary Affects* (Durham, NC: Duke University Press, 2007); Sara Ahmed, *The Cultural Politics of Emotion*, 2nd ed. (New York: Routledge, 2015); Berlant and Stewart, *The Hundreds*.

13 See Kimberlé Crenshaw, "Mapping the Margins: Intersectionality, Identity Politics, and Violence against Women of Color," *Stanford Law Review* 43, no. 6 (1991), 1241-99. Also see Patricia Hill Collins, *Black Feminist Thought: Knowledge, Consciousness, and the Politics of Empowerment* (London: Routledge, 2008); Vivian M. May, *Pursuing Intersectionality: Unsettling Dominant Imaginaries* (New York: Routledge, 2015); Jennifer Nash, *Black Feminism Reimagined after Intersectionality* (Durham, NC: Duke University Press, 2019); Patricia Hill Collins, *Intersectionality as Critical Social Theory* (Durham, NC: Duke University Press, 2019).

14 See Grace Kyungwon Hong and Roderick A. Ferguson, *Strange Affinities: The Gender and Sexual Politics of Comparative Racialization* (Minneapolis: University of Minnesota Press, 2011). Also see Jasbir Puar, *Terrorist Assemblages: Homonationalism in Queer Times* (Durham, NC: Duke University Press, 2007); Roderick A. Ferguson, *Aberrations in Black: Toward a Queer of Color Critique* (Minneapolis: University of Minnesota Press, 2003); José Esteban Muñoz, *Disidentifications: Queers of Color and the Performance of Politics* (Minneapolis: University of Minnesota Press, 1999); David L. Eng, Judith Halberstam, and José Esteban Muñoz, "What's Queer about Queer Studies Now?," *Social Text* 23, nos. 3-4 (2005): 1-17.

15 Dorothy J. Solinger, *Contesting Citizenship in Urban China: Peasant Migrants, the State, and the Logic of the Market* (Berkeley: University of California Press, 1999).

16 Dorothy J. Solinger, "The Floating Population in the Cities: Chances for Assimilation?," in *Urban Spaces in Contemporary China: The Potential for Autonomy and Community in Post-Mao China*, ed. Deborah S. Davis et al. (New York: Cambridge University Press, 1995), 113-48. See also Wanning Sun, *Subaltern China: Rural Migrants, Media, and Cultural Practices* (Lanham, MD: Rowman and Littlefield, 2014); Ngai Pun, *Made in China: Women Factory Workers in a Global Workplace* (Durham, NC: Duke University Press, 2005).

17 Recently scholars have noticed this analytical blank spot and begun to pay more attention to it. See Lisa Rofel, "Temporal-Spatial Migration: Workers in Transnational Supply-Chain Factories," in *Ghost Protocol: Development and Displacement in Global China*, ed. Carlos Rojas and Ralph A. Litzinger (Durham, NC: Duke University Press, 2016), 167-90; Carlos Rojas, "'I Am Great Leap Liu!': Circuits of Labor, Information, and Identity in Contemporary China," in *Ghost Protocol*, 205-23; Ralph A. Litzinger, "Regimes of Exclusion and Inclusion: Migrant Labor, Education, and Contested Futurities," in *Ghost Protocol*, 191-204.

18   Lisa Rofel, *Desiring China: Experiments in Neoliberalism, Sexuality, and Public Culture* (Durham, NC: Duke University Press, 2007).

19   Berlant, *Cruel Optimism*, 15.

20   Brian Massumi, *The Power at the End of the Economy* (Durham, NC: Duke University Press, 2014), 16.

21   Lisa Lowe, *The Intimacies of Four Continents* (Durham, NC: Duke University Press, 2015).

22   Nayan Shah, *Stranger Intimacy: Contesting Race, Sexuality, and the Law in the North American West* (Berkeley: University of California Press, 2012).

23   "Belt and Road Bedtime Stories," Episode 1, *China Daily*, May 8, 2017, https://www.chinadaily.com.cn/beltandroadinitiative/2017-05/08/content_29255516.htm.

24   Dambisa Moyo, "Is China the New Idol for Emerging Economies?," TED, June 2013, https://www.ted.com/talks/dambisa_moyo_is_china_the_new_idol_for_emerging_economies; Joseph E. Stiglitz, "Rethinking Globalization in the Trump Era: US-China Relations," *Frontiers of Economics in China* 13, no. 3 (2018): 133–46.

25   Simon Denyer, "Cheesy Song Praising Love of China's First Couple Goes Viral, Is Mocked," *Washington Post*, November 25, 2014, https://www.washingtonpost.com/news/worldviews/wp/2014/11/25/cheesy-song-praising-love-of-chinas-first-couple-goes-viral-is-mocked/?utm_term=.b250a08a77eb.

26   Austin Ramzy, "In Xi Jinping's Tears, a Message for China's People," *New York Times*, March 3, 2016, https://www.nytimes.com/2016/03/04/world/asia/china-xi-jinping-tears.html.

27   Andrew Jacobs and Chris Buckley, "Move Over Mao: Beloved 'Papa Xi' Awes China," *New York Times*, March 7, 2015, https://www.nytimes.com/2015/03/08/world/move-over-mao-beloved-papa-xi-awes-china.html.

28   "Yemen Crisis: China Evacuates Citizens and Foreigners from Aden," BBC, April 3, 2015, https://www.bbc.com/news/world-middle-east-32173811.

29   Charlie Campbell, "Xi Jinping's Party Congress Speech Leaves No Doubts over His Leadership Role," *Time*, October 18, 2017, http://time.com/4986999/xi-jinping-china-19th-congress-ccp/.

30   Adam Nossiter, "Marine Le Pen Leads Far-Right to Make France 'More French,'" *New York Times*, April 20, 2017, https://www.nytimes.com/2017/04/20/world/europe/france-election-marine-le-pen.html. See also "Europe's Rising Far Right: A Guide to the Most Prominent Parties," *New York Times*, December 6, 2016, https://www.nytimes.com/interactive/2016/world/europe/europe-far-right-political-parties-listy.html; "Jair Bolsonaro: Brazil's Firebrand Leader Dubbed the Trump of the Tropics," BBC, December 31, 2018, https://www.bbc.com/news/world-latin-america-45746013; Ari Khalidi, "Far-Right Turkish Nationalists to Back Erdogan in 2019 Turkey Election," Kurdistan 24, January 8, 2018, https://www.kurdistan24.net/en/news/44932dbc-9c05-405f-bd3d-815bae2c6998.

31   Kendall R. Phillips, "'The Safest Hands Are Our Own': Cinematic Affect, State Cruelty, and the Election of Donald J. Trump," *Communication and Critical/Cultural Studies* 15, no. 1 (2018): 85–89.

32   Simon Denyer and Luna Lin, "Mass Evictions in Freezing Beijing Winter Sparks Public Outrage but Little Official Remorse," *Washington Post*, November 27, 2017, https://

www.washingtonpost.com/news/worldviews/wp/2017/11/27/forced-evictions
-in-freezing-beijing-winter-sparks-public-outrage-but-little-official-remorse/
?noredirect=on&utm_term=.16df7ea9bb70.

33 Quoted in Denyer and Lin, "Mass Evictions in Freezing Beijing Winter Sparks Public
Outrage but Little Official Remorse."

34 Sara Ahmed, *The Promise of Happiness* (Durham, NC: Duke University Press, 2010),
14.

35 Ahmed, *The Promise of Happiness*, 2.

36 Mishuana Goeman, *Mark My Words: Native Women Mapping Our Nations* (Minneapolis: University of Minnesota Press, 2013), 45.

37 Elizabeth Povinelli, *The Empire of Love: Toward a Theory of Intimacy, Genealogy, and
Carnality* (Durham, NC: Duke University Press, 2006), 17.

38 Brian Massumi, "The Future Birth of the Affective Fact: The Political Ontology of
Threat," in *The Affect Theory Reader*, ed. Melissa Gregg and Gregory J. Seigwoth
(Durham, NC: Duke University Press, 2010), 54.

39 Tani Barlow, *The Question of Women in Chinese Feminism* (Durham, NC: Duke University Press, 2004), 2.

40 Bobby Benedicto, *Under Bright Lights: Gay Manila and the Global Scene* (Minneapolis: University of Minnesota Press, 2014), 2 and 4.

41 Stewart, "Atmospheric Attunements," 445.

42 Haiyan Lee, *Revolution of the Heart: A Genealogy of Love in China, 1900–1950* (Stanford, CA: Stanford University Press, 2007), 258.

43 Francis Fukuyama, *The End of History and the Last Man*, reissue ed. (New York: Free
Press, 2006).

44 Jinhua Dai, introduction to Jinhua Dai, *After the Post–Cold War: The Future of Chinese
History*, ed. Lisa Rofel and trans. Jie Li (Durham, NC: Duke University Press, 2018),
1–22.

45 Donald J. Trump, "Remarks by President Trump to the 73rd Session of the United
Nations General Assembly," September 25, 2018, https://uy.usembassy.gov/remarks
-by-president-trump-to-the-73rd-session-of-the-united-nations-general-assembly/.
Also see Nossiter, "Marine Le Pen Leads Far-Right to Make France 'More French'";
"Europe's Rising Far Right."

46 Panos Mourdoukoutas, "Can China Save the World Economy?," *Forbes*, August 18,
2011, http://www.forbes.com/sites/panosmourdoukoutas/2011/08/18/can-china
-save-the-world-economy/.

47 Zongze Li and Huan Wang, "Riben gongbu gdp shuju bei Zhongguo ganchao ju shijie
fisan (Japan's released GDP data shows it has been overtaken by China and regressed
to the world's no. 3)," Sina, February 14, 2011, http://finance.sina.com.cn/j/20110214
/08519369574.shtml.

48 Xi Jinping, "Full Text of Xi Jinping Keynote at the World Economic Forum," CGTV,
January 17, 2017, https://america.cgtn.com/2017/01/17/full-text-of-xi-jinping-keynote
-at-the-world-economic-forum.

49 Peter Martin, "Xi Pushes Chinese-Led Globalization after Pledging $78 Billion,"
Bloomberg, May 13, 2017, https://www.bloomberg.com/news/articles/2017-05-14
/xi-opens-china-s-globalization-forum-with-78-billion-in-pledges. Also see Jacob

Mardell, "The 'Community of Common Destiny' in Xi Jinping's New Era," *Diplomat*, October 25, 2017, https://thediplomat.com/2017/10/the-community-of-common -destiny-in-xi-jinpings-new-era/.

50 Daniel Bessner and Matthew Sparke, "Don't Let His Trade Policy Fool You: Trump Is a Neoliberal," *Washington Post*, March 22, 2017, https://www.washingtonpost.com /posteverything/wp/2017/03/22/dont-let-his-trade-policy-fool-you-trump-is-a -neoliberal/?utm_term=.bcf2247d38ef.

51 "Comprehensively Deepening Reform since Third Plenary Session of 18th CPC Central Committee," *Beijing Review*, accessed July 5, 2021, http://www.bjreview.com.cn /special/comprehensively_deepening_reform.html. Also see "China to Accelerate 'Hukou' System Reform: Document," Xinhua, November 15, 2013, http://en.people.cn /90785/8458115.html.

52 David Harvey, *A Brief History of Neoliberalism* (New York: Oxford University Press, 2005).

53 Robert A. Packenham and William Ratliff, "What Pinochet Did for Chile," *Hoover Digest*, no. 1 (January 30, 2007), http://www.hoover.org/research/what-pinochet-did-chile.

54 Stuart Hall, "The Neoliberal Revaluation," *Cultural Studies* 25, no. 6 (2011): 705–28; Harvey, *A Brief History of Neoliberalism*.

55 Aihwa Ong, *Neoliberalism as Exception: Mutations in Citizenship and Sovereignty* (Durham, NC: Duke University Press, 2006).

56 Dai, introduction, 4.

57 Barry Naughton, "Cities in the Chinese Economic System: Changing Roles and Conditions for Autonomy," in *Urban Spaces in Contemporary China: The Potential for Autonomy and Community in Post-Mao China*, ed. Deborah S. Davis et al. (New York: Cambridge University Press, 1995), 61–89.

58 Hui Wang, *China's New Order: Society, Politics, and Economy in Transition*, ed. Theodore Huters (Cambridge, MA: Harvard University Press, 2003).

59 Hui Wang, *The End of the Revolution: China and the Limits of Modernity* (London: Verso, 2009).

60 Hui Wang, *China's New Order*.

61 Joseph Stiglitz, *Globalization and Its Discontents* (New York: W. W. Norton, 2002); Harvey, *A Brief History of Neoliberalism*. Also see Michael Hardt, "Globalization and Democracy," GHC *Working Papers*, January (2011): 1–19; Maria Mies and Veronika Bennholdt-Thomsen, *The Subsistence Perspective: Beyond the Globalized Economy*, trans. Patrick Camiller, Maria Mies, and Gerd Weih (London: Zed Books, 1999).

62 Ong, *Neoliberalism as Exception*.

63 Chen Kuan-Hsing, *Asia as Method: Toward Deimperialization* (Durham, NC: Duke University Press, 2010), 12.

64 Charlie Yi Zhang, "Untangling the Intersectional Biopolitics of Neoliberal Globalization: Asia, Asian, and the Asia-Pacific Rim," *Feminist Formations* 26, no. 3 (2014): 167–96.

65 Rachel Heiman, Carla Freeman, and Mark Liechty, *The Global Middle Classes: Theorizing through Ethnography* (New York: School for Advanced Research Press, 2012); Ann Anagnost, "From 'Class' to 'Social Strata': Grasping the Social Totality in Reform-Era China," *Third World Quarterly* 29, no. 3 (2008): 497–519.

66　Charlie Yi Zhang, "Deconstructing the Hypermasculine National and Transnational Hegemony in Neoliberal China," *Feminist Studies* 40, no. 1 (2014): 13–38.

67　R. W. Connell and Julia Wood, "Globalization and Business Masculinities," *Men and Masculinities* 7, no. 4 (2005): 347–64.

68　Nancy Fraser, *The Fortunes of Feminism: From Women's Liberation to Identity Politics to Anti-Capitalism* (New York: Verso Books, 2013); Leta Hong Fincher, *Leftover Women: The Resurgence of Gender Inequality in China* (London: Zed Books, 2014).

69　Jan Jindy Pettman, "Globalization and the Gendered Politics of Citizenship," in *Women, Citizenship and Difference*, ed. Pnina Werbner and Nira Yuval-Davis (London: Zed Books, 1999), 212.

70　Rofel, *Desiring China*. See also Tze-Ian Deborah Sang, "At the Juncture of Censure and Mass Voyeurism: Narratives of Female Homoerotic Desire in Post-Mao China," *GLQ* 8, no. 4 (2002): 523–52; Tavis S. K. Kong, *Chinese Male Homosexualities: Memba, Tongzhi, and Golden Boy* (New York: Routledge, 2011).

71　On rebellions, the conflicts between the people of Wukan, a village in southern China, shocked the world in September 2011. To show their determination to fight the embezzlement of collective land by local officials, over twenty thousand villagers elected their own government officials and organized a fight against armed suppression by the police. Thereafter, several massive insurrections were kindled by corrupt local governments and increased class inequalities across China, from Zhongshan and Zengcheng in Guangdong province to Zhili and Zhuji in Zhejiang province, and then to Shifang in Sichuan province and Qidong in Jiangsu province, which mobilized tens of thousands of people to fight against the complicity of the state and the market. On suicidal protests and serial strikes, see Jack Linchuan Qiu, *Goodbye iSlave: A Manifesto for Digital Abolition* (Urbana: University of Illinois Press, 2017).

72　Stiglitz, *Globalization and Its Discontents.*

73　Bessner and Sparke, "Don't Let His Trade Policy Fool You."

74　Aihwa Ong, *Flexible Citizenship: The Cultural Logics of Transnationality* (Durham, NC: Duke University Press, 1999); Nancy Fraser, "Feminism, Capitalism and the Cunning of History," *New Left Review* 56, nos. 3–4 (2009): 97–117.

75　Kathleen Staudt and David Spener, "A View from the Frontier: Theoretical Perspectives Undisciplined," in *The U.S-Mexico Border: Transcending Divisions, Contesting Identities*, ed. David Spener and Kathleen Staudt (Boulder, CO: Lynne Rienner, 1998), 3–34.

76　Michel Foucault, *The Birth of Biopolitics: Lectures at the Collège de France, 1978–1979*, trans. Graham Burchell (Basingstoke, UK: Palgrave Macmillan, 2008).

77　Interview by the author, July 16, 2012, Wuxi, China.

78　Foucault, *The Birth of Biopolitics.*

79　Foucault, *The Birth of Biopolitics.*

80　Michel Foucault, *The History of Sexuality*, vol. 1: *The Will to Knowledge*, trans. Robert Hurley (London: Penguin, 1981). Also see Michel Foucault, *Society Must Be Defended: Lectures at the Collège de France, 1975–1976*, trans. David Macey (London: Picador, 2003).

81　Ann Laura Stoler, *Race and the Education of Desire: Foucault's History of Sexuality and the Colonial Order of Things* (Durham, NC: Duke University Press, 1995). Also see

Rey Chow, *The Protestant Ethnic and the Spirit of Capitalism* (New York: Columbia University Press, 2002).

82 Collins, *Black Feminist Thought.*

83 Chandra Talpade Mohanty, *Feminism without Borders: Decolonizing Theory, Practicing Solidarity* (Durham, NC: Duke University Press, 2003).

84 Mohanty, *Feminism without Borders*, 231.

85 Sumi Cho, Kimberlé Crenshaw, and Leslie McCall, "Toward a Field of Intersectionality Studies: Theory, Applications, and Praxis," *Signs* 38, no. 4 (2013): 788.

86 Focusing on the vectors of gender, class, and sexuality while strategically leaving out others, such as ethnicity (read here as the ethnic majority Han and minority groups, such as Tibetans and Mongolians), to be engaged in other places or by other scholars, it is by no means meant to downplay and ignore the egregious and horrendous domination and exploitation of ethnic minorities by the party-state to further its own agenda. See Carole McGranahan, *Arrested Histories: Tibet, the CIA, and Memories of a Forgotten War* (Durham, NC: Duke University Press, 2010). Also see Ralph A. Litzinger, *Other Chinas: The Yao and the Politics of National Belonging* (Durham, NC: Duke University Press, 2010); Louisa Schein, *Minority Rules: The Miao and the Feminine in China's Cultural Politics* (Durham, NC: Duke University Press, 2000); Kevin Carrico, *The Great Han: Race, Nationalism, and Tradition in China Today* (Oakland: University of California Press, 2017); Darren Byler, *Terror Capitalism: Uyghur Dispossession and Masculinity in a Chinese City* (Durham, NC: Duke University Press, 2021).

87 Grace Kyungwon Hong and Roderick A. Ferguson, introduction to *Strange Affinities: The Gender and Sexual Politics of Comparative Racialization*, ed. Grace Kyungwon Hong and Roderick A. Ferguson (Minneapolis: University of Minnesota Press, 2011), 1–22.

88 Puar, *Terrorist Assemblages.* Also see Jasbir Puar, "'I Would Rather Be a Cyborg than a Goddess': Becoming-Intersectional in Assemblage Theory," *philoSophia* 2, no. 1 (2012): 49–66; Brian Massumi, "The Autonomy of Affect," *Cultural Critique*, no. 31 (1995): 83–109.

89 Berlant, *Cruel Optimism*, 15 (emphasis in the original).

90 Berlant, *Cruel Optimism*, 24.

91 Berlant, *Cruel Optimism*, 3.

92 Berlant, *Cruel Optimism*, 3.

93 Berlant, *Cruel Optimism*, 3–4.

94 Massumi, "The Future Birth of the Affective Fact," 56.

95 Massumi, "The Future Birth of the Affective Fact," 52.

96 Massumi, *Parables for the Virtual*, 21.

97 Berlant and Stewart, *The Hundreds*, 17.

98 Gilles Deleuze and Félix Guattari, *Anti-Oedipus: Capitalism and Schizophrenia*, trans. Robert Hurley, Mark Seem, and Helen R. Lane (New York: Penguin Books, 1977).

99 Gilles Deleuze, "Ethology: Spinoza and Us," in *Incorporations*, ed. Jonathan Crary and Sanford Kwinter (New York: Zone Books, 1992), 626.

100 Bruno Latour, "How to Talk about the Body? The Normative Dimension of Science Studies," *Body and Society* 10, nos. 2–3 (2004): 205.

101 Elizabeth Freeman, *Time Binds: Queer Temporalities, Queer Histories* (Durham, NC: Duke University Press, 2010), 6.

102 Purnima Mankekar and Louisa Schein, "Mediations and Transmediations: Erotics, Sociality, and 'Asia,'" in *Media, Erotics, and Transnational Asia*, ed. Purnima Mankekar and Louisa Schein (Durham, NC: Duke University Press, 2012), 2.

103 Ferguson, *Aberrations in Black*.

104 Grace Kyungwon Hong, "Existentially Surplus: Women of Color Feminism and the New Crises of Capitalism," *GLQ* 18, no. 1 (2011): 87–106.

105 Harvey, *A Brief History of Neoliberalism*, 33.

106 Aimee Bahng, *Migrant Futures: Decolonizing Speculation in Financial Times* (Durham, NC: Duke University Press, 2017).

107 Sun, *Subaltern China*, 243.

108 Tania Branigan, "Five Chinese Feminists Held over International Women's Day Plans," *Guardian*, March 12, 2015, http://www.theguardian.com/world/2015/mar/12/five-chinese-feminists-held-international-womens-day.

109 Muñoz, *Disidentifications*.

110 Petrus Liu, *Queer Marxism in Two Chinas* (Durham, NC: Duke University Press, 2015), 31.

111 Eng, Halberstam, and Muñoz, "What's Queer about Queer Studies Now?"

112 Howard Chiang and Alvin Wong, "Asia Is Burning: Queer Asia as critique," *Culture, Theory and Critique* 58, no. 2 (2017): 122.

113 Emily Honig, *Creating Chinese Ethnicity: Subei People in Shanghai, 1850–1980* (New Haven, CT: Yale University Press, 1992).

114 Bei Tong, "Beijing Comrades: A Gay Chinese Love Story," trans. Scott Myers, *Amerasia Journal* 37, no. 2 (2011): 75–94. As the translator of the book, Myers, states, the pseudonymous author's "real-world identity has been a subject of debate since the story was first published on a gay Chinese website over a decade ago" and "is known variously as Beijing Comrade, Beijing Tongzhi, Xiao He, and Miss Wang" (76). In a review of the English translation, Hugh Ryan discussed the author's identity in detail ("The Controversial Chinese Gay Erotic Novel You Can Finally Read in English," March 16, 2016, Modern Chinese Literature and Culture Resource Center, Ohio State University, https://u.osu.edu/mclc/2016/03/17/beijing-comrades-review). Ryan writes: "In his 'Translator's Note,' Myers mentions three commonly discussed possibilities. First, that the author is . . . a 'heterosexual woman with the misfortune of unknowingly marrying a gay man.' Second, that the author is Wang Xiaobo, the 'late husband of prominent sociologist, queer activist, and public intellectual Li Yinhe.' And third, that the author was a female friend of a real-life couple who asked her to document their story online." After nearly six years of occasional correspondence (mostly through email), Myers is confident that he has been corresponding with the real author, who "he thought is likely a woman." According to Myers, the author "spent all of her days chatting with friends online and reading graphic [gay] porn fiction," and "she decided she could write something better. Why she felt that need, I don't know" (brackets in the original).

1. Love of the Zeitgeist

An earlier version of chapter 1 was published in *Frontiers: A Journal of Women's Studies* 37, no. 2 (2016): 1–27.

1   Gordon G. Chang, "Another Chinese Fib: 6.1% Growth," *Forbes*, April 22, 2009, https://www.forbes.com/2009/04/21/china-economic-statistics-growth-opinions-columnists-wen-jiabao.html#33428b9414ac.

2   Hu Jintao, "Speech at China's 60th Anniversary Ceremony," October 5, 2009, http://de.china-embassy.org/chn/zgyw/t618281.htm.

3   Heather Love, *Feeling Backward: Loss and the Politics of Queer History* (Cambridge, MA: Harvard University Press, 2009).

4   Xin Huang, "In the Shadow of Suku (Speaking-Bitterness): Master Scripts and Women's Life Stories," *Frontiers of History in China* 9, no. 4 (2014): 584–610. Also see Xin Huang, *The Gender Legacy of the Mao Era: Women's Life Stories in Contemporary China* (Albany: State University of New York Press, 2019).

5   Mark Rifkin, *Beyond Settler Time: Temporal Sovereignty and Indigenous Self-Determination* (Durham, NC: Duke University Press, 2017).

6   "Xi Jinping: Buneng fouren qian sanshinian lishi (Xi Jinping: We cannot deny the history of the first thirty years)," dw.com, May 1, 2013, https://www.dw.com/zh/%E4%B9%A0%E8%BF%91%E5%B9%B3%E4%B8%8D%E8%83%BD%E5%90%A6%E5%AE%9A%E5%89%8D30%E5%B9%B4%E5%8E%86%E5%8F%B2/a-16500930.

7   Jude Blanchette, *China's New Red Guards: The Return of Radicalism and the Rebirth of Mao Zedong* (New York: Oxford University Press, 2019); Shi Anshu, François Lachapelle, and Matthew Galway, "The Recasting of Chinese Socialism: The Chinese New Left since 2000," *China Information* 32, no. 1 (2018): 139–59.

8   Rifkin, *Beyond Settler Time*, viii.

9   Jinhua Dai, "Gender and Narration: Women in Contemporary Chinese Film," trans. Jonathan Noble, in *Cinema and Desire: Feminist Marxism and Cultural Politics in the Work of Dai Jinhua*, ed. Jing Wang and Tani E. Barlow (London: Verso, 2002), 123.

10 Charlie Yi Zhang, "Queering the National Body of Contemporary China," *Frontiers* 37, no. 2 (2016): 1–26.

11 Dai, "Gender and Narration," 102.

12 Elizabeth Freeman, *Time Binds: Queer Temporalities, Queer Histories* (Durham, NC: Duke University Press, 2010), 3.

13 Freeman, *Time Binds*, xi.

14 Xiaomei Chen, *Staging Chinese Revolution: Theater, Film, and the Afterlives of Propaganda* (New York: Columbia University Press, 2016), 3.

15 "China's 60th Anniversary Celebrations Not for 'the People,'" *Matière et révolution*, October 11, 2009, https://www.matierevolution.fr/spip.php?breve117.

16 Freeman, *Time Binds*, xv.

17 For the CCTV anchors' comments during the broadcast, see "China's Sixtieth Anniversary Ceremony," CCTV, accessed July 6, 2021, https://www.youtube.com/watch?v=SmSMQoTigos.

18 Zhang, "Queering the National Body of Contemporary China."

19   Dorothy J. Solinger, "China's Floating Population," in *The Paradox of China's Post-Mao Reforms*, ed. Merle Goldman and Roderick Macfarquhar (Cambridge, MA: Harvard University Press, 1999), 222.

20   Solinger, "China's Floating Population."

21   See Fei-Ling Wang, "Renovating the Great Floodgate: The Reform of China's Hukou System," in *One Country, Two Societies: Rural-Urban Inequality in Contemporary China*, ed. Martin King Whyte (Cambridge, MA: Harvard University Press, 2010), 335–64. Also see Martin King Whyte, "The Changing Role of Workers," in *The Paradox of China's Post-Mao Reforms*, 173–96.

22   Friedrich Engels, *The Origin of the Family, Private Property and the State*, intro. Tristram Hunt (London: Penguin Books, 2010).

23   Jacqui True, *Gender, Globalization and Postsocialism: The Czech Republic after Communism* (New York: Columbia University Press, 2003).

24   Dai, "Gender and Narration." Also see Tina Mai Chen, "Female Icons, Feminist Iconography? Socialist Rhetoric and Women's Agency in 1950s China," *Gender and History* 15, no. 2 (2003): 268–95.

25   Tyrsene White, "The Origins of China's Birth Planning Policy," in *Engendering China: Women, Culture, and the State*, ed. Christina K. Gilmartin et al. (Cambridge, MA: Harvard University Press, 1994), 250–78. Also see Susan Greenhalgh and Edwin A. Winckler, *Governing China's Population: From Leninist to Neoliberal Biopolitics* (Stanford, CA: Stanford University Press, 2005).

26   Zheng Wang, *Finding Women in the State: A Socialist Feminist Revolution in the People's Republic of China, 1949–1964* (Oakland: University of California Press, 2017), 222.

27   Ann Anagnost, "From 'Class' to 'Social Strata': Grasping the Social Totality in Reform-Era China," *Third World Quarterly* 29, no. 3 (2008): 497–519.

28   Jinhua Dai, introduction to Jinhua Dai, *After the Post–Cold War: The Future of Chinese History*, ed. Lisa Rofel and trans. Jie Li (Durham, NC: Duke University Press, 2018), 1–22.

29   Rachel Heiman, Carla Freeman, and Mark Liechty, *The Global Middle Classes: Theorizing through Ethnography* (New York: School for Advanced Research Press, 2012).

30   Charlie Yi Zhang, "Deconstructing the Hypermasculine National and Transnational Hegemony in Neoliberal China," *Feminist Studies* 40, no. 1 (2014): 13–38.

31   R. W. Connell and Julia Wood, "Globalization and Business Masculinities," *Men and Masculinities*, 7, no. 4 (2005), 347–64.

32   Leta Hong Fincher, *Leftover Women: The Resurgence of Gender Inequality in China* (London: Zed Books, 2014).

33   Jan Jindy Pettman, "Globalization and the Gendered Politics of Citizenship," in *Women, Citizenship and Difference*, ed. Pnina Werbner and Nira Yuval-Davis (London: Zed Books, 1999), 212.

34   Pettman, "Globalization and the Gendered Politics of Citizenship."

35   Lisa Rofel, *Desiring China: Experiments in Neoliberalism, Sexuality, and Public Culture* (Durham, NC: Duke University Press, 2007). Also see Tze-Ian Deborah Sang, "At the Juncture of Censure and Mass Voyeurism: Narratives of Female Homoerotic Desire in Post-Mao China," *GLQ* 8, no. 4 (2002): 523–52; Tiantian Zheng, *Tongzhi Living: Men Attracted to Men in Postsocialist China* (Minneapolis: University of Minnesota Press, 2015).

36   Chris Berry, Fran Martin, and Audrey Yue, "Introduction: Beep-Click-Link," in *Mobile Cultures: New Media in Queer Asia*, ed. Chris Berry, Fran Martin, and Audrey Yue (Durham, NC: Duke University Press, 2003), 1–20.

37   One of the hottest public affairs in early 2013—the rumored same-sex relationship between Leehom Wang, a Taiwanese pop star, and Yundi Li, an internationally famed Chinese pianist—surfaced after their first collaboration at the 2012 Spring Festival Gala sponsored by CCTV and became an open joke at the 2013 gala. Although the program director denied that this was an orchestrated script, this move proved quite conducive to the gala's endeavor to cater to a younger generation by addressing its members' interest in queerness. The viewing rate was later revealed to have reached its highest point with the queering scenario during the 2013 gala. See "Qian Liu: 'Zhao Lihong' zhihou de yanbian bushi wo neng kongzhi de (Qian Liu: I cannot control the aftereffects of 'Looking for Leehom')," sohu.com, March 1, 2013, http:// yule.sohu.com/20130301/n367512618.shtml.

38   Love, *Feeling Backward*.

39   Andrew F. Jones, *Yellow Music: Media Culture and Colonial Modernity in the Chinese Jazz Age* (Durham, NC: Duke University Press, 2001).

40   Dai, "Gender and Narration," 102.

41   Xinjun Liu, "Mao Zedong dui makesi zhuyi zhongguohua de gongxian (Mao Zedong's contribution to the localization of Marxism in China)," cssn.cn, May 5, 2018, http://sky.cssn.cn/skyskl/skyskl_yzfc/201805/t20180504_4226491.shtml.

42   Yiyan Wang, "Mr. Butterfly in Defunct Capital: 'Soft' Masculinity and (Mis)engendering in China," in *Asian Masculinities: The Meaning and Practice of Manhood in China and Japan*, ed. Kam Louie and Morris Low (London: Routledge, 2003), 41–58.

43   Dai, "Gender and Narration."

44   Evelyn Cheng, "Setting His Eyes on the Next 100 Years, Xi Seizes the Chance to Lead China to Greater Power," CNBC, July 1, 2021, https://www.cnbc.com/2021/07/02/ccp -100-years-xi-seizes-the-chance-to-lead-china-in-the-path-to-power.html.

45   C. J. Pascoe, *Dude, You're a Fag: Masculinity and Sexuality in High School* (Berkeley: University of California Press, 2007).

46   Alys Eve Weinbaum et al., "The Modern Girl as Heuristic Device: Collaboration, Connective Comparison, Multidirectional Citation," in *The Modern Girl around the World: Consumption, Modernity, and Globalization*, ed. Alys Eve Weinbaum et al. (Durham, NC: Duke University Press, 2008), 9.

47   Weinbaum et al., "The Modern Girl as Heuristic Device," 8.

48   Jing Wang and Tani Barlow, introduction to *Cinema and Desire: Feminist Marxism and Cultural Politics in the Work of Dai Jinhua*, ed. Jing Wang and Tani Barlow (London: Verso, 2002), 8.

49   Alvin K. Wong, "Gendering Intersubjectivity in New Chinese Documentary Feminist Multiplicity and Vulnerable Masculinity in Postsocialist China," in *Filming the Everyday: Independent Documentaries in Twenty-First-Century China*, ed. Paul G. Pickowicz and Yingjin Zhang (Lanham, MD: Rowman and Littlefield, 2017), 121.

50   Fan Yang, "The Politics of Exhibition: China's 'Fake' in the 2008 Beijing Olympics," *antiTHESIS* 19 (March 2009): 58.

51 Tania Branigan, "Olympics: Child Singer Revealed as Fake," *Guardian*, August 12, 2008, http://www.theguardian.com/sport/2008/aug/12/olympics2008.china1. Also see Yang, "The Politics of Exhibition."

52 "Sanjun nvbing fangdui: Junzhong 'huamulan' xiang nanren yiyang qu zhandou (Female soldier squads: 'Mulan' fighting like men)," Chinanews.com, October 1, 2009, http://news.fengone.com/b/20091001/100979.html.

53 Jun Lan, "Liushi zhounian dayuebing: Wanlvcongzhong de hongse lvbing (Military parade for China's sixtieth anniversary: Red female soldiers in green troops)," CNTV, October 9, 2012, http://news.cntv.cn/2012/10/09/ARTI1349772477529423.shtml.

54 Anne E. Gorsuch, "The Dance Class or the Working Class: The Soviet Modern Girl," in *The Modern Girl around the World*, 174–93.

55 See "China's Sixtieth Anniversary Ceremony."

56 Freeman, *Time Binds*.

57 Freeman, *Time Binds*, 3.

58 Walter Benjamin, *Illuminations: Essays and Reflections*, trans. Harry Zohn (New York: Schocken Books, 1969), 253.

59 Chin-Chuan Lee, "The Global and the National of the Chinese Media," in *Chinese Media, Global Context*, ed. Chin-Chuan Lee (London: Routledge, 2003), 8.

60 Shan Gao, "Zhongguo 1% jiating zhangwo quanguo 41.4% caifu pinfu chaju chengdu chaoguo meiguo (1% of Chinese families own 41.4% of wealth, social inequality surpasses that in the United States)," RFA, June 9, 2010, https://www.rfa.org/mandarin /yataibaodao/pinfu-06092010094151.html.

61 Jack Goodman, "Has China Lifted 100 Million People out of Poverty?" BBC, February 28, 2021, https://www.bbc.com/news/56213271.

62 Wei Guo, "Chengxia chaju zheng jinyibu kuoda bixu yinqi women de zhuyi (Urban-rural inequality enlarges and calls for our attention)," sohu.com, September 20, 2011, https://www.sohu.com/a/357939226_237819.

63 David Harvey, *A Brief History of Neoliberalism* (New York: Oxford University Press, 2005).

64 Charlie Yi Zhang, "Untangling the Intersectional Biopolitics of Neoliberal Globalization: Asia, Asian, and the Asia-Pacific Rim," *Feminist Formations* 26, no. 3 (2014): 167–96.

65 Zheping Huang, "What You Need to Know about Beijing's Crackdown on Its 'Low-End Population,'" November 27, 2017, Quartz, https://qz.com/1138395/low-end-population -what-you-need-to-know-about-chinas-crackdown-on-migrant-workers/.

66 Margaret Heffernan, "What Happened after the Foxconn Suicides," CBS News, August 7, 2013, https://www.cbsnews.com/news/what-happened-after-the-foxconn -suicides/.

67 Jack Linchuan Qiu, *Goodbye iSlave: A Manifesto for Digital Abolition* (Urbana: University of Illinois Press, 2017). Also see "Fushikang Taiyuang gongchang baofa daguimo saoluan (Massive revolts outburst in Taiyuan Foxconn)," mydrivers.com, September 24, 2012, https://news.mydrivers.com/1/242/242209.htm.

68 "Fushikang beibao fasheng laozi jiufen, bufen yuangong yangyan jiti zisha (Foxconn said to have labor-management conflict, some employees threatened to commit collective suicide)," Xinhua Network, January 12, 2012, http://news.sohu.com/20120112 /n332026451.shtml. Also see David Barboza, "Foxconn Resolves a Dispute with Some

Workers in China," January 12, 2012, *New York Times*, https://www.nytimes.com/2012 /01/13/technology/foxconn-resolves-pay-dispute-with-workers.html.

69 For instance, to stifle any potential uprising, all pigeons in Beijing were required to be caged and taxi windows to be kept closed during the CCP's eighteenth national congress. See Jonathan Kaiman, "China Congress: Toy Helicopters and Pigeons Vanish in Security Crackdown," *Guardian*, November 1, 2012, http://www.guardian.co.uk /world/2012/nov/01/china-party-congress-restrictions.

70 For instance, in 2010 *Dwelling Narrowness*, a soap opera exposing class inequality, was banned by Chinese authorities soon after it produced large-scale repercussions.

71 Zhang, "Deconstructing the Hypermasculine National and Transnational Hegemony in Neoliberal China."

72 Xiaomei Chen, *Staging Chinese Revolution*, 64.

73 Xiaomei Chen, *Staging Chinese Revolution*, 64.

74 As Zheng Wang reminds us, the Maoist state's appropriation of women's striving for gender egalitarianism should be distinguished from Chinese women's own endeavors to achieve and accomplishments of gender equality during the time. The homogenizing discourse that sees both as the masculinization of women is central to the neoliberal state's polarizing gender agenda, which in turn is key to its marketizing experiment (*Finding Women in the State*, 222–28).

75 Haiyan Lee, *Revolution of the Heart: A Genealogy of Love in China, 1900–1950* (Stanford, CA: Stanford University Press, 2007), 258.

76 Gilmartin et al., introduction to *Engendering China*, 1–24.

77 Susan Mann, *Gender and Sexuality in Modern Chinese History* (New York: Cambridge University Press, 2011), xvii.

78 In the Confucian canon, the three obediences require that a woman should obey her father before marriage, her husband when married, and her sons in widowhood. The four virtues are morality, proper speech, modest manner, and diligent work.

79 Francesca Bray, *Technology and Gender: Fabrics of Power in Late Imperial China* (Berkeley: University of California Press, 1997), 42.

80 Zhang, "Deconstructing the Hypermasculine National and Transnational Hegemony in Neoliberal China."

81 Lydia Liu, "The Female Body and Nationalist Discourse: The Field of Life and Death Revisited," in *Scattered Hegemonies: Postmodernity and Transnational Feminist Practices*, ed. Inderpal Grewal and Caren Kaplan (Minneapolis: University of Minnesota Press, 1994), 37–62.

82 Gail Hershatter, *Dangerous Pleasures: Prostitution and Modernity in Twentieth-Century Shanghai* (Berkeley: University of California Press, 1997).

83 Hershatter, *Dangerous Pleasures*, 7.

84 Christina K. Gilmartin, "Gender, Political Culture, and Women's Mobilization in the Chinese Nationalist Revolution, 1924–1927," in *Engendering China*, 195–225.

85 Tani Barlow, "Theorizing Woman: Funü, Guojia, Jiating (Chinese Women, Chinese State, Chinese Family)," in *Scattered Hegemonies*, 173–96.

86 For instance, as Joane Nagel argues, "masculinity and nationalism articulate well with one another, and the modern form of Western masculinity emerged at about the same time and place as modern nationalism" ("Masculinity and Nationalism:

Gender and Sexuality in the Making of Nations," *Ethnic and Racial Studies* 21, no. 2 [1998]: 242–69). Likewise, Cynthia Enloe notes that women are often relegated to minor symbolic roles in nationalist movements and conflicts, either as icons of nationhood to be elevated and defended, or as the booty or spoils of war to be denigrated and disgraced (*Bananas, Beaches and Bases: Making Feminist Sense of International Politics* [London: Pandora, 1999]).

87 See Anne McClintock, "'No Longer in a Future Heaven': Woman and Nationalism in South Africa," *Transition*, no. 51 (1991): 104–23. Also see Julie Skurski, "The Ambiguities of Authenticity: Dona Barbara and the Construction of National Identity," *Poetics Today* 15, no. 4 (1994): 605–42.

88 Norma Alarcón, Caren Kaplan, and Minoo Moallem, introduction to *Between Woman and Nation: Nationalisms, Transnational Feminisms, and the State*, ed. Caren Kaplan, Norma Alarcón, and Minoo Moallem (Durham, NC: Duke University Press, 1999), 1–16.

89 Shawn Michelle Smith, *American Archives: Gender, Race, and Class in Visual Culture* (Princeton, NJ: Princeton University Press, 1999).

90 Uma Narayan, *Dislocating Cultures: Identities, Traditions, and Third World Feminism* (New York: Routledge, 1997).

91 McClintock, "'No Longer in a Future Heaven.'"

92 Jianfen Gu and Jingting Han, "Today Is Your Birthday," mulanci.org, accessed August 12, 2021, https://www.mulanci.org/lyric/sl32915/, my translation.

93 Hui Wang, *China's New Order: Society, Politics, and Economy in Transition*, ed. Theodore Huters (Cambridge, MA: Harvard University Press, 2003).

94 Andrew F. Jones, *Like a Knife: Ideology and Genre in Contemporary Chinese Popular Music* (Ithaca, NY: Cornell University Press, 2010), 1.

95 Lynne Segal, *Why Feminism? Gender, Psychology, Politics* (Cambridge: Polity, 1999), 43.

96 Iris Marion Young, "The Logic of Masculinist Protection: Reflections on the Current Security State," *Signs* 29, no. 1 (2003): 1–25.

97 Xiaomei Chen, *Staging Chinese Revolution*.

98 Benedict Anderson, *Imagined Communities: Reflections on the Origin and Spread of Nationalism* (London: Verso, 2006).

99 Pheng Cheah, *Inhuman Conditions: On Cosmopolitanism and Human Rights* (Cambridge, MA: Harvard University Press, 2006).

100 Merle Goldman and Roderick Macfarquhar, "Dynamic Economy, Declining Party-State," in *The Paradox of China's Post-Mao Reforms*, 3–29.

101 Chin-Chuan Lee, "The Global and the National of the Chinese Media," 3.

102 Geng Song and Derek Hird, *Men and Masculinities in Contemporary China* (London: Brill, 2013).

103 Bin Ouyang, "Fanri youxing, Mao zhuxi he Bo Xilai (Anti-Japan protests, Chairman Mao and Bo Xilai)," *New York Times*, October 18, 2012, https://cn.nytimes.com/china/20121018/cc18ouyangbin/.

104 Giorgio Agamben, *Homo Sacer: Sovereign Power and Bare Life*, translated by Daniel Heller-Roazen (Stanford, CA: Stanford University Press, 1998), 6.

105 Aihwa Ong, "Cultural Citizenship as Subject-Making," *Current Anthropology* 37, no. 5 (1996): 738.

106   Eileen J. Suárez Findlay, *Imposing Decency: The Politics of Sexuality and Race in Puerto Rico, 1870–1920* (Durham, NC: Duke University Press, 2000), 11.

107   Achille Mbembe, *On the Postcolony*, trans. A. M. Berrett et al. (Berkeley: University of California Press, 2001).

108   Xiaomei Chen, "Staging Chinese Revolution: The Color Scheme of Socialist Epic Theater (1964–2006)," paper presented at the Languages, Literatures, and Cultures Conference, University of Kentucky, April 21, 2017.

109   Lee, *Revolution of the Heart*, 258.

110   Rofel, *Desiring China*; Everett Yuehong Zhang, *The Impotence Epidemic: Men's Medicine and Sexual Desire in Contemporary China* (Durham, NC: Duke University Press, 2015); Zheng, *Tongzhi Living*.

111   Rofel, *Desiring China*. Also see Sang, "At the Juncture of Censure and Mass Voyeurism."

112   Judith Butler, *Gender Trouble: Feminism and the Subversion of Identity* (New York: Routledge, 1999), 140–41.

113   Roderick A. Ferguson, *Aberrations in Black: Toward a Queer of Color Critique* (Minneapolis: University of Minnesota Press, 2003).

114   Ferguson, *Aberrations in Black*.

115   Ferguson, *Aberrations in Black*, 6.

116   To echo Tani Barlow's argument in the preface to *New Asian Marxisms*, my point here is not to develop a post-Marxist critique characterized by disillusionment, but to offer a postorthodox Marxist perspective to engage the local struggles that are commonly spawned by the difference-making machinery (particularly through sexuality) to reach for the universality through singularity (Tani Barlow, "Preface: Everything Diverges," in *New Asian Marxisms*, ed. Tani Barlow [Durham, NC: Duke University Press, 2002], vii–xv).

117   Engels, *The Origin of the Family, Private Property and the State*.

118   White, "The Origins of China's Birth Planning Policy," 254.

119   White, "The Origins of China's Birth Planning Policy."

120   See Zi'en Cui, "Queer China, 'Comrade' China," 2008, https://www.youtube.com/watch?v=2lrFdfLBTUY (accessed July 6, 2021).

121   See Cuncun Wu, "Beautiful Boys Made Up as Beautiful Girls: Anti-Masculine Taste in Qing China," in *Asian Masculinities*, 19–40. Also see Y. Wang, "Mr. Butterfly in Defunct Capital"); Wenqing Kang, *Obsession: Male Same-Sex Relations in China, 1900–1950* (Hong Kong: Hong Kong University Press, 2009); Howard Chiang and Ari Larissa Heinrich, *Queer Sinophone Cultures* (London: Routledge, 2014).

122   Greenhalgh and Winckler, *Governing China's Population*, 9.

123   Michel Foucault, *The History of Sexuality*, vol. 1: *The Will to Knowledge*, trans. Robert Hurley (London: Penguin, 1981).

2. Only If You Are the One!

1   Stefanie Knoll, "Why Australia Has Fallen Bizarrely in Love with a Chinese Dating Show," Public Radio International, October 9, 2015, https://www.pri.org/stories/2015-10-09/why-australia-has-fallen-bizarrely-love-chinese-dating-show.

2   "Shengnü chengwei shehui remen huati, jiemu tongguo chaozuo tigao shoushilv
      (Leftover women become a hot topic and TV program increases rating by sensation-
      alization)," *Xinmin Weekly*, June 2, 2010, http://news.sina.com.cn/s/sd/2010-06-02
      /120120395858.shtml.

3   Shaohua Guo, "When Dating Shows Encounter State Censors: A Case Study of *If You
      Are the One*," *Media, Culture and Society* 39, no. 4 (2017): 487–503.

4   See Guo, "When Dating Shows Encounter State Censors." Also see Shuyu Kong, "Are
      You the One? The Competing Public Voices of China's Post-1980s Generation," in
      Restless China, ed. Perry Link, Richard P. Madsen, and Paul G. Pickowicz (Lanham,
      MD: Rowman and Littlefield, 2013), 127–48; Luzhou Li, "*If You Are the One*: Dating
      Shows and Feminist Politics in Contemporary China," *International Journal of
      Cultural Studies* 18, no. 5 (2015): 519–35; Katherine Morrow, "Fei Cheng Wu Rao (非诚
      勿扰): Staging Global China through International Format Television and Overseas
      Special Episodes," *New Global Studies* 8, no. 3 (2014): 259–77.

5   Purnima Mankekar and Louisa Schein, "Mediations and Transmediations: Erotics,
      Sociality, and 'Asia,'" in *Media, Erotics, and Transnational Asia*, ed. Purnima
      Mankekar and Louisa Schein (Durham, NC: Duke University Press, 2012), 2.

6   Shu-mei Shih, "The Concept of the Sinophone," *PMLA* 126, no. 3 (2011): 710.

7   Howard Chiang, "(De)Provincializing China—Queer Historicism and Sinophone
      Postcolonial Critique," in *Queer Sinophone Cultures*, ed. Howard Chiang and Ari
      Larissa Heinrich (London: Routledge, 2014), 20. Also see Howard Chiang and Alvin
      Wong, "Asia Is Burning: Queer Asia as critique," *Culture, Theory and Critique* 58, no. 2
      (2017): 121–26; Petrus Liu, *Queer Marxism in Two Chinas* (Durham, NC: Duke Univer-
      sity Press, 2015).

8   Kong, "Are You the One?," 133.

9   Jiqiang Du, "Feichengwurao Ma Nuo yin 'baijin' bei maku, jin lunwei shengnü
      xianzhuang candan (Ma Nuo shed tears for criticisms of money worship and now
      becomes a miserable leftover woman)," China.com, April 12, 2017, http://news.china
      .com/socialgd/10000169/20170412/30411884_all.html.

10   Jinhua Dai, introduction to Jinhua Dai, *After the Post–Cold War: The Future of
      Chinese History*, ed. Lisa Rofel and trans. Jie Li (Durham, NC: Duke University Press,
      2018), 1–22.

11   Lisa Rofel, *Desiring China: Experiments in Neoliberalism, Sexuality, and Public Cul-
      ture* (Durham, NC: Duke University Press, 2007); Everett Yuehong Zhang, *The Impo-
      tence Epidemic: Men's Medicine and Sexual Desire in Contemporary China* (Durham,
      NC: Duke University Press, 2015); Tiantian Zheng, *Tongzhi Living: Men Attracted to
      Men in Postsocialist China* (Minneapolis: University of Minnesota Press, 2015).

12   Lauren Berlant, *Cruel Optimism* (Durham, NC: Duke University Press, 2012), 4.

13   Kong, "Are You the One?"

14   Feiyu, "Shijijiayuan IPO shouri shoupan 10.52 meiyuan (Jiayuan.com wrapped up at
      $10.52 after its first day of IPO)," *Sina*, May 12, 2011, http://tech.sina.com.cn/i/2011-05
      -12/04055511496.shtml.

15   Andrew F. Jones, *Yellow Music: Media Culture and Colonial Modernity in the Chinese
      Jazz Age* (Durham, NC: Duke University Press), 8 and 18.

16   Zhang, *The Impotence Epidemic*.

17 Anne Alison, *Nightwork: Sexuality, Pleasure, and Corporate Masculinity in a Tokyo Hostess Club* (Chicago: University of Chicago Press, 1994). Also see Kimberly Kay Hoang, *Dealing in Desire: Asian Ascendancy, Western Decline, and the Hidden Currencies of Global Sex Work* (Oakland: University of California Press, 2015).

18 Rofel, *Desiring China.*

19 Lai Lin Thomala, "Film Industry in China—Statistics and Facts," Statista, June 18, 2021, https://www.statista.com/topics/5776/film-industry-in-china/.

20 Silvia Wong, "'The Mermaid' Becomes China's Highest-Grossing Film," *Screen Daily*, February 23, 2016, https://www.screendaily.com/news/the-mermaid-becomes-chinas-highest-grossing-film/5100768.article.

21 Entgroup, "China Film Industry Report 2013–2014," accessed April 29, 2021, http://english.entgroup.cn/uploads/reports/ChinaFilmIndustryReport2013-2014(sharedversion)490.pdf.

22 Tania Lewis, Fran Martin, and Wanning Sun, *Telemodernities: Television and Transforming Lives in Asia* (Durham, NC: Duke University Press, 2016).

23 Purnima Mankekar and Louisa Schein, "Mediations and Transmediations: Erotics, Sociality, and 'Asia,'" in *Media, Erotics, and Transnational Asia*, ed. Purnima Mankekar and Louisa Schein (Durham, NC: Duke University Press, 2012), 2.

24 Yuezhi Zhao, *Media, Market, and Democracy in China: Between the Party Line and the Bottom Line* (Urbana: University of Illinois Press, 1998).

25 Zhao, *Media, Market, and Democracy in China.*

26 Chin-Chuan Lee, "Chinese Communication: Prisms, Trajectories, and Modes of Understanding," in *Power, Money, and Media: Communication Patterns and Bureaucratic Control in Cultural China*, ed. Chin-Chuan Lee, 3–44 (Evanston, IL: Northwestern University Press, 2000).

27 Chin-Chuan Lee, "The Global and the National of the Chinese Media," in *Chinese Media, Global Context*, ed. Chin-Chuan Lee (London: Routledge, 2003), 10.

28 Zhao, *Media, Market, and Democracy in China.*

29 "A Brief Introduction of JSBC," jsbc.com, April 15, 2021, http://www.jsbc.com/info/1608534497285.shtml.

30 According to JSBC's website, the organization contains "14 television channels, including 2 satellite television channels (Jiangsu Satellite Channel and International Channel), 7 terrestrial television channels (City Channel, Variety Show Channel, Film and TV Channel, Public Channel, Channel Win, Children's Channel, and Business Channel), and 4 digital pay TV channels (Fashion Channel, Kid's Education Channel, English Education Channel, and Fortune Channel), as well as a mobile TV channel (Jiangsu Mobile TV)" ("A Brief Introduction of JSBC").

31 Yuezhi Zhao, *Communication in China: Political Economy, Power, and Conflict* (Lanham, MD: Rowman and Littlefield, 2008), 112.

32 Zhao, *Communication in China*, 112.

33 Zhao, *Communication in China.*

34 Yuezhi Zhao, "Transnational Capital, the Chinese State, and China's Communication Industries in a Fractured Society," *Public/Javnost* 10, no. 4 (2003): 53–74.

35 Zhao, "Transnational Capital, the Chinese State, and China's Communication Industries in a Fractured Society."

36   Lee, "The Global and the National of the Chinese Media."

37   Zhao, *Communication in China*, 87.

38   Anthony Fung, *Global Capital, Local Culture: Transnational Media Corporations in China* (New York: Peter Lang, 2008), vx.

39   Chin-Chuan Lee, Zhou He, and Yu Huang, "'Chinese Party Publicity Inc.' Conglomerated: The Case of the Shenzhen Press Group," *Media, Culture and Society* 28, no. 4 (2006): 581–602.

40   Jing Wang, "Culture as Leisure and Culture as Capital," *Positions* 9, no. 1 (2001): 70.

41   Despite some slight changes in the program's design, Jiangsu Star TV was sued by Hunan Satellite TV for violating its copyright. See Yuan Ma and Jingjing Bo, "Feichengwurao xianru banquan zhengduozhan (*If You Are the One* gets into trouble for copyright issue)," *Xinhua Daily*, April 8, 2010, http://www.chinadaily.com.cn/dfpd /2010-04/08/content_9701054.htm.

42   Ning Zhan, "'Feichengwurao' dianshi xiangqin jiemu xushi huayu fenxi (Discursive analysis of the narrative paradigm of the TV dating game show *If You Are the One*)," crsqa.com, accessed July 15, 2021, https://www.crsqa.com/3DZvRB7D/.

43   Guo, "When Dating Shows Encounter State Censors," 491.

44   Michael Kimmel, *Manhood in America: A Cultural History* (New York: Free Press, 1996).

45   R. W. Connell, *Masculinities* (Cambridge: Polity Press, 2005); C. J. Pascoe, *Dude, You're a Fag: Masculinity and Sexuality in High School* (Berkeley: University of California Press, 2007).

46   For competition-based Western dating game shows, see *The Bachelor* of the United States and *Take Me Out* of Australia and the United Kingdom.

47   Alain Badiou and Peter Bush, *In Praise of Love* (New York: New Press, 2012).

48   Herbert Marcuse, *Eros and Civilization: A Philosophical Inquiry into Freud* (New York: Beacon Press, 1974).

49   Donovan Schaefer, *Religious Affects: Animality, Evolution, and Power* (Durham, NC: Duke University Press, 2015), 58.

50   Kathleen Stewart, *Ordinary Affects* (Durham, NC: Duke University Press, 2007), 4.

51   Jasbir Puar, *The Right to Maim: Debility, Capacity, Disability* (Durham, NC: Duke University Press, 2017), 19.

52   Max Horkheimer, *Eclipse of Reason* (New York: Seabury Press, 1974).

53   Charlie Yi Zhang, "Deconstructing the Hypermasculine National and Transnational Hegemony in Neoliberal China," *Feminist Studies* 40, no. 1 (2014): 13–38.

54   Biao Zeng, "Feichengwurao de kandian (Things to see in *If You Are the One*)," BBC, August 7, 2011, https://www.bbc.com/ukchina/simp/uk_education/2011/08/110805 _zengbiao_tv_show.

55   Rachel E. Dubrofsky, "The Bachelor: Whiteness in the Harem," *Critical Studies in Media Communication* 23, no. 1 (2006): 39–56.

56   "Meng Fei didiao xianshen wei dashigao cheng fengcheng zhengshidu chao xinwen (Meng Fei shows up in low profile and claims *If You Are the One* is more real than news)," CFC, June 12, 2012, https://bbs.comefromchina.com/threads/1096439/.

57   "Ways of Registration," official website of *If You Are the One*, accessed July 8, 2021, http://tv.jstv.com/fcwr/.

58　Jingyuan Shi, "Guangdianzongju zhengshi dianshi xiangqin jiemu jinzhi chaozuo baijin deng disu neirong (SARFT rectifies TV dating programs and prohibits worship of money and other vulgar content)," Sohu.com, June 10, 2010, https://yule.sohu.com /20100610/n272690377.shtml.

59　Michel Foucault, *The Birth of Biopolitics: Lectures at the Collège de France, 1978–1979*, trans. Graham Burchell (Basingstoke, UK: Palgrave Macmillan, 2008).

60　Mark Leonard, *What Does China Think?* (New York: Public Affairs, 2008).

61　Isaac Stone Fish, "Chinese Coup Watching," *Foreign Policy*, March 21, 2012, https:// foreignpolicy.com/2012/03/21/chinese-coup-watching/.

62　Foucault, *The Birth of Biopolitics*.

63　Kimmel, *Manhood in America*.

64　R. W. Connell and Julia Wood, "Globalization and Business Masculinities," *Men and Masculinities* 7, no. 4 (2005): 347–64.

65　Kimberly Kay Hoang, "Flirting with Capital: Negotiating Perceptions of Pan-Asian Ascendency and Western Decline in Global Sex Work," *Social Problems* 61, no. 4 (2014): 507–29.

66　David Harvey, *The New Imperialism* (New York: Oxford University Press, 2003).

67　Aradhana Sharma, *Logics of Empowerment: Development, Gender, and Governance in Neoliberal India* (Minneapolis: University of Minnesota Press, 2008).

68　Aihwa Ong, *Neoliberalism as Exception: Mutations in Citizenship and Sovereignty* (Durham, NC: Duke University Press, 2006).

69　Pun Ngai, *Made in China: Women Factory Workers in a Global Workplace* (Durham, NC: Duke University Press, 2005).

70　Jan Jindy Pettman, "Globalization and the Gendered Politics of Citizenship," in *Women, Citizenship and Difference*, ed. Pnina Werbner and Nira Yuval-Davis (London: Zed Books, 1999), 212.

71　Jane H. Bayes, Mary Hawkesworth, and Rita Mae Kelly, "Globalization, Democratization and Gender Regimes," in *Globalization, Democratization and Gender Regimes*, ed. Jane H. Bayes, Mary Hawkesworth, and Rita Mae Kelly (Boulder, CO: Rowman and Littlefield, 2001), 1–14.

72　Marianne H. Marchand and Anne Sisson Runyan, introduction to *Gender and Global Restructuring: Sightings, Sites, and Resistances*, ed. Marianne H. Marchand and Anne Sisson Runyan (New York: Routledge, 2000), 15.

73　Wei-hsin Yu, *Gendered Trajectories: Women, Work, and Social Change in Japan and Taiwan* (Stanford, CA: Stanford University Press, 2009). Also see Amanda ReCupido, "'Leftover Christmas Cake' and Other Anti-Feminist Expressions," *HuffPost*, August 31, 2009, https://www.huffingtonpost.com/amanda-recupido/leftover -christmas-cake-a_b_248364.html.

74　Nicole Tan, "Our Response to 'A PhD's Fine, but What about Love and Babies?,'" Association of Women for Action and Research, September 13, 2011, http://www.aware .org.sg/2011/09/our-response-to-a-phds-fine-but-what-about-love-and-babies/.

75　Leta Hong Fincher, *Leftover Women: The Resurgence of Gender Inequality in China* (London: Zed Books, 2014).

76　Mishuana Goeman, *Mark My Words: Native Women Mapping Our Nations* (Minneapolis: University of Minnesota Press, 2013).

77 Friedrich Engels, *The Origin of the Family, Private Property and the State*, intro. Tristram Hunt (London: Penguin Books, 2010).

78 Harvey, *The New Imperialism*.

79 Berlant, *Cruel Optimism*, 3.

80 Raquel Vidales, "Sanmao: A Chinese Woman's Tragic Love Story in Spain," *El Pais*, October 26, 2016, https://elpais.com/elpais/2016/10/25/inenglish/1477405923_390849.html.

81 Manya Koetse, "Remembering San Mao—the Bohemian Writer That Captured the Hearts of Millions of Chinese," Weibo, January 5, 2018, https://www.whatsonweibo.com/remembering-san-mao-beautiful-bohemian-writer-captured-hearts-millions-chinese/.

82 Sara Ahmed, "Happy Objects," in *The Affect Theory Reader*, ed. Melissa Gregg and Gregory J. Seigwoth (Durham, NC: Duke University Press, 2010), 33.

83 Stuart Elliott, "Sign of Arrival, for Xinhua, Is 60 Feet Tall," *New York Times*, July 25, 2011, http://www.nytimes.com/2011/07/26/business/media/xinhuas-giant-sign-to-blink-on-in-times-square.html.

84 Anton Troianovski, "China Agency Nears Times Square," *Wall Street Journal*, June 30, 2010, https://www.wsj.com/articles/SB10001424052748704334604575339281420753918.

85 J. Wang, "Culture as Leisure and Culture as Capital."

86 Knoll, "Why Australia Has Fallen Bizarrely in Love with a Chinese Dating Show."

87 Hong Liu, "New Migrants and the Revival of Overseas Chinese Nationalism," *Journal of Contemporary China* 14, no. 43 (2005): 291–316.

88 Peter Stalker, *Workers without Frontiers—The Impact of Globalization on International Migration* (Geneva: International Labour Organization, 2000).

89 Charlie Yi Zhang, "Untangling the Intersectional Biopolitics of Neoliberal Globalization: Asia, Asian, and the Asia-Pacific Rim," *Feminist Formations* 26, no. 3 (2014): 167–96.

90 Jie Zong and Jeanne Batalova, "Chinese Immigrants in the United States," Migration Policy Institute, September 29, 2017, https://www.migrationpolicy.org/article/chinese-immigrants-united-states-2016.

91 Liu, "New Migrants and the Revival of Overseas Chinese Nationalism."

92 Liu, "New Migrants and the Revival of Overseas Chinese Nationalism," 295.

93 Liu, "New Migrants and the Revival of Overseas Chinese Nationalism."

94 Liu, "New Migrants and the Revival of Overseas Chinese Nationalism."

95 Min Zhou and Rebecca Y. Kim, "Formation, Consolidation, and Diversification of the Ethnic Elite: The Case of the Chinese Immigrant Community in the United States," *Journal of International Migration and Integration* 2, no. 2 (2001): 227–47.

96 Zhang, "Untangling the Intersectional Biopolitics of Neoliberal Globalization."

97 Mike Swift, "Blacks, Latinos and Women Lose Ground at Silicon Valley Tech Companies," *Mercury News*, 2010, February 11, 2010, http://www.mercurynews.com/ci_14383730.

98 Aihwa Ong, *Flexible Citizenship: The Cultural Logics of Transnationality* (Durham, NC: Duke University Press, 1999).

99 Grace Kyungwon Hong, *The Ruptures of American Capital: Women of Color Feminism and the Culture of Immigrant Labor* (Minneapolis: University of Minnesota Press, 2006).

100 Ann Laura Stoler, *Race and the Education of Desire: Foucault's History of Sexuality and the Colonial Order of Things* (Durham, NC: Duke University Press, 1995). Also see Rey Chow, *The Protestant Ethnic and the Spirit of Capitalism* (New York: Columbia University Press, 2002); Michel Foucault, *The Government of Self and Others*, trans. Graham Burchell (New York: Picador, 2011).

101 Grace Kyungwon Hong and Roderick A. Ferguson, *Strange Affinities: The Gender and Sexual Politics of Comparative Racialization* (Minneapolis: University of Minnesota Press, 2011).

102 Catherine Lee, "'Where the Danger Lies': Race, Gender, and Chinese and Japanese in the United States, 1870–1924," *Sociological Forum* 25, no. 2 (2010): 248–71. Also see Nayan Shah, *Stranger Intimacy: Contesting Race, Sexuality, and the Law in the North American West* (Berkeley: University of California Press, 2012).

103 Ara Wilson, *The Intimate Economies of Bangkok: Tomboys, Tycoons, and Avon Ladies in the Global City* (Berkeley: University of California Press, 2004). See also Kwai-cheung Lo, *Excess and Masculinity in Asian Cultural Productions* (Albany: State University of New York Press, 2010); Hui Wang, "The Politics of Imagining Asia: A Genealogical Analysis," *Inter-Asia Cultural Studies* 8, no. 1 (2007): 1–33; Ong, *Flexible Citizenship*.

104 Aihwa Ong, *Buddha Is Hiding: Refugees, Citizenship, the New America* (Berkeley: University of California Press, 2003), 14.

105 Eduardo Bonilla-Silva, *Racism without Racists: Color-Blind Racism and the Persistence of Racial Inequality in the United States* (Lanham, MD: Rowman and Littlefield, 2010).

106 Daryl Maeda, *Rethinking the Asian American Movement* (London: Routledge, 2011).

107 Ong, *Flexible Citizenship*.

108 See Stoler, *Race and the Education of Desire*. Also see Chow, *The Protestant Ethnic and the Spirit of Capitalism*; Cedric J. Robinson, *Black Marxism: The Making of the Black Radical Tradition*, 2nd ed. (Chapel Hill: University of North Carolina Press, 2000).

109 Puar, *The Right to Maim*.

110 David Harvey, *A Brief History of Neoliberalism* (New York: Oxford University Press, 2005).

111 Ong, *Flexible Citizenship*.

112 David Kang, *China Rising: Peace, Power, and Order in East Asia* (New York: Columbia University Press, 2007), 6.

113 Huiyao Wang, David Zweig, and Xiaohua Lin, "Returnee Entrepreneurs: Impact on China's Globalization Process," *Journal of Contemporary China* 20, no. 70 (2011), 413.

114 Delia Lin, "The CCP's Exploitation of Confucianism and Legalism," in *Routledge Handbook of the Chinese Communist Party*, ed. Willy Wo-Lap Lam (London: Routledge, 2020), 47–58.

115 Morrow, "Fei Cheng Wu Rao."

116 Xinrui Zhu and Shuai Yan, "The State Press, Publication, Radio, Film and Television Administration Issued a Document to Promote the Independent Innovation of the TV Program," People.cn, June 20, 2016, http://media.people.com.cn/n1/2016/0620/c40606-28456837.html.

117 "Australia Battles Chinese Political Influence," *Economist*, June 17, 2017, https://www
.economist.com/news/asia/21723454-it-will-be-uphill-struggle-australia-battles
-chinese-political-influence. Also see David Fisher and Matt Nippert, "Revealed:
China's Network of Influence in New Zealand," *NZ Herald*, September 19, 2017,
http://www.nzherald.co.nz/business/news/article.cfm?c_id=3&objectid=11924169;
Elizabeth Redden, "China's 'Long Arm,'" *Inside Higher Ed*, January 3, 2018, https://
www.insidehighered.com/news/2018/01/03/scholars-and-politicians-raise-concerns
-about-chinese-governments-influence-over.

118 Steven Ward, "Because China Isn't 'Caucasian,' the U.S. Is Planning for a 'Clash of
Civilizations.' That Could Be Dangerous," *Washington Post*, May 4, 2019, https://www
.washingtonpost.com/politics/2019/05/04/because-china-isnt-caucasian-us-is
-planning-clash-civilizations-that-could-be-dangerous/?noredirect=on&utm_term=
.b91caaae7483.

119 Zhen Liu, "Chinese Americans on Supporting Trump: 'There's Nothing to Be
Ashamed of,'" *Business Insider*, November 1, 2016, https://www.businessinsider.com
/chinese-americans-supporting-donald-trump-2016-11.

120 J. Weston Phippen, "Asians Now Outpace Mexicans in Terms of Undocumented
Growth," *Atlantic*, August 20, 2015, https://www.theatlantic.com/politics/archive
/2015/08/asians-now-outpace-mexicans-in-terms-of-undocumented-growth
/432603/.

121 Vivian Yee, Kenan Davis, and Jugal K. Patel, "Here's the Reality about Illegal Immigrants in the United States," *New York Times*, March 6, 2017, https://www.nytimes.com
/interactive/2017/03/06/us/politics/undocumented-illegal-immigrants.html?_r=0.

122 Jie Li, "Zichan guoyi furen 27% yi yimin jinsannian chao 170 yi liuxiang guowai (27%
of China's billionaires already migrated with the flight of over 17 billion yuan to
foreign countries in recent three years)," *Global Times*, January 6, 2013, http://finance
.huanqiu.com/life/2013-01/3450050.html.

123 Iyko Day, *Alien Capital: Asian Racialization and the Logic of Settler Colonial Capitalism* (Durham, NC: Duke University Press, 2016).

124 Maximilian Kärnfelt, "China's Tight Capital Controls Fail to Address Underlying Problems," *Financial Times*, November 10, 2017, https://www.ft.com/content/1d288888
-c613-11e7-b2bb-322b2cb39656.

125 Demetri Sevastopulo, "China Cracks Down on 'Naked Officials,'" *Financial Times*,
June 8, 2014, https://www.ft.com/content/9d1f3a88-ef01-11e3-acad-00144feabdc0.

3. The Woeful Landscape of Love

Epigraphs: Yihong Tang, "Returning Home Backwards," in *Iron Moon: An Anthology
of Chinese Migrant Worker Poetry*, ed. Qin Xiaoyu and trans. Eleanor Goodman
(Buffalo, NY: White Pine Press, 2016), 51, and Yihong Tang, "It Seems I'm Really His
Father," in *Iron Moon*, 52.

1   Lauren Berlant, *Cruel Optimism* (Durham, NC: Duke University Press, 2012), 1.

2   Aimee Bahng, *Migrant Futures: Decolonizing Speculation in Financial Times*
(Durham, NC: Duke University Press, 2017).

3 Zhi Fei, "Zhongguoshi xiangqin: Wo erzi cai 33, bukaolnü mei Beijing hukou de guniang (Chinese-style blind date: My son is only 33 and won't consider any girls without
Beijing *hukou*)," *Phoenix Weekly*, July 11, 2017. https://chinadigitaltimes.net/chinese
/2017/07/%E5%87%A4%E5%87%Boweekly-%E4%B8%AD%E5%9B%BD%E5%BC%8F%
E7%9B%B8%E4%BA%B2%E4%BB%B7%E7%9B%AE%E8%A1%A8/.

4 Pinhui Zhuang, "The Beijing Marriage Market: Putting a Price on a Perfect Match
in a Chinese Park," *South China Morning Post*, July 14, 2017, http://www.scmp.com
/news/china/society/article/2102712/beijing-marriage-market-putting-price-perfect
-match-chinese-park.

5 Zhuang, "The Beijing Marriage Market."

6 He-Yin Zhen, "Economic Revolution and Women's Revolution," in *The Birth of Chinese Feminism: Essential Texts in Transnational Theory*, ed. Lydia H. Liu, Rebecca E.
Karl, and Dorothy Ko, 92–104 (New York: Columbia University Press, 2013).

7 Lydia H. Liu, Rebecca E. Karl, and Dorothy Ko, "Introduction: Toward a Transnational Theory," in *The Birth of Chinese Feminism*, 7.

8 Deborah Davis and Steven Harrell, "Introduction: The Impact of Post-Mao Reforms
on Family Life," in *Chinese Families in the Post-Mao Era*, ed. Deborah Davis and
Steven Harrell (Berkeley: University of California Press, 1992), 1–22.

9 Interview by the author, May 18, 2012, Hai'an, China.

10 Jinhua Dai, introduction to Jinhua Dai, *After the Post–Cold War: The Future of Chinese
History*, ed. Lisa Rofel and trans. Jie Li (Durham, NC: Duke University Press, 2018),
1–22.

11 Cheng Li, *Rediscovering China: Dynamics and Dilemmas of Reform* (Lanham, MD:
Rowman and Littlefield, 1997), 3.

12 Fulong Wu, "Real Estate Development and the Transformation of Urban Space in
China's Transitional Economy, with Special Reference to Shanghai," in *The New
Chinese City: Globalization and Market Reform*, ed. John Logan (Oxford: Blackwell,
2002), 153–66.

13 Ding Ding, Xiaoyu Huang, Tao Jin, and W. Raphael Lam, "Assessing China's Residential Real Estate Market" International Monetary Fund Working Paper, November 2017,
https://www.imf.org/~/media/Files/Publications/WP/2017/wp17248.ashx.

14 Fulong Wu, Jiang Xu, and Anthony Gar-On Yeh, *Urban Development in Post-Reform
China: State, Market, and Space* (London: Routledge, 2006), 14.

15 Jinyue Dong and Le Xia, "China: How Resilient Is the Economy to Housing Price
Fall?" BBVA Research, March 2018, https://www.bbvaresearch.com/wp-content
/uploads/2018/03/20180326_China-Housing-market_edi.pdf.

16 Informal interview by the author, May 21, 2012, Hai'an, China.

17 Shenghui Weng, "Shishang zuiqiang maifang guanggao: Meifang zhineng jiao ayi
(The most impressive housing ad in history: You can only call 'aunt' if you have no
property)," HouseFun, March 7, 2017, https://news.housefun.com.tw/news/article
/184617156227.html.

18 Mingyu, "Danshennan gongxian 2% jingji zengzhang: Hunyin yu jingji de aimei
guanxi (Single men contribute to 2% of the GDP growth: The ambiguous relationship
between marriage and the economy)," CCTV, February 24, 2013, http://jingji.cntv.cn
/2013/02/24/ARTI1361687207280124.shtml.

19 Yuxi Zhang, "Quanguo chengzhen fangjia shinian zhangfu 143%: Huobi bianzhi fang-jia shiji zai die? (A 143% growth of China's urban housing price in the last decade: An actual price drop with inflation?)," ChinaNews.com, February 26, 2013, http://www.chinanews.com/house/2013/02-26/4597511.shtml.

20 Economist Intelligence Unit, "China's Supply-Side Structural Reforms: Progress and Outlook," 2017, https://www.eiu.com/public/topical_report.aspx?campaignid=ChinaSSSR2017.

21 Interview by the author, May 30, 2012, Hai'an, China.

22 Friedrich Engels, *The Origin of the Family, Private Property and the State*, intro. Tristram Hunt (London: Penguin Books, 2010).

23 Informal interview by the author, May 22, 2012, Hai'an, China.

24 Informal Interview by the author, May 30, 2012, Hai'an, China.

25 Lee Edelman, "The Future Is Kid Stuff: Queer Theory, Disidentification, and the Death Drive," *Narrative* 6, no. 1 (1998): 18–31.

26 Simon Denyer and Luna Lin, "Mass Evictions in Freezing Beijing Winter Sparks Public Outrage but Little Official Remorse," *Washington Post*, November 27, 2017, https://www.washingtonpost.com/news/worldviews/wp/2017/11/27/forced-evictions-in-freezing-beijing-winter-sparks-public-outrage-but-little-official-remorse/?noredirect=on&utm_term=.16df7ea9bb70.

27 Hilary Whiteman, "Deaths in Dumpster Expose Plight of China's Street Kids," CNN, November 22, 2012, https://www.cnn.com/2012/11/21/world/asia/china-boys-dead-dumpster/index.html.

28 Tom Phillips, "Chinese Police 'Find Suicide Note' in Case of 'Left Behind' Children Deaths," *Guardian*, June 14, 2015, https://www.theguardian.com/world/2015/jun/14/chinese-police-investigating-deaths-of-left-behind-children-find-suicide-note.

29 Lijia Zhang, "One of 60 Million: Life as a 'Left-Behind' Child in China," *South China Morning Post*, January 21, 2018, http://www.scmp.com/week-asia/society/article/2128700/one-60-million-life-left-behind-child-china.

30 Berlant, *Cruel Optimism*, 95.

31 Lixin Fan, dir., *Last Train Home* (Montreal: EyeSteelFilm, 2019).

32 Dorothy J. Solinger, "China's Floating Population," in *The Paradox of China's Post-Mao Reforms*, ed. Merle Goldman and Roderick Macfarquhar (Cambridge, MA: Harvard University Press, 1999), 225.

33 Solinger, "China's Floating Population," 222.

34 Solinger, "China's Floating Population."

35 Martin King Whyte, "The Paradoxes of Rural-Urban Inequality in Contemporary China," in *One Country, Two Societies: Rural-Urban Inequality in Contemporary China*, ed. Martin King Whyte (Cambridge, MA: Harvard University Press, 2010), 1–25.

36 Barry Naughton, "China's Transition in Economic Perspective," in *The Paradox of China's Post-Mao Reforms*, 40.

37 Interview by the author, July 28, 2012, Wuxi, China.

38 Solinger, "China's Floating Population."

39 Interview by the author, June 18, 2012, Wuxi, China.

40 Anita Chan, *China's Workers under Assault: The Exploitation of Labor in a Globalizing Economy* (Armonk, NY: East Gate Press, 2001), 8.

41 Merle Goldman and Roderick Macfarquhar, "Dynamic Economy, Declining Party-State," in *The Paradox of China's Post-Mao Reforms*, 3–29; Whyte, "The Paradoxes of Rural-Urban Inequality in Contemporary China."

42 Helen Gao, "China's Education Gap," *New York Times*, September 4, 2014, https://www.nytimes.com/2014/09/05/opinion/sunday/chinas-education-gap.html.

43 Qiang Wang, "Rural Students Are Being Left behind in China," *Nature*, June 25, 2014, https://www.nature.com/news/rural-students-are-being-left-behind-in-china-1.15448.

44 Ruth Wilson Gilmore, *Golden Gulag: Prisons, Surplus, Crisis, and Opposition in Globalizing California* (Berkeley: University of California Press, 2007).

45 Whyte, "The Paradoxes of Rural-Urban Inequality in Contemporary China."

46 "Europe and Right-Wing Nationalism: A Country-by-Country Guide," bbc, November 13, 2019, https://www.bbc.com/news/world-europe-36130006.

47 Naughton, "China's Transition in Economic Perspective," 43.

48 Emily Honig and Gail Hershatter, *Personal Voices: Chinese Women in the 1980's* (Stanford, CA: Stanford University Press, 1988); Elizabeth J. Perry and Mark Selden, "Introduction: Reform and Resistance in Contemporary China," in *Chinese Society: Change, Conflict and Resistance*, ed. Elizabeth J. Perry and Mark Selden, 1–30 (London: Routledge, 2010); Heying Jenny Zhan and Rhonda J. V. Montgomery, "Gender and Elder Care in China: The Influence of Filial Piety and Structural Constraints," *Gender and Society* 17, no. 2 (2003): 209–29.

49 Xiangming Chen, "A Globalizing City on the Rise: Shanghai's Transformation in Comparative Perspective," in *Shanghai Rising: State Power and Local Transformations in a Global Megacity*, ed. Xiangming Chen, xv–xxxv (Minneapolis: University of Minnesota Press, 2009).

50 Delia Davin, "The Impact of Export-Oriented Manufacturing on the Welfare Entitlements of Chinese Women Workers," in *Globalization, Export-Oriented Employment and Social Policy*, ed. Shahra Razavi, Ruth Pearson, and Caroline Danloy (New York: Palgrave Macmillan, 2004), 67–90.

51 Xun Lian, "Qiye wei jianzhu nügong pai xiezhen, nühanzi bian nüshen (Corporation takes photos of female construction workers, female men turned into goddesses)," Xinhua, March 3, 2015. http://www.xinhuanet.com/politics/2015-03/03/c_1114494569.

52 Honig and Hershatter, *Personal Voices*.

53 Ngai Pun, *Made in China: Women Factory Workers in a Global Workplace* (Durham, NC: Duke University Press, 2005).

54 Interview by the author, July 26, 2012, Wuxi, China.

55 Interview by the author, July 26, 2012, Wuxi, China.

56 Pun, *Made in China*, 136.

57 Aihwa Ong, *Neoliberalism as Exception: Mutations in Citizenship and Sovereignty* (Durham, NC: Duke University Press, 2006).

58 Saskia Sassen, "The Global City Perspective: Theoretical Implications for Shanghai," in *Shanghai Rising*, 3–29; Yan Hairong, *New Masters, New Servants: Migration, Development, and Women Workers in China* (Durham, NC: Duke University Press, 2008).

59 Bahng, *Migrant Futures*, 128–29.

60 Ong, *Neoliberalism as Exception*.

61 "Xi'an Chengdu Wuhan deng shiliu cheng qiang rencai song hukou gei xianjin buxiangou (Sixteen cities including Xi'an, Chengdu, and Wuhan vying to attract talents with offers of *hukou*, cash, and unrestricted rights to buy property)," Sina .com.cn, January 15, 2018, http://finance.sina.com.cn/china/gncj/2018-01-15/doc -ifyqqciz7104848.shtml.

62 Fan, *Last Train Home*.

63 Janet Collins, *Threads: Gender, Labor, and Power in the Global Apparel Industry* (Chicago: University of Chicago Press, 2003), 13–14.

64 Davin, "The Impact of Export-Oriented Manufacturing on the Welfare Entitlements of Chinese Women Workers," 78.

65 Shixing Liu, "Shengxia sanqianwan: Nongcun shengnan diaocha baogao zhiyi (Thirty million unmarried: An investigation of China's rural single men)," Huanqiu.com, February 23, 2016, https://china.huanqiu.com/article/9CaKrnJU2jJ.

66 "Demand for Wives in China Endangers Women Who Live on Its Borders," *Economist*, November 4, 2017, https://www.economist.com/china/2017/11/04/demand-for -wives-in-china-endangers-women-who-live-on-its-borders.

67 Yihong Tang, "Hide That Uniform Away," in *Iron Moon*, 53.

68 Interview by the author, August 3, 2012, Wuxi, China.

69 Interview by the author, August 3, 2012, Wuxi, China.

70 Roderick A. Ferguson, *Aberrations in Black: Toward a Queer of Color Critique* (Minneapolis: University of Minnesota Press, 2003).

71 Quoted in "Housing Should Be for Living In, Not for Speculation, Xi Says," Bloomberg News, October 18, 2017, https://www.bloomberg.com/news/articles/2017-10-18/xi -renews-call-housing-should-be-for-living-in-not-speculation.

72 Bahng, *Migrant Futures*, 5. Also see Brian Massumi, *The Power at the End of the Economy* (Durham, NC: Duke University Press, 2014).

73 Jasbir Puar, *The Right to Maim: Debility, Capacity, Disability* (Durham, NC: Duke University Press, 2017), 81.

74 Frank Fang, "Russian Media Is Harshly Critical of China's 'One Belt, One Road' Projects in Eurasia," *Epoch Times*, August 8, 2018, https://www.theepochtimes.com/russian -media-harshly-criticizes-chinas-one-belt-one-road-projects-in-eurasia_2618886.html; Liu Xinyu, "Tepuhui hou e yulun zhuanxiang pi yidaiyilu (Russia starting to criticize Belt and Road Initiative after Trump-Putin meeting)," Radio Free Asia, August 7, 2018, https://www.rfa.org/mandarin/yataibaodao/junshiwaijiao/lxy-08072018102247.html.

75 Naughton, "China's Transition in Economic Perspective."

76 Philip Martin, *Promise Unfulfilled: Unions, Immigration, and Farm Workers* (Ithaca, NY: Cornell University Press, 2003); Souad Mekhennet, "A 50-Year Journey for Turkey and Germany," *New York Times*, October 30, 2011, https://www.nytimes.com/2011/10 /31/world/europe/turks-recall-german-guest-worker-program.html.

77 Aihwa Ong, *Buddha Is Hiding: Refugees, Citizenship, the New America* (Berkeley: University of California Press, 2003).

78 Interview by the author, August 8, 2012, Chengdu, China.

79 A. Chan, *China's Workers under Assault*.

80 Ngai Pun and Anita Koo, "A 'World-Class' (Labor) Camp/us: Foxconn and China's New Generation of Labor Migrants," *Positions* 23, no. 3 (2015): 417.

81 Susan Naquin and Evelyn S. Rawski, *Chinese Society in the Eighteenth Century* (New Haven, CT: Yale University Press, 1989), 47.

82 Wanning Sun, "Suzhi on the Move: Body, Place and Power," *Positions* 17, no.,3 (2009): 617–42.

83 Emily Honig, *Creating Chinese Ethnicity: Subei People in Shanghai, 1850–1980* (New Haven, CT: Yale University Press, 1992).

84 Honig, *Creating Chinese Ethnicity*, 4.

85 Focus group by the author, June 22, 2012, Hai'an, China.

86 Nayan Shah, *Stranger Intimacy: Contesting Race, Sexuality, and the Law in the North American West* (Berkeley: University of California Press, 2012).

87 Interview by the author, July 26, 2012, Wuxi, China. Also see Bing Ye, "Shenzhen weiquan shengyuantuan zao qingchang, shengyuanzhe shilian (Shenzhen solidarity groups supporting workers' rights suppressed by the state, supporters disappearing)," Voice of America, August 24, 2018, https://www.voachinese.com/a/voanews -20180824-china-police-raided-students-backing-shenzhen-workers/4542455.html.

88 Alexandra Dobrowolsky and Evangelia Tastsoglou, *Women, Migration and Citizenship: Making Local, National and Transnational Connections* (Aldershot, UK: Ashgate, 2006), 5.

89 Interview by the author, July 26, 2012, Wuxi, China.

90 Donovan Schaefer, *Religious Affects: Animality, Evolution, and Power* (Durham, NC: Duke University Press, 2015), 67.

91 Brian Massumi, "The Future Birth of the Affective Fact: The Political Ontology of Threat," in *The Affect Theory Reader*, ed. Melissa Gregg and Gregory J. Seigworth (Durham, NC: Duke University Press, 2010), 54 (emphasis in the original).

92 Berlant, *Cruel Optimism*, 2.

4. Lessons from the Polarizing Love

1 David Harvey, *The New Imperialism* (New York: Oxford University Press, 2003), 43.

2 Harvey, *The New Imperialism*, 91.

3 Finbarr Bermingham and Jeong-ho Lee, "How the Trade War Led to Samsung and Other South Korean Companies' Exodus from China," *South China Morning Post*, July 4, 2019, https://www.scmp.com/economy/china-economy/article/3017110 /samsung-and-other-south-korean-firms-exodus-china-example. Also see Mark Gongloff, "The Next Reboot: Cold War, This Time with China," Bloomberg, August 13, 2018, https://www.bloomberg.com/opinion/articles/2018-08-13/trump-s-china -trade-war-could-be-the-first-step-in-a-cold-war; Peter Beinart, "Trump Is Preparing for a New Cold War," *Atlantic*, February 27, 2018, https://www.theatlantic.com /international/archive/2018/02/trump-is-preparing-for-a-new-cold-war/554384/.

4 Fareed Zakaria, "Trump Is Right: China's a Trade Cheat," *Washington Post*, April 5, 2018, https://www.washingtonpost.com/opinions/global-opinions/trump-is-right -chinas-a-trade-cheat/2018/04/05/6cd69054-390f-11e8-8fd2-49fe3c675a89_story.html.

5 Zakaria, "Trump Is Right."

6 John Micklethwait, Margaret Talev, and Jennifer Jacobs, "Trump Threatens to Pull U.S. out of WTO If It Doesn't 'Shape Up,'" Bloomberg, August 30, 2018, https://

www.bloomberg.com/news/articles/2018-08-30/trump-says-he-will-pull-u-s-out-of
-wto-if-they-don-t-shape-up.

7 Michael Graham, "Commentary: Here's One Reason Trump's Average Approval Rating Is Going Up," CBS News, September 3, 2018, https://www.cbsnews.com/news /commentary-heres-one-reason-trumps-average-approval-rating-is-going-up/.

8 "The GDP Data of Nantong Areas, 1978–2017," Wordpress.com, June 16, 2018, https:// malooo0.wordpress.com/2018/06/16/1978%E5%B9%B4%E8%87%B32017%E5%8D%97 %E9%80%9A%E5%9C%B0%E5%8C%BA%E5%90%84%E5%8E%BF%E5%B8%82%E5%8 E%86%E5%B9%B4gdp%E6%95%B0%E6%8D%AE/.

9 Malcolm Moore, "Communist Party Congress: A Decade under Hu Jintao and Wen Jiabao," Telegraph, November 14, 2012, https://www.telegraph.co.uk/news/worldnews /asia/china/9677748/Communist-Party-Congress-a-decade-under-Hu-Jintao-and -Wen-Jiabao.html.

10 National Bureau of Statistics of China, "2012 guomin jingji fazhan wenzhongyoujin (China's national economy developed with stability in 2012)," January 18, 2013, http:// www.stats.gov.cn/tjsj/zxfb/201301/t20130118_12924.html.

11 Alice Luo, "Ten Years of China under Hu Jintao and Wen Jiabao," Ever, November 19, 2012, http://blogs.ubc.ca/aliceqianluo/2012/11/19/ten-years-of-china-under-hu -jintao-and-wen-jiabao/.

12 Informal conversation by the author, May 31, 2012, Hai'an, China.

13 Informal conversation by the author, July 8, 2012, Wuxi, China. Also see informal conversations by the author, July 12 and 18, 2012, Wuxi, China.

14 Fulong Wu, Jiang Xu, and Anthony Gar-On Yeh, Urban Development in Post-Reform China: State, Market, and Space (London: Routledge, 2006).

15 Mariana Mazzucato, The Entrepreneurial State: Debunking Public vs. Private Sector Myths (London: Anthem Press, 2013).

16 Wu, Xu, and Yeh, Urban Development in Post-Reform China.

17 Martin King Whyte, "The Changing Role of Workers," in The Paradox of China's Post-Mao Reforms, ed. Merle Goldman and Roderick Macfarquhar (Cambridge, MA: Harvard University Press, 1999), 173–96. Also see Yasheng Huang, Capitalism with Chinese Characteristics: Entrepreneurship and the State (New York: Cambridge University Press, 2008).

18 Harvey, The New Imperialism, 146.

19 Ramón Grosfoguel and Ana Margarita Cervantes-Rodríguez, "Unthinking Twentieth-Century Eurocentric Mythologies: Universal Knowledges, Decolonialization, and Developmentalism," in The Modern/Colonial/Capitalist World-System in the Twentieth Century: Global Processes, Antisystemic Movements and the Geopolitics of Knowledge, ed. Ramón Grosfoguel and Ana Margarita Cervantes-Rodríguez (Westport, CT: Greenwood Press, 2002), 11–30.

20 Elizabeth J. Perry and Mark Selden, "Introduction: Reform and Resistance in Contemporary China," in Chinese Society: Change, Conflict and Resistance, ed. Elizabeth J. Perry and Mark Selden (London: Routledge, 2010), 1–30.

21 Sari Wahyuni, Esther Sri Astuti, and Karina Miaprajna Utari, "Critical Outlook at Special Economic Zone in Asia: A Comparison between Indonesia, Malaysia, Thailand and China," Journal of Indonesian Economy and Business 28, no. 3 (2013): 336–46.

22 "China Plans to Build Hainan into Pilot Free Trade Zone," Xinhua, April 14, 2018, http://www.xinhuanet.com/english/2018-04/14/c_137109412.htm.

23 Janet Collins, *Threads: Gender, Labor, and Power in the Global Apparel Industry* (Chicago: University of Chicago Press, 2003).

24 J. Collins, *Threads*.

25 Interview by the author, June 6, 2012, Hai'an, China.

26 Michael Hardt and Antonio Negri, *Empire* (Cambridge, MA: Harvard University Press, 2000).

27 Joseph Stiglitz, *Globalization and Its Discontents* (New York: W. W. Norton, 2002).

28 Jeff Stein and Erica Werner, "White House Floats Large Corporate Tax Cut for Firms That Bring Jobs Back from Overseas," *Washington Post*, May 15, 2020, https://www.washingtonpost.com/business/2020/05/15/white-house-floats-large-corporate-tax-cut-firms-that-bring-jobs-back-overseas/.

29 Henry Blodget, "Foxconn Explains Cause of iPhone 5 Shortages That Are Hammering Apple's Stock," October 17, 2012, Insider, https://www.businessinsider.com/foxconn-explains-trouble-making-iphone-5-2012-10.

30 Michael Hardt, "Globalization and Democracy," GHC *Working Papers*, January (2011): 13.

31 Charlie Yi Zhang, "Mapping the Will for Otherwise: Towards an Intersectional Critique of the Biopolitical System of Neoliberal Governmentality," in *Biopolitical Governance: Gender, Race and Economy*, ed. Hannah Richter (Lanham, MD: Rowman and Littlefield, 2018), 155.

32 Focus group by the author, June 15, 2012, Hai'an, China.

33 Focus group by the author, June 22, 2012, Hai'an, China.

34 Charlie Yi Zhang, "Untangling the Intersectional Biopolitics of Neoliberal Globalization: Asia, Asian, and the Asia-Pacific Rim," in *Feminist Formations* 26, no. 3 (2014): 167–96.

35 Laura Hyun Yi Kang, "The Uses of Asianization: Figuring Crises, 1997–8 and 2007–?," in "Race, Empire and the Crisis of the Subprime," special issue, *American Quarterly* 64, no.3 (September 2012): 413.

36 Pheng Cheah, *Inhuman Conditions: On Cosmopolitanism and Human Rights* (Cambridge, MA: Harvard University Press, 2006).

37 Interview by the author, July 26, 2012, Wuxi, China.

38 Interview by the author, July 26, 2012, Wuxi, China.

39 Jenny Chan, "Shenzhen Jasic Technology: Towards a Worker-Student Coalition in China," *New Politics*, August 31, 2018, http://newpol.org/content/shenzhen-jasic-technology-towards-workerstudent-coalition-china. Also see Mimi Lau, "Chinese Maoists Join Students in Fight for Workers' Rights at Jasic Technology," *South China Morning Post*, August 10, 2018, https://www.scmp.com/news/china/policies-politics/article/2158991/chinese-maoists-join-students-fight-workers-rights.

40 Sue-Lin Wong and Christian Shepherd, "Some Chinese Student Activists Released after Police Raid," Reuters, August 28, 2018, https://ca.reuters.com/article/topNews/idCAKCN1LD1DQ-OCATP.

41 Charlie Yi Zhang, "Deconstructing the Hypermasculine National and Transnational Hegemony in Neoliberal China," *Feminist Studies* 40, no. 1 (2014): 13–38.

42 Ann Anagnost, "From 'Class' to 'Social Strata': Grasping the Social Totality in Reform-Era China," *Third World Quarterly* 29, no. 3 (2008): 497–519.

43 Wanning Sun, *Subaltern China: Rural Migrants, Media, and Cultural Practices* (Lanham, MD: Rowman and Littlefield, 2014), 243.

44 Feng Wang, "In the Spring," mulanci.org, accessed August 12, 2021, https://www.mulanci.org/lyric/sh176604/, my translation.

45 Andrew F. Jones, *Like a Knife: Ideology and Genre in Contemporary Chinese Popular Music* (Ithaca, NY: Cornell University Press, 2010), 3–4.

46 Xuri Yanggang, "In the Spring," Youku.com, November 19, 2010, https://v.youku.com/v_show/id_XMjIzNDk3MTY4.html.

47 "Hunan shengwei shuji cheng ting nonminggong chang 'chuntianli' releiyingkuang (Secretary of Hunan Provincial Committee of the CCP moved to tears by the migrant worker vocal duo)," Sohu.com, November 11, 2010, http://cul.sohu.com/20101111/n277535229.shtml.

48 Zhang, "Mapping the Will for Otherwise."

49 Yunxiang Yan, *Private Life under Socialism: Love, Intimacy, and Family Change in a Chinese Village 1949–1999* (Stanford, CA: Stanford University Press, 2003).

50 Yan, *Private Life under Socialism*.

51 Judith Stacey, *Patriarchy and Socialist Revolution in China* (Berkeley: University of California Press, 1983). Also see Phyllis Andors, *The Unfinished Liberation of Chinese Women, 1949–1980* (Bloomington: Indiana University Press, 1983); Margery Wolf, *Revolution Postponed: Women in Contemporary China* (Stanford, CA: Stanford University Press, 1985).

52 Deborah Davis and Steven Harrell, "Introduction: The Impact of Post-Mao Reforms on Family Life," in *Chinese Families in the Post-Mao Era*, ed. Deborah S. Davis and Steven Harrell (Berkeley: University of California Press, 1992), 1–2.

53 Zhang, "Untangling the Intersectional Biopolitics of Neoliberal Globalization."

54 Interview by the author, May 29, 2012, Hai'an, China.

55 Deborah S. Davis, "Introduction: Urban China," in *Urban Spaces in Contemporary China: The Potential for Autonomy and Community in Post-Mao China*, ed. Deborah S. Davis et al. (New York: Cambridge University Press, 1995), 5.

56 Davis, "Introduction."

57 Rob Brooks, "China's Biggest Problem? Too Many Men," CNN, March 4, 2013, http://www.cnn.com/2012/11/14/opinion/china-challenges-one-child-brooks.

58 Kathleen E. McLaughlin, "China and the Worst-Ever, Man-Made Gender Gap," World, January 3, 2013, https://www.pri.org/stories/2013-01-03/china-and-worst-ever-man-made-gender-gap.

59 Eugene K. Chow, "China's Trafficked Brides," *Diplomat*, July 19, 2017, https://thediplomat.com/2017/07/chinas-trafficked-brides/.

60 Yunxiang Yan, "Intergenerational Intimacy and Descending Familism in Rural North China," *American Anthropologist* 118, no. 2 (2016): 244–57.

61 Informal conversation by the author, May 30, 2012, Hai'an, China.

62 Alec Ash, "Is China's Gaokao the World's Toughest School Exam?," *Guardian*, October 12, 2016, https://www.theguardian.com/world/2016/oct/12/gaokao-china-toughest-school-exam-in-world.

63 Interview by the author, July 17, 2012, Wuxi, China.

64 Interview by the author, July 17, 2012, Wuxi, China.

65 Pengying Zhu, "Zhusanjiao xinyilun mingonghuang diaocha: Jingji huinuan qiye que zhaobudao ren (Investigation into the new round of labor shortages in the Pearl River Delta: Hard to recruit workers despite economic recovery)," ChinaNews.com, January 25, 2010, http://www.chinanews.com/gn/news/2010/01-25/2088900.shtml.

66 "Daxuesheng qiangzhi zai fushikang shixi xu: Xiaofang cheng shi tiyan shenghuo (Enforced college interns in Foxconn: To get more lived experience as alleged by the school)," *Beijing Times*, October 12, 2013, https://tech.qq.com/a/20131012/000980.htm.

67 Arthur W. Lewis, "Economic Development with Unlimited Supplies of Labor," *Manchester School of Economic and Social Studies* 22 (May 1954): 139–91.

68 For instance, see Hong Chang, "Zhuanjia: 2013 zhongguo renkou hongli huo jiang xiaoshi dierci renkou hongli keneng zailai (Expert: China's population dividend will be ending in 2013 and might be rebuilt)," People.com.cn, August 24, 2012, http://politics.people.com.cn/n/2012/0824/c1001-18820528.html.

69 Dong Li and He Xia, "Mingnian zhongguo laodongli renkou shouchao shiyi dadao fengzhi (China's labor force exceeding one billion and reaching the peak next year)," People.com.cn, December 24, 2012, http://finance.people.com.cn/money/n/2012/1224/c218900-19993387.html.

70 A. C. S., "China Approaching the Turning Point," *Economist*, January 31, 2013, https://www.economist.com/free-exchange/2013/01/31/china-approaching-the-turning-point.

71 Bill Birtles, "China's Birth Rate Drops Despite End of One-Child Policy," ABC, January 19, 2018, http://www.abc.net.au/news/2018-01-19/chinas-birth-rate-drops-despite-end-of-one-child-policy/9344634.

72 Quoted in Associated Press, "China Scraps Family Planning Agencies in Hint at End to Birth Limits," *South China Morning Post*, September 11, 2018, https://www.scmp.com/news/china/politics/article/2163722/china-scraps-family-planning-agencies-hint-end-birth-limits.

73 Xiaoyi Wang, "Tongjiju: 2013 nian renkou zengzhang 4.92% laodong renkou jiang 244 wan (Bureau of Statistics: 4.92 percent population growth rate in 2013, labor population decreased by 2.44 million)," 163.com, January 20, 2014, http://money.163.com/14/0120/10/9J1BH251002550O9.html.

74 Lu Zhang, "2013 nian daxuesheng jiuye baogao: Benkesheng qianyuelnü buzu sicheng (2013 employment report of college graduates: Under 40 percent among undergraduate students)," Sohu.com, June 10, 2013, http://roll.sohu.com/20130610/n378558623.shtml.

75 Reuters, "China's 'Jobless Rate' Hits 15-Year Low but Flood of Graduates on Horizon," *South China Morning Post*, January 26, 2018, https://www.scmp.com/news/china/society/article/2130699/chinas-jobless-rate-hits-15-year-low-flood-graduates-horizon.

76 Interview by the author, June 8, 2012, Hai'an, China.

77 Brian Massumi, *The Power at the End of the Economy* (Durham, NC: Duke University Press, 2014), 6.

78 Massumi, *The Power at the End of the Economy*, 6.

79 Massumi, *The Power at the End of the Economy*, 23.

80 Lauren Berlant, *Cruel Optimism* (Durham, NC: Duke University Press, 2012).

81 Sara Ahmed, "Affective Economies," *Social Text* 79, no. 2 (Summer 2004): 119.

82 Ahmed, "Affective Economies," 120.

83 Ahmed, "Affective Economies," 120.

84 Ahmed, "Affective Economies," 121.

85 Sara Ahmed, "A Phenomenology of Whiteness," *Feminist Theory* 8, no. 2 (2007): 150.

86 Bob Bryan, "An Under-the-Radar Provision in the US-Mexico-Canada Trade Deal Looks Like a Direct Shot at China," Insider, October 2, 2018, https://www.businessinsider.com/trump-us-mexico-canada-nafta-trade-deal-china-2018-10.

87 Siobhan Hughes and Josh Zumbrun, "Senate Approves Plan to Double Funding for Global Infrastructure Projects," *Wall Street Journal*, October 3, 2018, https://www.wsj.com/articles/senate-approves-plan-to-double-funding-for-global-infrastructure-projects-1538595889.

88 Zhang, "Mapping the Will for Otherwise."

89 Zhang, "Mapping the Will for Otherwise."

90 Roderick A. Ferguson, *The Reorder of Things: The University and Its Pedagogies of Minority Difference* (Minneapolis: University of Minnesota Press, 2012).

91 Angela Xiao Wu and Yige Dong, "What Is Made-in-China Feminism(s)? Gender Discontent and Class Friction in Post-Socialist China," *Critical Asian Studies* 51, no. 4 (2019): 471–92.

92 Sun, *Subaltern China*, 24.

5. Love with an Unspeakable Name

An earlier version of chapter 5 was published in *Feminist Formations* 29, no. 2 (2017): 121–46.

1 Quoted in Alison Flood, "Chinese Writer Tianyi Sentenced to Decade in Prison for Gay Erotic Novel," *Guardian*, November 20, 2018, https://www.theguardian.com/books/2018/nov/20/chinese-writer-tianyi-sentenced-to-decade-in-prison-for-gay-erotic-novel.

2 Alan Williams, "Rethinking *Yaoi* on the Regional and Global Scale," *Intersections*, no. 37 (March 2015), http://intersections.anu.edu.au/issue37/williams.htm.

3 Charlie Yi Zhang, "When Feminist Falls in Love with Queer: *Danmei* Culture as a Transnational Apparatus of Love," *Feminist Formations* 29, no. 2 (2017): 123.

4 Ling Yang and Yanrui Xu, "Chinese *Danmei* Fandom and Cultural Globalization from Below," in *Boys' Love, Cosplay, and Androgynous Idols: Queer Fan Cultures in Mainland China, Hong Kong, and Taiwan*, ed. Maud Lavin, Ling Yang, and Jing Jamie Zhao (Hong Kong: Hong Kong University Press, 2017), 3.

5 Wanning Sun, *Subaltern China: Rural Migrants, Media, and Cultural Practices* (Lanham, MD: Rowman and Littlefield, 2014), 24.

6 Jing Jamie Zhao, Ling Yang, and Maud Lavin, introduction to *Boys' Love, Cosplay, and Androgynous Idols*, xxi.

7 Quoted in Christian Shepherd, "Ten Years' Jail Term for Chinese Author of Homo-erotic Novel Sparks Outcry," Reuters, November 19, 2018, https://www.reuters.com/article/us-china-censorship/ten-years-jail-term-for-chinese-author-of-homoerotic-novel-sparks-outcry-idUSKCN1NO0RH.

8 Hongwei Bao, *Queer Comrades: Gay Identity and Tongzhi Activism in Postsocialist China* (Copenhagen: NIAS Press, 2018).

9   Zheng Wang, "Detention of the Feminist Five in China," *Feminist Studies* 41, no. 2 (2015): 476.

10   Leta Hong Fincher, "China's Feminist Five," *Dissent*, Fall 2016, https://www .dissentmagazine.org/article/china-feminist-five.

11   Shuyuan Zhou, "From Online BL Fandom to the CCTV Spring Festival Gala: The Transforming Power of Online Carnival," in *Boys' Love, Cosplay, and Androgynous Idols*, 91–110. Also see Egret Lulu Zhou, "Dongfang Bubai, Online Fandom, and the Gender Politics of a Legendary Queer Icon," in *Boys' Love, Cosplay, and Androgynous Idols*, 111–27.

12   My empirical data verify an observation that has been stated in most literature on queer fandom cultures, particularly the literature on boys' love: a growing number of gay male readers and viewers, alongside heterosexual women, are interested in queer fandom cultures. See Kazumi Nagaike, "Fudanshi ('Rotten Boys') in Asia: A Cross-Cultural Analysis of Male BL Fandoms," paper presented at the Annual Conference of the Association for Asian Studies, Chicago, March 28, 2015.

13   Angela Xiao Wu and Yige Dong, "What Is Made-in-China Feminism(s)? Gender Discontent and Class Friction in Post-Socialist China," *Critical Asian Studies* 51, no. 4 (2019): 471–92.

14   Bill Birtles, "China's Birth Rate Drops Despite End of One-Child Policy," ABC, January 19, 2018, http://www.abc.net.au/news/2018-01-19/chinas-birth-rate-drops -despite-end-of-one-child-policy/9344634.

15   Yanrui Xu and Ling Yang, "Funü 'fu' nan: Kuaguo wenhua liudongzhong de danmei, fuwenhua yu nanxing qizhi zaizao (Queering men by *funü*: Reconstructing masculinity in transnational circulation of *danmei* and *fu* culture)," *Wenhua yanjiu* (Cultural studies), no. 3 (2014): 3–25.

16   See Fran Martin, "Girls Who Love Boys' Love: Japanese Homoerotic Manga as Transnational Taiwan Culture," *Inter-Asia Cultural Studies* 13, no. 3 (2012): 365–84. Also see Yanrui Xu and Ling Yang, "Forbidden Love: Incest, Generational Conflict, and the Erotics of Power in Chinese BL Fiction," *Journal of Graphic Novels and Comics* 4, no. 1 (2013): 30–43; Maud Lavin, Ling Yang, and Jing Jamie Zhao, *Boys' Love, Cosplay, and Androgynous Idols*.

17   Bei Tong, *Beijing Comrades: A Novel*, trans. Scott Myers, afterword by Petrus Liu (New York: Feminist Press at the City University of New York, 2016).

18   Bing Zhang, "Lun 'danmei' xiaoshuo de jige zhuti (On the themes of *danmei* fictions)," *Wenxue pinglun* (Literary review), no. 5 (2012): 171–79.

19   See Laura Mulvey, "Visual Pleasure and Narrative Cinema," *Screen* 16, no. 3 (1975): 6–18. Also see John Berger, *Ways of Seeing* (London: Penguin Books, 1972).

20   Timothy Perper and Martha Cornog, "Non-Western Sexuality Comes to the U.S.: A Crash Course in Manga and Anime for Sexologists," *Contemporary Sexuality* 39, no. 3 (2005): 5.

21   Mark McLelland, "No Climax, No Point, No Meaning? Japanese Women's Boy-Love Sites on the Internet," *Journal of Communication Inquiry* 24, no. 3 (2000): 277.

22   McLelland, "No Climax, No Point, No Meaning?," 278

23   Zhao, Yang, and Lavin, introduction, xv.

24   Online interview by the author, October 12, 2011.

25 Fran Martin, *Backward Glances: Contemporary Chinese Cultures and the Female Homoerotic Imaginary* (Durham, NC: Duke University Press, 2010), 8.

26 Petrus Liu, *Queer Marxism in Two Chinas* (Durham, NC: Duke University Press, 2015), 31.

27 Howard Chiang, "(De)Provincializing China—Queer Historicism and Sinophone Postcolonial Critique," in *Queer Sinophone Cultures*, ed. Howard Chiang and Ari Larissa Heinrich (London: Routledge, 2014), 36.

28 Phone interview by the author, February 8, 2009.

29 The only exception among my interviewees was a woman who was in a relationship with another woman when the interview was conducted.

30 Phone interview by the author, April 19, 2009.

31 Interview by the author, May 5, 2013, Phoenix, Arizona.

32 Zhao, Yang, and Lavin, introduction, xviii.

33 Mulvey, "Visual Pleasure and Narrative Cinema."

34 Patricia Hill Collins, *Black Feminist Thought: Knowledge, Consciousness, and the Politics of Empowerment* (London: Routledge, 2008).

35 Yukari Fujimoto, "Shōjo manga ni okeru 'shōnen ai' no imi' (The meaning of 'boys' love' in Shōjo Manga)," *New Feminism Review* 2 (May 1991): 283.

36 Steve Susoyev, "'Beijing Comrades' by Bei Tong," Lambda Literary, March 13, 2016, https://www.lambdaliterary.org/2016/03/beijing-comrades-by-bei-tong/.

37 Petrus Liu, "From Identity to Social Protest: The Cultural Politics of Beijing Comrades," in Bei Tong, *Beijing Comrades*, 374.

38 Liu, "From Identity to Social Protest," 374.

39 Bei Tong, *Beijing Comrades*, 282.

40 Liu, "From Identity to Social Protest," 375.

41 Hugh Ryan, "The Controversial Chinese Gay Erotic Novel You Can Finally Read in English," March 16, 2016, Modern Chinese Literature and Culture Resource Center, Ohio State University, https://u.osu.edu/mclc/2016/03/17/beijing-comrades-review/.

42 Nina Sparling, "*Beijing Comrades* by Bei Tong," Rumpus, April 26, 2016, https://therumpus.net/2016/04/beijing-comrades-by-bei-tong/.

43 Sparling, "*Beijing Comrades* by Bei Tong."

44 Liu, "From Identity to Social Protest," 373.

45 Liu, "From Identity to Social Protest," 374.

46 See Ryan, "The Controversial Chinese Gay Erotic Novel You Can Finally Read in English."

47 Quoted in Ryan, "The Controversial Chinese Gay Erotic Novel You Can Finally Read in English."

48 Quoted in Ryan, "The Controversial Chinese Gay Erotic Novel You Can Finally Read in English."

49 Hongwei Bao, "Haunted Chinese Gay Identity: Sexuality, Masculinity, and Class in *Beijing Story*," in *The Cosmopolitan Dream: Transnational Chinese Masculinities in a Global Age*, ed. Derek Hird and Geng Song (Hong Kong: Hong Kong University Press, 2018), 80.

50 In my engagement with several social-media-based *funü* chat groups, I documented a few skirmishes deriving from female *danmei* fans' participation in online

gay communities to acquire some real-life knowledge to improve their writing. To understand the opinion of men having same-sex experiences about *danmei*, I also tried to interview a few men who identified themselves as gay, but my requests were declined because none of them was interested in this topic. In casual conversations, a few friends who also identified themselves as gay on other occasions expressed their bafflement about *danmei* and its heterosexual female fans. All my ethnographic work was done before 2013, and with the recent popularization of several TV dramas based on *danmei* fiction, such as *Go Princess Go* (2015) and *Addicted* (2016), gay men's attitudes might have changed in *danmei*'s favor.

51 Alain Badiou and Peter Bush, *In Praise of Love* (New York: New Press, 2012), 14–15.

52 Friedrich Engels, *The Origin of the Family, Private Property and the State*, intro. Tristram Hunt (London: Penguin Books, 2010).

53 Sara L. Friedman, *Intimate Politics: Marriage, the Market, and the State Power in Southeastern China* (Cambridge, MA: Harvard University Press, 2006), 3.

54 Quoted in Leta Hong Fincher, *Leftover Women: The Resurgence of Gender Inequality in China* (London: Zed Books, 2014).

55 Quoted in Nicole Tan, "Our Response to 'A PhD's Fine, but What about Love and Babies?,'" Association of Women for Action and Research, September 13, 2011, http://www.aware.org.sg/2011/09/our-response-to-a-phds-fine-but-what-about-love-and-babies/.

56 Tan, "Our Response to 'A PhD's Fine, but What about Love and Babies?'"

57 Elisabeth Croll, *Changing Identities of Chinese Women: Rhetoric, Experience and Self-Perception in 20th Century China* (London: Hong Kong University Press, 1995). Also see Harriet Evans, *Women and Sexuality in China* (London: Polity, 1997).

58 Jan Jindy Pettman, "Globalization and the Gendered Politics of Citizenship," in *Women, Citizenship and Difference*, ed. Pnina Werbner and Nira Yuval-Davis (London: Zed Books, 1999), 212.

59 Informal conversations by the author, April 15 and 18, 2009, Phoenix, Arizona.

60 Xu and Yang, "Queering Men by *Funü*."

61 Judith Butler, *Gender Trouble: Feminism and the Subversion of Identity* (New York: Routledge, 1999).

62 Hoang Tan Nguyen, *A View from the Bottom: Asian American Masculinity and Sexual Representation* (Durham, NC: Duke University Press, 2014).

63 Zhang, "When Feminist Falls in Love with Queer," 132.

64 Kam Louie, "Chinese, Japanese and Global Masculine Identities, in *Asian Masculinities: The Meaning and Practice of Manhood in China and Japan*, ed. Kam Louie and Morris Low (London: Routledge Curzon, 2003), 6.

65 Chiang, "(De)Provincializing China," 35.

66 Michel Foucault, *The History of Sexuality*, vol. 1: *The Will to Knowledge*, trans. Robert Hurley (London: Penguin, 1981). Also see Michel Foucault, *The Birth of Biopolitics: Lectures at the Collège de France, 1978–1979*, trans. Graham Burchell (Basingstoke, UK: Palgrave Macmillan, 2008).

67 Butler, *Gender Trouble*.

68 Jonathan Ned Katz, *The Invention of Heterosexuality* (Chicago: University of Chicago Press, 2007).

69 Katz, *The Invention of Heterosexuality*, 54.

70 Louie, "Chinese, Japanese and Global Masculine Identities."

71 Timothy Perper and Martha Cornog, "Eroticism for the Masses: Japanese Manga Comics and Their Assimilation into the U.S.," *Sexuality and Culture* 6, no. 1 (2002): 9.

72 Jason G. Karlin, "The Gender of Nationalism: Competing Masculinities in Meiji Japan," *Journal of Japanese Studies* 28, no. 1 (Winter 2002): 41–77.

73 Geng Song, *The Fragile Scholar: Power and Masculinity in Chinese Culture* (Hong Kong: Hong Kong University Press, 2004).

74 Cuncun Wu, "Beautiful Boys Made Up as Beautiful Girls: Anti-Masculine Taste in Qing China," in *Asian Masculinities*, 19–40; Yiyan Wang, "Mr. Butterfly in Defunct Capital: 'Soft' Masculinity and (Mis)engendering in China," in *Asian Masculinities*, 41–58; Lingzhen Wang, "Other Genders, Other Sexualities: Chinese Difference," *Difference* 24, no. 2 (2013): 1–7; Chengzhou He, "Trespassing, Crisis, and Renewal: Li Yugang and Cross-Dressing Performance," *Difference* 24, no. 2 (2013), 150–71; Howard Chiang, *Transgender China* (New York: Palgrave Macmillan, 2012).

75 Wenqing Kang, *Obsession: Male Same-Sex Relations in China, 1900–1950* (Hong Kong: Hong Kong University Press, 2009).

76 Phone interview by the author, March 16, 2009.

77 Jack Halberstam, *Female Masculinity* (Durham, NC: Duke University Press, 1998).

78 Nicholas Rose, "The Human Sciences in a Biological Age," *Theory, Culture and Society* 30, no. 1 (2013): 3–34.

79 Butler, *Gender Trouble*, 187.

80 Butler, *Gender Trouble*, 187.

81 Butler, *Gender Trouble*, 175.

82 Butler, *Gender Trouble*, 187.

83 Hui-Ling Chou, "Striking Their Own Poses: The History of Cross-Dressing on the Chinese Stage," *TDR* 44, no. 2 (1997): 130–52.

84 Anna Wing-Bo Tso, "Female Cross-Dressing in Chinese Literature Classics and Their English Versions," *International Studies* 16, no. 1 (2014): 115.

85 Tso, "Female Cross-Dressing in Chinese Literature Classics and Their English Versions," 114.

86 Leslie Nguyen-Okwu, "The Tragic Romance of China's Romeo and Juliet," Ozy, December 18, 2016, https://www.ozy.com/true-and-stories/the-tragic-romance-of-chinas-romeo-and-juliet/74598/.

87 See Kaige Chen, dir., *Farewell My Concubine* (Beijing Film Studio, 1993). Also see Siu-Leung Li, *Cross-Dressing in Chinese Opera* (Hong Kong: Hong Kong University Press, 2003); See-Kam Tan, "The Cross-Gender Performances of Yam Kim-Fei, or the Queer Factor in Postwar Hong Kong Cantonese Opera/Opera Films," *Journal of Homosexuality* 39, nos. 3–4 (2000): 201–11.

88 Chou, "Striking Their Own Poses."

89 Quoted in Li, *Cross-Dressing in Chinese Opera*, 216.

90 Chou, "Striking Their Own Poses," 135.

91 Chou, "Striking Their Own Poses," 136.

92 Chou, "Striking Their Own Poses," 130–31.

93 Chou, "Striking Their Own Poses."

94   Jin Jiang, *Women Playing Men: Yue Opera and Social Change in Twentieth-Century Shanghai* (Seattle: University of Washington Press, 2009), 7.

95   Charlie Yi Zhang, "Deconstructing the Hypermasculine National and Transnational Hegemony in Neoliberal China," *Feminist Studies* 40, no. 1 (2014): 13–38.

96   Interview by the author, January 29, 2013, Phoenix, Arizona.

97   Eve Kosofsky Sedgwick, *Epistemology of the Closet* (Berkeley: University of California Press, 1993), 8.

98   Jasbir Puar, *Terrorist Assemblages: Homonationalism in Queer Times* (Durham, NC: Duke University Press, 2007), 205.

99   Aihwa Ong, *Neoliberalism as Exception: Mutations in Citizenship and Sovereignty* (Durham, NC: Duke University Press, 2006); Pheng Cheah, *Inhuman Conditions: On Cosmopolitanism and Human Rights* (Cambridge, MA: Harvard University Press, 2006).

100 Martin, *Backward Glances*, 15.

101 Online interview by the author, June 7, 2011.

102 José Esteban Muñoz, *Cruising Utopia: The Then and There of Queer Futurity* (New York: New York University Press, 2009), 161.

103 Phone interview by the author, June 15, 2011.

104 Interview by the author, April 8, 2009, Phoenix, Arizona.

105 Liu, "From Identity to Social Protest," 377.

106 Ann Anagnost, "From 'Class' to 'Social Strata': Grasping the Social Totality in Reform-Era China," *Third World Quarterly* 29, no. 3 (2008): 497–519.

107 Interview by the author, January 29, 2013, Phoenix, Arizona.

108 Chiang, "(De)Provincializing China," 37.

109 David L. Eng, "The Queer Space of China: Expressive Desire in Stanley Kwan's *Lan Yu*," *Positions* 18, no. 2 (2010): 459–87. Also see Stanley Kwan, dir., *Lan Yu* (Yongning Creation Workshop, 2001).

110 Bao, "Haunted Chinese Gay Identity."

111 Bobby Benedicto, "The Haunting of Gay Manila: Global Space-Time and the Specter of Kabaklaan," *GLQ* 14, nos. 2–3 (2008): 321.

112 For instance, see Mariko Hihara, *The Sundered: Yaoi Novel* (Enjugroup, 2016). Also see Hikaru Masaki, *The Lonely Egotist* (Gardena, CA: Digital Manga, 2009).

113 Benedicto, "The Haunting of Gay Manila," 318.

114 Lisa Duggan, *The Twilight of Equality: Neoliberalism, Cultural Politics, and the Attack on Democracy* (Boston: Beacon Press, 2003), 50.

115 David L. Eng, *The Feeling of Kinship: Queer Liberalism and the Racialization of Intimacy* (Durham, NC: Duke University Press, 2010); Chandan Reddy, "Asian Diasporas, Neoliberalism, and Family: Reviewing the Case for Homosexual Asylum in the Context of Family Rights," *Social Text* 23, nos. 3–4 (2005): 101–9; Jasbir Puar, "Circuits of Queer Mobility: Tourism, Travel, and Globalization," *GLQ* 8, nos. 1–2 (2002): 101–37, and *Terrorist Assemblages*.

116 R. W. Connell, "The History of Masculinity," in *The Masculinity Studies Reader*, ed. Rachel Adams and David Savran (Hoboken, NJ: Wiley-Blackwell, 2002), 245–61; Zhang, "Deconstructing the Hypermasculine National and Transnational Hegemony in Neoliberal China."

117   The popularization of the British TV soap opera *Sherlock* in *danmei* communities is a good example, which caught the attention of the BBC. See "Pianai jiqing 'shentan xialuoke' zhongguo funü zouhong (Chinese funü earn reputation for their preference of gay love in 'Sherlock')," Kekenet.com, September 1, 2015, https://m.kekenet.com /read/201509/396578.shtml.

118   See Zhang, "When Feminist Falls in Love with Queer."

119   Eric Baculinao, "China Tackles 'Masculinity Crisis,' Tries to Stop 'Effeminate' Boys," NBC, January 9, 2017, https://www.nbcnews.com/news/china/china-tackles -masculinity-crisis-tries-stop-effeminate-boys-n703461.

120   Jasbir Puar, *The Right to Maim: Debility, Capacity, Disability* (Durham, NC: Duke University Press, 2017), 36.

Conclusion

1   Henry Farrell and Abraham Newman, "Will the Coronavirus End Globalization as We Know It?," *Foreign Affairs*, March 16, 2020, https://www.foreignaffairs.com/articles /2020-03-16/will-coronavirus-end-globalization-we-know-it.

2   Tobias Burgers and Scott N. Romaniuk, "Can the Coronavirus Strengthen China's Authoritarian Regime?," *Diplomat*, March 10, 2020, https://thediplomat.com/2020 /03/can-the-coronavirus-strengthen-chinas-authoritarian-regime/.

3   Josh Horwitz and Ryan Woo, "China's SOE Regulator Calls for Continued Overseas Expansion Despite Trade War: CSJ," Reuters, May 30, 2019, https://www.reuters.com /article/us-usa-trade-china-soe/chinas-soe-regulator-calls-for-continued-overseas -expansion-despite-trade-war-csj-idUSKCN1T1044.

4   Philippe Legrain, "The Coronavirus Is Killing Globalization as We Know It," *Foreign Policy*, March 12, 2020, https://foreignpolicy.com/2020/03/12/coronavirus-killing -globalization-nationalism-protectionism-trump/.

5   In the Public Interest, "The Trump Administration Privatized Coronavirus Testing, and Now the U.S. Is Paying the Price," March 16, 2020, http://www.inthepublicinterest .org/the-trump-administration-privatized-coronavirus-testing-and-now-the-u-s-is -paying-the-price/.

6   Neil Irwin, "It's the End of the World Economy as We Know It," *New York Times*, April 16, 2020, https://www.nytimes.com/2020/04/16/upshot/world-economy -restructuring-coronavirus.html.

7   Barbara Starr and Ryan Browne, "US Increases Military Pressure on China as Tensions Rise Over Pandemic," CNN, May 15, 2020, https://www.cnn.com/2020/05/14 /politics/us-china-military-pressure/index.html.

8   Chela Sandoval, *Methodology of the Oppressed* (Minneapolis: University of Minnesota Press, 2000).

9   Sandoval, *Methodology of the Oppressed*, 139–40.

10   Brian Massumi, *The Power at the End of the Economy* (Durham, NC: Duke University Press, 2014)

11   Massumi, *The Power at the End of the Economy*, 88.

12   Daniel Bessner and Matthew Sparke, "Don't Let His Trade Policy Fool You: Trump Is a Neoliberal," *Washington Post*, March 22, 2017, https://www.washingtonpost.com

/posteverything/wp/2017/03/22/dont-let-his-trade-policy-fool-you-trump-is-a
-neoliberal/?utm_term=.bcf2247d38ef.

13   Michel Foucault, *Discipline and Punish: The Birth of the Prison*, trans. Alan Sheridan
(New York: Vintage Books, 1995).

14   Joyce Liu, prod., "In Your Face: China's All-Seeing State," BBC, December 10, 2017,
https://www.bbc.com/news/av/world-asia-china-42248056.

15   Tara Francis Chan, "One Chinese City Is Using Facial-Recognition That Can Help
Police Detect and Arrest Criminals in as Little as 2 Minutes," Insider, March 19, 2018,
https://www.businessinsider.com/china-guiyang-using-facial-recognition-to-arrest
-criminals-2018-3.

16   Liu, "In Your Face."

17   Bernhard Zand, "A Surveillance State Unlike Any the World Has Ever Seen," *Spiegel*,
July 26, 2018, http://www.spiegel.de/international/world/china-s-xinjiang-province
-a-surveillance-state-unlike-any-the-world-has-ever-seen-a-1220174.html.

18   Zand, "A Surveillance State Unlike Any the World Has Ever Seen."

19   Jasbir Puar, *The Right to Maim: Debility, Capacity, Disability* (Durham, NC: Duke
University Press, 2017), 57.

20   Beatriz [Paul] Preciado, "The Pharmaco-Pornographic Regime: Sex, Gender, and
Subjectivity in the Age of Punk Capitalism," in *Transgender Studies Reader* 2, ed.
Susan Stryker and Aren Z. Aizura (New York: Routledge, 2013), 271, quoted in Puar,
The Right to Maim, 57.

21   Ryan Grenoble, "Welcome to the Surveillance State: China's AI Cameras See All,"
Huffpost, December 12, 2017, https://www.huffpost.com/entry/china-surveillance
-camera-big-brother_n_5a2ff4dfe4b01598ac484acc.

22   "How Tiananmen Square Cemented China's Obsession with Control," *Bloomberg*,
May 31, 2019, https://www.bloomberg.com/news/articles/2019-05-31/how-tanks-on
-tiananmen-square-defined-china-s-model-for-control. Also see Robert Lawrence
Kuhn, "Xi Jinping's Chinese Dream," *New York Times*, June 4, 2013, https://www
.nytimes.com/2013/06/05/opinion/global/xi-jinpings-chinese-dream.html.

23   Lily Kuo, "'The New Normal': China's Excessive Coronavirus Public Monitoring
Could Be Here to Stay," *Guardian*, March 8, 2020, https://www.theguardian.com
/world/2020/mar/09/the-new-normal-chinas-excessive-coronavirus-public
-monitoring-could-be-here-to-stay.

24   Nectar Gan, "Outcasts in Their Own Country, the People of Wuhan Are the Unwanted
Faces of China's Coronavirus Outbreak," CNN, February 2, 2020, https://www.cnn
.com/2020/02/01/asia/coronavirus-wuhan-discrimination-intl-hnk/index.html.

25   Paul Mozur, Jonah M. Kessel, and Melissa Chan, "Made in China, Exported to the
World: The Surveillance State," *New York Times*, April 24, 2019, https://www.nytimes
.com/2019/04/24/technology/ecuador-surveillance-cameras-police-government
.html#. Also see Qiang Xiao, "The Road to Digital Unfreedom: President Xi's Surveillance State," *Journal of Democracy* 30, no. 1 (2019): 53–67.

26   Lingling Wei, "China's Coronavirus Response Toughens State Control and Weakens the Private Market," *Wall Street Journal*, March 18, 2020, https://www.wsj.com
/articles/chinas-coronavirus-response-toughens-state-control-and-weakens-the
-private-market-11584540534.

Bibliography

A. C. S. "China Approaching the Turning Point." *Economist*, January 31, 2013. https://www
.economist.com/free-exchange/2013/01/31/china-approaching-the-turning-point.

Agamben, Giorgio. *Homo Sacer: Sovereign Power and Bare Life*. Translated by Daniel
Heller-Roazen. Stanford, CA: Stanford University Press, 1998.

Ahmed, Sara. "Affective Economies." *Social Text* 79, no. 2 (Summer 2004): 117–39.

Ahmed, Sara. *The Cultural Politics of Emotion*. 2nd ed. New York: Routledge, 2015.

Ahmed, Sara. "Happy Objects." In *The Affect Theory Reader*, edited by Melissa Gregg and
Gregory J. Seigworth, 29–51. Durham, NC: Duke University Press, 2010.

Ahmed, Sara. "A Phenomenology of Whiteness." *Feminist Theory* 8, no. 2 (2007): 149–68.

Ahmed, Sara. *The Promise of Happiness*. Durham, NC: Duke University Press, 2010.

Alarcón, Norma, Caren Kaplan, and Minoo Moallem. Introduction to *Between Woman and
Nation: Nationalisms, Transnational Feminisms, and the State*, edited by Caren Kaplan,
Norma Alarcón, and Minoo Moallem, 1–16. Durham, NC: Duke University Press, 1999.

Alison, Anne. *Nightwork: Sexuality, Pleasure, and Corporate Masculinity in a Tokyo Hostess Club*. Chicago: University of Chicago Press, 1994.

Anagnost, Ann. "From 'Class' to 'Social Strata': Grasping the Social Totality in Reform-Era
China." *Third World Quarterly* 29, no. 3 (2008): 497–519.

Anderson, Benedict. *Imagined Communities: Reflections on the Origin and Spread of
Nationalism*. London: Verso, 2006.

Andors, Phyllis. *The Unfinished Liberation of Chinese Women, 1949–1980*. Bloomington:
Indiana University Press, 1983.

Andrews, Julia F., and Kuiyi Shen. "The New Chinese Woman and Lifestyle Magazines in
the Late 1990s." In *Popular China: Unofficial Culture in a Globalizing Society*, edited by
Perry Link, Richard P. Madsen, and Paul G. Pickowicz, 137–61. Lanham, MD: Rowman
and Littlefield, 2002.

Ash, Alec. "Is China's Gaokao the World's Toughest School Exam?" *Guardian*, October 12,
2016. https://www.theguardian.com/world/2016/oct/12/gaokao-china-toughest
-school-exam-in-world.

Associated Press. "China Scraps Family Planning Agencies in Hint at End to Birth Limits." *South China Morning Post*, September 11, 2018. https://www.scmp.com/news/china /politics/article/2163722/china-scraps-family-planning-agencies-hint-end-birth -limits.

"Australia Battles Chinese Political Influence." *Economist*, June 17, 2017. https://www .economist.com/news/asia/21723454-it-will-be-uphill-struggle-australia-battles -chinese-political-influence.

Baculinao, Eric. "China Tackles 'Masculinity Crisis,' Tries to Stop 'Effeminate' Boys." NBC, January 9, 2017. https://www.nbcnews.com/news/china/china-tackles-masculinity -crisis-tries-stop-effeminate-boys-n703461.

Badiou, Alain, and Peter Bush. *In Praise of Love*. New York: New Press, 2012.

Bahng, Aimee. *Migrant Futures: Decolonizing Speculation in Financial Times*. Durham, NC: Duke University Press, 2017.

Bao, Hongwei. "Haunted Chinese Gay Identity: Sexuality, Masculinity, and Class in *Beijing Story*." In *The Cosmopolitan Dream: Transnational Chinese Masculinities in a Global Age*, edited by Derek Hird and Geng Song, 73–86. Hong Kong: Hong Kong University Press, 2018.

Bao, Hongwei. *Queer Comrades: Gay Identity and Tongzhi Activism in Postsocialist China*. Copenhagen: NIAS Press, 2018.

Barboza, David. "Foxconn Resolves a Dispute with Some Workers in China." *New York Times*, January 12, 2012. https://www.nytimes.com/2012/01/13/technology/foxconn -resolves-pay-dispute-with-workers.html.

Barlow, Tani. "Preface: Everything Diverges." In *New Asian Marxisms*, edited by Tani Barlow, vii–xv. Durham, NC: Duke University Press, 2002.

Barlow, Tani. *The Question of Women in Chinese Feminism*. Durham, NC: Duke University Press, 2004.

Barlow, Tani. "Theorizing Woman: Funü, Guojia, Jiating (Chinese Women, Chinese State, Chinese Family)." In *Scattered Hegemonies: Postmodernity and Transnational Feminist Practices*, edited by Inderpal Grewal and Caren Kaplan, 173–96. Minneapolis: University of Minnesota Press, 1994.

Bayes, Jane H., Mary Hawkesworth, and Rita Mae Kelly. "Globalization, Democratization and Gender Regimes." In *Globalization, Democratization and Gender Regimes*, edited by Jane H. Bayes, Mary Hawkesworth, and Rita Mae Kelly, 1–14. Boulder, CO: Rowman and Littlefield, 2001.

Bei Tong. "Beijing Comrades: A Gay Chinese Love Story." Translated by Scott Myers. *Amerasia Journal* 37, no. 2 (2011), 75–94.

Bei Tong. *Beijing Comrades: A Novel*. Translated by Scott Myers, with an afterword by Petrus Liu. New York: Feminist Press at the City University of New York, 2016.

Beinart, Peter. "Trump Is Preparing for a New Cold War." *Atlantic*, February 27, 2018. https://www.theatlantic.com/international/archive/2018/02/trump-is-preparing-for -a-new-cold-war/554384/.

"Belt and Road Bedtime Stories." Episode 1, *China Daily*, May 8, 2017. https://www .chinadaily.com.cn/beltandroadinitiative/2017-05/08/content_29255516.htm.

Benedicto, Bobby. "The Haunting of Gay Manila: Global Space-Time and the Specter of Kabaklaan." *GLQ* 14, nos. 2–3 (2008): 317–38.

Benedicto, Bobby. *Under Bright Lights: Gay Manila and the Global Scene*. Minneapolis: University of Minnesota Press, 2014.

Benjamin, Walter. *Illuminations: Essays and Reflections*. Translated by Harry Zohn. New York: Schocken Books, 1969.

Berger, John. *Ways of Seeing*. London: Penguin Books, 1972.

Berlant, Lauren. *Cruel Optimism*. Durham, NC: Duke University Press, 2012.

Berlant, Lauren, and Kathleen Stewart. *The Hundreds*. Durham, NC: Duke University Press, 2019.

Bermingham, Finbarr, and Jeong-ho Lee. "How the Trade War Led to Samsung and Other South Korean Companies' Exodus from China." *South China Morning Post*, July 4, 2019. https://www.scmp.com/economy/china-economy/article/3017110/samsung -and-other-south-korean-firms-exodus-china-example.

Berry, Chris, Fran Martin, and Audrey Yue. "Introduction: Beep-Click-Link." In *Mobile Cultures: New Media in Queer Asia*, edited by Chris Berry, Fran Martin, and Audrey Yue, 1–20. Durham, NC: Duke University Press, 2003.

Bessner, Daniel, and Matthew Sparke. "Don't Let His Trade Policy Fool You: Trump Is a Neoliberal." *Washington Post*, March 22, 2017. https://www.washingtonpost.com /posteverything/wp/2017/03/22/dont-let-his-trade-policy-fool-you-trump-is-a -neoliberal/?utm_term=.bcf2247d38ef.

Birtles, Bill. "China's Birth Rate Drops Despite End of One-Child Policy." ABC, January 19, 2018. http://www.abc.net.au/news/2018–01–19/chinas-birth-rate-drops-despite-end -of-one-child-policy/9344634.

Blanchette, Jude. *China's New Red Guards: The Return of Radicalism and the Rebirth of Mao Zedong*. New York: Oxford University Press, 2019.

Blodget, Henry. "Foxconn Explains Cause of iPhone 5 Shortages That Are Hammering Apple's Stock." Insider, October 17, 2012. https://www.businessinsider.com/foxconn -explains-trouble-making-iphone-5-2012-10.

Bonilla-Silva, Eduardo. *Racism without Racists: Color-Blind Racism and the Persistence of Racial Inequality in the United States*. Lanham, MD: Rowman and Littlefield, 2010.

Branigan, Tania. "Five Chinese Feminists Held over International Women's Day Plans." *Guardian*, March 12, 2015. http://www.theguardian.com/world/2015/mar/12/five -chinese-feminists-held-international-womens-day.

Branigan, Tania. "Olympics: Child Singer Revealed as Fake." *Guardian*, August 12, 2008. http://www.theguardian.com/sport/2008/aug/12/olympics2008.china1.

Bray, Francesca. *Technology and Gender: Fabrics of Power in Late Imperial China*. Berkeley: University of California Press, 1997.

"A Brief Introduction of JSBC." Jsbc.com. April 15, 2021. http://www.jsbc.com/info /1608534497285.shtml.

Brooks, Rob. "China's Biggest Problem? Too Many Men." CNN, March 4, 2013. http://www .cnn.com/2012/11/14/opinion/china-challenges-one-child-brooks.

Burgers, Tobias, and Scott N. Romaniuk. "Can the Coronavirus Strengthen China's Authoritarian Regime?" *Diplomat*, March 10, 2020. https://thediplomat.com/2020/03/can-the -coronavirus-strengthen-chinas-authoritarian-regime/.

Butler, Judith. *Gender Trouble: Feminism and the Subversion of Identity*. New York: Routledge, 1999.

Byler, Darren. *Terror Capitalism: Uyghur Dispossession and Masculinity in a Chinese City*. Durham, NC: Duke University Press, 2021.

Campbell, Charlie. "Xi Jinping's Party Congress Speech Leaves No Doubts over His Leadership Role." *Time*, October 18, 2017. http://time.com/4986999/xi-jinping-china-19th-congress-ccp/.

Carrico, Kevin. *The Great Han: Race, Nationalism, and Tradition in China Today*. Oakland: University of California Press, 2017.

Chan, Anita. *China's Workers under Assault: The Exploitation of Labor in a Globalizing Economy*. Armonk, NY: East Gate Press, 2001.

Chan, Jenny. "Shenzhen Jasic Technology: Towards a Worker-Student Coalition in China." *New Politics*, August 31, 2018. http://newpol.org/content/shenzhen-jasic-technology-towards-workerstudent-coalition-china.

Chan, Tara Francis. "One Chinese City Is Using Facial-Recognition That Can Help Police Detect and Arrest Criminals in as Little as 2 Minutes." Insider, March 19, 2018. https://www.businessinsider.com/china-guiyang-using-facial-recognition-to-arrest-criminals-2018-3.

Chang, Gordon G. "Another Chinese Fib: 6.1% Growth." *Forbes*, April 22, 2009. https://www.forbes.com/2009/04/21/china-economic-statistics-growth-opinions-columnists-wen-jiabao.html#33428b9414ac.

Chang, Hong. "Zhuanjia: 2013 zhongguo renkou hongli huo jiang xiaoshi dierci renkou hongli keneng zailai (Expert: China's population dividend will be ending in 2013 and might be rebuilt)." People.com.cn, August 24, 2012. http://politics.people.com.cn/n/2012/0824/c1001-18820528.html.

Cheah, Pheng. *Inhuman Conditions: On Cosmopolitanism and Human Rights*. Cambridge, MA: Harvard University Press, 2006.

Chen, Kaige, dir. *Farewell My Concubine*. Beijing Film Studio, 1993.

Chen, Kuan-Hsing. *Asia as Method: Toward Deimperialization*. Durham, NC: Duke University Press, 2010.

Chen, Tina Mai. "Female Icons, Feminist Iconography? Socialist Rhetoric and Women's Agency in 1950s China." *Gender and History* 15, no .2 (2003): 268–95.

Chen, Xiangming. "A Globalizing City on the Rise: Shanghai's Transformation in Comparative Perspective." In *Shanghai Rising: State Power and Local Transformations in a Global Megacity*, edited by Xiangming Chen, xv–xxxv. Minneapolis: University of Minnesota Press, 2009.

Chen, Xiaomei. "Staging Chinese Revolution: The Color Scheme of Socialist Epic Theater (1964–2006)." Paper presented at the Languages, Literatures, and Cultures Conference, University of Kentucky, April 21, 2017.

Chen, Xiaomei. *Staging Chinese Revolution: Theater, Film, and the Afterlives of Propaganda*. New York: Columbia University Press, 2016.

Cheng, Evelyn. "Setting His Eyes on the Next 100 Years, Xi Seizes the Chance to Lead China to Greater Power." CNBC, July 1, 2021. https://www.cnbc.com/2021/07/02/ccp-100-years-xi-seizes-the-chance-to-lead-china-in-the-path-to-power.html.

Chiang, Howard. "(De)Provincializing China—Queer Historicism and Sinophone Postcolonial Critique." In *Queer Sinophone Cultures*, edited by Howard Chiang and Ari Larissa Heinrich, 18–51. London: Routledge, 2014.

Chiang, Howard, ed. *Transgender China*. New York: Palgrave Macmillan, 2012.

Chiang, Howard, and Ari Larissa Heinrich, eds. *Queer Sinophone Cultures*. London: Routledge, 2014.

Chiang, Howard, and Alvin Wong. "Asia Is Burning: Queer Asia as critique." *Culture, Theory and Critique* 58, no. 2 (2017): 121–26.

"China Plans to Build Hainan into Pilot Free Trade Zone." Xinhua, April 14, 2018. http://www.xinhuanet.com/english/2018-04/14/c_137109412.htm.

"China to Accelerate 'Hukou' System Reform: Document." Xinhua, November 15, 2013. http://en.people.cn/90785/8458115.html.

"China's 60th Anniversary Celebrations Not for 'the People.'" *Matière et révolution*, October 11, 2009. https://www.matierevolution.fr/spip.php?breve117.

"China's Sixtieth Anniversary Ceremony." CCTV. Accessed July 6, 2021. https://www.youtube.com/watch?v=SmSMQoTigos.

Cho, Sumi, Kimberlé Crenshaw, and Leslie McCall. "Toward a Field of Intersectionality Studies: Theory, Applications, and Praxis." *Signs* 38, no. 4 (2013): 785–810.

Chou, Hui-Ling. "Striking Their Own Poses: The History of Cross-Dressing on the Chinese Stage." *TDR* 44, no. 2 (1997): 130–52.

Chow, Eugene K. "China's Trafficked Brides." *Diplomat*, July 19, 2017. https://thediplomat.com/2017/07/chinas-trafficked-brides/.

Chow, Rey. *The Protestant Ethnic and the Spirit of Capitalism*. New York: Columbia University Press, 2002.

Clough, Patricia Ticineto. *The Affective Turn: Theorizing the Social*. Durham, NC: Duke University Press, 2007.

Collins, Janet. *Threads: Gender, Labor, and Power in the Global Apparel Industry*. Chicago: University of Chicago Press, 2003.

Collins, Patricia Hill. *Black Feminist Thought: Knowledge, Consciousness, and the Politics of Empowerment*. London: Routledge, 2008.

Collins, Patricia Hill. *Intersectionality as Critical Social Theory*. Durham, NC: Duke University Press, 2019.

"Comprehensively Deepening Reform since Third Plenary Session of 18th CPC Central Committee." *Beijing Review*. Accessed July 5, 2021. http://www.bjreview.com.cn/special/comprehensively_deepening_reform.html.

Connell, R. W. "The History of Masculinity." In *The Masculinity Studies Reader*, edited by Rachel Adams and David Savran, 245–61. Hoboken, NJ: Wiley-Blackwell, 2002.

Connell, R. W. *Masculinities*. Cambridge: Polity Press, 2005.

Connell, R. W., and Julia Wood. "Globalization and Business Masculinities." *Men and Masculinities* 7, no. 4 (2005): 347–64.

Crenshaw, Kimberlé. "Mapping the Margins: Intersectionality, Identity Politics, and Violence against Women of Color." *Stanford Law Review* 43, no. 6 (1991), 1241–99.

Croll, Elisabeth. *Changing Identities of Chinese Women: Rhetoric, Experience and Self-Perception in 20th Century China*. London: Hong Kong University Press, 1995.

Cui, Zi'en. "Queer China, 'Comrade' China." 2008. https://www.youtube.com/watch?v=2lrFdfLBTUY. Accessed July 6, 2021.

Dai, Jinhua. "Gender and Narration: Women in Contemporary Chinese Film." Translated by Jonathan Noble. In *Cinema and Desire: Feminist Marxism and Cultural Politics in the Work of Dai Jinhua*, edited by Jing Wang and Tani Barlow, 99–150. London: Verso, 2002.

Dai, Jinhua. Introduction to Jinhua Dai, *After the Post–Cold War: The Future of Chinese History*, edited by Lisa Rofel and translated by Jie Li, 1–22. Durham, NC: Duke University Press, 2018.

Davin, Delia. "The Impact of Export-Oriented Manufacturing on the Welfare Entitlements of Chinese Women Workers." In *Globalization, Export-Oriented Employment and Social Policy*, edited by Shahra Razavi, Ruth Pearson, and Caroline Danloy, 67–90. New York: Palgrave Macmillan, 2004.

Davis, Deborah S. "Introduction: Urban China." In *Urban Spaces in Contemporary China: The Potential for Autonomy and Community in Post-Mao China*, edited by Deborah S. Davis, Richard Kraus, Barry Naughton, and Elizabeth J. Perry, 1–21. New York: Cambridge University Press, 1995.

Davis, Deborah, and Steven Harrell. "Introduction: The Impact of Post-Mao Reforms on Family Life." In *Chinese Families in the Post-Mao Era*, edited by Deborah Davis and Steven Harrell, 1–22. Berkeley: University of California Press, 1992.

"Daxuesheng qiangzhi zai fushikang shixi xu: Xiaofang cheng shi tiyan shenghuo (Enforced college interns in Foxconn: To get more lived experience as alleged by the school)." *Beijing Times*, October 12, 2013. https://tech.qq.com/a/20131012/000980.htm.

Day, Iyko. *Alien Capital: Asian Racialization and the Logic of Settler Colonial Capitalism*. Durham, NC: Duke University Press, 2016.

Deleuze, Gilles. "Ethology: Spinoza and Us." In *Incorporations*, edited by Jonathan Crary and Sanford Kwinter, 625–33. New York: Zone Books, 1992.

Deleuze, Gilles, and Félix Guattari. *Anti-Oedipus: Capitalism and Schizophrenia*. Translated by Robert Hurley, Mark Seem, and Helen R. Lane. New York: Penguin Books, 1977.

"Demand for Wives in China Endangers Women Who Live on Its Borders." *Economist*, November 4, 2017. https://www.economist.com/china/2017/11/04/demand-for-wives-in-china-endangers-women-who-live-on-its-borders.

Denyer, Simon. "Cheesy Song Praising Love of China's First Couple Goes Viral, Is Mocked." *Washington Post*, November 25, 2014. https://www.washingtonpost.com/news/worldviews/wp/2014/11/25/cheesy-song-praising-love-of-chinas-first-couple-goes-viral-is-mocked/?utm_term=.b250a08a77eb.

Denyer, Simon, and Luna Lin. "Mass Evictions in Freezing Beijing Winter Sparks Public Outrage but Little Official Remorse." *Washington Post*, November 27, 2017. https://www.washingtonpost.com/news/worldviews/wp/2017/11/27/forced-evictions-in-freezing-beijing-winter-sparks-public-outrage-but-little-official-remorse/?noredirect=on&utm_term=.16df7ea9bb70.

Ding, Ding, Xiaoyu Huang, Tao Jin, and W. Raphael Lam. "Assessing China's Residential Real Estate Market." International Monetary Fund Working Paper, November 2017. https://www.imf.org/~/media/Files/Publications/WP/2017/wp17248.ashx.

Dobrowolsky, Alexandra, and Evangelia Tastsoglou. *Women, Migration and Citizenship: Making Local, National and Transnational Connections*. Aldershot, UK: Ashgate, 2006.

Dong, Jinyue, and Le Xia. "China: How Resilient Is the Economy to Housing Price Fall?" BBVA Research, March 2018. https://www.bbvaresearch.com/wp-content/uploads/2018/03/20180326_China-Housing-market_edi.pdf.

Du, Jiqiang. "Feichengwurao Ma Nuo yin 'baijin' bei maku, jin lunwei shengnü xian-zhuang candan (Ma Nuo shed tears for criticisms of money worship and now becomes a miserable leftover woman)." China.com, April 12, 2017. http://news.china .com/socialgd/10000169/20170412/30411884_all.html.

Dubrofsky, Rachel E. "The Bachelor: Whiteness in the Harem." *Critical Studies in Media Communication* 23, no. 1 (2006): 39–56.

Duggan, Lisa. *The Twilight of Equality: Neoliberalism, Cultural Politics, and the Attack on Democracy.* Boston: Beacon Press, 2003.

Echeverria-Estrada, Carlos, and Jeanne Batalova. "Chinese Immigrants in the United States." Migration Policy Institute, January 15, 2020. http://www.migrationinformation .org/USFocus/display.cfm?id=876.

Economist Intelligence Unit. "China's Supply-Side Structural Reforms: Progress and Outlook." 2017. https://www.eiu.com/public/topical_report.aspx?campaignid =ChinaSSSR2017.

Edelman, Lee. "The Future Is Kid Stuff: Queer Theory, Disidentification, and the Death Drive." *Narrative* 6, no. 1 (1998): 18–31.

Elliott, Stuart. "Sign of Arrival, for Xinhua, Is 60 Feet Tall." *New York Times*, July 25, 2011. http://www.nytimes.com/2011/07/26/business/media/xinhuas-giant-sign-to-blink -on-in-times-square.html.

Eng, David L. *The Feeling of Kinship: Queer Liberalism and the Racialization of Intimacy.* Durham, NC: Duke University Press, 2010.

Eng, David L. "The Queer Space of China: Expressive Desire in Stanley Kwan's *Lan Yu*." *Positions* 18, no. 2 (2010): 459–87.

Eng, David L., Judith Halberstam, and José Esteban Muñoz. "What's Queer about Queer Studies Now?" *Social Text* 23, nos. 3–4 (2005): 1–17.

Engels, Friedrich. *The Origin of the Family, Private Property and the State.* Introduction by Tristram Hunt. London: Penguin Books, 2010.

Enloe, Cynthia H. *Bananas, Beaches and Bases: Making Feminist Sense of International Politics.* London: Pandora, 1999.

Entgroup. "China Film Industry Report 2013–2014." Accessed April 29, 2021. http://english .entgroup.cn/uploads/reports/ChinaFilmIndustryReport2013-2014(sharedversion)490 .pdf.

"Europe and Right-Wing Nationalism: A Country-by-Country Guide." BBC, November 13, 2019. https://www.bbc.com/news/world-europe-36130006.

"Europe's Rising Far Right: A Guide to the Most Prominent Parties." *New York Times,* December 6, 2016. https://www.nytimes.com/interactive/2016/world/europe/europe -far-right-political-parties-listy.html.

Evans, Harriet. *Women and Sexuality in China.* London: Polity, 1997.

Fan, Lixin, dir. *Last Train Home.* Montreal: EyeSteelFilm, 2019.

Fang, Frank. "Russian Media Is Harshly Critical of China's 'One Belt, One Road' Projects in Eurasia." *Epoch Times*, August 8, 2018. https://www.theepochtimes.com/russian-media -harshly-criticizes-chinas-one-belt-one-road-projects-in-eurasia_2618886.html.

Farrell, Henry, and Abraham Newman. "Will the Coronavirus End Globalization as We Know It?" *Foreign Affairs*, March 16, 2020. https://www.foreignaffairs.com/articles /2020-03-16/will-coronavirus-end-globalization-we-know-it.

Fei, Zhi. "Zhongguoshi xiangqin: Wo erzi cai 33, bukaolnü mei Beijing hukou de guniang (Chinese-style blind date: My son is only 33 and won't consider any girls without Beijing *hukou*)." *Phoenix Weekly*, July 11, 2017. https://chinadigitaltimes.net/chinese/2017/07/%E5%87%A4%E5%87%B0weekly-%E4%B8%AD%E5%9B%BD%E5%BC%8F%E7%9B%B8%E4%BA%B2%E4%BB%B7%E7%9B%AE%E8%A1%A8/.

Feiyu. "Shijijiayuan IPO shouri shoupan 10.52 meiyuan (Jiayuan.com wrapped up at $10.52 after its first day of IPO)." *Sina*, May 12, 2011. http://tech.sina.com.cn/i/2011-05-12/04055511496.shtml.

Ferguson, Roderick A. *Aberrations in Black: Toward a Queer of Color Critique*. Minneapolis: University of Minnesota Press, 2003.

Ferguson, Roderick A. *The Reorder of Things: The University and Its Pedagogies of Minority Difference*. Minneapolis: University of Minnesota Press, 2012.

Fincher, Leta Hong. "China's Feminist Five." *Dissent*, Fall 2016. https://www.dissentmagazine.org/article/china-feminist-five.

Fincher, Leta Hong. *Leftover Women: The Resurgence of Gender Inequality in China*. London: Zed Books, 2014.

Findlay, Eileen J. Suárez. *Imposing Decency: The Politics of Sexuality and Race in Puerto Rico, 1870–1920*. Durham, NC: Duke University Press, 2000.

Fish, Isaac Stone. "Chinese Coup Watching." *Foreign Policy*, March 21, 2012. https://foreignpolicy.com/2012/03/21/chinese-coup-watching/.

Fisher, David, and Matt Nippert. "Revealed: China's Network of Influence in New Zealand." *NZ Herald*, September 19, 2017. http://www.nzherald.co.nz/business/news/article.cfm?c_id=3&objectid=11924169.

Flood, Alison. "Chinese Writer Tianyi Sentenced to Decade in Prison for Gay Erotic Novel." *Guardian*, November 20, 2018. https://www.theguardian.com/books/2018/nov/20/chinese-writer-tianyi-sentenced-to-decade-in-prison-for-gay-erotic-novel.

Foucault, Michel. *The Birth of Biopolitics: Lectures at the Collège de France, 1978–1979*. Translated by Graham Burchell. Basingstoke, UK: Palgrave Macmillan, 2008.

Foucault, Michel. *Discipline and Punish: The Birth of the Prison*. Translated by Alan Sheridan. New York: Vintage Books, 1995.

Foucault, Michel. *The Government of Self and Others*. Translated by Graham Burchell. New York: Picador, 2011.

Foucault, Michel. *The History of Sexuality*. Volume 1: *The Will to Knowledge*. Translated by Robert Hurley. London: Penguin, 1981.

Foucault, Michel. *Society Must Be Defended: Lectures at the Collège de France, 1975–1976*. Translated by David Macey. London: Picador, 2003.

Fraser, Nancy. "Feminism, Capitalism and the Cunning of History." *New Left Review* 56, nos. 3–4 (2009): 97–117.

Fraser, Nancy. *The Fortunes of Feminism: From Women's Liberation to Identity Politics to Anti-Capitalism*. New York: Verso Books, 2013.

Freeman, Elizabeth. *Time Binds: Queer Temporalities, Queer Histories*. Durham, NC: Duke University Press, 2010.

Friedman, Sara L. *Intimate Politics: Marriage, the Market, and the State Power in Southeastern China*. Cambridge, MA: Harvard University Press, 2006.

Fukuyama, Francis. *The End of History and the Last Man*. Reissue ed. New York: Free Press, 2006.

Fung, Anthony. *Global Capital, Local Culture: Transnational Media Corporations in China*. New York: Peter Lang, 2008.

"Fushikang beibao fasheng laozi jiufen bufen, yuangong yangyan jiti zisha (Foxconn said to have labor-management conflict, some employees threatened to commit collective suicide)." Xinhua Network, January 12, 2012. http://news.sohu.com/20120112 /n332026451.shtml.

"Fushikang Taiyuan gongchang baofa daguimo saoluan (Massive revolts outburst in Taiyuan Foxconn)." Mydrivers.com, September 24, 2012 https://news.mydrivers.com/1 /242/242209.htm.

Gan, Nectar. "Outcasts in Their Own Country, the People of Wuhan Are the Unwanted Faces of China's Coronavirus Outbreak." CNN, February 2, 2020. https://www.cnn.com /2020/02/01/asia/coronavirus-wuhan-discrimination-intl-hnk/index.html.

Gao, Helen. "China's Education Gap." *New York Times*, September 4, 2014. https://www .nytimes.com/2014/09/05/opinion/sunday/chinas-education-gap.html.

Gao, Shan. "Zhongguo 1% jiating zhangwo quanguo 41.4% caifu pinfu chaju chengdu chaoguo meiguo (1% of Chinese Families Own 41.4% of Wealth Social Inequality Surpasses That in the United States)." RFA, June 9, 2010. https://www.rfa.org/mandarin /yataibaodao/pinfu-06092010094151.html.

"The GDP Data of Nantong Areas, 1978–2017." Wordpress.com, June 16, 2018. https:// maloooo.wordpress.com/2018/06/16/1978%E5%B9%B4%E8%87%B32017%E5%8D%97 %E9%80%9A%E5%9C%B0%E5%8C%BA%E5%90%84%E5%8E%BF%E5%B8%82%E5%8E %86%E5%B9%B4gdp%E6%95%B0%E6%8D%AE/.

Gilmartin, Christina K. "Gender, Political Culture, and Women's Mobilization in the Chinese Nationalist Revolution, 1924–1927." In *Engendering China: Women, Culture, and the State*, edited by Christina K. Gilmartin, Gail Hershatter, Lisa Rofel, and Tyrsene White, 195–225. Cambridge, MA: Harvard University Press, 1994.

Gilmartin, Christina K., et al. Introduction to *Engendering China: Women, Culture, and the State*, edited by Christina K. Gilmartin, Gail Hershatter, Lisa Rofel, and Tyrsene White, 1–24. Cambridge, MA: Harvard University Press, 1994.

Gilmore, Ruth Wilson. *Golden Gulag: Prisons, Surplus, Crisis, and Opposition in Globalizing California*. Berkeley: University of California Press, 2007.

Goeman, Mishuana. *Mark My Words: Native Women Mapping Our Nations*. Minneapolis: University of Minnesota Press, 2013.

Goldman, Merle, and Roderick Macfarquhar. "Dynamic Economy, Declining Party-State." In *The Paradox of China's Post-Mao Reforms*, edited by Merle Goldman and Roderick Macfarquhar, 3–29. Cambridge, MA: Harvard University Press, 1999.

Gongloff, Mark. "The Next Reboot: Cold War, This Time with China." Bloomberg, August 13, 2018. https://www.bloomberg.com/view/articles/2018-08-13/trump-s-china -trade-war-could-be-the-first-step-in-a-cold-war.

Goodman, Jack. "Has China Lifted 100 Million People out of Poverty?" BBC, February 28, 2021. https://www.bbc.com/news/56213271.

Gorsuch, Anne E. "The Dance Class or the Working Class: The Soviet Modern Girl." In *The Modern Girl around the World*, edited by Alys Eve Weinbaum, Lynn M. Thomas, Priti

Ramamurthy, Uta G. Poiger, Madeleine Yue Dong, and Tani Barlow, 174–93. Durham, NC: Duke University Press, 2008.

Graham, Michael. "Commentary: Here's One Reason Trump's Average Approval Rating Is Going Up." CBS News, September 3, 2018. https://www.cbsnews.com/news /commentary-heres-one-reason-trumps-average-approval-rating-is-going-up/.

Greenhalgh, Susan, and Edwin A. Winckler. *Governing China's Population: From Leninist to Neoliberal Biopolitics.* Stanford, CA: Stanford University Press, 2005.

Gregg, Melissa, and Gregory J. Seigwoth, eds. *The Affect Theory Reader.* Durham, NC: Duke University Press, 2010.

Grenoble, Ryan. "Welcome to the Surveillance State: China's AI Cameras See All." Huffpost, December 12, 2017. https://www.huffpost.com/entry/china-surveillance-camera -big-brother_n_5a2ff4dfe4b01598ac484acc.

Grosfoguel, Ramón, and Ana Margarita Cervantes-Rodríguez. "Unthinking Twentieth-Century Eurocentric Mythologies: Universal Knowledges, Decolonialization, and Developmentalism." In *The Modern/Colonial/Capitalist World-System in the Twentieth Century: Global Processes, Antisystemic Movements and the Geopolitics of Knowledge,* edited by Ramón Grosfoguel and Ana Margarita Cervantes-Rodríguez, 11–30. Westport, CT: Greenwood Press, 2002.

Gu, Jianfen, and Jingting Han. "Today Is Your Birthday." mulanci.org. Accessed August 12, 2021. https://www.mulanci.org/lyric/sl32915/.

Guo, Shaohua. "When Dating Shows Encounter State Censors: A Case Study of *If You Are the One.*" *Media, Culture and Society* 39, no. 4 (2017): 487–503.

Guo, Wei. "Chengxia chaju zheng jinyibu kuoda bixu yinqi women de zhuyi (Urban-rural inequality enlarges and calls for our attention)." Sohu.com, September 20, 2011. https://www.sohu.com/a/357939226_237819.

Halberstam, Jack. *Female Masculinity.* Durham, NC: Duke University Press, 1998.

Hall, Stuart. "The Neoliberal Revaluation." *Cultural Studies* 25, no. 6 (2011): 705–28.

Hardt, Michael. "Globalization and Democracy." GHC *Working Papers,* January (2011): 1–19.

Hardt, Michael, and Antonio Negri. *Empire.* Cambridge, MA: Harvard University Press, 2000.

Harvey, David. *A Brief History of Neoliberalism.* New York: Oxford University Press, 2005.

Harvey, David. *The New Imperialism.* New York: Oxford University Press, 2003.

He, Chengzhou. "Trespassing, Crisis, and Renewal: Li Yugang and Cross-Dressing Performance." *Difference* 24, no. 2 (2013): 150–71.

He, Zhou. "How Do the Chinese Media Reduce Organizational Incongruence? Bureaucratic Capitalism in the Name of Communism." In *Chinese Media, Global Context,* edited by Chin-Chuan Lee, 196–214. London: Routledge, 2003.

Heffernan, Margaret. "What Happened after the Foxconn Suicides." CBS News, August 7, 2013. https://www.cbsnews.com/news/what-happened-after-the-foxconn-suicides/.

Heiman, Rachel, Carla Freeman, and Mark Liechty, eds. *The Global Middle Classes: Theorizing through Ethnography.* New York: School for Advanced Research Press, 2012.

Hershatter, Gail. *Dangerous Pleasures: Prostitution and Modernity in Twentieth-Century Shanghai.* Berkeley: University of California Press, 1997.

Hikaru Masaki. *The Lonely Egotist.* Gardena, CA: Digital Manga, 2009.

Hoang, Kimberly Kay. *Dealing in Desire: Asian Ascendancy, Western Decline, and the Hidden Currencies of Global Sex Work*. Oakland: University of California Press, 2015.

Hoang, Kimberly Kay. "Flirting with Capital: Negotiating Perceptions of Pan-Asian Ascendency and Western Decline in Global Sex Work." *Social Problems* 61, no.4 (2014): 507–29.

Hong, Grace Kyungwon. "Existentially Surplus: Women of Color Feminism and the New Crises of Capitalism." *GLQ* 18, no. 1 (2011): 87–106.

Hong, Grace Kyungwon. *The Ruptures of American Capital: Women of Color Feminism and the Culture of Immigrant Labor*. Minneapolis: University of Minnesota Press, 2006.

Hong, Grace Kyungwon, and Roderick A. Ferguson. Introduction to *Strange Affinities: The Gender and Sexual Politics of Comparative Racialization*, edited by Grace Kyungwon Hong and Roderick A. Ferguson, 1–22. Minneapolis: University of Minnesota Press, 2011.

Hong, Grace Kyungwon, and Roderick A. Ferguson, eds. *Strange Affinities: The Gender and Sexual Politics of Comparative Racialization*. Minneapolis: University of Minnesota Press, 2011.

Honig, Emily. *Creating Chinese Ethnicity: Subei People in Shanghai, 1850–1980*. New Haven, CT: Yale University Press, 1992.

Honig, Emily, and Gail Hershatter. *Personal Voices: Chinese Women in the 1980's*. Stanford, CA: Stanford University Press, 1988.

Horkheimer, Max. *Eclipse of Reason*. New York: Seabury Press, 1974.

Horwitz, Josh, and Ryan Woo. "China's SOE Regulator Calls for Continued Overseas Expansion Despite Trade War: CSJ." Reuters, May 30, 2019. https://www.reuters.com/article/us-usa-trade-china-soe/chinas-soe-regulator-calls-for-continued-overseas-expansion-despite-trade-war-csj-idUSKCN1T1044.

"Housing Should Be for Living In, Not for Speculation, Xi Says." Bloomberg News, October 18, 2017. https://www.bloomberg.com/news/articles/2017-10-18/xi-renews-call-housing-should-be-for-living-in-not-speculation.

"How Tiananmen Square Cemented China's Obsession with Control." Bloomberg, May 31, 2019. https://www.bloomberg.com/news/articles/2019-05-31/how-tanks-on-tiananmen-square-defined-china-s-model-for-control.

Hu Jintao. "Speech at China's 60th Anniversary Ceremony." October 5, 2009. http://de.china-embassy.org/chn/zgyw/t618281.htm.

Huang, Xin. *The Gender Legacy of the Mao Era: Women's Life Stories in Contemporary China*. Albany: State University of New York Press, 2019.

Huang, Xin. "In the Shadow of Suku (Speaking-Bitterness): Master Scripts and Women's Life Stories." *Frontiers of History in China* 9, no. 4 (2014): 584–610.

Huang, Yasheng. *Capitalism with Chinese Characteristics: Entrepreneurship and the State*. New York: Cambridge University Press, 2008.

Huang, Zheping. "What You Need to Know about Beijing's Crackdown on Its 'Low-End Population.'" Quartz, November 27, 2017. https://qz.com/1138395/low-end-population-what-you-need-to-know-about-chinas-crackdown-on-migrant-workers/.

Hughes, Siobhan, and Josh Zumbrun. "Senate Approves Plan to Double Funding for Global Infrastructure Projects." *Wall Street Journal*, October 3, 2018. https://www.wsj.com

/articles/senate-approves-plan-to-double-funding-for-global-infrastructure-projects
-1538595889.

"Hunan shengwei shuji cheng ting nonminggong chang 'chuntianli' releiyingkuang
(Secretary of Hunan Provincial Committee of the CCP moved to tears by the migrant
worker vocal duo)." Sohu.com, November 11, 2010. http://cul.sohu.com/20101111
/n277535229.shtml.

In the Public Interest. "The Trump Administration Privatized Coronavirus Testing, and
Now the U.S. Is Paying the Price." March 16, 2020. http://www.inthepublicinterest
.org/the-trump-administration-privatized-coronavirus-testing-and-now-the-u-s-is
-paying-the-price/.

Irwin, Neil. "It's the End of the World Economy as We Know It." *New York Times*, April 16,
2020. https://www.nytimes.com/2020/04/16/upshot/world-economy-restructuring
-coronavirus.html.

Jacobs, Andrew, and Chris Buckley. "Move Over Mao: Beloved 'Papa Xi' Awes China." *New
York Times*, March 7, 2015. https://www.nytimes.com/2015/03/08/world/move-over
-mao-beloved-papa-xi-awes-china.html.

"Jair Bolsonaro: Brazil's Firebrand Leader Dubbed the Trump of the Tropics." BBC, December 31, 2018. https://www.bbc.com/news/world-latin-america-45746013.

Jin, Jiang. *Women Playing Men: Yue Opera and Social Change in Twentieth-Century
Shanghai.* Seattle: University of Washington Press, 2009.

Jones, Andrew F. *Like a Knife: Ideology and Genre in Contemporary Chinese Popular Music.*
Ithaca, NY: Cornell University Press, 2010.

Jones, Andrew F. *Yellow Music: Media Culture and Colonial Modernity in the Chinese Jazz
Age.* Durham, NC: Duke University Press, 2001.

Kaiman, Jonathan. "China Congress: Toy Helicopters and Pigeons Vanish in Security
Crackdown." *Guardian*, November 1, 2012. http://www.guardian.co.uk/world/2012
/nov/01/china-party-congress-restrictions.

Kang, David. *China Rising: Peace, Power, and Order in East Asia.* New York: Columbia
University Press, 2007.

Kang, Laura Hyun Yi. "The Uses of Asianization: Figuring Crises, 1997–8 and 2007–?."
"Race, Empire and the Crisis of the Subprime," special issue, *American Quarterly* 64,
no. 3 (September 2012): 411–436.

Kang, Wenqing. *Obsession: Male Same-Sex Relations in China, 1900–1950.* Hong Kong:
Hong Kong University Press, 2009.

Karlin, Jason G. "The Gender of Nationalism: Competing Masculinities in Meiji Japan."
Journal of Japanese Studies 28, no. 1 (Winter 2002), 41–77.

Kärnfelt, Maximilian. "China's Tight Capital Controls Fail to Address Underlying Problems." *Financial Times*, November 10, 2017. https://www.ft.com/content/1d288888
-c613-11e7-b2bb-322b2cb39656.

Katz, Jonathan Ned. *The Invention of Heterosexuality.* Chicago: University of Chicago
Press, 2007.

Khalidi, Ari. "Far-Right Turkish Nationalists to Back Erdogan in 2019 Turkey Election."
Kurdistan 24, January 8, 2018. http://www.kurdistan24.net/en/news/44932dbc-9c05
-405f-bd3d-815bae2c6998.

Kimmel, Michael. *Manhood in America: A Cultural History.* New York: Free Press, 1996.

Knoll, Stefanie. "Why Australia Has Fallen Bizarrely in Love with a Chinese Dating Show." *Public Radio International*, October 9, 2015. https://www.pri.org/stories/2015-10-09/why-australia-has-fallen-bizarrely-love-chinese-dating-show.

Koetse, Manya. "Remembering San Mao—the Bohemian Writer That Captured the Hearts of Millions of Chinese." *Weibo*, January 5, 2018. https://www.whatsonweibo.com/remembering-san-mao-beautiful-bohemian-writer-captured-hearts-millions-chinese/.

Kong, Shuyu. "Are You the One? The Competing Public Voices of China's Post-1980s Generation." In *Restless China*, edited by Perry Link, Richard P. Madsen, and Paul G. Pickowicz, 127–48. Lanham, MD: Rowman and Littlefield, 2013.

Kong, Tavis S. K. *Chinese Male Homosexualities: Memba, Tongzhi, and Golden Boy*. New York: Routledge, 2011.

Kuhn, Robert Lawrence. "Xi Jinping's Chinese Dream." *New York Times*, June 4, 2013. https://www.nytimes.com/2013/06/05/opinion/global/xi-jinpings-chinese-dream.html.

Kuo, Lily. "'The New Normal': China's Excessive Coronavirus Public Monitoring Could Be Here to Stay." *Guardian*, March 8, 2020. https://www.theguardian.com/world/2020/mar/09/the-new-normal-chinas-excessive-coronavirus-public-monitoring-could-be-here-to-stay.

Kwan, Stanley, dir. *Lan Yu*. Yongning Creation Workshop, 2001.

Lan, Jun. "Liushi zhounian dayuebing: Wanlvcongzhong de hongse lvbing (Military parade for China's sixtieth anniversary: Red female soldiers in green troops)." CNTV, October 9, 2012. http://news.cntv.cn/2012/10/09/ARTI1349772477529423.shtml.

Latour, Bruno. "How to Talk about the Body? The Normative Dimension of Science Studies." *Body and Society* 10, nos. 2–3 (2004): 205–29.

Lau, Mimi. "Chinese Maoists Join Students in Fight for Workers' Rights at Jasic Technology." *South China Morning Post*, August 10, 2018. https://www.scmp.com/news/china/policies-politics/article/2158991/chinese-maoists-join-students-fight-workers-rights.

Lavin, Maud, Ling Yang, and Jing Jamie Zhao, eds. *Boys' Love, Cosplay, and Androgynous Idols: Queer Fan Cultures in Mainland China, Hong Kong, and Taiwan*. Hong Kong: Hong Kong University Press, 2017.

Lee, Catherine. "'Where the Danger Lies': Race, Gender, and Chinese and Japanese in the United States, 1870–1924." *Sociological Forum* 25, no. 2 (2010): 248–71.

Lee, Chin-Chuan. "Chinese Communication: Prisms, Trajectories, and Modes of Understanding." In *Power, Money, and Media: Communication Patterns and Bureaucratic Control in Cultural China*, edited by Chin-Chuan Lee, 3–44. Evanston, IL: Northwestern University Press, 2000.

Lee, Chin-Chuan. "The Global and the National of the Chinese Media." In *Chinese Media, Global Context*, edited by Chin-Chuan Lee, 1–31. London: Routledge, 2003.

Lee, Chin-Chuan, Zhou He, and Yu Huang. "'Chinese Party Publicity Inc.' Conglomerated: The Case of the Shenzhen Press Group." *Media, Culture and Society* 28, no. 4 (2006): 581–602.

Lee, Haiyan. *Revolution of the Heart: A Genealogy of Love in China, 1900–1950*. Stanford, CA: Stanford University Press, 2007.

Legrain, Philippe. "The Coronavirus Is Killing Globalization as We Know It." *Foreign Policy*, March 12, 2020. https://foreignpolicy.com/2020/03/12/coronavirus-killing -globalization-nationalism-protectionism-trump/.

Leonard, Mark. *What Does China Think?* New York: Public Affairs, 2008.

Lewis, Arthur W. "Economic Development with Unlimited Supplies of Labor." *Manchester School of Economic and Social Studies* 22 (May 1954): 139–91.

Lewis, Tania, Fran Martin, and Wanning Sun. *Telemodernities: Television and Transforming Lives in Asia*. Durham, NC: Duke University Press, 2016.

Li, Cheng. *Rediscovering China: Dynamics and Dilemmas of Reform*. Lanham, MD: Rowman and Littlefield, 1997.

Li, Dong, and He Xia. "Mingnian zhongguo laodongli renkou shouchao shiyi dadao fengzhi (China's labor force exceeding one billion and reaching the peak next year)." People.com.cn, December 24, 2012. http://finance.people.com.cn/money/n/2012 /1224/c218900-19993387.html.

Li, Jie. "Zichan guoyi furen 27% yi yimin jinsannian chao 170 yi liuxiang guowai (27% of China's billionaires already migrated with the flight of over 17 billion yuan to foreign countries in recent three years)." *Global Times*, January 6, 2013. http://finance .huanqiu.com/life/2013-01/3450050.html.

Li, Luzhou. "*If You Are the One*: Dating Shows and Feminist Politics in Contemporary China." *International Journal of Cultural Studies* 18, no. 5 (2015): 519–35.

Li, Siu-Leung. *Cross-Dressing in Chinese Opera*. Hong Kong: Hong Kong University Press, 2003.

Li, Zongze, and Huan Wang. "Riben gongbu gdp shuju bei Zhongguo ganchao ju shijie disan (Japan's released GDP data shows it has been overtaken by China and regressed to the world's no. 3)." Sina, February 14, 2011. http://finance.sina.com.cn/j/20110214 /08519369574.shtml.

Lian, Xun. "Qiye wei jianzhu nügong pai xiezhen, nühanzi bian nüshen (Corporation takes photos of female construction workers, female men turned into goddesses)." Xinhua, March 3, 2015. http://www.xinhuanet.com/politics/2015-03/03/c_1114494569. htm.

Lin, Delia. "The ccp's Exploitation of Confucianism and Legalism." In *Routledge Handbook of the Chinese Communist Party*, edited by Willy Wo-Lap Lam, 47–58. London: Routledge, 2020.

Litzinger, Ralph A. *Other Chinas: The Yao and the Politics of National Belonging*. Durham, NC: Duke University Press, 2010.

Litzinger, Ralph A. "Regimes of Exclusion and Inclusion: Migrant Labor, Education, and Contested Futurities." In *Ghost Protocol: Development and Displacement in Global China*, edited by Carlos Rojas and Ralph A. Litzinger, 191–204. Durham, NC: Duke University Press, 2016.

Liu, Hong. "New Migrants and the Revival of Overseas Chinese Nationalism." *Journal of Contemporary China* 14, no. 43 (2005): 291–316.

Liu, Joyce, prod. "In Your Face: China's All-Seeing State." BBC, December 10, 2017. https:// www.bbc.com/news/av/world-asia-china-42248056.

Liu, Lydia. "The Female Body and Nationalist Discourse: The Field of Life and Death Revisited." In *Scattered Hegemonies: Postmodernity and Transnational Feminist Prac-*

tices, edited by Inderpal Grewal and Caren Kaplan, 37–62. Minneapolis: University of Minnesota Press, 1994.

Liu, Lydia H., Rebecca E. Karl, and Dorothy Ko. "Introduction: Toward a Transnational Theory." In *The Birth of Chinese Feminism: Essential Texts in Transnational Theory*, edited by Lydia H. Liu, Rebecca E. Karl, and Dorothy Ko, 1–26. New York: Columbia University Press, 2013.

Liu, Petrus. "From Identity to Social Protest: The Cultural Politics of Beijing Comrades." In Bei Tong, *Beijing Comrades: A Novel*, translated by Scott Myers, with an afterword by Petrus Liu, 372–81. New York: Feminist Press at the City University of New York, 2016.

Liu, Petrus. *Queer Marxism in Two Chinas*. Durham, NC: Duke University Press, 2015.

Liu, Shixing. "Shengxia sanqianwan: Nongcun shengnan diaocha baogao zhiyi (Thirty million unmarried: An investigation of China's rural single men)." Huanqiu.com, February 23, 2016. https://china.huanqiu.com/article/9CaKrnJU2jJ.

Liu, Xinjun. "Mao Zedong dui makesi zhuyi zhongguohua de gongxian (Mao Zedong's contribution to the localization of Marxism in China)." Cssn.cn, May 5, 2018. http://sky .cssn.cn/skyskl/skyskl_yzfc/201805/t20180504_4226491.shtml.

Liu, Xinyu. "Tepuhui hou e yulun zhuanxiang pi yidaiyilu (Russia starting to criticize Belt and Road Initiative after Trump-Putin meeting)." Radio Free Asia, August 7, 2018. https://www.rfa.org/mandarin/yataibaodao/junshiwaijiao/lxy-08072018102247.html.

Liu, Zhen. "Chinese Americans on Supporting Trump: 'There's Nothing to Be Ashamed of.'" *Business Insider*, November 1, 2016. http://www.businessinsider.com/chinese -americans-supporting-donald-trump-2016-11.

Lo, Kwai-cheung. *Excess and Masculinity in Asian Cultural Productions*. Albany: State University of New York Press, 2010.

Louie, Kam. "Chinese, Japanese and Global Masculine Identities." In *Asian Masculinities: The Meaning and Practice of Manhood in China and Japan*, edited by Kam Louie and Morris Low, 1–16. London: Routledge, 2003.

Love, Heather. *Feeling Backward: Loss and the Politics of Queer History*. Cambridge, MA: Harvard University Press, 2009.

Lowe, Lisa. *The Intimacies of Four Continents*. Durham, NC: Duke University Press, 2015.

Luo, Alice. "Ten Years of China under Hu Jintao and Wen Jiabao." Ever, November 19, 2012. http://blogs.ubc.ca/aliceqianluo/2012/11/19/ten-years-of-china-under-hu-jintao-and -wen-jiabao/.

Ma, Yuan, and Jingjing Bo. "Feichengwurao xianru banquan zhengduozhan (*If You Are the One* gets into trouble for copyright issue)." *Xinhua Daily*, April 8, 2010. http://www .chinadaily.com.cn/dfpd/2010-04/08/content_9701054.htm.

Maeda, Daryl. *Rethinking the Asian American Movement*. London: Routledge, 2011.

Mankekar, Purnima, and Louisa Schein. "Mediations and Transmediations: Erotics, Sociality, and 'Asia.'" In *Media, Erotics, and Transnational Asia*, edited by Purnima Mankekar and Louisa Schein, 1–31. Durham, NC: Duke University Press, 2012.

Mann, Susan. *Gender and Sexuality in Modern Chinese History*. New York: Cambridge University Press, 2011.

Marchand, Marianne H., and Anne Sisson Runyan. Introduction to *Gender and Global Restructuring: Sightings, Sites and Resistances*, edited by Marianne H. Marchand and Anne Sisson Runyan, 1–23. New York: Routledge, 2000.

Marcuse, Herbert. *Eros and Civilization: A Philosophical Inquiry into Freud*. New York: Beacon Press, 1974.

Mardell, Jacob. "The 'Community of Common Destiny' in Xi Jinping's New Era." *Diplomat*, October 25, 2017. https://thediplomat.com/2017/10/the-community-of-common -destiny-in-xi-jinpings-new-era/.

Mariko Hihara. *The Sundered: Yaoi Novel*. Enjugroup, 2016.

Martin, Fran. *Backward Glances: Contemporary Chinese Cultures and the Female Homo- erotic Imaginary*. Durham, NC: Duke University Press, 2010.

Martin, Fran. "Girls Who Love Boys' Love: Japanese Homoerotic Manga as Transnational Taiwan Culture." *Inter-Asia Cultural Studies* 13, no. 3 (2012): 365–84.

Martin, Peter. "Xi Pushes Chinese-Led Globalization after Pledging $78 Billion." Bloomberg, May 13, 2017. https://www.bloomberg.com/news/articles/2017-05-14/xi -opens-china-s-globalization-forum-with-78-billion-in-pledges.

Martin, Philip. *Promise Unfulfilled: Unions, Immigration, and Farm Workers*. Ithaca, NY: Cornell University Press, 2003.

Massumi, Brian. "The Autonomy of Affect." *Cultural Critique*, no. 31 (1995): 83–109.

Massumi, Brian. "The Future Birth of the Affective Fact: The Political Ontology of Threat." In *The Affect Theory Reader*, edited by Melissa Gregg and Gregory J. Seigwoth, 52–70. Durham, NC: Duke University Press, 2010.

Massumi, Brian. *Parables for the Virtual: Movement, Affect, Sensation*. Durham, NC: Duke University Press, 2002.

Massumi, Brian. *The Power at the End of the Economy*. Durham, NC: Duke University Press, 2014.

May, Vivian M. *Pursuing Intersectionality: Unsettling Dominant Imaginaries*. New York: Routledge, 2015.

Mazzucato, Mariana. *The Entrepreneurial State: Debunking Public vs. Private Sector Myths*. London: Anthem Press, 2013.

Mbembe, Achille. *On the Postcolony*. Translated by A. M. Berrett, Janet Toitman, Murray Last, and Steven Rendall. Berkeley: University of California Press, 2001.

McClintock, Anne. "'No Longer in a Future Heaven': Woman and Nationalism in South Africa." *Transition*, no. 50 (1991): 104–23.

McCormack, Derek. "Remotely Sensing Affective Afterlives: The Spectral Geographies of Material Remains." *Annals of the Association of American Geographers* 100, no. 3 (2010): 640–54.

McGranahan, Carole. *Arrested Histories: Tibet, the CIA, and Memories of a Forgotten War*. Durham, NC: Duke University Press, 2010.

McLaughlin, Kathleen E. "China and the Worst-Ever, Man-Made Gender Gap." World, January 3, 2013. https://www.pri.org/stories/2013-01-03/china-and-worst-ever-man -made-gender-gap.

McLelland, Mark. "No Climax, No Point, No Meaning? Japanese Women's Boy-Love Sites on the Internet." *Journal of Communication Inquiry* 24, no. 3 (2000): 274–291.

Mekhennet, Souad. "A 50-Year Journey for Turkey and Germany." *New York Times*, Octo- ber 30, 2011. https://www.nytimes.com/2011/10/31/world/europe/turks-recall-german -guest-worker-program.html.

"Meng Fei didiao xianshen wei dashigao cheng fengcheng zhengshidu chao xinwen (Meng Fei shows up in low profile and claims *If You Are the One* is more real than news)." CFC, June 12, 2012. https://bbs.comefromchina.com/threads/1096439/.

Micklethwait, John, Margaret Talev, and Jennifer Jacobs. "Trump Threatens to Pull U.S. out of WTO If It Doesn't 'Shape Up.'" Bloomberg, August 30, 2018. https://www.bloomberg.com/news/articles/2018-08-30/trump-says-he-will-pull-u-s-out-of-wto-if-they-don-t-shape-up.

Mies, Maria, and Veronika Bennholdt-Thomsen. *The Subsistence Perspective: Beyond the Globalized Economy*. Translated by Patrick Camiller, Maria Mies, and Gerd Weih. London: Zed Books, 1999.

Mingyu. "Danshennan gongxian 2% jingji zengzhang: Hunyin yu jingji de aimei guanxi (Single men contribute to 2% of the GDP growth: The ambiguous relationship between marriage and the economy)." CCTV, February 24, 2013. http://jingji.cntv.cn/2013/02/24/ARTI1361687207280124.shtml.

Mohanty, Chandra Talpade. *Feminism without Borders: Decolonizing Theory, Practicing Solidarity*. Durham, NC: Duke University Press, 2003.

Moore, Malcolm. "Communist Party Congress: A Decade under Hu Jintao and Wen Jiabao." *Telegraph*, November 14, 2012. https://www.telegraph.co.uk/news/worldnews/asia/china/9677748/Communist-Party-Congress-a-decade-under-Hu-Jintao-and-Wen-Jiabao.html.

Morrow, Katherine. "Fei Cheng Wu Rao (非诚勿扰): Staging Global China through International Format Television and Overseas Special Episodes." *New Global Studies* 8, no. 3 (2014): 259–77.

Mourdoukoutas, Panos. "Can China Save the World Economy?" *Forbes*, August 18, 2011. http://www.forbes.com/sites/panosmourdoukoutas/2011/08/18/can-china-save-the-world-economy/.

Moyo, Dambisa. "Is China the New Idol for Emerging Economies?" TED, June 2013. https://www.ted.com/talks/dambisa_moyo_is_china_the_new_idol_for_emerging_economies.

Mozur, Paul, Jonah M. Kessel, and Melissa Chan. "Made in China, Exported to the World: The Surveillance State." *New York Times*, April 24, 2019.https://www.nytimes.com/2019/04/24/technology/ecuador-surveillance-cameras-police-government.html#.

Mulvey, Laura. "Visual Pleasure and Narrative Cinema." *Screen* 16, no. 3 (1975): 6–18.

Muñoz, José Esteban. *Cruising Utopia: The Then and There of Queer Futurity*. New York: New York University Press, 2009.

Muñoz, José Esteban. *Disidentifications: Queers of Color and the Performance of Politics*. Minneapolis: University of Minnesota Press, 1999.

Nagaike, Kazumi. "Fudanshi ('Rotten Boys') in Asia: A Cross-Cultural Analysis of Male BL Fandoms." Paper presented at the Annual Conference of the Association for Asian Studies, Chicago, March 28, 2015.

Nagel, Joane. "Masculinity and Nationalism: Gender and Sexuality in the Making of Nations." *Ethnic and Racial Studies* 21, no. 2 (1998): 242–69.

Naquin, Susan, and Evelyn S. Rawski. *Chinese Society in the Eighteenth Century*. New Haven, CT: Yale University Press, 1989.

Narayan, Uma. *Dislocating Cultures: Identities, Traditions, and Third World Feminism.* New York: Routledge, 1997.

Nash, Jennifer. *Black Feminism Reimagined after Intersectionality.* Durham, NC: Duke University Press, 2019.

National Bureau of Statistics of China. "2012 guomin jingji fazhan wenzhongyoujin (China's national economy developed with stability in 2012)." January 18, 2013. http://www .stats.gov.cn/tjsj/zxfb/201301/t20130118_12924.html.

Naughton, Barry. "China's Transition in Economic Perspective." In *The Paradox of China's Post-Mao Reforms*, edited by Merle Goldman and Roderick Macfarquhar, 30–44. Cambridge, MA: Harvard University Press, 1999.

Naughton, Barry. "Cities in the Chinese Economic System: Changing Roles and Conditions for Autonomy." In *Urban Spaces in Contemporary China: The Potential for Autonomy and Community in Post-Mao China*, edited by Deborah S. Davis, Richard Kraus, Barry Naughton, and Elizabeth J. Perry, 61–89. New York: Cambridge University Press, 1995.

Nguyen, Hoang Tan. *A View from the Bottom: Asian American Masculinity and Sexual Representation.* Durham, NC: Duke University Press, 2014.

Nguyen-Okwu, Leslie. "The Tragic Romance of China's Romeo and Juliet." Ozy, December 18, 2016. https://www.ozy.com/true-and-stories/the-tragic-romance-of-chinas -romeo-and-juliet/74598/.

Nossiter, Adam. "Marine Le Pen Leads Far-Right to Make France 'More French.'" *New York Times*, April 20, 2017. https://www.nytimes.com/2017/04/20/world/europe/france -election-marine-le-pen.html.

Ong, Aihwa. *Buddha Is Hiding: Refugees, Citizenship, the New America.* Berkeley: University of California Press, 2003.

Ong, Aihwa. "Cultural Citizenship as Subject-Making." *Current Anthropology* 37, no. 5 (1996): 737–62.

Ong, Aihwa. *Flexible Citizenship: The Cultural Logics of Transnationality.* Durham, NC: Duke University Press, 1999.

Ong, Aihwa. *Neoliberalism as Exception: Mutations in Citizenship and Sovereignty.* Durham, NC: Duke University Press, 2006.

Ouyang, Bin. "Fanri youxing, Mao zhuxi he Bo Xilai (Anti-Japan protests, Chairman Mao and Bo Xilai)." *New York Times*, October 18, 2012. https://cn.nytimes.com/china /20121018/cc18ouyangbin/.

Packenham, Robert A., and William Ratliff. "What Pinochet Did for Chile." *Hoover Digest*, no. 1 (January 30, 2007). http://www.hoover.org/research/what-pinochet-did-chile.

Pascoe, C. J. *Dude, You're a Fag: Masculinity and Sexuality in High School.* Berkeley: University of California Press, 2007.

Perper, Timothy, and Martha Cornog. "Eroticism for the Masses: Japanese Manga Comics and Their Assimilation into the U.S." *Sexuality and Culture* 6, no. 1 (2002): 3–126.

Perper, Timothy, and Martha Cornog. "Non-Western Sexuality Comes to the U.S.: A Crash Course in Manga and Anime for Sexologists." *Contemporary Sexuality* 39, no. 3 (2005): 3–7.

Perry, Elizabeth J., and Mark Selden. "Introduction: Reform and Resistance in Contemporary China." In *Chinese Society: Change, Conflict and Resistance*, edited by Elizabeth J. Perry and Mark Selden, 1–30. London: Routledge, 2010.

Pettman, Jan Jindy. "Globalization and the Gendered Politics of Citizenship." In *Women, Citizenship and Difference*, edited by Pnina Werbner and Nira Yuval-Davis, 207–20. London: Zed Books, 1999.

Phillips, Kendall R. "'The Safest Hands Are Our Own': Cinematic Affect, State Cruelty, and the Election of Donald J. Trump." *Communication and Critical/Cultural Studies* 15, no. 1 (2018): 85–89.

Phillips, Tom. "Chinese Police 'Find Suicide Note' in Case of 'Left Behind' Children Deaths." *Guardian*, June 14, 2015. https://www.theguardian.com/world/2015/jun/14/chinese-police-investigating-deaths-of-left-behind-children-find-suicide-note.

Phippen, J. Weston. "Asians Now Outpace Mexicans in Terms of Undocumented Growth." *Atlantic*, August 20, 2015. https://www.theatlantic.com/politics/archive/2015/08/asians-now-outpace-mexicans-in-terms-of-undocumented-growth/432603/.

"Pianai jiqing 'shentan xialuoke' zhongguo funü zouhong (Chinese funü earn reputation for their preference of gay love in 'Sherlock')." Kekenet.com, September 1, 2015. https://m.kekenet.com/read/201509/396578.shtml.

Povinelli, Elizabeth. *The Empire of Love: Toward a Theory of Intimacy, Genealogy, and Carnality.* Durham, NC: Duke University Press, 2006.

Preciado, Beatriz [Paul]. "The Pharmaco-Pornographic Regime: Sex, Gender, and Subjectivity in the Age of Punk Capitalism." In *Transgender Studies Reader 2*, edited by Susan Stryker and Aren Z. Aizura, 266–77. New York: Routledge, 2013.

Puar, Jasbir. "Circuits of Queer Mobility: Tourism, Travel, and Globalization." *GLQ* 8, nos. 1–2 (2002): 101–37.

Puar, Jasbir. "'I Would Rather Be a Cyborg than a Goddess': Becoming-Intersectional in Assemblage Theory." *philoSophia* 2, no. 1 (2012): 49–66.

Puar, Jasbir. *The Right to Maim: Debility, Capacity, Disability.* Durham, NC: Duke University Press, 2017.

Puar, Jasbir. *Terrorist Assemblages: Homonationalism in Queer Times.* Durham, NC: Duke University Press, 2007.

Pun, Ngai. *Made in China: Women Factory Workers in a Global Workplace.* Durham, NC: Duke University Press, 2005.

Pun, Ngai, and Anita Koo. "A 'World-Class' (Labor) Camp/us: Foxconn and China's New Generation of Labor Migrants." *Positions* 23, no. 3 (2015): 411–35.

"Qian Liu: 'Zhao Lihong' zhihou de yanbian bushi wo neng kongzhi de (Qian Liu: I cannot Control the Aftereffects of 'Looking for Leehom')." sohu.com, March 1, 2013. http://yule.sohu.com/20130301/n367512618.shtml.

Qiu, Jack Linchuan. *Goodbye iSlave: A Manifesto for Digital Abolition.* Urbana: University of Illinois Press, 2017.

Ramzy, Austin. "In Xi Jinping's Tears, a Message for China's People." *New York Times*, March 3, 2016. https://www.nytimes.com/2016/03/04/world/asia/china-xi-jinping-tears.html.

ReCupido, Amanda. "'Leftover Christmas Cake' and Other Anti-Feminist Expressions." *HuffPost*, August 31, 2009. https://www.huffingtonpost.com/amanda-recupido/leftover-christmas-cake-a_b_248364.html.

Redden, Elizabeth. "China's 'Long Arm.'" *Inside Higher Ed*, January 3, 2018. https://www.insidehighered.com/news/2018/01/03/scholars-and-politicians-raise-concerns-about-chinese-governments-influence-over.

Reddy, Chandan. "Asian Diasporas, Neoliberalism, and Family: Reviewing the Case for Homosexual Asylum in the Context of Family Rights." *Social Text* 23, nos. 3–4 (2005): 101–9.

Reuters. "China's 'Jobless Rate' Hits 15-Year Low but Flood of Graduates on Horizon." *South China Morning Post*, January 26, 2018. https://www.scmp.com/news/china/society/article/2130699/chinas-jobless-rate-hits-15-year-low-flood-graduates-horizon.

Rifkin, Mark. *Beyond Settler Time: Temporal Sovereignty and Indigenous Self-Determination.* Durham, NC: Duke University Press, 2017.

Robinson, Cedric J. *Black Marxism: The Making of the Black Radical Tradition.* 2nd ed. Chapel Hill: University of North Carolina Press, 2000.

Rofel, Lisa. *Desiring China: Experiments in Neoliberalism, Sexuality, and Public Culture.* Durham, NC: Duke University Press, 2007.

Rofel, Lisa. "Temporal-Spatial Migration: Workers in Transnational Supply-Chain Factories." In *Ghost Protocol: Development and Displacement in Global China*, edited by Carlos Rojas and Ralph A. Litzinger, 167–90. Durham, NC: Duke University Press, 2016.

Rojas, Carlos. "'I Am Great Leap Liu!': Circuits of Labor, Information, and Identity in Contemporary China." In *Ghost Protocol: Development and Displacement in Global China*, edited by Carlos Rojas and Ralph A. Litzinger, 205–23. Durham, NC: Duke University Press, 2016.

Rose, Nicholas. "The Human Sciences in a Biological Age." *Theory, Culture and Society* 30, no. 1 (2013): 3–34.

Ryan, Hugh. "The Controversial Chinese Gay Erotic Novel You Can Finally Read in English." March 16, 2016. Modern Chinese Literature and Culture Resource Center, Ohio State University. https://u.osu.edu/mclc/2016/03/17/beijing-comrades-review/.

Sandoval, Chela. *Methodology of the Oppressed.* Minneapolis: University of Minnesota Press, 2000.

Sang, Tze-Ian Deborah. "At the Juncture of Censure and Mass Voyeurism: Narratives of Female Homoerotic Desire in Post-Mao China." *GLQ* 8, no. 4 (2002): 523–52.

"Sanjun nvbing fangdui: Junzhong 'huamulan' xiang nanren yiyang qu zhandou (Female soldier squads: 'Mulan' fighting like men)." Chinanews.com, October 1, 2009. http://news.fengone.com/b/20091001/100979.html.

Sassen, Saskia. "The Global City Perspective: Theoretical Implications for Shanghai." In *Shanghai Rising: State Power and Local Transformations in a Global Megacity*, edited by Xiangming Chen, 3–29. Minneapolis: University of Minnesota Press, 2009.

Schaefer, Donovan. *Religious Affects: Animality, Evolution, and Power.* Durham, NC: Duke University Press, 2015.

Schein, Louisa. *Minority Rules: The Miao and the Feminine in China's Cultural Politics.* Durham, NC: Duke University Press, 2000.

Sedgwick, Eve Kosofsky. *Epistemology of the Closet.* Berkeley: University of California Press, 1993.

Segal, Lynne. *Why Feminism? Gender, Psychology, Politics.* Cambridge: Polity, 1999.

Serres, Michel. *The Parasite.* Translated by Lawrence R. Schehr. Baltimore, MD: Johns Hopkins University Press, 1982.

Sevastopulo, Demetri. "China Cracks Down on 'Naked Officials.'" *Financial Times*, June 8, 2014. https://www.ft.com/content/9d1f3a88-ef01-11e3-acad-00144feabdc0.

Shah, Nayan. *Stranger Intimacy: Contesting Race, Sexuality, and the Law in the North American West*. Berkeley: University of California Press, 2012.

Sharma, Aradhana. *Logics of Empowerment: Development, Gender, and Governance in Neoliberal India*. Minneapolis: University of Minnesota Press, 2008.

"Shengnü chengwei shehui remen huati, jiemu tongguo chaozuo tigao shoushilv (Leftover women become a hot topic and TV program increases rating by sensationalization)." *Xinmin Weekly*, June 2, 2010. http://news.sina.com.cn/s/sd/2010-06-02/120120395858 .shtml.

Shepherd, Christian. "Ten Years' Jail Term for Chinese Author of Homoerotic Novel Sparks Outcry." Reuters, November 19, 2018. https://www.reuters.com/article/us-china -censorship/ten-years-jail-term-for-chinese-author-of-homoerotic-novel-sparks -outcry-idUSKCN1NOoRH.

Shi, Anshu, François Lachapelle, and Matthew Galway. "The Recasting of Chinese Socialism: The Chinese New Left since 2000." *China Information* 32, no. 1 (2018): 139–59.

Shi, Jingyuan. "Guangdianzongju zhengshi dianshi xiangqin jiemu jinzhi chaozuo baijin deng disu neirong (SARFT rectifies TV dating programs and prohibits worship of money and other vulgar content)." Sohu.com, June 10, 2010. https://yule.sohu.com /20100610/n272690377.shtml.

Shih, Shu-mei. "The Concept of the Sinophone." *PMLA* 126, no. 3 (2011): 709–18.

Skurski, Julie. "The Ambiguities of Authenticity: Dona Barbara and the Construction of National Identity." *Poetics Today* 15, no. 4 (1994): 605–42.

Smith, Shawn Michelle. *American Archives: Gender, Race, and Class in Visual Culture*. Princeton, NJ: Princeton University Press, 1999.

Solinger, Dorothy J. "China's Floating Population." In *The Paradox of China's Post-Mao Reforms*, edited by Merle Goldman and Roderick Macfarquhar, 220–40. Cambridge, MA: Harvard University Press, 1999.

Solinger, Dorothy J. *Contesting Citizenship in Urban China: Peasant Migrants, the State, and the Logic of the Market*. Berkeley: University of California Press, 1999.

Solinger, Dorothy J. "The Floating Population in the Cities: Chances for Assimilation?" In *Urban Spaces in Contemporary China: The Potential for Autonomy and Community in Post-Mao China*, edited by Deborah S. Davis, Richard Kraus, Barry Naughton, and Elizabeth J. Perry, 113–48. New York: Cambridge University Press, 1995.

Sommer, Matthew. *Sex, Law, and Society in Late Imperial China*. Stanford, CA: Stanford University Press, 2002.

Song, Geng. *The Fragile Scholar: Power and Masculinity in Chinese Culture*. Hong Kong: Hong Kong University Press, 2004.

Song, Geng, and Derek Hird, eds. *Men and Masculinities in Contemporary China*. London: Brill, 2013.

Sparling, Nina. "*Beijing Comrades* by Bei Tong." Rumpus, April 26, 2016. https:// therumpus.net/2016/04/beijing-comrades-by-bei-tong/.

Stacey, Judith. *Patriarchy and Socialist Revolution in China*. Berkeley: University of California Press, 1983.

Stalker, Peter. *Workers without Frontiers—The Impact of Globalization on International Migration*. Geneva: International Labour Organization, 2000.

Starr, Barbara, and Ryan Browne. "US Increases Military Pressure on China as Tensions Rise Over Pandemic." CNN, May 15, 2020. https://www.cnn.com/2020/05/14/politics/us-china-military-pressure/index.html.

Staudt, Kathleen, and David Spener. "A View from the Frontier: Theoretical Perspectives Undisciplined." In *The U.S.-Mexico Border: Transcending Divisions, Contesting Identities*, edited by David Spener and Kathleen Staudt, 3–34. Boulder, CO: Lynne Rienner, 1998.

Stein, Jeff, and Erica Werner. "White House Floats Large Corporate Tax Cut for Firms That Bring Jobs Back from Overseas." *Washington Post*, May 15, 2020. https://www.washingtonpost.com/business/2020/05/15/white-house-floats-large-corporate-tax-cut-firms-that-bring-jobs-back-overseas/.

Stewart, Kathleen. "Arresting Images." In *Aesthetic Subjects*, edited by Pamela R. Mathews and David McWhirter, 431–38. Minneapolis: University of Minnesota Press, 2003.

Stewart, Kathleen. "Atmospheric Attunements." *Environment and Planning D* 29, no. 3 (2011): 445–53.

Stewart, Kathleen. *Ordinary Affects*. Durham, NC: Duke University Press, 2007.

Stewart, Kathleen. "Weak Theory in an Unfinished World." *Journal of Folklore Research* 45, no. 1 (2008): 71–82.

Stiglitz, Joseph. *Globalization and Its Discontents*. New York: W. W. Norton, 2002.

Stiglitz, Joseph E. "Rethinking Globalization in the Trump Era: US-China Relations." *Frontiers of Economics in China* 13, no. 3 (2018): 133–46.

Stoler, Ann Laura. *Race and the Education of Desire: Foucault's History of Sexuality and the Colonial Order of Things*. Durham, NC: Duke University Press, 1995.

Sun, Wanning. *Subaltern China: Rural Migrants, Media, and Cultural Practices*. Lanham, MD: Rowman and Littlefield, 2014.

Sun, Wanning. "Suzhi on the Move: Body, Place and Power." *Positions* 17, no. 3 (2009): 617–42.

Susoyev, Steve. "'Beijing Comrades' by Bei Tong." Lambda Literary, March 13, 2016. https://www.lambdaliterary.org/2016/03/beijing-comrades-by-bei-tong/.

Swift, Mike. "Blacks, Latinos and Women Lose Ground at Silicon Valley Tech Companies." *Mercury News*, February 11, 2010. http://www.mercurynews.com/ci_14383730.

Tan, Nicole. "Our Response to 'A PhD's Fine, but What about Love and Babies?'" Association of Women for Action and Research, September 13, 2011. http://www.aware.org.sg/2011/09/our-response-to-a-phds-fine-but-what-about-love-and-babies/.

Tan, See-Kam. "The Cross-Gender Performances of Yam Kim-Fei, or the Queer Factor in Postwar Hong Kong Cantonese Opera/Opera Films." *Journal of Homosexuality* 39, nos. 3–4 (2000): 201–11.

Tang, Yihong. "Hide That Uniform Away." In *Iron Moon: An Anthology of Chinese Migrant Worker Poetry*, edited by Qin Xiaoyu and translated by Eleanor Goodman, 53. Buffalo, NY: White Pine Press, 2016.

Tang, Yihong. "It Seems I'm Really His Father." In *Iron Moon: An Anthology of Chinese Migrant Worker Poetry*, edited by Qin Xiaoyu and translated by Eleanor Goodman, 52. Buffalo, NY: White Pine Press, 2016.

Tang, Yihong. "Returning Home Backwards." In *Iron Moon: An Anthology of Chinese Migrant Worker Poetry*, edited by Qin Xiaoyu and translated by Eleanor Goodman, 51. Buffalo, NY: White Pine Press, 2016.

Thomala, Lai Lin. "Film Industry in China—Statistics and Facts." Statista, June 18, 2021. https://www.statista.com/topics/5776/film-industry-in-china/.

Troianovski, Anton. "China Agency Nears Times Square." *Wall Street Journal*, June 30, 2010. https://www.wsj.com/articles/SB10001424052748704334604575339281420753918.

True, Jacqui. *Gender, Globalization and Postsocialism: The Czech Republic after Communism*. New York: Columbia University Press, 2003.

Trump, Donald J. "Remarks by President Trump to the 73rd Session of the United Nations General Assembly." September 25, 2018. https://uy.usembassy.gov/remarks-by -president-trump-to-the-73rd-session-of-the-united-nations-general-assembly/.

Tso, Anna Wing-Bo. "Female Cross-Dressing in Chinese Literature Classics and Their English Versions." *International Studies* 16, no. 1 (2014): 111–24.

Vidales, Raquel. "Sanmao: A Chinese Woman's Tragic Love Story in Spain." *El Pais*, October 26, 2016. https://elpais.com/elpais/2016/10/25/inenglish/1477405923_390849 .html.

Wahyuni, Sari, Esther Sri Astuti, and Karina Miaprajna Utari. "Critical Outlook at Special Economic Zone in Asia: A Comparison between Indonesia, Malaysia, Thailand and China." *Journal of Indonesian Economy and Business* 28, no. 3 (2013): 336–46.

Wang, Fei-Ling. "Renovating the Great Floodgate: The Reform of China's Hukou System." In *One Country, Two Societies: Rural-Urban Inequality in Contemporary China*, edited by Martin King Whyte, 335–64. Cambridge, MA: Harvard University Press, 2010.

Wang, Feng. "In the Spring." mulanci.org. Accessed August 12, 2021. https://www.mulanci .org/lyric/sl176604/.

Wang, Hui. *China's New Order: Society, Politics, and Economy in Transition*. Edited by Theodore Huters. Cambridge, MA: Harvard University Press, 2003.

Wang, Hui. *The End of the Revolution: China and the Limits of Modernity*. London: Verso, 2009.

Wang, Hui. "The Politics of Imagining Asia: A Genealogical Analysis." *Inter-Asia Cultural Studies* 8, no. 1 (2007): 1–33.

Wang, Huiyao, David Zweig, and Xiaohua Lin. "Returnee Entrepreneurs: Impact on China's Globalization Process." *Journal of Contemporary China* 20, no. 70 (2011): 413–31.

Wang, Jing. "Culture as Leisure and Culture as Capital." *Positions* 9, no. 1 (2001): 69–104.

Wang, Jing, and Tani Barlow. Introduction to *Cinema and Desire: Feminist Marxism and Cultural Politics in the Work of Dai Jinhua*, edited by Jing Wang and Tani Barlow, 1–12. London: Verso, 2002.

Wang, Lingzhen. "Other Genders, Other Sexualities: Chinese Difference." *Difference* 24, no. 2 (2013): 1–7.

Wang, Qiang. "Rural Students Are Being Left behind in China." *Nature*, June 25, 2014. https://www.nature.com/news/rural-students-are-being-left-behind-in-china-1.15448.

Wang, Xiaoyi. "Tongjiju: 2013 nian renkou zengzhang 4.92% laodong renkou jiang 244 wan (Bureau of Statistics: 4.92 percent population growth rate in 2013, labor population decreased by 2.44 million)." 163.com, January 20, 2014. http://money.163.com/14/0120 /10/9J1BH25100255009.html.

Wang, Yiyan. "Mr. Butterfly in Defunct Capital: 'Soft' Masculinity and (Mis)engendering in China." In *Asian Masculinities: The Meaning and Practice of Manhood in China and Japan*, edited by Kam Louie and Morris Low, 41–58. London: Routledge, 2003.

Wang, Zheng. "Detention of the Feminist Five in China." *Feminist Studies* 41, no. 2 (2015): 476–82.

Wang, Zheng. *Finding Women in the State: A Socialist Feminist Revolution in the People's Republic of China, 1949–1964.* Oakland: University of California Press, 2017.

Ward, Steven. "Because China Isn't 'Caucasian,' the U.S. Is Planning for a 'Clash of Civilizations.' That Could Be Dangerous." *Washington Post,* May 4, 2019. https://www.washingtonpost.com/politics/2019/05/04/because-china-isnt-caucasian-us-is-planning-clash-civilizations-that-could-be-dangerous/?noredirect=on&utm_term=.b91caaae7483.

"Ways of Registration." Official website of *If You Are the One.* Accessed July 8, 2021. http://tv.jstv.com/fcwr/.

Wei, Lingling. "China's Coronavirus Response Toughens State Control and Weakens the Private Market." *Wall Street Journal,* March 18, 2020. https://www.wsj.com/articles/chinas-coronavirus-response-toughens-state-control-and-weakens-the-private-market-11584540534.

Weinbaum, Alys Eve, Lynn M. Thomas, Priti Ramamurthy, Uta G. Poiger, Madeleine Yue Dong, and Tani Barlow. "The Modern Girl as Heuristic Device: Collaboration, Connective Comparison, Multidirectional Citation." In *The Modern Girl around the World: Consumption, Modernity, and Globalization,* edited by Alys Eve Weinbaum, Lynn M. Thomas, Priti Ramamurthy, Uta G. Poiger, Madeleine Yue Dong, and Tani Barlow, 1–24. Durham, NC: Duke University Press, 2008.

Weng, Shenghui. "Shishang zuiqiang maifang guanggao: Meifang zhineng jiao ayi (The most impressive housing ad in history: You can only call 'aunt' if you have no property)." HouseFun, March 7, 2017. https://news.housefun.com.tw/news/article/184617156227.html.

White, Tyrsene. "The Origins of China's Birth Planning Policy." In *Engendering China: Women, Culture, and the State,* edited by Christina K. Gilmartin, Gail Hershatter, Lisa Rofel, and Tyrsene White, 250–78. Cambridge, MA: Harvard University Press, 1994.

Whiteman, Hilary. "Deaths in Dumpster Expose Plight of China's Street Kids." CNN, November 22, 2012. https://www.cnn.com/2012/11/21/world/asia/china-boys-dead-dumpster/index.html.

Whyte, Martin King. "The Changing Role of Workers." In *The Paradox of China's Post-Mao Reforms,* edited by Merle Goldman and Roderick Macfarquhar, 173–96. Cambridge, MA: Harvard University Press, 1999.

Whyte, Martin King. "The Paradoxes of Rural-Urban Inequality in Contemporary China." In *One Country, Two Societies: Rural-Urban Inequality in Contemporary China,* edited by Martin King Whyte, 1–25. Cambridge, MA: Harvard University Press, 2010.

Williams, Alan. "Rethinking *Yaoi* on the Regional and Global Scale." *Intersections,* no. 37 (March 2015). http://intersections.anu.edu.au/issue37/williams.htm.

Wilson, Ara. *The Intimate Economies of Bangkok: Tomboys, Tycoons, and Avon Ladies in the Global City.* Berkeley: University of California Press, 2004.

Wolf, Margery. *Revolution Postponed: Women in Contemporary China.* Stanford, CA: Stanford University Press, 1985.

Wong, Alvin K. "Gendering Intersubjectivity in New Chinese Documentary Feminist Multiplicity and Vulnerable Masculinity in Postsocialist China." In *Filming the Everyday:*

Independent Documentaries in Twenty-First-Century China, edited by Paul G. Pickowicz and Yingjin Zhang, 119–33. Lanham, MD: Rowman and Littlefield, 2017.

Wong, Silvia. "'The Mermaid' Becomes China's Highest-Grossing Film." *Screen Daily*, February 23, 2016. https://www.screendaily.com/news/the-mermaid-becomes-chinas-highest-grossing-film/5100768.article.

Wong, Sue-Lin, and Christian Shepherd. "Some Chinese Student Activists Released after Police Raid." Reuters, August 28, 2018. https://ca.reuters.com/article/topNews/idCAKCN1LD1DQ-OCATP.

Wu, Angela Xiao, and Yige Dong. "What Is Made-in-China Feminism(s)? Gender Discontent and Class Friction in Post-Socialist China." *Critical Asian Studies* 51, no. 4 (2019): 471–92.

Wu, Cuncun. "Beautiful Boys Made Up as Beautiful Girls: Anti-Masculine Taste in Qing China." In *Asian Masculinities: The Meaning and Practice of Manhood in China and Japan*, edited by Kam Louie and Morris Low, 19–40. London: Routledge, 2003.

Wu, Fulong. "Real Estate Development and the Transformation of Urban Space in China's Transitional Economy, with Special Reference to Shanghai." In *The New Chinese City: Globalization and Market Reform*, edited by John Logan, 153–66. Oxford: Blackwell, 2002.

Wu, Fulong, Jiang Xu, and Anthony Gar-On Yeh. *Urban Development in Post-Reform China: State, Market, and Space.* London: Routledge, 2006.

Xi Jinping. "Full Text of Xi Jinping Keynote at the World Economic Forum." CGTV, January 17, 2017. https://america.cgtn.com/2017/01/17/full-text-of-xi-jinping-keynote-at-the-world-economic-forum.

"Xi Jinping: Buneng fouren qian sanshinian lishi (Xi Jinping: We cannot deny the history of the first thirty years)." May 1, 2013. https://www.dw.com/zh/%E4%B9%A0%E8%BF%91%E5%B9%B3%E4%B8%8D%E8%83%BD%E5%90%A6%E5%AE%9A%E5%89%8D30%E5%B9%B4%E5%8E%86%E5%8F%B2/a-16500930.

"Xi'an Chengdu Wuhan deng shiliu cheng qiang rencai song hukou gei xianjin buxiangou (Sixteen cities including Xi'an, Chengdu, and Wuhan vying to attract talents with offers of *hukou*, cash, and unrestricted rights to buy property)." Sina.com.cn, January 15, 2018. http://finance.sina.com.cn/china/gncj/2018-01-15/doc-ifyqqciz7104848.shtml.

Xiao, Qiang. "The Road to Digital Unfreedom: President Xi's Surveillance State." *Journal of Democracy* 30, no. 1 (2019): 53–67.

Xu, Yanrui, and Ling Yang. "Forbidden Love: Incest, Generational Conflict, and the Erotics of Power in Chinese BL Fiction." *Journal of Graphic Novels and Comics* 4, no. 1 (2013): 30–43.

Xu, Yanrui, and Ling Yang. "Funü 'fu' nan: Kuaguo wenhua liudongzhong de danmei, fuwenhua yu nanxing qizhi zaizao (Queering men by *funü*: Reconstructing masculinity in transnational circulation of *danmei* and *fu* culture)." *Wenhua yanjiu* (Cultural studies), no. 3 (2014): 3–25.

Xuri Yanggang. "In the Spring." Youku.com, November 19, 2010. https://v.youku.com/v_show/id_XMjIzNDk3MTY4.html.

Yan, Hairong. *New Masters, New Servants: Migration, Development, and Women Workers in China.* Durham, NC: Duke University Press, 2008.

Yan, Yunxiang. "Intergenerational Intimacy and Descending Familism in Rural North China." *American Anthropologist* 118, no. 2 (2016): 244–57.

Yan, Yunxiang. *Private Life Under Socialism: Love, Intimacy, and Family Change in a Chinese Village 1949–1999*. Stanford, CA: Stanford University Press, 2003.

Yang, Fan. "The Politics of Exhibition: China's 'Fake' in the 2008 Beijing Olympics." *antiTHESIS* 19 (March 2009): 56–70.

Yang, Ling, and Yanrui Xu. "Chinese *Danmei* Fandom and Cultural Globalization from Below." In *Boys' Love, Cosplay, and Androgynous Idols: Queer Fan Cultures in Mainland China, Hong Kong, and Taiwan*, edited by Maud Lavin, Ling Yang, and Jing Jamie Zhao, 3–19. Hong Kong: Hong Kong University Press, 2017.

Ye, Bing. "Shenzhen weiquan shengyuantuan zao qingchang, shengyuanzhe shilian (Shenzhen solidarity groups supporting workers' rights suppressed by the state, supporters disappearing)." Voice of America, August 24, 2018. https://www.voachinese.com/a/voanews -20180824-china-police-raided-students-backing-shenzhen-workers/4542455.html.

Yee, Vivian, Kenan Davis, and Jugal K. Patel. "Here's the Reality about Illegal Immigrants in the United States." *New York Times*, March 6, 2017. https://www.nytimes.com /interactive/2017/03/06/us/politics/undocumented-illegal-immigrants.html?_r=0.

"Yemen Crisis: China Evacuates Citizens and Foreigners from Aden." BBC, April 3, 2015. https://www.bbc.com/news/world-middle-east-32173811.

Young, Iris Marion. "The Logic of Masculinist Protection: Reflections on the Current Security State." *Signs* 29, no. 1 (2003): 1–25.

Yu, Wei-hsin. *Gendered Trajectories: Women, Work, and Social Change in Japan and Taiwan*. Stanford, CA: Stanford University Press, 2009.

Yukari Fujimoto. "Shōjo manga ni okeru 'shōnen ai' no imi' (The meaning of 'boys' love' in Shōjo Manga)." *New Feminism Review* 2 (May 1991): 280–84.

Zakaria, Fareed. "Trump Is Right: China's a Trade Cheat." *Washington Post*, April 5, 2018. https://www.washingtonpost.com/opinions/global-opinions/trump-is-right-chinas -a-trade-cheat/2018/04/05/6cd69054-390f-11e8-8fd2-49fe3c675a89_story.html?utm _term=.7b8ce17bf9bd.

Zand, Bernhard. "A Surveillance State Unlike Any the World Has Ever Seen." *Spiegel*, July 26, 2018. http://www.spiegel.de/international/world/china-s-xinjiang-province-a -surveillance-state-unlike-any-the-world-has-ever-seen-a-1220174.html.

Zeng, Biao. "Feichengwurao de kandian (Things to see in *If You Are the One*)." BBC, August 7, 2011. https://www.bbc.com/ukchina/simp/uk_education/2011/08/110805 _zengbiao_tv_show.

Zhan, Heying Jenny, and Rhonda J. V. Montgomery. "Gender and Elder Care in China: The Influence of Filial Piety and Structural Constraints." *Gender and Society* 17, no. 2 (2003): 209–29.

Zhan, Ning. "'Feichengwurao' dianshi xiangqin jiemu xushi huayu fenxi (Discursive analysis of the narrative paradigm of the TV dating game show *If You Are the One*)." Crsqa.com. Accessed July 15, 2021. https://www.crsqa.com/3DZvRB7D/.

Zhang, Bing. "Lun 'danmei' xiaoshuo de jige zhuti (On the themes of *danmei* fictions)." *Wenxue pinglun* (Literary review), no. 5 (2012): 171–79.

Zhang, Charlie Yi. "Deconstructing the Hypermasculine National and Transnational Hegemony in Neoliberal China." *Feminist Studies* 40, no. 1 (2014): 13–38.

Zhang, Charlie Yi. "Mapping the Will for Otherwise: Towards an Intersectional Critique of the Biopolitical System of Neoliberal Governmentality." In *Biopolitical Governance:*

Gender, Race and Economy, edited by Hannah Richter, 139–59. Lanham, MD: Rowman and Littlefield, 2018.

Zhang, Charlie Yi. "Queering the National Body of Contemporary China." *Frontiers* 37, no. 2 (2016): 1–26.

Zhang, Charlie Yi. "Untangling the Intersectional Biopolitics of Neoliberal Globalization: Asia, Asian, and the Asia-Pacific Rim." *Feminist Formations* 26, no. 3 (2014): 167–96.

Zhang, Charlie Yi. "When Feminist Falls in Love with Queer: *Danmei* Culture as a Transnational Apparatus of Love." *Feminist Formations* 29, no. 2 (2017): 121–46.

Zhang, Everett Yuehong. *The Impotence Epidemic: Men's Medicine and Sexual Desire in Contemporary China*. Durham, NC: Duke University Press, 2015.

Zhang, Lijia. "One of 60 Million: Life as a 'Left-Behind" Child in China." *South China Morning Post*, January 21, 2018. http://www.scmp.com/week-asia/society/article/2128700/one-60-million-life-left-behind-child-china.

Zhang, Lu. "2013 nian daxuesheng jiuye baogao: Benkesheng qianyuelnü buzu sicheng (2013 employment report of college graduates: Under 40 percent among undergraduate students)." Sohu.com, June 10, 2013. http://roll.sohu.com/20130610/n378558623.shtml.

Zhang, Yuxi. "Quanguo chengzhen fangjia shinian zhangfu 143%: Huobi bianzhi fangjia shiji zai die? (A 143% growth of China's urban housing price in the last decade: An actual price drop with inflation?)." ChinaNews.com, February 26, 2013. http://www.chinanews.com/house/2013/02-26/4597511.shtml.

Zhao, Jing Jamie, Ling Yang, and Maud Lavin. Introduction to *Boys' Love, Cosplay, and Androgynous Idols: Queer Fan Cultures in Mainland China, Hong Kong, and Taiwan*, edited by Maud Lavin, Ling Yang, and Jing Jamie Zhao, xi–xxxiii. Hong Kong: Hong Kong University Press, 2017.

Zhao, Yuezhi. *Communication in China: Political Economy, Power, and Conflict*. Lanham, MD: Rowman and Littlefield, 2008.

Zhao, Yuezhi. *Media, Market, and Democracy in China: Between the Party Line and the Bottom Line*. Urbana: University of Illinois Press, 1998.

Zhao, Yuezhi. "Transnational Capital, the Chinese State, and China's Communication Industries in a Fractured Society." *Public/Javnost* 10, no. 4 (2003): 53–74.

Zhen, He-Yin. "Economic Revolution and Women's Revolution." In *The Birth of Chinese Feminism: Essential Texts in Transnational Theory*, edited by Lydia H. Liu, Rebecca E. Karl, and Dorothy Ko, 92–104. New York: Columbia University Press, 2013.

Zheng, Tiantian. *Red Lights: The Lives of Sex Workers in Postsocialist China*. Minneapolis: University of Minnesota Press, 2009.

Zheng, Tiantian. *Tongzhi Living: Men Attracted to Men in Postsocialist China*. Minneapolis: University of Minnesota Press, 2015.

Zhou, Egret Lulu. "Dongfang Bubai, Online Fandom, and the Gender Politics of a Legendary Queer Icon." In *Boys' Love, Cosplay, and Androgynous Idols: Queer Fan Cultures in Mainland China, Hong Kong, and Taiwan*, edited by Maud Lavin, Ling Yang, and Jing Jamie Zhao, 111–27. Hong Kong: Hong Kong University Press, 2017.

Zhou, Min, and Rebecca Y. Kim. "Formation, Consolidation, and Diversification of the Ethnic Elite: The Case of the Chinese Immigrant Community in the United States." *Journal of International Migration and Integration* 2, no. 2 (2001): 227–47.

Zhou, Shuyuan. "From Online BL Fandom to the CCTV Spring Festival Gala: The Trans-
forming Power of Online Carnival." In *Boys' Love, Cosplay, and Androgynous Idols:
Queer Fan Cultures in Mainland China, Hong Kong, and Taiwan*, edited by Maud
Lavin, Ling Yang, and Jing Jamie Zhao, 91–110. Hong Kong: Hong Kong University
Press, 2017.

Zhu, Pengying. "Zhusanjiao xinyilun mingonghuang diaocha: Jingji huinuan qiye que
zhaobudao ren (Investigation into the new round of labor shortages in the Pearl River
Delta: Hard to recruit workers despite economic recovery)." ChinaNews.com, January 25, 2010. http://www.chinanews.com/gn/news/2010/01-25/2088900.shtml.

Zhu, Xinrui, and Shuai Yan. "The State Press, Publication, Radio, Film and Television
Administration Issued a Document to Promote the Independent Innovation of the
TV Program." People.cn, June 20, 2016. http://media.people.com.cn/n1/2016/0620
/c40606-28456837.html.

Zhuang, Pinhui. "The Beijing Marriage Market: Putting a Price on a Perfect Match in a
Chinese Park." *South China Morning Post*, July 14, 2017. http://www.scmp.com/news
/china/society/article/2102712/beijing-marriage-market-putting-price-perfect-match
-chinese-park.

Zong, Jie, and Jeanne Batalova. "Chinese Immigrants in the United States." Migration
Policy Institute, September 29, 2017. https://www.migrationpolicy.org/article/chinese
-immigrants-united-states-2016.

Index

Bush, George W., 51
Butler, Judith, 55–56, 164, 166, 168–69
The Butterfly Lovers, 169

cadres, 94, 132, 142
Cambodia, transnational marriage market, 118
Canada, 6, 84, 87, 91, 161
Cheah, Pheng, 171
Chen, Handong, 161–62, 165
Chen, Xiaomei, 37, 47
Chengdu, 97, 116, 143
Chiang, Howard, 159
Chicago, 56, 120
Chile, 14
China: education system in, 110, 113, 117; market reforms, 40; one-child policy, 57, 111; pursuit of education, 7–8, 40, 79, 91, 105, 118, 147, 157; real estate market, 120–21; state heteronormativity, 58–59; transition from socialism to neoliberalism, 2, 27, 58, 62, 81, 141, 144, 163, 181; two-child policy, 149, 157; the world's factory, 16, 31, 148, 177
China Central Television (CCTV), 35, 38, 44, 61, 67, 197n37
China's Got Talent (TV show), 66
Chinese Communist Party (CCP): abuse/corruption, 132, 138; anti-corruption campaign, 36; censorship, 61; COVID-19 narrative, 178, 184; factions in, 77; gender ideology, 49–58; hypermasculinity, 129; public pageantry, 38–39; similarity to Western right-wing politicians, 178, 183; temporal management, 77–78; vision of the future, 185. *See also* cadres; Sixteenth CCP National Congress; Seventeenth CCP National Congress; Eighteenth CCP National Congress
Chinese Men's and Boy's Paradise (website), 161
Chinese Nationalist Party, 49
Chinese New Left, 36, 77
Chongqing, 36
Chow, Stephen, 65
chronobiopolitical techniques (rewinding in the class-based revolutionary festivities, spotlighting by the gendered ballroom dancing, and fast-forwarding that brings the future of the People's Republic of China into the awareness of the audiences), 23, 37, 44, 46, 54

chrononormative, 46, 62
Chung, Wallace, 172
class, 39–41, 106–11; social stratification, 40
Cold War, 11–12, 14, 17–18, 80, 126, 130, 178, 181
Collins, Patricia Hill, 19, 160
Connell, R. W., and Julia Wood, 40
COVID-19, coronavirus, 177, 184. *See also* Chinese Communist Party (CCP)
Cultural Revolution, 47, 52, 139

Dagong (town), 135
Dai, Jinhua, 12, 42
danmei ("Boys Love" or BL), 26, 29, 155–76; as escape, 155–59; as homosexual desire, 159–67. *See also* queer fandom culture
daochamen ("marrying into one's wife's family" or matrilocal change of residency for men), 144. *See also* matrilocal
Deleuze, Gilles, and Félix Guattari, 22
Deng Xiaoping, 14–15, 39, 44; economic reform, 7, 43; one-child policy, 57, 111
desire, 4–7, 10–14, 29, 37, 64–65; desire and intimacy, 5, 7, 10, 11, 29, 36, 37, 43, 55, 166, 167; heteronormative desire, 55–58; love potentialities, 99, 157; male desire, 42–43; personal desire, 43–48, 55; same-sex desire/homoerotic desire/queer desire, 157–58, 166–67, 171, 174; temporalized desire, 35, 41
difference-making machinery/the differentiating machinery/the polarizing machinery/the difference-making mechanism, 17–25, 27, 31, 37, 62–63, 69, 86, 92, 99, 107, 127–129, 136, 145–48, 152–54, 171, 175–81; CCP manipulation of, 182–85; definition of, 6–7; gender, race, sexuality, and class as indexes of, 12, 14, 16, 23, 29, 58–59, 78–79, 105, 112–21, 124–26, 159
disenfranchised citizens, 2, 7, 17–20, 47, 99, 153; rural migrant workers, 109–21, 125–28, 156
Dubrofsky, Rachel, 74
Duggan, Lisa, 175
Dwelling Narrowness (TV soap opera), 40, 199n70

The East Is Red, 47, 52, 54
Edelman, Lee, 105
Eighteenth CCP National Congress, 199n69

55, 58, 62, 82, 94, 105, 145; affective and rational attachment to, 5–8; barometer of the Loveland, 99–101, 179; Chinese emigration flows, 87–90; Chinese state-engineered media marketization, 67–69; fueled by the difference-making machinery, 11–18, 116, 127, 129, 183; restructuring *danmei*, 171

Martin, Fran, 158, 171

Marx, Karl, 56–57, 140, 152, 158; Marxist-Leninist orthodoxy in China, 39, 42, 47, 49, 52

Massumi, Brian, 6, 21–22, 151, 178

matrilocal, 144. See also *daochamen*

May Fourth Movement (anti-imperialist, 1920s), 170

McClintock, Anne, 50

Mei, Lanfang, 169

Meiji Era, 167

Meng, Fei, 75–76, 85

migration/migrant workers, 7, 9, 98, 119, 141; rural migration restrictions, 108

mother-in-law economics, 103

Mulvey, Laura, 160

Muñoz, José Esteban, 172

Musical Records of Old and New, 169

Myers, Scott, 161, 194

My Hero (reality TV show), 165

Nagel, Joane, 199n86

Narayan, Uma, 50

national bodies: gendered, 45–46, 51; performers, 23; the PRC historiography, 37, 62

National Health Commission (Division of Population Monitoring and Family Development, family planning policies), 149

National Informatics Center and Chinese Academy of Social Sciences, 149. *See also* Lewis, Arthur ("Lewis turning point")

nationalism/nationalist, 25, 50; backlash to neoliberalism, 5–14, 92, 111, 128, 130, 135–36, 153; Chinese state mobilization of, 18, 27, 38, 52–53; economic, 25; gendered forms of, 43, 51–55, 78, 170, 199n86; parades, 41–48

neoliberal governmentality/governance, 17, 18, 21, 26, 52, 74, 77, 80, 126, 128, 134, 139, 155, 178. *See also* marketization/neoliberal transition/neoliberal restructuring

neolocal (familial model), 146–47

New Zealand, 87

Nezavisimaya Gazeta (Russian newspaper), 121. *See also* Belt and Road Initiative (BRI)

Nguyen, Hoang Tan, 165

Occupy Wall Street Movement, 90

one-child policy, 57, 111. *See also* Deng Xiaoping

Ong, Aihwa, 17, 53, 171

patrilineal, 82; connection to private property, 84, 104; patriarchy, 144; under Mao, 111

patrilocal: connection to private property, 129; familial model, 143; heteropatriarchal system, 145; one-child policy, 115; sexism, 26, 129; under Mao, 111; women, 146

Pédri, Jean-Roch, 61

Peng, Liyuan, 55

People's Daily: *nühanzi* ("female men") report, 113. *See also* Xinhua News Agency

Philippines, *bakla* tradition, 175

Pinochet, Augusto, 14. *See also* Chile

Povinelli, Elizabeth, 10

private property, 11, 79, 102, 111, 146; citizenship/human value, 84–85; connection to intimacy and desire, 102–4, 125, 152; Engels, Friedrich, 163; homepatriarchal love, 85, 101, 129; under Mao, 143

protest/rebellion/uprising, 15, 17, 53, 90, 132, 134, 140, 150, 192n71, 199n69

Puar, Jasbir, 4, 176

Pun, Ngai, 115

Qing dynasty, 101, 170

Qinghai province (Xining, capital city), 131

queer fandom culture, 26, 41, 219n12; gay men's attitude towards, 220n50. See also *danmei*

queer of color critique/analysis, 5, 27. *See also* Ferguson, Roderick

rationality, 6, 73, 113, 151–52; biopolitical, 24–26, 57; difference-making machinery, 14, 179; neoliberal globalization, 17

Reagan, Ronald, 14

Red Detachment of Women, 40

reproductive futurism, 105, 147

Rifkin, Mark, 36
Rofel, Lisa, 6
The Rose Date (*Meigui zhiyue*, TV show), 71
Ryan, Hugh, 194n114

Sandoval, Chela, 178
Sanmao (novelist), 84
Saturday Rendezvous (*Xiangyue xingqiliu*, TV show), 71
Sedgwick, Eve Kosofsky, 171
Segal, Lynne, 51
Seventeenth CCP National Congress, 86
sexuality. See *danmei*; heterosexuality; homosexuality
Shah, Nayan, 6
Shanghai, 28, 104, 112, 123–24; hub city, 116; sex workers, 49; Shanghai Dragon TV, 165; Shanghai TV, 71; Yue opera, 170
Shenzhen, 97, 104, 140
Sichuan province, 98, 122, 124, 192n71
Singapore, 82; gender expectations, 83, 163; human rights, 138; investment in China, 92; neoliberalism, 138
Sixteenth CCP National Congress, 67
Smith, Shawn Michelle, 50
sociospaces, 5, 27; the edgeless Loveland, 59, 62–63
Song dynasty, 48
Southeast Asia, 16, 29, 87, 113, 134; diaspora, 122
South Korea, 66, 87, 93
sovereign power/totalizing power, 180; Chinese government adoption of neoliberal governance as, 18, 25, 109–11, 113, 123, 133–34, 139; gender discipline, 164; Loveland as, 10–11, 22, 58, 80; neoliberalism as, 6, 20–21, 79, 128, 135; state power as, 53, 79, 128; US-China rivalry, 136–37, 40
Spain, 87
spatiality, 74–86, 128, 134; love as, 11, 23, 30, 59, 63; queer, 171
speculative: capital, 24–25; love, 73, 105–6, 121; manipulation of affect, Loveland, 12, 20, 27, 99, 125, 129; spatiality, 11
State Administration of Radio, Film, and Television of China (SARFT, a governmental agency in charge of all media-related issues), 77
Strictly Come Dancing (reality TV show), 66

Subei (now northern Jiangsu), 28, 124
subjectivistic reason, 4, 17–18, 74, 141
Sun, Wanning, 26, 141

Taiwan, 65–66, 71, 89, 91, 161; investment in China, 92
Take Me Out (Chinese version of British dating game show named *Women yuehui ba* or "Let's date"), 64, 66, 69, 74, 204n46
Tang, Yihong, 98
Tang dynasty, 28
temporality, 27; logic, 5, 127; Loveland, 29, 36–38, 58; the PRC temporal logic, 36, 38–41, 45–46, 77–78; reconstruction of the PRC as a timeless entity, 48–55; queer, 171
Teng, Teresa, 65
Thailand, special economic zone, 134
Thatcher, Margaret, 14
Tian'anmen Square, 38; massacre (June 4th democracy movement), 15, 51, 66, 174
Tianjin, 116
Tianyi (*danmei* writer, sentenced to prison), 155
Times Square (New York City), 86
transnational feminism, 19
Trump, Donald J., 9, 180, 184
two-child policy, 149, 157

United Kingdom, 204n46. *See also* Britain
United States, 87, 91, 112, 130, 132; American dream, 9; anti-China sentiment, 15; Belt and Road Initiative, 8; China's adversary, 153; the Cold War, 80; economy, 13; financial crisis, 14; gender/women, 2–3, 83, 165; immigration, 6, 87–90, 93, 122, 124, 137, 153; industrial revolution, 166; neoliberalization, 16, 19, 21, 84; queerness, 175; racialized prison-industrial complex, 110; right-wing politics, 135; September 11, 51; settler colonialism, 84; trade war with China, 130, 136; Treasury Department, 15; university tuition, 147. *See also* Bush, George W; Reagan, Ronald; Trump, Donald J.
Uyghurs, 182. *See also* Xinjiang province

Vietnam, 112, 148; transnational marriage market, 118; special economic zone, 134
The Voice of China (reality TV show), 66, 87